Financial Systems

This book examines financial system activity in market economies from both a theoretical and a practical perspective. The discussion explains why typical financial systems exhibit their contemporary organisational forms, why that organisation is currently changing so rapidly and how those changes present the professional with opportunities for profit.

The book consists of five parts. Part I describes how a financial system is organised, the clients it serves and how system organisation tends to change over time. Part II gives a detailed examination of the economic principles according to which financial deals are done and financial firms are organised. Part III examines markets for raising funds and for managing risks, as well as some of the financial firms trading in these markets. Part IV examines financial intermediaries in both domestic and international terms. Finally, Part V examines government financial activity and supervision and the question of assessing and improving financial system performance in the future.

Each chapter contains policy-oriented questions linking the theory explained in the chapter with important topical questions. The provision of a glossary and solutions section at the back of the book help to make this text an extremely effective learning resource for students of finance and business.

Edwin H. Neave is Professor of Finance at Queen's University, Kingston, Ontario. He is also an Honorary Fellow of the Institute of Canadian Bankers. Neave's profit planning simulations are used by the Institute in its banking education programs in more than forty countries. Neave is also currently Editor-in-Chief of a Treasury Management Program being designed by the Institute.

Financial Systems

Principles and Organisation

Edwin H. Neave

London and New York

332
N35f

FOR LIZ

First published 1998
by Routledge
11 New Fetter Lane, London EC4P 4EE

Simultaneously published in the USA and Canada
by Routledge
29 West 35th Street, New York, NY 10001

Typeset in Times by Florencetype Ltd, Stoodleigh, Devon
Printed and bound in Great Britain by MPG Books Ltd,
Bodmin, Cornwall

British Library Cataloguing in Publication Data

A catalogue record for this book is available from the
British Library

Library of Congress Cataloguing in Publication Data
Neave, Edwin H.
Financial systems : principles and organisation / Edwin H.
Neave.
p. cm.
Includes bibliographical references and index.
1. Finance. 2. Financial institutions. I. Title.
HG173.N332   1998
332–dc21   97–32079
                                            CIP

ISBN 0–415–11056–4 (hbk)
ISBN 0–415–11057–2 (pbk)

Contents

List of figures		vii
List of tables		viii
Preface		x

Part I Overview

1	Introduction	3
2	Roles and clients	9
3	Financial system organisation	25
4	Change	40
5	Financial systems: an empirical overview	51

Part II Concepts

6	Principles of asset pricing	69
7	Dividing and pricing risks	94
8	Financial governance	119
9	Portfolio governance	135
10	Deals' terms	156
11	Market trading and intermediation	170

Part III Financial markets

12	Domestic financial markets	189
13	Markets for risk trading	213
14	International financial markets	235

Part IV Financial intermediaries

15 Principles of intermediation   259

16 Domestic intermediation   279

17 International intermediation   296

Part V Assessing and improving performance

18 Government financial activity   311

19 Supervision   322

20 Toward the future   335

    Appendix: solutions to exercises   346
    Glossary   378
    Notes   386
    References   397
    Index   402

Figures

2.1	Flow of funds diagram	13
3.1	Governance capabilities, deal attributes and alignment	34
6.1	The security market line and arbitrage possibilities	81
6.2	Examples of yield curves for government and corporate bonds	89
10.1	Deal attributes and governance structures	158
14.1	Balance of payments accounts	237
14.2	Covered interest arbitrage activities	246
15.1	Liquidity management	268
15.2	Structure of intermediary balance sheet	270
15.3	The balance sheet restated	271
15.4	Balance sheet showing relations to total assets	271
15.5	Income statement	272
15.6	Effect of reserve and capital requirements on ITE	273
15.7	Effects of interest rates on ITE	274
15.8	Effects of b and k on ITE and σ^2(ITE)	274

Tables

2.1	Securities market and credit market financings, United States, 1994	13
5.1	Condensed balance sheets	58
5.2	Typical patterns of sources and uses	58
5.3	Domestic savings and investment as percentages of GNP, 1994	61
5.4	Percentages of household financial assets	62
5.5	Household debt/GNP	62
5.6	Stock market capitalisation, November 30, 1995	63
5.7	Non-financial companies, debt–equity ratios	63
5.8	Changes in relative importance of financial intermediaries	64
6.1	Real and nominal UK interest rates, 1993	87
6.2	Comparisons of changes in bond prices	90
7.1	Profits or losses on a forward contract with forward price of $100.00	98
7.2	Values of asset and forward contract with a forward price of $100.00	99
7.3	Valuing a contract with a forward price of $97.90	99
7.4	Options with exercise price of $100.00	101
7.5	Valuing the call by the riskless hedge method	104
7.6	Devising a portfolio with a certainty payoff: illustration of put-call parity	106
7.7	Finding a put and a call with the same value	107
7.8	Payoffs when debt with principal and interest payment of $95.00 is issued	109
7.9	Valuing debt and equity	110
7.10	Payoffs when debt with principal and interest payment of $99.00 is issued	110
7.11	Payoffs when risky debt with principal and interest payment of $99.00 is issued	111
7.12	Options with exercise price of $99.00	111
7.13	Forward and futures contracts	113
7.14	Values of long position in forward and futures contracts	114
7.15	Present values of long position in forward and futures contracts	114

8.1	Illustration of efficiency concepts	122
8.2	Attributes and deal types	127
8.3	Financiers' governance capabilities	128
9.1	Returns on perfectly positively correlated securities	138
9.2	Attainable stock prices	141
9.3	Insured portfolio	142
9.4	Synthetic insured portfolio	143
9.5	Net earnings of two banks, before swap	151
9.6	Swap payments from Bank B to Bank A (+), from Bank A to Bank B (–)	152
12.1	Claims of debtholders and stockholders (first example)	204
12.2	Claims of debtholders and stockholders (second example)	205
12.3	Interest sensitivity of level payments on mortgages	209
13.1	Approximate daily turnover, all derivatives contracts (foreign and interest rate instruments), April 1995	215
13.2	A risky investment proposition	216
13.3	Relations between share and call prices	218
13.4	Trans Canada Options: quotations for June 20, 1995	220
13.5	Interest hedging with a futures contract	223
13.6	Daily quotations for Chicago Mercantile Exchange Eurodollar Futures three month contract, $1 million	224
13.7	A risky investment proposition (Exercise 1)	233
14.1	International bond issues and placements, 1989–92	253
15.1	Example of an intermediary's profit planning problem	275

Preface

This book surveys financial system activity at both the theoretical and the practical levels. Using a transactions economics theory of how financing arrangements are governed, the book explains how market-oriented financial systems are organised and how that organisation evolves. At the theoretical level, the book argues that financial system organisation results principally from the ways that financings of different types are structured: informed choices among governance methods can be used to explain financial system organisation.

At the practical level, the book applies its theory to describe the workings of typical financial systems. This discussion is relevant to the professional practice of finance, because it explains how financial deals are structured and shows how these structural choices affect the well-being of the financial firm. More broadly, the book helps financial executives and students of finance to understand why typical financial systems exhibit their contemporary organisational forms, why that organisation is currently changing so rapidly, and how those changes present the professional with opportunities for profit.

There are several excellent books giving specialised accounts of financial markets or financial intermediaries, but currently there are no other books which examine financial systems with a view to analysing the relations between different kinds of financial activities. This book addresses such questions as: why are some financial arrangements made in markets while others are made with intermediaries? Why did swaps evolve from specialised arrangements into a standardised market transaction?

The book is intended as a capstone survey, and is aimed at students who are already familiar with the basic ideas of financial theory and financial practice. The book is intended to help finance students use theory to analyse financial system activity. For example, it shows students the basic ideas underlying the design and valuation of risk management instruments, and it shows students why some financial deals are structured as market transactions while others must be arranged in negotiations with one or more financial intermediaries. It explains how securitisation has evolved, and shows why securitisation does not, as is sometimes conjectured, indicate the demise of banking activity.

Whether the students are undergraduate or graduate, whether they are in economics or in business, is not as important as is familiarity with the theories and subject matter of finance. The writer's undergraduate and masters' students customarily use the book to help understand the principal elements of modern financial systems, to explain what economic forces shape these systems, and to sketch how financial systems change. The book is also used with financial system professionals continuing their education, and members of this audience are able to use the material most productively if they are already familiar with basic theoretical courses in finance.

Through their insight, interest and persistent inquiries, many students have helped to shape the form in which this material is now presented. I hope this book does justice to their enthusiasm and to their insights. It is also a pleasure to acknowledge the support of a sabbatical leave from Queen's University, Kingston, which greatly accelerated the preparation of the manuscript. The hospitality of the University of St Andrews, Fife, was of material assistance during the early stages of the writing. My friend and secretary, Lilly Lloyd, has patiently endured the preparation of many drafts of this work over the years, and I am particularly grateful for her help. Finally, my sincere thanks to the people at Routledge who helped bring this work to fruition: Alan Jarvis and Alison Kirk. Their enthusiasm, professionalism and continuing support have been invaluable.

Kingston, Ontario
January, 1998

Part I

Overview

Part I is an introductory overview which examines the roles of a financial system and explains how a typical financial system is organised. Chapter 1 outlines the structure of the book. Chapter 2 examines the roles a financial system performs and the clients it serves, while Chapter 3 explains how a typical financial system is organised. Chapter 4, which contends that change is one of the most important features of a modern financial system, outlines the factors contributing to change and explains why the effects of change are registered so rapidly in a modern financial system. The last chapter of the overview, Chapter 5, examines prominent features of the financial systems of four major countries – Germany, Japan, the UK and the US – to give the reader an initial idea of some of the similarities, and some of the differences, among the world's principal financial systems.

1 Introduction

1.1 The book's purposes 5

1.2 The book's organisation 7

1.3 Summary of approach 7

LEARNING OBJECTIVES

After reading this chapter you will understand

● that a financial system helps savers to invest their funds
● that financial system organisation is determined according to the ways different forms of financial deals are governed
● that the kinds of financial deals done, and the ways they are done, can affect economic growth
● that financiers' pursuit of new profit sources is the principal determinant of financial system change
● how knowledge of financial system activity can help financial managers perform their roles more effectively

---

This book is intended to help future managers understand the kinds of activities that take place in a financial system, and to understand why certain kinds of organisations are set up to carry out those activities. The book explains that financial systems in market-oriented economies have a typical structure that is determined by economics: the economics of governing the transactions they take on, and the operating economics of the firms effecting the transactions. The book further explains that financial system change is driven by the same economic forces that determine system organisation. As you gain an understanding of how these economics work, you will become better able to discern directions of future financial system change. This knowledge will in turn help you to deal more effectively with the opportunities that the changes will likely bring.

This book argues that the world's financial systems are largely shaped by the same forces, and develop in quite similar ways. To be sure, there are also important differences among financial systems. But most of the differences among domestic financial systems result principally from details of an economy's development, or even from historical accident. Moreover, the differences are continually being mitigated by the same economic forces, thus causing the world's major financial systems to converge toward a common type. The book uses examples from financial systems throughout the world to illustrate this process of convergence, and to explain how the same kinds of changes are transmitted from one economy to another.

The study of a financial system is a more vital matter than commonly realised. A financial system's importance is not limited to the people working in it. Rather, financial system performance can and will importantly affect business capital formation decisions, and these decisions in turn affect economic development and international competitiveness. The terms on which financing is made available affect both the amount and type of capital formation that takes place in an economy. If business cannot obtain funds as readily and as cheaply in one country as in another, it will attempt either to raise the funds where the terms are better, or may even relocate the entire business to another part of the world. Moreover, the terms on which business can obtain financing will depend on the skills and insights of financiers who must decide whether or not to put funds into different kinds of projects.

Since the mid-1970s, change has been the most prominent feature of the world's financial systems. Change has been and continues to be driven by two principal forces: technological development and the increased competition which follows on it. In nearly all developed economies, technological change and evolving competition affect the economics of doing financial transactions, or 'deals' as the rest of this book usually calls them. As financiers discern these changes, they alter their ways of doing business in response. Even regulators respond to the workings of the same forces, principally by proposing legislative changes to recognise evolving forms of domestic financial business. In addition, as international finance continues to increase in importance a body of international law, and a number of international organisations, are being developed to supervise the growing international activity.

1.1 THE BOOK'S PURPOSES

Today's financial managers find it more urgent than ever to understand the basic forces driving financial system change. As the world's financial markets increasingly become more competitive, and more closely integrated, new profit opportunities need to be exploited quickly if they are not to be lost to competitors. Indeed, new products may need to be introduced with speed just to ensure that existing business can be retained. In such an environment the manager without an understanding of how and why change occurs is a manager who will quickly become outdated, and therefore one who will likely fail to prosper. For example, during the 1980s management personnel in some of the larger securities firms earned much of their companies' revenue by arranging mergers and acquisitions. During the later 1980s and early 1990s the pace of this activity tailed off, and earnings declined commensurately. At the present time, the later 1990s, interest in merger activity is again increasing. This book will explain why such cycles in financial activity occur. It will also discuss the potential for profiting from cycles, as well as some of the dangers to be encountered along the way.

Understanding how and why change occurs is not simply a matter of describing what is happening today: description is not explanation. Explanation demands a more organised picture of the forces driving change, and of how those forces influence financial activity. This book uses the economics of financial transactions to develop such a picture. It explains why financial systems take their manifest forms, and why these forms change over time. For example, readers of this book will learn why there was a virtual explosion in **derivatives** trading over the 1970s and 1980s,[1] and will therefore come to understand the reasons for this immense increase in derivatives' popularity. While some press accounts suggest that the growth of derivatives trading is largely due to a willingness to speculate, the real reasons are to be found in the changing risks within the financial system and the corresponding changes in the economics of their management.

To help the reader apply its theory, the book refers to activities in a number of financial systems, especially those of Germany, Japan, the UK and the US. Examples from these and other countries show how profit opportunities arise as financial systems change, and how managers interested in setting up and operating financial firms can take advantage of these opportunities. By understanding how the forces of change operate, readers planning private sector careers can learn to profit from them. Equally, readers whose careers are likely to be in the public service can use the same knowledge to devise and implement better, more effective ways of supervising financial activity. For example, the book will show that the rapid increases in the size of the Japanese banking system, and the more recent increases in its loan losses, are not unique events. Rather, they are examples of a recurring form of crisis that recurs regularly, to greater or lesser degrees, in most economies' banking systems. The book will show that some of the difficulties currently facing Japanese banks are explained by the same factors that led to difficulties encountered previously in other banking systems.

The book begins by explaining how individual financial transactions or deals differ, and what this means for the ways in which deals can be structured. Second, the book explains the basic ideas underlying the use of derivative securities, and shows why their importance for risk management has grown so rapidly since the early 1970s. Third, the book explains why it is so important for financiers to have different kinds of deal-making capabilities. An understanding of these issues helps the reader appreciate how financial system development occurs and where profit opportunities are likely to arise as the changes take place.

Even though many examples are used, the book's explanations emphasise principles rather than descriptive detail. Many readers will probably agree that explanations can convey a more powerful understanding than descriptions, but some may object that analysing a financial system in terms of principles omits so many practical details that it cannot be of much help to the everyday manager. Yet, practical details must be omitted if the reader is to make real headway in understanding financial systems. First, in today's rapidly changing financial environment descriptions become dated so quickly that it is almost impossible to keep them current. Second, even if it were possible to keep descriptions current, they are not enough. Every analyst needs to have a theory (road map) to understand the broad outlines of, and the major forces at work within, a financial system. Without the organisation provided by theory, an analyst can assemble a mass of detail but still fail to understand either how the details relate to each other or what causes them to keep changing. Finally, the reader who has learned to apply the theory has a set of ideas that remain valid for a much longer time than does current description.

1.2 THE BOOK'S ORGANISATION

This book consists of five parts. The first, overview part describes the users of a financial system, how the system is organised, and how that organisation changes over time. Selected data from four major systems – Germany, Japan, the US and the UK – are used to identify the principal financial system features examined in the rest of the book. The second part of the book is an examination of the economic principles according to which deals are done and financial firms are organised.

The remaining three parts of the book apply the theory. The third part, financial markets, examines markets for raising funds and for managing risks, as well as some of the financial firms trading in these markets. The fourth part examines financial intermediaries. Intermediaries are often active in many financial markets, but much of their importance is attributable to their non-market negotiations with clients. Intermediaries administer, or govern, deals differently than do market agents. These differences mean intermediaries actually agree to different kinds of deals than do market agents, and hence their activities are complementary to market trading. The book's fifth and final part examines the questions of assessing and improving financial system performance.

1.3 SUMMARY OF APPROACH

This book develops a theory of how financial deals differ, and of how different deals are structured. The theory explains how the size and nature of the financial firms doing the deals are determined, and thus shows how the financial system emerges as an aggregate of these firms' activities. The theory also explains why financial system change occurs, and discusses some of the reasons why many forms of financial activity are cyclical in nature. These explanations can help future managers to function effectively in a financial environment, whether they intend to work in profit-making firms or as public servants.

REVIEW QUESTIONS

Exercise 1 Suppose you can make a loan to an impeccable credit risk for one year at a rate of 7 percent. Would the rate you charge on a higher risk loan be less, the same, or more?

Exercise 2 Why do you suppose banks are so eager to sell insurance in their branches nowadays?

Exercise 3 The huge growth in risk management instruments (swaps, options, futures) has almost all taken place since the early 1970s. Try to list some of the reasons why there would be an increased demand for risk management since the early 1970s.

Exercise 4 Some of the following activities are mainly fund raising, while others are mainly aimed at risk management. Try to classify them accordingly: buying insurance; selling bonds to fund the purchase of a new computer system; buying an option; borrowing to finance a new venture; arranging an interest rate swap. (If you don't know exactly what's involved in some of these transactions, you will be learning more about each at a later point in the book.)

Exercise 5 Suppose a bank buys some treasury bills that it intends to hold until maturity, and that it also makes a long term loan to a fairly risky new business. Would the second deal require more continuing attention than the first? Why?

Exercise 6 If you invest in government bonds and hold them to maturity, they represent a relatively low risk investment. Stocks typically represent a higher risk investment, because the returns on them usually fluctuate over a wider range than do the returns on bonds. Suppose you are considering putting your money either into a five year US Savings Bond currently offering an 8 percent return, or a bank equity fund that has a historical return of 8 percent. Which do you think is the better deal, and why?

Exercise 7 Give an example of some kind of financial deal to which a bank would typically pay little continuing attention. Do you think the same would be true of a venture capital investment in a new company? Why or why not?

Exercise 8 What are the major forces contributing to financial system change? Why do these forces contribute to change?

Exercise 9 Why are these forces having similar impacts on most market economies' financial systems?

Exercise 10 Why has the pace of change increased within the world's financial systems?

Exercise 11 Find at least one article on changing financial regulation in the United States or the United Kingdom. Who wants these regulatory changes? Why do you think they are wanted?

2 Roles and clients

2.1	What roles does a financial system perform?	10
	2.1.1 Payments system	10
	2.1.2 Store of wealth	11
	2.1.3 Primary and secondary transactions	12
	2.1.4 Risk management	14
	2.1.5 Finance and economic activity	16
2.2	Who uses the financial system?	18
	2.2.1 Consumers	18
	2.2.2 Businesses	19
	2.2.3 Governments	21
	2.2.4 Residents of other countries	21
2.3	Summary	22

LEARNING OBJECTIVES

After reading this chapter, you will understand

- that the financial system serves several different types of clients – consumers, business and governments
- how the financial system serves to effect payments
- how the financial system serves as a store of value
- how the financial system facilitates risk management
- some of the ways in which finance affects economic activity

---

The workings of a country's financial system are not readily apparent to casual observers. Readers of the financial press probably think of a financial system as a set of markets in which shares and exotic instruments such as financial derivatives are traded. They are less likely to think about the importance of the financial system for providing new funding of projects, and about whether that funding comes mainly through financial markets or financial intermediaries. They are also less likely to realise that the financial system helps an economy to run smoothly, and is a vital contributor to the economy's development.

2.1 WHAT ROLES DOES A FINANCIAL SYSTEM PERFORM?

Financial systems perform most of their everyday operations so quickly and smoothly that their importance is not always well readily recognised. Few observers notice how easily a well functioning financial system performs its principal roles: effecting payments, facilitating the investment of accumulated wealth, making funds available to finance viable new projects, and providing risk management facilities.[1] Yet, when you begin to consider how important each of these functions is, the vital roles played by the financial system start to become apparent. When in addition you realise that the financial system can contribute to economic growth, the importance of its functioning becomes still more evident.[2]

2.1.1 Payments system

The financial system effects payments by responding to the instructions of individuals, businesses and governments to transfer funds to other parties. When a traveller uses a credit card to obtain cash in a foreign country, or when a firm pays for imports from abroad, the financial system completes the transaction. The financial system also makes it possible for countries' governments to deposit funds directly into individuals' bank accounts. Indeed, the system makes it easy and cheap to transfer funds quickly between almost any two points in the world, usually in whatever currency the payer desires to use. The traveller appreciates this most acutely when communications are disrupted and the banking machines on which she is relying for her weekend expenditures do not dispense the cash she expected to obtain.

2.1.2 Store of wealth

Individuals who earn more than they spend,[3] and businesses whose profits exceed their capital expenditures, are both classified as savers. There is also an obverse definition: those who spend more than they earn are said to dissave. When individuals save, they usually place some of their surplus funds in cash or non-interest-bearing deposits, some in return-bearing forms such as interest-bearing securities or deposits or other securities expected to yield a combination of dividend income and capital gains. In most developed countries, individuals' savings are distributed among bank deposits, investments in pension and mutual funds, and marketable securities. The proportions held in each type of investment vary according to which types are available to the consumer, and according to the average returns each type yields. As discussed extensively below, greater average returns almost always mean greater risks as well, and consumers make tradeoffs between expected return and the risk of earning that return.

Like individuals, businesses hold a combination of liquid assets having no or low returns, and other financial assets such as securities, typically bearing higher returns. However, the investment goals of businesses are usually different from those of individuals and as a result the particular combinations of financial assets they hold are also different. For example, the proportion of liquid assets held by either a business or a consumer will depend, at least to some extent, on how unpredictable its short term cash inflows and outflows are likely to be.

While savers want to earn a reasonable rate of return on their savings, most also want to ensure that their funds are invested safely. Indeed since most investors are risk averse, they demand asset returns commensurate with the perceived risk of the investment. The hypothesis that investors demand a yield premium that increases with investment risk is one of the most important conclusions of modern financial theory, and one that is well confirmed by empirical research. For example, stocks usually yield higher expected returns than bonds because most investors consider stocks to be riskier than bonds.

Even though most investors behave as risk averters, one can still find cases of contradictory behaviour. For example, some savers pay little attention to potential risk when faced with an investment promising an unusually high return. Savers who make these decisions may fail to recognise that the promised rewards are almost always associated with taking great risks. The next time you read that a financial institution somewhere in the world is paying extremely high rates of return to depositors, and that it is growing extremely quickly, you will probably be witness to an example of savers taking very great risks. Some of the savers you will be reading about will likely lose most or all of their funds when the scheme eventually goes bankrupt. In the 1990s notable frauds were perpetrated in both Albania and Romania, with some depositors losing as much as two years' income when the fraudulent institutions failed. While they are more likely to be quickly terminated by supervisory authorities, attempts at defrauding savers are not always confined to transition economies. For example, a scheme similar to the Albanian and Romanian ones was closed down, after just a few weeks of operation, by Canadian authorities in 1996.

2.1.3 Primary and secondary transactions

A financial system raises funds from lenders or investors, making them available to borrowers or other users. Lenders and other investors are called suppliers of funds, while borrowers and other users are known as demanders for funds. The funds may be used either to finance current expenditures, say on consumer goods, or capital expenditures, say on business plant and equipment. In either case, the transactions are measured using a system of accounts called the **funds flow accounts** or **financial flow accounts**.[4]

---

funds flow accounts trace net borrowing or lending transactions between major sectors in the economy. The sectors defined in the accounts are households and unincorporated business, private non-financial business, government, private financial business and the rest of the world.

While the details of the funds flow accounts will be examined further in Chapter 5, at this point it is useful to point out how they can help display the broad outlines of financial activity. Funds flow accounts measure transfers of funds between a number of sectors, as shown in Figure 2.1. For most of the market-oriented economies which gather the data, the funds flow accounts show that funds financing new investment flow mainly through intermediaries, with only a relatively small proportion being transmitted directly through financial markets. Table 2.1 gives a representative example for the United States. As Table 2.1 indicates, the data give a rather different impression of financial activity than is usually conveyed by the financial press, since much of the discussion in a typical financial newspaper is devoted, not to new financing, but to takeovers, mergers and market trading of previously issued securities. The typical financial newspaper also tends to emphasise security market financings more heavily than it stresses the financings provided through intermediaries.

Any economic agent who spends more than current earnings must either sell assets or borrow funds to finance the difference. Deals for raising new funds are called **primary transactions**,[5] and involve creating new financial assets. The new securities may be shares, bonds, promissory notes, loan contracts or variants of these instruments. The securities may be sold to investors through the securities markets, or they may be acquired by financial institutions which advance funds directly to their clients.

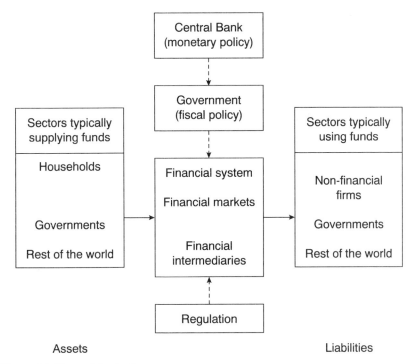

Figure 2.1 Flow of funds diagram

Table 2.1 Securities market and credit market financings, United States, 1994 (amounts in US $billion; net new issues)

Transaction type	Amount	Percentage of total
Federal government borrowing from public	185.0	12.4
State and local government	106.0	7.1
US corporations – bonds	498.0	33.4
US corporations – stocks	85.1	5.7
Credit market issues, domestic non-financial sector	618.9	41.5
Total	1,493.0	100.0

Source: *Federal Reserve Bulletin* August 1996.

> **primary transaction** one involving the raising of new funds by the creation of new financial instruments.

Primary transactions that finance new capital formation activity are particularly important because of their effects on economic growth. If a domestic financial system does not finance certain kinds of deals, capital formation will be inhibited – unless the necessary funds can be raised offshore. If neither domestic nor foreign financing is available, the proposed capital formation will be postponed until it can be financed from retained earnings, or else may be abandoned. In either case, economic growth is normally affected adversely (see King and Levine 1993).

Deals involving trades in outstanding instruments are called **secondary transactions**. Secondary market purchases of securities are used to invest surplus funds, secondary market sales of securities are used to raise funds. Secondary transactions almost always take place in the stock markets, the bond markets or the money markets. The instruments representing loans provided by banks or other intermediaries are rarely resold in the marketplace, for reasons explained at several later points in the book.

---

secondary transaction one involving trades in existing securities. It represents a reallocation of existing financing rather than the creation of a new arrangement.

Active secondary trading of a company's or government's securities both improves the liquidity of its primary securities issues and helps evaluate new information about the issuer. Secondary transactions enhance the liquidity of primary issues because they indicate it will likely prove relatively easy to trade the securities at some subsequent point in time. The changing prices at which secondary transactions are consummated help to assess the value of emerging information, at or near the time it is released.

2.1.4 Risk management

Instead of being used to raise new funds, some financial deals are struck with the principal purpose of dividing up and trading risks. Although risk management is often regarded as having emerged in the 1970s and 1980s, that view stems principally from observations of the very rapid growth of risk trading during those decades. Indeed, the idea of risk management has been familiar to at least some financiers for a much longer time. For example, some risks have been insured since long distance trading first became a reality. From this historical beginning, insurance companies were formed principally to assume risks that others were unwilling to bear.

When an individual or a business buys a policy that insures assets against loss through fire or damage, the client is in effect selling risks to the insurance company. Typically, the risks assumed by insurance companies are not actively traded, but rather remain on the books as untraded liabilities. Other instruments such as commodities futures have long been used to trade risks actively. For example, crop growers sell commodities futures allowing them to hedge against the risks of fluctuating crop prices, while speculators buy the same futures contracts to assume the risks. The commodities futures markets were originated by securities firms that were both familiar and comfortable with the idea of secondary market trading. These innovative firms realised that risks could be exchanged through market trading, in much the same manner that funds are traded when securities are bought and sold.

In the late 1960s, and even more so in the 1970s and 1980s, risk management expanded greatly in volume and importance, first in the United States, then soon after in Great Britain, Japan and other countries. The explosive growth of risk management, particularly the trade in derivative securities, is due both to shifts in the demand for risk management and to changes in the supply of instruments suitable for risk management.

On the demand side, risk management became increasingly popular as the financial environment became increasingly more turbulent in the late 1960s and 1970s, and continued to remain turbulent through the 1980s and early 1990s. At the same time, the internationalisation of business implied very rapid increases in foreign currency transactions, increasing the demand for managing these kinds of risks. As one example, the increasing strength of the Japanese yen in the late 1970s and early 1980s meant Japanese investors suffered large capital losses on their US dollar denominated investments, many of which took the form of US government securities. These losses were one of the major factors stimulating the Japanese to develop their current high volume, sophisticated risk trading activities.

On the supply side, market trading of such risk management instruments as derivative securities is based on the same considerations that led insurance companies to write liabilities and commodities traders to purchase futures contracts. But, in the early 1970s two important supply side changes, both technological, greatly increased the volume of risk trading. First, traders in the instruments learned the importance of standardising terms, which lowered the costs of both contract origination and of subsquent trading. Second, traders learned the importance of guaranteeing contract performance.[6] Performance guarantees centralise the screening activity, lower the probability of default faced in secondary market trading, and thus obviate the need for numerous separate checks of creditworthiness. That is, the client who buys an instrument traded on a well-known exchange almost always obtains a performance guarantee that the instrument will be honoured as written. This means the purchaser does not have to investigate the creditworthiness of the issuer before deciding whether or not to buy the instrument.

Growth in the market trading of risks does not represent the only supply side change. Over-the-counter trading of non-standardised risk instruments has also increased substantially,[7] especially during the later 1980s and 1990s. During this period, standardised instruments proved inadequate to meet the demands of some clients, and intermediaries willing to negotiate forms of over-the-counter risk trading increased in number, as discussed further in Chapter 13.

Secondary market risk trading facilitates the primary undertaking of risky projects, just as secondary markets for securities improve the functioning of primary markets for raising funds. An economy with access to cheap and easy secondary trading of risk instruments will undertake more viable risky projects than one without secondary markets, mainly because the parties originally under-taking to face the risk find it easier to divide into different components that are attractive to purchasers with specialised requirements.

2.1.5 Finance and economic activity

Macroeconomic theory explains that consumption, investment and government spending are the major determinants of economic activity over the near term. In particular, changes in the rate of investment (capital formation) importantly affect the rate of economic growth. Moreover, the kind of investment under-taken affects the kind of productive capability the economy acquires. By making primary financings easier to arrange, the financial system can encourage economic growth.[8] Financiers do not directly stimulate capital formation by deciding to put up funds for projects, but they can certainly constrain decisions to acquire long term capital if they refuse to provide funding. If funds are not available domestically, business can seek financing offshore, but business that is unknown to the financiers of a foreign country may not always be successful in obtaining funds. In such cases underdevelopment of the domestic financial system clearly impedes economic growth. In addition to being able to affect the rate of economic growth, the financial system can also affect its type. Whether funds are provided offshore or domestically, financiers may favour some types of projects over others, even if the riskier ones offer higher returns.[9]

Economic growth can also stimulate financial system growth. Both financial system development, and many individual financing decisions, are driven by attempts to respond to changing demands for funds. In addition, the financial system evolves to overcome emerging impediments to financing new kinds of deals. For example, over the 1970s a world-wide increase in the demand for more risk management services was met by increased trading activity and the development of many new risk management products, as already mentioned.

Both interest costs and the availability of finance differ between countries. As already mentioned, differences in financiers' capabilities (having their roots in differing patterns of trade, differing governmental restrictions, differing entre-preneurial skills and the like) affect the availability and the cost of finance. A second source of differences in cost and availability is the cost of producing deal information in differing milieux (dependent, for instance, on financial infra-structure: legal frameworks, accounting standards and the like).

High financing costs (relative to competitive market returns for similarly risky projects) or limited availability of funds signal financial underdevelopment. Improving an economy's growth prospects means improving its existing finan-cial system capabilities, its access to offshore finance, or both. The interests of any economy are served by overcoming financial underdevelopment, but that is not an easy task since it requires building up new capabilities to screen and govern financial deals. Financial system development is most likely to occur in an already sophisticated financial system, because that is where innovation is least costly and most likely to be profitable.

Another manifestation of the relations between economic and financial activity is that as they evolve, financial systems develop differing capabilities to assess and to administer financial deals. At any given time, the possibility of being able to fund a given deal depends on financiers' evolved capabilities to assess or screen it, as well as on the financiers' capabilities to administer or govern it profitably.

In most developed economies, established large businesses with profitable track records do not have much difficulty finding financing. For such businesses, the most important consideration about obtaining financing is usually its cost. Smaller businesses' short term financing needs can also be satisfied relatively easily, at least so long as the business has marketable assets to offer as security. For instance, small businesses have little difficulty in raising funds to finance acquisitions of inventory or accounts receivable, being able to rely on bank loans or trade credit to do so. Similarly, small businesses can readily acquire some kinds of equipment by offering the equipment as security, say using a lease or conditional sales contract. A financial system will usually offer some way of funding a relatively routine deal that is secured by liquid assets or a readily quantified earnings stream.

However, not all deals, even potentially viable ones, can be financed easily. Consider, for example, what happens when smaller businesses seek to obtain long term debt or startup equity. Such proposals present financiers with the problem of valuing a highly uncertain earnings potential. The potential earnings may depend critically on the skills of an entrepreneur, or on purchasing specialised fixed assets with no ready secondary market. When financiers have little other than relatively uncertain earnings prospects to secure their positions, they are unlikely to find the deal attractive unless they know the industry well and can assure themselves that in the event of success they will be likely to share in the rewards.

Financial systems vary in their capability to fund innovative or unfamiliar projects backed only by uncertain earnings or illiquid assets. In some economies, creative financiers know how to fund technologically innovative projects, and hence are able efficiently to allocate financial capital toward high risk or uncertain proposals. Other economies have relative few imaginative financiers capable of looking at such kinds of deals constructively as well as critically. Countries whose financial systems foster diverse financing arrangements normally do a better job of encouraging creative financiers. It follows that the more diverse the capabilities of a financial system, and the more its regulatory climate encourages responsible experimentation with new forms of financing, the more likely the economy will be able to maintain international competitiveness through updating its productive capacity.

Growth is important to all economies, but particularly to less developed ones where both infrastructural and business capital are likely to be in relatively short supply. Unfortunately, financial system development is relatively difficult in underdeveloped countries, placing them at an additional disadvantage that can only be overcome with patiently building up the elements of a sound financial system over time. Moreover, when underdeveloped economies rely on external capital, the decisions of offshore financiers can determine the kinds of projects that will be funded, and it will not always be the case that the most highly productive projects are first in line to obtain whatever limited funds are available from the offshore sources.

In addition to affecting the rate and kind of economic growth that occurs, the financial system works to value assets, to increase liquidity and to produce information, including information about sources of financing. Securities trading in the primary and secondary markets determines the prices of both the securities and the productive assets to which they convey title. Securities valuations are largely based on expectations of the assets' future earnings, and are based on current information regarding those earnings prospects. As a result, securities valuations can change as new or additional information becomes available. Secondary market trading increases the liquidity of both financial assets and risk instruments, and increases in the liquidity of outstanding securities can also make new issues easier to sell. Both securities trading and the activities of financial intermediaries produce information, but markets produce information that is publicly disseminated while the information produced by intermediaries is not generally available to other agents. Finally, the presence of financial markets and financial firms means that the cost of searching for an accommodating financier is less than it would otherwise be.

2.2 WHO USES THE FINANCIAL SYSTEM?

The principal users of any financial system are consumers, businesses, governments and residents of other countries. Each of these client classes has its own goals, and consequently uses the financial system to achieve particular ends. Understanding the goals of individual client classes is a first step to understanding the kinds of products and services delivered by the firms constituting a typical financial system.

2.2.1 Consumers

Individuals or householders borrow or lend as a means of adjusting their expenditures toward their long term income prospects rather than their current incomes. That is, householders enter financial transactions to transfer purchasing power from one point in time. Through using financial transactions, households can arrange their expenditures with greater flexibility than would otherwise be possible, and thus gain greater satisfaction from the ways they spend their incomes. The existence of a well-functioning financial system makes such adjustments possible, and as a result the existence of such a system contributes to enhancing consumer satisfaction. Nearly all householders will enter financial transactions of some type. At any point in time, some householders will be net borrowers (i.e., their borrowing will exceed their lending or investment) while others will be net lenders or investors.

Consumers use banks and other depository intermediaries to hold both their cash or payments balances and, usually, some of their short term savings. Their cash balances are used primarily to cover cheques, pre-authorised payment orders, and electronically originated payments. Their cash balances are usually held in some form of chequing account, which may be interest-bearing, and their short term savings are almost always placed in interest-bearing accounts. Consumers also use their savings to purchase or contribute to such longer investments as mutual funds or pension funds. Finally, consumers buy life insurance, fire and accident insurance on their properties, and motor insurance to protect their earning power and their assets against various forms of loss.

Mortgage loans are households' principal source of longer term finance, while consumer credit is the principal medium term source. Consumers use mortgage loans to finance the construction, purchase or alteration of a primary residence. Consumers also borrow against their homes to finance purchases of cottages or other investment in rental housing, but such loans are less common. Still more rarely at the present time, some mortgage loans are used to finance consumption expenditures. However, this last form of financing may become more common as the ageing populations of the next few decades seek new sources of retirement financing.

Consumer credit originally financed retail purchases of consumer durables, and was mainly provided by department stores. Currently, however, personal lines of credit and credit card facilities extended by financial institutions are most common. Of the two types, credit card advances are usually the more frequently used. These funds so raised are used to finance anything from consumption expenditures to securities purchases.

2.2.2 Businesses

Businesses borrow to finance both short term transactions (i.e., for working capital reasons) and capital expenditures that are intended to increase the business's long term profitability. Firms raise funds from a variety of external sources, selecting among them on the basis of cost and availability. For example, many larger businesses can either borrow from their bankers or sell securities in the public markets, permitting them to use the two sources of funds as substitutes.

Like any other client group, businesses must pay market interest rates to raise funds. However, in contrast to other client groups, large corporations are less likely to face limits on the amounts of funds they can raise. Large businesses can usually raise funds quite readily so long as they can show financiers that proposed expenditure plans are likely to prove profitable. Nevertheless, even large firms may find fund raising difficult if they are entering new lines of business and financiers are not fully familiar with their proposed projects. The time periods needed for financiers to become familiar with new types of business can be relatively long (in rare instances years), and during that time funds may be either expensive or limited when viewed from the perspective of the business trying to raise the funds.

When they can do so, businesses will select among sources according to which they judge to offer the better terms. Different sources and different terms of borrowing can thus sometimes serve as substitutes. For example, a firm may wish to raise long term funds, but believe that long term borrowing rates are excessively high. In such cases it may initially borrow short term with the intention of subsequently refinancing on a longer term basis at a later time, when interest rates might be lower. As a second example, stock prices may seem low to management. Implicitly, this means that management see the rate at which future earnings are being discounted as relatively high. In such cases, especially if long term borrowing rates are also judged to be high, management may use internal financing with the hope of later raising external funds on more favourable terms. In other instances a project may be deferred in the hope that subsequently external financing will be available at lower effective rates.

Project finance means obtaining funds for a specific activity rather than for the firm conducting it. Such deals are secured by project assets and repaid from project returns rather than from the cash flows of the entire company. Thus a large project can be financed on its own merits rather than as a part of overall corporate activity. Project financing is sometimes **off-balance sheet**,[10] in which case it may have little effect on the undertaking firm's credit standing. It may also be based on cost plus contracts with purchasers of the project outputs, thus reducing the risk of cost overruns and providing financiers with greater security. It may also reduce financing costs.

---

off-balance sheet financing   a process of raising funds in such a manner that the client does not incur a direct financial obligation. As an example of incurring a direct financial obligation, a client may purchase an asset and borrow the funds to pay for it. The same transaction could be financed off-balance sheet if the client arranged to lease the asset from a financial leasing firm. In this case both the ownership of the asset and the direct liability for the asset are found on the balance sheet of the leasing company and not on that of the client actually using the asset.

Small business makes relatively heavier use of short term and conditional sales contract financing, because small business typically has much more difficulty than large business in raising longer term funds. These financing problems usually arise because small business has fewer liquid assets to secure loans or investments, and because the fixed costs of public financing are large enough to imply that raising small amounts of equity funds will be relatively expensive. These problems of small business finance are discussed at a number of subsequent points in the book.

2.2.3 Governments

Fiscal policy determines the difference between government revenues and expenditures, and thus whether a government saves or dissaves. A government with a budgetary surplus collects more than it spends, while a government with a budgetary deficit spends more than it collects. When government has a budgetary deficit, the excess of its expenses over revenues is covered by borrowings which usually take the form of bond or bill issues. The securities may be sold either to public or, if the government in question is a national one, to the central bank. In the first case, the deficit is financed by borrowing from the public, in the second through monetary expansion. Consider each in turn.

Government borrowing in domestic financial markets can cause interest rates to increase because the borrowing competes directly with the funds demands of the private sector. As the amount of public sector borrowing increases relative to total borrowing, the demands of the private sector may either be curtailed or met only at increased interest rates.[11]

A national government might sell its bonds to the central bank rather than borrow from the public. In this case the public's existing cash balances are not paid over to the government in exchange for bonds. Rather, the central bank prints extra money which is then used to buy the bonds. As a result the money supply increases when the government spends the funds. Interest rates may not be affected immediately by this type of deficit financing, but the expansion of the money supply will almost always prove inflationary over the longer run. In turn, inflation usually leads to eventually higher nominal interest rates.

Finally, government may bid up prices for goods or services when it spends the borrowed funds. Since fewer real resources then remain available to meet private sector demands, the spending can create inflationary pressures.[12] Hence a government deficit can result in relatively scarcer supplies of funds, higher interest rates, fewer resources available to the private sector, or any combination of the foregoing.

2.2.4 Residents of other countries

International transactions are important to every major financial system. Some countries are net lenders on the international scene, some are net borrowers. From the perspective of the net borrowing country, it is convenient to regard foreign investors as providers of residual funds. If foreign investors lose confidence in the borrowing country, its ability to raise funds will be impaired, and it will typically have to make a number of domestic adjustments to restore investor confidence. The adjustments are of the type that any over-extended borrower must make – cutting back on spending (usually government spending), reducing imports, promoting longer run economic growth and the like.

2.3 SUMMARY

This chapter introduced the roles performed by a financial system, and discussed the nature of typical financial system clients. With regard to roles, the chapter explained that a typical financial system effects payments, acts to help savers invest their accumulated wealth, facilitates both fund raising and risk management transactions. The most important relation between finance and economic activity – the role of the financial system in raising funds to finance economic growth – was also discussed. The principal users of financial system services are consumers, businesses, governments and residents of other countries. Transactions typically entered by each type of client were identified and discussed.

REVIEW QUESTIONS

Exercise 1 The relation between government expenditures and revenues can have an effect on the international value of the US dollar. For example, the mid-1990s' attempts to reduce federal budget deficits have helped to strengthen the dollar somewhat. Try to think of at least two ways in which a stronger US dollar affects your own financial position.

Exercise 2 Most currency dealers charge about 10 percent (included either in the difference between their rates and/or in the fee they charge) to exchange your funds for another currency. Some (but not all, you have to check the prices carefully) automated teller machines (ATMs) will dispense local currency for you, at or near current exchange rates, for a flat fee of about $2.00, debiting your account with the value of the currency and the fee. Which is the better deal? What if the ATM routes the transaction through your credit card, on which the rate is 18 percent?

Exercise 3 In the fall of 1993 the Romanian financial institution Caritas (no connection to the Catholic charity of the same name) promised a 100 percent return on savings left with them for three months. At the end of the first three months, they renewed the promise. If you had been able to, would you have deposited money with this institution?

Exercise 4 Suppose an economy had no financial markets or financial institutions. If you needed funds to finance some project, what would you have to do? Would the economy's level of capital formation be likely to change if there were a financial system? Why or why not?

Exercise 5 This book will later show you that debt is usually less risky than equity. If you are setting up a new venture, and some of your initial financing is by way of debt, who is likely to be taking the greater risk – the debtholders or yourself? Who ought to get the higher returns, the debtholders or yourself? How does this help you to understand why banks do not like to put too much money into a small business?

Exercise 6 If a company issues publicly traded stocks, what kind of information is available to investors? If the same company borrowed all its money privately, would the information available to the public at large be different? In what ways?

Exercise 7 Suppose you need $1 million for five years, at which time the funds will be repaid in full. No interim instalment payments are made. You can borrow for the full five years at 11 percent simple interest. As an alternative, you can borrow for one year at 12 percent, and then there is an equal chance that the rate for the remaining four years will be either 10 percent or 6 percent. What are your expected borrowing costs under each alternative?

Exercise 8 In China companies that lose money have been permitted to borrow the losses from the state banking system. The state banks must make the loans, so in effect they create new deposits which the money-losing companies then spend. In effect, the system increases the money supply by the amount of each year's losses. What effects ought this to have on Chinese interest rates?

Exercise 9 How does the existence of a financial system affect possibilities for capital formation?

Exercise 10 What do the following transactions have in common?

● Fuelling your car at a pump operated by a credit card.
● Using the phone's keypad to obtain the current value of your credit card account.
● Using the phone's keypad to find out, from the tax authorities, how much you can contribute this year to a tax-free retirement account.

Exercise 11 Use a price index to determine how much consumer prices have increased over the past twenty years. Using the index, if someone had bought you a $1,000 bond twenty years ago, how would its buying power have changed?

Exercise 12 Using the price index information from Exercise 11 and an estimate of average wages, calculate how long the average wage earner worked to buy a $1,000 bond twenty years ago. How long would the same person work for the same amount today?

Exercise 13 In the 1970s many persons bought travellers' cheques before travelling to other countries. They would usually exchange the travellers' cheques in local banks for local currency. Today many of the same persons carry a credit card and draw local currency from ATMs as they travel. What does this suggest about changes in the international payments system?

Exercise 14 In the late 1960s and early 1970s, risk management tools such as interest rate swaps were almost unheard of, but their use is now widespread. Try to outline several kinds of economic benefits to the greater use of risk management instruments.

Exercise 15 If you were trying to start a small business, how important do you think a financier who could make a clearheaded assessment of your firm's earnings potential would likely be? Why?

3 Financial system organisation

3.1	Introduction		26
	3.1.1	The parties to a deal	26
	3.1.2	Clients	27
	3.1.3	Financiers	27
3.2	Deal attributes		28
	3.2.1	Risk versus uncertainty	29
	3.2.2	Risky deals	29
	3.2.3	Deals under uncertainty	30
	3.2.4	Symmetries and asymmetries	30
	3.2.5	Asset liquidity	31
3.3	Governance mechanisms		31
	3.3.1	Market governance	31
	3.3.2	Financial intermediaries	32
	3.3.3	Internal governance	33
3.4	Cost-effective governance		33
	3.4.1	Alignment	33
	3.4.2	Deal terms	36
	3.4.3	Financial firms	36
	3.4.4	System organisation	37
3.5	Summary		37

LEARNING OBJECTIVES

After reading this chapter you will understand

- that financiers and their clients reconcile differing objectives as they enter a deal
- that deals can be regarded as presenting different combinations of a few important attributes
- that a deal can be administered using any one of three principal mechanisms: markets, financial intermediaries and internal organisation
- that cost-effective governance involves a deliberate alignment of governance mechanism capabilities and deal attributes
- that financial system organisation results from these alignments

---

3.1 INTRODUCTION

This chapter describes how a typical financial system is organised, and explains why this organisational form evolves. First, the chapter examines the parties to a typical financial deal and the objectives they strive to achieve. Next, the chapter contends that different deals can be regarded as presenting varying combinations of a few important attributes. The chapter then describes three principal types of governance mechanisms. Each mechanism can be used to administer financial deals, but each has its own distinctive capabilities that render it more or less well suited to governing deals of a particular type. The principal governance task faced by financiers is to determine which mix of governance capabilities can be used most effectively, given a deal's particular attributes. Finding this mix is described as alignment of deal attributes with governance capabilities. Finally, the chapter shows that a financial system's organisation at a point in time results from these cost-effective alignments. Over time, cost-effective forms of governance can change as the economics of doing deals changes.

3.1.1 The parties to a deal

Chapter 2 pointed out that the parties to any deal are a client and one or more financiers. Normally, clients will be individuals or non-financial firms, although sometimes one financial business will also be the client of another. Clients act as lenders or investors when they place funds, as borrowers when they raise funds. Financiers are individuals or business firms whose principal purpose is to profit from completing financial deals, either by selling financial products or by performing financial services. Financiers act as borrowers when they raise funds, as lenders or investors when they put funds to work. Some financiers function principally as agents, facilitating deals but not investing their own funds in the deals. Other financiers act as principals, both arranging the deal and providing some or all of the funds from their own resources.

3.1.2 Clients

As Chapter 2 indicated, data from the **funds flow accounts** show that the principal original suppliers of funds in market-oriented economies are households. Households are both lenders and borrowers. As lenders, households put savings to work when they acquire financial assets. As borrowers, they use others' savings. On a net basis, household saving exceeds household borrowing, and therefore households as a group are net suppliers of funds to the financial system. Households invest some funds through direct securities purchases, but larger proportions of their funds are entrusted to financial intermediaries, which then in turn lend the funds to clients. Business saving is also a source of financial system funds, but one that is relatively less important than household saving, and indeed on a net basis business is a user rather than a supplier of funds. In a typical market-oriented economy, the chief users of funds are corporations, households and governments (at all levels, from national to local). When clients deposit or invest their funds, they seek the most attractive terms they can find. Equally, when clients borrow they try to find the necessary funds at low interest rates, and on terms that are otherwise as attractive as they can find.

3.1.3 Financiers

Financiers raise their funds through both market and non-market transactions, the exact mix of their sources depending on the type of financial business they conduct. Financiers lend or invest the funds they raise in one of three principal ways. They purchase securities in the market place, they lend or invest on a negotiated basis, and they also invest directly, either in their own subsidiaries or in other firms.

While all financiers are concerned with the same tasks – raising funds and putting them to work as profitably as possible – there are important differences in the functions they perform. Financiers differ in their capabilities to screen potential deals, as well as in their capabilities to monitor and control deals they have already agreed. Differences among financiers arise both from the differing capabilities they acquire, and from their operating economics, which determines the mix of products and services they provide. Typically, the operations of financial firms are characterised by **scale economies**, **scope economies**, or both.[1] As shown later, these cost characteristics of financial firms explain both why large multiproduct firms are commonplace and why some some small, specialised financial institutions emerge.

Students sometimes have the impression that, in market-oriented economies like those of the US or the UK, most funds are raised in the securities markets. In fact, however, intermediaries are the principal suppliers of funds to business. While the proportions vary widely from one economy to the next, and from one year to the next within a given economy, about half the business funds required to finance new investment are raised internally, through the business's operations. Of the remaining, externally raised half, some 80 percent is raised from intermediaries in North American economies, while the rest is provided through the securities markets. The typical forms of these transactions are illustrated by Table 2.1 in the previous chapter.

3.2 DEAL ATTRIBUTES

The casual observer of financial activity is likely to be impressed by the enormous variety of deals mentioned in descriptive accounts. However, the descriptions create a misleading impression, because it is possible to describe a multitude of seemingly different deals in terms of a few distinguishing economic attributes. To be sure, the attributes may appear in different combinations, but this does not mean that deals with a few novel features differ very much in principle. Indeed, many of the arrangements described in the press as new are actually variants of familiar deals.[2] The rapidity with which such deals appear offers evidence that the same attributes are being recombined, usually in only slightly different ways. For example, in later chapters an **interest rate swap** will be shown notionally to be made up of several **forward contracts**. That is, both will be shown to be risk management instruments that employ similar ideas in similar ways.

In other words, different deals can be regarded as different mixes of the same principal attributes. The list of principal attributes changes very little, either over time or among different financial systems. On the other hand, new deals incorporate existing attributes in possibly unfamiliar combinations. Even a given type of deal may exhibit changes in the relative importance of its attributes over time. For example, a type of deal that is initially difficult to describe quantitatively may become less so as financiers become more familiar with doing it. In the early 1970s **swaps** were quite unfamiliar, and were usually negotiated individually. In the 1990s swaps are so familiar that whole families of related instruments can be negotiated on standard terms agreed to by institutions throughout the world.

The list of principal deal attributes can usefully be regarded as three-fold.[3] First, a deal can be regarded as presenting either risk or uncertainty.[4] For example, a deal such as purchasing a US treasury security can most usefully be regarded as risky, while financing the Channel Tunnel represented (and still represents) a deal under uncertainty. The profitability of a deal under risk can be described quantitatively, but the profitability of a deal under uncertainty is so difficult to determine that quantitative descriptions are of little help. Second, most deals involve financing the acquisition of some kinds of assets, and it matters considerably whether the assets are liquid or illiquid. For example, a working capital loan secured by an inventory of readily marketable clothing is a loan against liquid assets. In contrast, consider the provision of startup financing for a new high-technology venture whose success depends principally on the skills of an entrepreneur. Such a deal represents financing human capital, an illiquid asset that is notoriously difficult to value.[5] Third, deals can vary in legal and institutional features such as tax status, and these differences in detail can exert an important influence on a deal's profitability. For example, the interest on US municipal bonds is not treated as taxable income in the hands of a US investor, and as a result the market required rates of return on these bonds are much lower than on bonds of similar risk but different tax status.

3.2.1 Risk versus uncertainty

One way of comprehending the difference between risk and uncertainty is to view it in terms of the financier's capability to understand and manage events relevant to a deal's profitability. Financiers are quite often willing to describe their capabilities in such terms, and use their beliefs to decide how they will govern the deals they accept. For example, if an agent regards herself as highly competent to handle a given type of deal, she probably regards the deal as risky, feeling relatively confident that she can describe its payoffs satisfactorily in a quantitative sense. On the other hand, an agent who does not feel competent to understand a given deal may regard it as presenting considerable uncertainty. If an agent does decide to take on an uncertain deal, its governance will be quite different from the governance of a risky deal, as explained further below.

3.2.2 Risky deals

Risky deals are the kinds of deals described in numerous finance textbooks, that is deals that are structured well enough to permit describing their payoffs as probability distributions. Risky deals can present **profitability risk**, **default risk** or both. Profitability risk means that the earnings on the deal can vary randomly, in a way that can be described quantitatively using a probability distribution. Thus profitability risk refers to the probability of earning a relatively low or even negative return on the investment. Default risk refers to the possibility that a lender or investor faces the risk of not recovering anything at all.

---

profitability risk the risk that a loan or investment will not yield its rate of return with certainty.

---

default risk the risk that a loan or investment will not be repaid, usually because the client has no funds with which to repay it.

Profitability risk and default risk are not unrelated, but for descriptive purposes it is useful to distinguish them. Profitability risk is most closely related to such features as the possible magnitude of fluctuations in asset earnings, the maturity of the deal, whether the interest rate on it is fixed or floating, and the currency in which the deal is expressed. Default risk is most closely related to the credit rating of the obligant and to the illiquidity of assets whose acquisition is being financed. Deals financing the purchase of liquid assets are less likely to pose default risk than those financing the purchase of illiquid assets. Liquid assets can be seized and sold to repay all or at least part of the loan or investment extended to finance their purchase.

3.2.3 Deals under uncertainty

Uncertainty means that an agent does not regard himself as understanding a deal well. Deals most likely to present uncertainty are those involving a strategic change in business operations, or those financing a technological innovation. As already mentioned, a startup investment in a new, high-technology business offers an example of a deal under uncertainty. It is often observed that such projects are particularly difficult to finance, mainly because agents find it difficult to make quantitative analyses of their likely payoffs. First, neither clients nor financiers may be able to determine a proposed deal's key profitability features. Second, the possible reactions of competitors to carrying out the project may be difficult to predict. Despite these difficulties, deals presenting uncertainties are the essence of both business and financial innovation, and analysing how financiers overcome the difficulties is profoundly important to studying financial activity.

3.2.4 Symmetries and asymmetries

Financiers and clients do not always have the same deal information. The differences may arise because the two parties do not have access to the same data, or because they both have the same data but interpret them differently. These differences in interpretation can stem from differing levels of competence, or because differing experiences colour their interpretations of the data. In addition to these differing views of the deal itself, each agent forms a view of how counterparties regard the deal, complicating the picture further. Thus a deal's informational attributes can be classified in at least the following different ways:

- agents perceive risks symmetrically (i.e., they have the same view of the risks)
- agents perceive risks asymmetrically
- at least one agent perceives uncertainty.

Except where otherwise indicated specifically, the rest of this book assumes the client's information is at least as precise as that of any financier.

Whenever informational asymmetries are perceived to have economically important consequences for financiers, they will attempt to obtain more information, at least if the information's value is expected to be greater than the cost of gathering it. Cost-benefit analysis of information acquisition can be difficult under risk, and even more so under uncertainty. In the latter case, financiers may not even know how to frame relevant questions regarding any benefits to gathering more information. In this latter case, financiers may decide that they cannot learn enough about a given deal to assess its profitability even roughly, and as a result may decline to enter the deal.

3.2.5 Asset liquidity

Financiers find it easiest to fund projects whose assets have readily determined market values.[6] If the underlying assets trade actively in competitive secondary markets, financiers are likely to regard their financing as a risky rather than an uncertain deal. If the assets are liquid enough to be resold or redeployed readily, financiers can rely on their market value as a form of security. In the event of default they can seize and sell the assets (whose market values are relatively easy to estimate) to recover their funds. On the other hand, financing the acquisition and operation of illiquid assets[7] almost always involves uncertainty. For example, financing projects whose success rests on the talent and commitment of given individuals really amounts to financing human capital, as already mentioned. Human capital is best regarded as an illiquid asset, principally because the potential value of entrepreneurial skills is especially difficult to estimate.

3.3. GOVERNANCE MECHANISMS

Three principal kinds of governance mechanisms, each offering a unique set of capabilities for governing financial deals, can be distinguished.

3.3.1 Market governance

Markets and market agents are well equipped to handle deals whose terms can be specified fully at the outset. Thus markets are an effective mechanism for governing risky deals, and particularly deals which involve financing the acquisition of liquid assets. In such deals, the financier's main function is to determine the market price of the securities involved, mainly by using information publicly available to market participants. Such deals normally require only a minimal degree of subsequent monitoring, since their terms can be specified relatively completely at the time when funds are first advanced. Deals of this type are said to be implemented using **complete contracting**.

---

complete contracting a situation under risk in which all important outcomes can be described completely, and in which terms governing the actions to be taken in the event of such outcomes can also be described completely.

Within the category of market governance, finer distinctions can also be made. For example, private markets, in which securities are sold to one or a small group of investors, typically permit more detailed initial screening and more detailed negotiation of a deal's terms than do public markets in which securities are sold to a relatively large number of investors.

3.3.2 Financial intermediaries

All financial intermediaries raise funds in order to relend them, and as a group intermediaries raise most of the funds that a financial system provides to ultimate users. All intermediaries repackage loans or investments, and perform information processing functions as they do so. For the present discussion the most important aspects of these functions are the governance capabilities the intermediaries can muster.

Intermediaries usually have governance capabilities not possessed by market agents. First, they may sometimes have greater initial screening capabilities than do market agents. But even if they have only the same screening capabilities as market agents, intermediaries almost always have greater capabilities for monitoring, control and subsequent adjustment of deal terms. The principal means of adjustment available to market agents is to sell out an investment position,[8] but intermediaries have at least some capability to require their clients to adjust operations to reflect changing circumstances. As a result, intermediaries are better equipped to govern deals whose successful conclusion is likely to involve adjustment after a deal is agreed. In particular, intermediaries' capabilities for continued monitoring and adjustment render the consequences of learning from mistakes less costly than they would be for market agents.

Intermediary portfolios can be varied in both composition and type. For example, an important proportion of bank assets takes the form of illiquid loans, while life insurance company assets are mainly liquid securities. On the liability side, banks have many deposit obligations, while the principal liabilities of insurance companies are determined by the risks they assume. Although financial institutions are exhibiting an increasing tendency to combine portfolios of different types, say through mergers of bank and insurance company operations, many intermediaries still assemble relatively specialised asset and liability portfolios.

There are several economic reasons for specialising portfolios to some degree. First, specialised skills and experience may be required in order to be able to do deals profitably, and only a few intermediaries can justify incurring these expenses. For example, some banks specialise in foreign exchange transactions involving their home currencies, while other banks trade in most major foreign currencies. Second, certain types of deals can be done only in relatively small volumes, so that only a few firms can profitably service that market. Venture capital investments offer a case in point. Third, regulation may restrict intermediaries to only certain types of transactions. For example, North American trust companies have been restricted by legislation to having only a small proportion of their assets in consumer or commercial loans.

Financial intermediaries produce a great deal of information, some of it quite distinct from the kind normally used for accounting purposes. Intermediaries produce client information both when they first screen loan applications and when they monitor previously agreed deals. Unlike market information, the information produced by financial intermediaries typically remains private, because intermediaries do not trade most of the financial assets they originate. Thus any valuation of firms based on the information intermediaries produce is not subjected to the same public scrutiny as is the valuation information developed in the financial markets.[9] For the same reasons, the value of intermediary assets is not subject to the same public scrutiny as is a portfolio of marketable securities.

3.3.3 Internal governance

Hierarchical (internal) governance offers the greatest potential for intensive screening, continued monitoring, control over operations, and adjustment of deal terms. As a result, internal governance will normally be used to govern deals whose uncertainties are greater than those acceptable to intermediaries. In particular, the use of hierarchy is relatively more common in the case of incomplete contracting. As with intermediaries, hierarchical governance involves information production, but in this case the information produced remains almost entirely in private hands.

3.4 COST-EFFECTIVE GOVERNANCE

Financiers try to do deals as profitably as possible, which implies they agree only to deals they can govern cost-effectively. A market agent will not usually take on deals which require the specialised governance capabilities of a financial intermediary. If intermediaries take on these kinds of deals and exercise additional governance capabilities, their loan administration costs will be higher than the administration costs of market agents, and they will have to charge a higher interest rate to cover the costs and do the deal profitably. On the demand side, clients attempt to seek out a financier who offers the most attractive terms available. For example, clients will not willingly pay a higher fee to an intermediary if their deal can be handled more cheaply, or more effectively, by a market agent.

3.4.1 Alignment

The process by which financiers' capabilities and deal attributes are matched up is called alignment. Alignment choices represent a matching between a deal's attributes and the capabilities needed to govern those attributes. Financiers attempt to make alignment choices as cost-effectively as they are able, and Figure 3.1 shows how alignment can be regarded as the results of an interplay between deal attributes, financiers' governance capabilities and the costs of employing those capabilities.

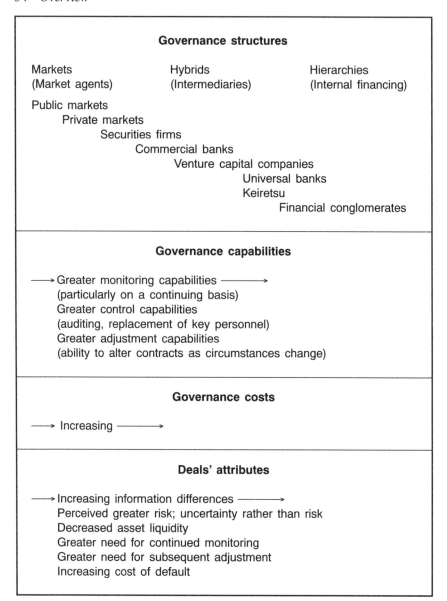

Figure 3.1 Governance capabilities, deal attributes and alignment

The first section of Figure 3.1 arranges the three basic governance mechanisms – markets, hybrids such as financial intermediaries, and hierarchical arrangements such as internal financing – in increasing order of governance capability. For example, public markets are recorded to the left of private markets, because private market agents can muster certain governance capabilities not possessed by public market agents. Private market agents usually have greater investigative capability, and in some cases greater freedom to negotiate terms, than do public market agents. Similarly, even though commercial banks and venture capital firms are both intermediaries, commercial banks usually have less highly developed screening and monitoring capabilities than do venture capital firms. In particular, venture capital firms make greater use of discretionary arrangements, which usually include obtaining a seat on the board of any company to which they extend funds. Finally, hierarchical governance means governance within a given organisation or group. Western financial conglomerates sometimes offer examples of hierarchical organisations, as do the Japanese keiretsu.[10] Similarly, the universal banks found in Germany use something closer to hierarchical governance when they both purchase the shares of, and make long term loans to, the same clients.[11]

Figure 3.1's second section indicates that different governance mechanisms have differing degrees of capabilities. For example, hierarchical mechanisms have greater monitoring and control capabilities than do market agents. The figure's governance costs section is a reminder that greater capabilities are normally mustered at increasing cost.

Reading from left to right in Figure 3.1's attributes section shows that deals characterised by greater informational differences between the two parties (the financiers typically having less information) are viewed by financiers as involving higher degrees of risk, or as presenting uncertainty instead of risk. Higher risk deals, and deals with uncertain payoffs, pose greater needs for continuing governance than lower risk deals, in part because they carry increasing expected costs of default. Similarly, greater uncertainty, a lower degree of asset liquidity or both make it more difficult to establish market values for the underlying assets,[12] and consequently make it more difficult for financiers to determine the breakup value of a firm in financial difficulty. If they cannot readily establish a breakup value for the firm, financiers do not know what they might be able to realise if the firm should fail. Therefore, deals with such firms appear less secure than, say, deals that finance purchases of liquid assets with readily established market values.

Financiers accept some deals, and reject others, on the basis of whether the capabilities they can muster make it likely they will be able to administer the deal profitably. Financiers strive to make their alignment choices cost-effectively, as shown by the arrangements in the different parts of the figure. For example, in comparison to hybrid or hierarchically governed deals, market deals tend to be more standardised, and to exhibit less important informational differences between client and financier. As a result, market governance uses relatively few monitoring and control capabilities, and market-governed deals typically present lower administration costs than do hierarchically governed deals.

To put the same issue in different words, since financings under uncertainty present the most difficult governance problems, they are likely to have the highest governance costs. Naturally these higher governance costs must be recovered from gross returns on the investment, just as greater possibilities of default losses must be compensated for. For example, administering a portfolio of short term liquid securities principally requires market governance, while administering the financing of conglomerate subsidiaries that are entering new ventures can require a much more intensive, and higher capability, form of governance. As a result, the second kind of deal must offer higher gross returns if it is to generate expected net profits.

3.4.2 Deal terms

Deal terms are varied both in attempts to ensure profitability and to fine tune governance. One of the most important deal terms is the effective interest rate charged for using the funds. The effective interest rate on a deal increases with its risk, and will be higher for uncertainty than for risk, because financiers require larger returns to compensate for greater risks or for assuming uncertainty rather than risk. Analogously, the tax status of a deal can affect both the financier's return and the client's cost of funds.

Other terms of a deal include its maturity (fixed or variable), the collateral taken, the currency used and specific contract provisions. These kinds of terms are varied in attempts to govern particular deal attributes. For example, a deal offering uncertain payoffs can be much easier to finance if the client can offer marketable securities as collateral. In this case a loan can be made against the value of the securities, and the financier, who can rely on the securities' market value as collateral for the loan, will likely view the deal as merely risky rather than uncertain.

3.4.3 Financial firms

Financial firms assemble agreed deals into portfolios whose size and composition are determined by the firms' operating economics. Financiers specialise in particular types of deals as a means of realising scale economies in screening and in information production. They realise additional **scale economies** by increasing the numbers of deals in their portfolios, and **scope economies** by taking on related types of deals. In other words, these actions reduce unit costs and, if unit revenue remains the same, profitability is improved.

When a firm assumes a greater number of deals, as well as when it assumes additional types of deals, it can usually diversify portfolio risks.[13] Since diversifying portfolio risk reduces earnings risk relative to the expected level of earnings, the firm's performance is thereby improved.

Limits to the size of a financial firm depend mainly on the costs of coordinating the governance of different deal types. When coordination costs begin to rise on a unit basis, taking on more business generating the same unit revenue means that the profitability of additional business begins to fall. When incremental profitability falls to zero, it does not pay the firm to take on still further business: firms can be expected to grow only until coordination costs become large enough to impair the profitability of taking on more deals.

scale economies the ability to produce additional units of output at a decreasing average cost per unit. Scale economies frequently arise from spreading fixed production costs over a larger number of units of output.

scope economies the ability to obtain combinations of goods or services at a lower average cost per unit than can be achieved if the goods or services are produced individually. Scope economies, sometimes called cost complementarities, usually result from the ability to share common inputs.

3.4.4 System organisation

The alignment of deal attributes and governance capabilities, and the consequent assembly of portfolios to take advantage of the associated firms' operating economies, explain the static organisation of the financial services industry. In the aggregate, the structure of a financial system will reflect a mix of alignments determined by the deals agreed and the capabilities of the economy's financiers. The sizes of individual firms will be determined by their operating economics.

Although there is a natural evolution of any particular deal type from the right to the left in Figure 3.1 (due to financier learning, increasing volume of deals, standardisation of deals over time, more nearly precise and cheaper information production), a continual infusion of new deals means that high capability governance structures continue to be needed, even in advanced economies.

3.5 SUMMARY

This chapter explained that different types of deals are most cost-effectively governed by using governance mechanisms appropriate to the deal's attributes. The chapter first explained that financial deals differ principally in whether they present risky or uncertain payoffs, and in whether the assets financed by a loan or investment are liquid or illiquid. The chapter then continued by explaining that the three principal governance mechanisms are markets, financial intermediaries and internal organisation. Markets offer the most cost-effective method of governing standardised deals. Standardised deals take place under risk, and are sufficiently well specified at the outset that they can be represented by complete contracts. Intermediaries are more cost-effective for governing deals that present some uncertainties, and therefore require a greater degree of continued monitoring and adjustment than market-governed deals. Internal allocation is more cost-effective for governing deals that present considerable uncertainty and require a relatively intensive degree of continued monitoring and adjustment capabilities.

REVIEW QUESTIONS

Exercise 1 You can set down most of what matters about a risky deal at the outset, but cannot set down most of what matters about an uncertain deal, because the deal may be new and what matters may not be knowable. Suppose you have agreed to extend funds to one client under risk, and to another under uncertainty. The first might be a working capital loan, the second an equity investment in a new business. In which of the two deals will your learning likely be greater?

Exercise 2 Consider another form in which the alternatives of a risky and an uncertain deal might arise. Suppose the risky deal involves financing an airplane purchase to add one more flight on an already profitable airline route, while the uncertain deal involves financing the same airplane purchase, but the plane will now be used to open up a new and untried route. In this case, even though operating the new route might present uncertain payoffs, the financier's position is not the same as in Exercise 1. Why?

Exercise 3 Government treasury bills are promissory notes that evidence short term borrowing by a government. When a small business borrows from a bank, it too issues a promissory note. Why does the first promissory note sell in an active marketplace, while the second does not?

Exercise 4 Small business loans are not individually sold in the marketplace, but a bank might be able to securitise a portfolio of small business loans, which means that the bank can raise funds in markets by selling its own securities against a portfolio of small business loans. What economic function has the bank performed to make the securitisation possible?

Exercise 5 Suppose your firm financed a new project undertaken by one of its subsidiaries. How would the firm's capability to monitor and control the investment differ from the monitoring and control that could be exercised by a venture capital firm?

Exercise 6 Why would it be too costly to have the financial division of a conglomerate headquarters supervise a short term investment in treasury bills?

Exercise 7 Imagine that you own a holding company that in turn owns several different kinds of businesses, and suppose the holding company has $1 million to invest. Suppose that you could either put the money into bonds, or into a new project controlled by the holding company. List some of the ways your control over the investments would differ.

Exercise 8 Suppose you were setting up a company and seeking to obtain startup capital. What financiers would you approach, and why?

Exercise 9 What are some of the most important differences between a risky deal and a deal under uncertainty? If you wanted to put funds into an uncertain investment project, what kinds of questions would you want to ask your client?

Exercise 10 How can financiers' decisions to fund or not fund projects affect a country's ability to compete in world markets?

Exercise 11 Some commentators on restructuring the former planned economies place heavy emphasis on opening a stock market to achieve financial reform. Why might it also be important to strengthen the banking system?

4 Change

4.1	Forces of change		41
4.2	Processes of change		42
	4.2.1	Experimentation	43
	4.2.2	Profitability	43
	4.2.3	Regulation	44
4.3	Short term change		45
4.4	Current issues		46
	4.4.1	Is there a continuing role for banks?	46
	4.4.2	Mitigating underdevelopment	46
4.5	Summary		48

LEARNING OBJECTIVES

After reading this chapter you will understand

- what kinds of forces drive financial system evolution
- how the search for new profit opportunities drives change
- how regulation usually adapts to change, rather than causing it
- that even while change continues, the same financial system functions continue to be performed
- that understanding the forces of change can help refine the search for new profit opportunities
- that understanding the forces of change can be used to help design better financial systems

Financiers continually seek to improve their profit positions, both by looking to increase margins on the types of deals they are already doing and by finding new forms of profitable deals. Financiers are so interested in new profit opportunities that they sometimes take on new deals whose likely profitability has only been suggested rather than confirmed. When a new type of deal is first taken on, it will likely be structured through negotiation with an intermediary. If the new type of product or service proves to meet a previously unsatisfied client demand, the new type of deal is likely to become increasingly familiar, and its terms are likely to become increasingly standardised. If enough deals are done, it may eventually become possible to carry them out in the marketplace rather than through negotiation with intermediaries. The emergence of the standardised, plain vanilla **swap** to be discussed in Chapter 13 is an example. If the new types of deals become common practice, they can contribute to permanent changes in financial system organisation. For example, virtually all of the world's major banks and securities firms now have facilities for trading in risk management instruments, but none of these same firms traded risks to any appreciable degree prior to 1970.

4.1 FORCES OF CHANGE

Changes in deals' profitability can result either from changes in demand for the product or service, or from changes in the terms on which financiers supply it. Changes in demand can occur in at least two forms: a shift in the demand curve for deals of a given type, or the emergence of demand for deals of new types. Demand changes derive principally from changes in the environmental conditions clients face. For example, both increases in international trade and increasing volatility in the foreign exchange markets led to increased demands for foreign currency hedging.

Changes in the terms on which financiers offer new products or services mainly arise as new forms of technology, either electronic or purely financial, make them possible. Changes in technology change deals' risk–return ratios, usually by making their governance cheaper. As an example of a change in electronic technology, computers permit supervising a credit card portfolio on a management by exception basis, and thus create new sources of scale economies in governing a portfolio of credit card debt. Before computers became widely available, records had to be reviewed manually to identify slow payers and other accounts needing personal attention. As an example of a change in financial technology, development loans were rarely made to small private borrowers until about the mid-1980s, because it was thought the credit risks of this type of business were too great. However, at that time the International Finance Corporation began extending loans to villages rather than to individual borrowers, and it was found that the default risk of these loans was much less than had been expected. Thus a technical change in the way financing was supplied made possible the emergence of what had previously been thought to be an unprofitable business.

Financiers will not always respond immediately to changes in demand. Sometimes proposed new deals are not profitable, and sometimes financiers do not realise that they can actually do new deals at a profit. For example, if a certain deal's risk is perceived as too high in relation to its expected returns, financiers will not entertain it no matter how actively clients seek the financing. Prior to the mid-1980s, the requests for certain forms of development financing were usually regarded in this light, as the previous paragraph explained.

4.2 PROCESSES OF CHANGE

Technological change has profoundly affected the world's financial system. The changes, which began in the early 1980s, have continued apace through the 1990s and appear likely to continue for at least another decade. Reductions in computing and communications costs have contributed to the financial system's becoming increasingly integrated and increasingly international in character. As the information processing elements common to traditionally different financial functions have come increasingly to be recognised, traditional boundaries between formerly separate parts of the financial industry have weakened or dissolved. This development has been a gradual one, in that it was first pointed out by such observers as Walter Wriston (a former chairman of Citibank) in the 1970s. Wriston recognised that many seemingly different kinds of financial activities could usefully be viewed as variants of a scorekeeping function that can cheaply and easily be performed by computers. Despite the concept's gradual acceptance, the effects of treating financial activity as an information processing function have now become widespread, and many formerly specialised financial intermediaries have merged to form multiproduct organisations. The rapidly changing computing and communications environment has also led to a proliferation of new products as financial institutions have strived to retain or even increase their market shares through exploiting technological advances.

4.2.1 Experimentation

Financiers differ in their abilities to govern deals and in their readiness to adapt to change. Some experiment, others do not. Whether financiers are conservative or innovative, their choice can be explained as a rational conclusion drawn from their own assessments of deal attributes and their ability to administer those attributes profitably. For example, some merchant bankers have actively sought to arrange **leveraged buyouts**, even arranging bridging finance in order to capture additional merger and acquisition business. These innovative merchant bankers hoped to be able to earn new profits, but since they were experimenting with unfamiliar new forms of business, they could not always characterise their expected returns quantitatively. Other merchant bankers avoided making the same choices, again because of the difficulties they had in describing quantitatively the kinds of earnings they expected to generate.

When they experiment, financiers understand that they are taking unquantified risks, may feel uncomfortable with taking them, but regard the game as worth the candle nevertheless.[1] Financial system change represents intendedly rational action, but it is very often taken in an atmosphere of uncertainty. Decisions to enter new businesses are based on anticipated net benefits of some kind, but at the time the decisions are being taken it may not be possible to describe these benefits in very precise terms.[2]

4.2.2 Profitability

A financier with a new product or method can retain a monopolistic advantage (even in a competitive market) for the time it takes competing institutions to emulate the innovation. During this period, the innovator may be able to earn above normal profits, or to capture new shares of profitable business. As competition for new profit opportunities continued to increase throughout the 1970s and 1980s, the average time over which monopoly profits could be earned on a new product gradually shortened. Thus the financiers of the 1990s are under increasingly greater pressure to learn to detect new profit opportunities and to exploit them as quickly as possible. For example, in recent years competition in retail banking has forced participants to adopt new technology quickly, even if it did not offer the prospect of temporary monopoly profits. Financiers have found themselves forced to adopt new technologies just to retain their ability to compete effectively with other firms in the industry.

Innovative deals can demand new governance capabilities, needed to administer the uncertainties that experimental ventures present. While it can be relatively easy to describe quantitatively the distribution of profits on routine deals, it is usually much harder to describe the returns to innovative forms of deals with anything like the same degree of quantitative precision. For example, the banks and securities firms which tried to take advantage of London's Big Bang (1986) through rapid expansion into new areas could not always justify their moves in profitability terms.[3] Yet, many felt they had to make such moves simply to keep even with the competition. The late 1980s' and early 1990s' retrenchments of international banks and securities firms are adjustments reflecting the same banks' subsequent learning, from experience, that the market opportunities were not large enough to sustain all the new entrants.

Even though it has become increasingly important to exploit new profit opportunities quickly, supply changes are not always instantaneous. Innovation is costly, and learning how to adapt established routines to new circumstances can be a lengthy process. Accordingly, both innovative deals and innovative governance structures often evolve relatively slowly from well-established technologies. Some viable new deals may be avoided, at least for a time, either because their gross returns are underestimated or because their governance costs are overestimated. Financiers are sometimes less likely to innovate under competition than under monopoly, because under competition an innovative financier can have less opportunity to recover unanticipated cost increases.

Finally, temporary advantages to innovation may not always be exploited as immediate monopoly profits. Tufano (1989) argues that investment banks which create new products do not always charge higher prices in the period before imitative products appear. Rather, some innovative firms charge prices below those of their rivals, and by so doing capture a larger share of new business than is enjoyed by their imitators. Tufano's finding may mean that innovative firms can enjoy lower costs of trading, underwriting and marketing. Innovation may be cost reducing, permitting the innovator to realise economies of scale and of scope. Alternatively, innovation may signal intangible forms of skill or creativity that attract new business. Finally, innovators may become skilled at learning by doing, and can thus develop new products more cheaply than their imitative rivals. Taking all the foregoing factors into account, a financial system's innovativeness can be said to depend on a delicate and shifting balance of the forces favouring and impeding innovation.

4.2.3 Regulation

Regulation is usually aimed at improving system performance. Changes to regulation are best looked on as a dynamic process of adaptation between the regulators and the regulated, a process which might be termed a regulatory dialectic. New regulation increases the cost of conducting or combining certain types of business, and profitable financial activity may sometimes be restricted by regulation. But if the benefits to the business are sufficiently large, and if they can be captured in the interest rates financiers can collect, new business very often springs up in spite of regulation intended to prevent it. Indeed, a substantial proportion of managerial effort may be devoted to finding ways of carrying out transactions that are restricted by regulation, but are nevertheless perceived to be potentially profitable.

Sometimes management is successful in finding new ways to avoid or frustrate regulation, and when this occurs regulation is usually revised to recognise the new reality. Such regulatory validations of a newly established status quo occur partly because much of the initiative for regulatory change takes the form of a response to existing problems, and partly because regulations are usually revised infrequently. The possibility that infrequent revisions can inhibit change has led at least some financiers to plead for more frequent, or even continuous, revision of regulation.

4.3 SHORT TERM CHANGE

There are usually predictable relations among short term interest rates. For example, Chapter 6 will show that rates on higher risk instruments are usually higher than rates on lower risk, but otherwise comparable, instruments. Rates will depart from their typical patterns as the quantity of funds supplied changes relative to the quantity demanded, but these departures from typical patterns are also signals for their elimination. As soon as unusual interest rate differentials emerge, funds are diverted from markets where rates are atypically low to markets where they are atypically high (in relation to the instruments' perceived risk). These reallocations usually eliminate the atypical interest differential relatively quickly. Transactions aimed at profiting from atypical interest differentials take two principal forms. First, financial intermediaries change the emphasis of their activities, lending more where rates are atypically high and less where rates are atypically low. Second, arbitrageurs (persons seeking **arbitrage opportunities**: see p. 75) begin selling securities with relatively low interest rates, in order to buy securities bearing higher rates.

While short term funds flows usually respond quickly to unusual short term interest rate differentials, they respond much more slowly, if at all, to changes in legislation. Indeed, legislation to control profitable types of business is usually ineffective. Adjustment processes may be impeded by legislation, but profitable transactions cannot usually be stopped. For example, when limitations on deposit interest rates (Regulation Q ceilings) were imposed on US financial intermediaries by the US Federal Reserve System in the late 1960s, the banks moved to booking the same deposits in London, where the maximal rates were not subject to Federal Reserve restrictions.

Regulatory attempts to control either the type of business done, or the quantity of a given type, are quite likely to meet a similar fate. For example, if banks are requested to make more loans to homeowners for improvement purposes, and if they are required to extend the loans at below-market interest rates, they will offer only token compliance. The banks may claim there is no demand for this type of loan, they may disqualify applicants on the basis of technical irregularities in their loan applications, or they may simply delay processing applications. As a second example, foreign exchange controls cannot readily prevent transactions outside the country. Most countries' citizens find it easy to open bank accounts in other countries and to transport cash across the national borders, both actions that can circumvent foreign exchange controls.

4.4 CURRENT ISSUES

Two questions, concerning the future role of banks and ways of mitigating underdevelopment, illustrate how the foregoing discussion of change can be used to help understand current financial market developments.

4.4.1 Is there a continuing role for banks?

Although this book will argue that screening, monitoring and adjustment will continue to be part of the financial activity of the future, some observers suggest that in the future banks may play a sharply diminished role. These observers place little emphasis on the functions of screening, monitoring and adjustment performed by banks, and merely note a contemporary manifestation of an ever present phenomenon: that banks keep changing the forms of their business. First, the current version of the argument often notes that there have been increasing amounts of asset securitisation over the 1980s and 1990s, suggesting that the funds for lending are increasingly coming from the capital markets rather than from depositors. Second, over the same period corporations have used proportionately more capital market financing and proportionately less bank financing. Third, banks have recently begun selling credit derivatives which transfer some of their credit risks to other agents.

Yet none of these observations argues that banks will spend less time on screening, monitoring and adjustment in the future, nor do the observations argue that these latter functions will become economically less valuable. As savers place more of their funds in marketable securities, banks will likely respond by raising greater proportions of their funds from other institutions, or from their own offerings of investment funds rather than deposits. Moreover, banks will undoubtedly see a continuing migration of some clients toward market financings. In addition, banks are tailoring the risks they bear on their own books by selling credit derivatives. The theory of Chapter 3 recognised such developments, suggesting that the logical progression of certain kinds of deals was from right to left in Figure 3.1. In other words, this change in the qualitative nature of some deals means only that the deals banks can govern cost-effectively keep changing. It does not mean the banks will be left without any deals to govern in the future. Rather, banks will continue to enjoy scale economies in screening and monitoring firms, and to have an advantage in restructuring firms.

4.4.2 Mitigating underdevelopment

A number of problems related to financial underdevelopment are exemplified by the so-called transition economies, that is the formerly planned economies now adopting market-oriented economic systems. Most transition economies have only rudimentary financial systems, mainly because their financial products and services were formerly provided by state organisations that did not generally price products or services at market rates of interest. The transition economies can derive at least three benefits from further financial system development. First, further development will bring greater availability of financing and of risk management services. Second, the emergence of more active trading in equities should lead to greater investor control over firms' management. Third, financial system development should help to attract foreign investment, thus helping overcome domestic capital shortages.

It is sometimes argued that the transitional economies primarily need new equities markets. As the theory of Chapter 3 suggests, market governance plays an important role in financing relatively simple, well-understood kinds of deals. Equities markets do make it possible to capitalise firms publicly and to diversify the resulting investment risks. They produce information regarding the value of firms' activities, and influence firms' managers through the possibility of merger and takeover threats that publicly traded equity provides. Developed equity markets also aid in attracting foreign capital, because they offer new investment opportunities to foreign investors. These advantages are important for at least two reasons. First, management is a scarce resource, and changes that encourage developing management capabilities are beneficial. Second, additional information helps agents make resource allocation decisions more efficiently, and these kinds of improvements can bring significant payoffs.

On the other hand, the developing equity markets typical of transitional economies do not usually stimulate more than small amounts of secondary market trading, and the costs of trading may be high. In addition, if accounting practices are not well developed, it will be difficult for agents in these thinner markets to place market values on the securities traded. Both these features of developing equity markets impair their ability to assist in raising primary financing. Even if these difficulties are ultimately overcome, however, equity markets cannot perform all financial system functions equally well.

Chapter 3 explained that intermediary financing can bring advantages complementary to those of market financing, and also that most new financing in developed economies comes from intermediaries rather than from new share issues. For these reasons, promoting intermediary as well as market financing is likely to benefit the transition economies. There is another, more controversial reason, as well. Albert (1993: 72–74) and others suggest that equity markets tend to emphasise short term rather than long term results, and thus leave some kinds of viable deals unfunded.To the extent this observation is empirically valid,[4] it provides another reason for encouraging the development of intermediaries as well as markets.

Some skeptical observers argue that banks mainly lend to well-established, safe borrowers, and avoid riskier propositions, but these objections do not recognise that intermediaries in different countries can exercise quite different degrees of non-market governance. For example, German and Japanese banks typically have closer connections to major clients, both through shareholdings and positions on client boards, than do banks in, say, the United States or the United Kingdom. As a result of their close connections with clients, the German and

Japanese banks can sometimes[5] fund specific forms of long term, high risk investments that would be more difficult to finance in the equities markets of the US or the UK.

Both markets and intermediaries provide information about the value of firms' activities. A functioning equity market provides short term valuations of assets, while intermediaries provide longer term, more discriminating, and less public evaluations. Bank-dominated financial systems produce less public information than do market-dominated systems, and thus do not always provide the up-to-date valuation information characteristic of securities markets. The kinds of information most critical to a given transition economy depend on its structure and the types of financing deals sought. If the deals are relatively easy to value, market governance will be useful. If longer term horizons and monitoring are needed to complete the valuation process, intermediaries using a longer term governance perspective will be needed. In most transition economies, it seems likely that both an equities market and a banking system will play the complementary roles they play in developed market economies.

The role of the financial system may be more important to economic growth in industrialising countries than has previously been realised. Singh (1995), who compares the kinds of funding used by firms in developed and developing countries, argues that in developed countries corporations mostly use retained profits to finance their investment needs. When they turn to external sources, corporations in developed countries turn first to long term debt and only as a last resort to the stock market, as indicated by funds flow data introduced in Chapter 2 and discussed more fully in Chapter 5. In developing countries, Singh finds that corporations rely less on retained earnings, and more on external funds, including new issues of shares, to finance growth of net assets. If Singh's findings are supported by further analyses, they would suggest that an absence of financial system development is likely to have even more importance to financing the economic growth of industrialising countries than it has in already developed economies.

4.5 SUMMARY

This chapter sketched the processes of financial system change. It began by discussing the forces of change, both those affecting the demands for financial services and those affecting the ways financiers supply their services. The chapter then examined processes of change, stressing the uncertainties financiers face as they attempt to manage change. Financiers balance factors that favour change against other factors that inhibit it. To some extent, regulation can affect the economics of change, but usually for relatively short periods of time. Regulation that attempts to curb profitable activity over the longer term contains the seeds of its own destruction, as financial managers have incentives to circumvent it.

The book's theory of financial system activity was used to examine two current issues regarding change. First, it was argued that banks will not disappear even though they are currently losing corporate lending business and at the same time securitising their own assets. Since banks are skilled at non-market types of governance, they will instead turn to new deals requiring those types of governance skills. Negotiated risk management deals offer a current example. Second, the chapter contended that financial system development requires a mix of markets and financial intermediaries if it is to handle successfully the mix of deals that a developing economy typically needs to finance.

REVIEW QUESTIONS

Exercise 1 Since the mid-1980s, banks have increasingly used ATMs, and they have also increasingly used securitisation. Which of these represents learning regarding how to use governance methods?

Exercise 2 In 1993, the damages claims resulting from one hurricane in Florida wiped out all the underwriting profits the State Farm Insurance Company had earned over the previous fifty years. Some insurers, observing the losses and revising their estimates of hurricane damage, decided to leave the business. Can you think of an alternative that would involve staying in business and changing the insurers' methods of risk management?

Exercise 3 Would computer processing of a credit card account be likely to differ from computer processing of a business loan account? What about computer records for a mutual fund and for an insurance policy with a savings element? Assuming that big computer installations can be made only for a large fixed cost, what does this suggest to you about combining different types of financial business?

Exercise 4 Suppose your boss wants you to manage a new product development campaign whose payoffs, in your view, are quite uncertain. Your boss wants to go ahead, but has been muttering that a five year development campaign would cost about $50 million, and that five years is a long time to wait to see if that kind of investment pays off. There is no real market research that will help assess product profitability, but you think you can trim the uncertainties and impress your boss anyhow. What kind of proposal might do this?

Exercise 5 Deposits in US banks were at one time subjected to interest rate ceilings that did not apply to the London offices of these US banks. London rates rose above the ceilings. What happened to the domestic deposits?

Exercise 6 Rates on mortgages have just risen, and rates on bonds have fallen a little. What would you expect to see banks doing? What about securities firms that carry inventories of bonds?

Exercise 7 What forces are currently causing most financial system change?

Exercise 8 Will the financial system attempt to promote financial products that consumers or businesses do not want?

Exercise 9 Small business persons often talk about how difficult it is to raise funds to finance growth. In the mid-1960s they said much the same thing. Is this evidence that the financial system does not adapt?

Exercise 10 One form of asset securitisation currently used by mortgage lenders (banks, near banks) involves their making mortgage loans and then selling instruments secured by the mortgage loan portfolio to other financial institutions. Effectively, this kind of deal means the banks raise funds from, say, pension or mutual funds, and invest them in mortgages. This kind of deal is currently so popular that some observers think banks may not have a role to play in the future. Do you agree? Why or why not?

5 Financial systems: an empirical overview

5.1	Introduction	52
5.2	Bases for comparison	52
5.3	Financial system effects	53
	5.3.1 Finance and economic activity	53
	5.3.2 Governance and long term finance	55
5.4	Interpreting funds flows	57
	5.4.1 Funds flow accounts	57
	5.4.2 Financial system growth	60
	5.4.3 Linkages with the rest of the world	60
5.5	Interpreting asset data	61
	5.5.1 Household financial assets	61
	5.5.2 Corporate finance	62
	5.5.3 Financial intermediaries	63
5.6	Summary	64

LEARNING OBJECTIVES

After reading this chapter you will understand

- how funds flow data help trace short term financial activity
- how outstanding balances data help trace longer term trends
- some of the important similarities and differences among the financial systems of Germany, Japan, the US and the UK

5.1 INTRODUCTION

Most readers find it easier to apply a theory if they can examine data that describe broadly their field of study. For this reason, the present chapter compares and contrasts aspects of financial activity in Germany, Japan, the UK and the US. The overview is designed to point out some of the similarities among the four countries' financial systems, as well as to identify some of their more important differences.

5.2 BASES FOR COMPARISON

The financial systems of the four countries considered in this chapter all perform the roles discussed in Chapters 2 and 3. Each of the four financial systems raises funds from agents who wish to save, and makes the funds available to other agents who wish to borrow or to finance long term investments. Each of the four systems employs the three types of governance identified in Chapter 3, although in varying ways that depend on both historical accident and the differing features of the four economies.

Two kinds of data will be used to indicate the quantitative importance of different financial activities. The first type, funds flow data, quantitatively describes the sources of funds raised in any given period and the uses to which the funds are put. Funds are supplied mainly from household savings, and enter the financial system through three channels: direct securities purchases, deposits in intermediaries such as banks, and payments to savings intermediaries such as pension funds and insurance companies. The funds raised by intermediaries are in turn lent to or invested in activities of the intermediaries' clients. These clients are businesses, governments that have spent more than they raised in taxes and other charges, and households availing themselves of mortgage loans or consumer credit.

The flows in a financial system are the borrowing or lending transactions taking place over a given period of time, usually a year. The funds flow accounts, which are used principally to trace the channels through which funds are transmitted from original suppliers to final users, show that most funds are provided by households. While households invest some funds directly, most of their savings flows through financial intermediaries before being made available to final users. Within any given country, the quantity of funds saved domestically does not usually equal the quantity of funds employed in financing domestic investment. If a country's domestic savings is less than its domestic investment, the country must on balance raise funds from abroad; if domestic savings exceeds investment, the country will lend or invest its surplus funds to other countries' users.

Flow data are useful for tracing the customary channels through which funds flow, but they also have their limitations. First, flow data are constructed using changes in balance sheets drawn up at successive points in time, and as a result show only the net borrowing or lending transactions that occurred during the intervening period. That is, the accounts do not separately report total lending and total borrowing, but only the difference between them. Second, any economy's flow data change over relatively wide ranges from one year to the next, meaning that funds flow accounts are more useful for describing current events than for making historical comparisons. Third, the reported data are estimated from a number of sources and therefore embody relatively large errors.[1] Finally, the rapid and wide-ranging changes in successive years' accounts mean that the data are not well suited to making definitive comparisons among different economies.

The second type of data indicates the ownership distribution of financial assets, that is the cumulative effects of funds flows over many time periods. These cumulated flows, or amounts outstanding, can be interpreted as indicating who owes whom, and how much, at a given point in time. Data for amounts outstanding, or balances data, are considerably more stable than funds flows. Thus, they can be used to provide informative comparisons of how the market shares of different financial businesses, and of different financial instruments, change over time. The stability of asset data also means they are useful for comparing some aspects of financial activity among different countries. Asset data are used both by financial managers for competitive purposes and by regulatory authorities for supervisory purposes.

5.3 FINANCIAL SYSTEM EFFECTS

Determining how a financial system influences economic activity poses a number of complex and difficult questions, mainly because the influences of financing are confounded by many other factors, including the structure of the economy, its pattern of evolution, and the technical and cultural differences which affect it. Comparison among economies does not fully resolve the difficulties, since it is difficult to assess the factors' relative importance in the countries being compared. Despite these cautions, however, an outline of typical financial activity can be developed using the data.

5.3.1 Finance and economic activity

Relative to the US and the UK, Japan and Germany show much higher rates of economic growth between 1930 and 1995 and, generally much higher rates of savings as well. Germany and Japan have displayed low percentages of government consumption and high percentages of government savings relative to gross national product (GNP) (Organisation for Economic Cooperation and Development (OECD) 1989; Sakakibara and Feldman 1990). Finally, rates of capital formation have been considerably higher, in both Germany and Japan, than in either the UK or the US. Japan greatly restricted the growth of consumer credit, so that available savings have been used either to finance acquisitions of new plant and equipment, or to purchase securities from overseas. The German picture is not dissimilar: consumer credit has traditionally been much less important than in either the US or the UK.

The four countries' financial systems also exhibit characteristic differences. Both **nominal rates of interest** and **real rates of interest** have generally been lower in Japan and Germany than in the US or the UK. To some extent real interest rates have been lower in Japan and Germany because of the greater supply of savings relative to demand for it. Real rates may also have been lower because both countries have traditionally run surpluses on capital account, making funds available to other countries rather than having to raise funds abroad. In addition, particularly in Japan, a combination of fiscal monetary and regulatory policies has worked to keep interest rates relatively low. Nominal rates have been lower in Japan and Germany since the end of World War II mainly because inflation has been kept lower by relatively conservative monetary and fiscal policies.

---

nominal rate of interest the rate of interest on a transaction collected in contemporary currency units without any adjustment for changes in price levels, that is the purchasing power of the currency units.

---

real rate of interest the rate of interest on a transaction after it is adjusted for any changes in the purchasing power of the currency, that is the interest rate in constant purchasing power terms.

Although the similarities among the four financial systems have been increasing at least since the 1970s, some noteworthy differences still remain. First, the major banks in Japan and Germany are predominantly **universal banks**, that is banks which make loans to client companies, own shares in client companies, arrange securities underwritings for their clients, engage in secondary market trading, and provide brokerage and trust services for their clients (Coleman 1996: 21). In contrast, the predominantly **commercial banks** of the US and the UK emphasise deposit gathering, retail and commercial lending. In both the UK and the US, especially in the US where legislative prohibitions have slowed adaptation, the involvement of commercial banks in the securities business is currently less than in Japan or Germany. However, this picture is changing. As in most countries, banks in the US are becoming increasingly involved in the securities business, as will be discussed further in Parts IV and V.

---

universal banks banks which make loans to client companies, own shares in client companies, arrange securities underwritings for their clients, engage in secondary market trading, and provide brokerage and trust services for their clients. Some, especially German, universal banks have also long been active in selling insurance.

---

commercial banks banks which emphasise deposit gathering, retail and commercial lending, but do not generally participate actively in the securities business.

In the mid-1990s, Japan and Germany still used bank financing more heavily than did the UK or the US, where greater emphasis is placed on securities market funding. Banks in Japan and Germany frequently take share positions in their client companies, while banks in the UK and the US have been and to some extent still are constrained from taking similar positions. German and Japanese banks are noted for having closer and longer term relations with some of their clients than are their counterparts in the US or the UK (Sheard 1992), and debt–equity ratios are generally higher in Japan and Germany than they are in the UK and the US; see Table 5.8.[2]

5.3.2 Governance and long term finance

The theory of Chapter 3 argues that governance differences can play a significant role in financing certain types of projects, especially those whose asset values are difficult to establish through market transactions. Intermediaries capable of exercising intensive monitoring and adjustment capabilities are likely to take a longer term perspective of their clients' fortunes than are market agents. In part, intermediaries can take these longer term views because they can both advise their clients and renegotiate the terms of financial arrangements as the clients' fortunes evolve. On the other hand, market financings can offer the advantages of greater adaptability and faster restructuring of firms in difficulty.

Close and continuing governance can be particularly important to profitably financing technologically innovative projects where the payoff is difficult to establish in advance, and where continuing supervision is important to ensuring the deal's eventually satisfactory resolution. The universal banks of Germany and Japan may sometimes offer more intensive monitoring and more highly developed capabilities for adjustment than can the banks in the US or the UK, and if so these differences in capabilities could create some differences in the ways longer term projects with uncertain payoffs can be financed.

Japanese and German universal banks also have disadvantages, however. In particular, providing financing through a universal banking system does not produce the same kind or amount of public information as is produced by securities market trading in the US and the UK. Relative to the US and the UK, Japanese and German banking practice may also reduce competition, both between financial firms and between the industrial companies these financial firms typically fund.

In the context of US finance, Williamson (1988) argues that equity comes closer to providing the high capability governance of the previous paragraph than does debt. It does not follow, however, that lower debt–equity ratios in the UK and the US (see Table 5.7) indicate those countries make greater use of intensive governance than do Germany or Japan. Transactions economics stresses the importance of analysing the individual deal rather than the aggregate statistics, and hence the question to be resolved is whether Japan and Germany offer greater possibilities for intensive and cost-effective governance of certain, specific types of deals than do the US or the UK. Since non-market governance is largely based on understandings and informal arrangements, comparison of financial data for different countries can be misleading unless these qualitative features of financial arrangements are taken into account.

Edwards and Fischer (1994) are skeptical about the German financial system's providing different forms of financing from those provided in the US or the UK. However, they also suggest that German banks are more likely to advise management, or to ask for additional collateral, than to call the loans of firms the banks deem to be experiencing financial distress (Edwards and Fischer 1994: 167). Such attempts to counsel clients and to support client operations reflect the kind of informal and intensive governance stressed by transactions analysis.

It may not prove possible to reach definitive conclusions regarding the effectiveness of nationally different forms of practice, but it may be possible to establish through future research the kinds of deals for which each different form of governance is likely to prove cost-effective. For example, an OECD study (1995) concludes that closer ties between financiers and their clients can make possible more financing of projects with longer term paybacks, especially in an atmosphere of implicit contracts. It may prove to be the case that the more intensive forms of governance characteristic of Japan and Germany are more cost-effective for some types of deals, while for other types the less intensive forms characteristic of the US or the UK are most cost-effective.

A similar possibility is raised by Houston and James (1996), who suggest the existence of a tradeoff between bank-supplied and market-supplied finance. In a US-based empirical study, these authors find that if firms have a single bank relationship, the reliance on bank debt is negatively related to growth opportunities, but that when firms borrow from multiple banks, debt and growth opportunities are positively related. The authors conclude that 'banks create durable transaction-specific information as part of an ongoing relationship. While this private information may have important benefits, it can also impose costs when borrowing is concentrated with a single borrower.' However, for 'smaller firms without publicly traded common stock, the benefits of bank monitoring are likely to be large relative to the potential adverse incentive effects of information monopolies' (Houston and James 1996: 1888). Mayer (1997) argues that the continental European and Japanese financial systems may be 'superior at implementing policies which involve relations with stakeholders,' while the US and the UK systems 'may be more responsive to change.' Finally, Levine concludes that 'the evidence suggests complex interactions between the functioning of stock markets and corporate decisions to borrow from banks that depend on the overall level of economic development. . . . We need considerably more research into the links among stock markets, banks, and corporate financing decisions to understand the relationship between financial structure and economic growth' (1997: 720).

5.4 INTERPRETING FUNDS FLOWS

Further information regarding the similarities and differences among financial systems can be obtained by examining funds flow data. The usefulness of examining these data will be enhanced by first considering how the accounts are constructed.

5.4.1 Funds flow accounts

Funds flow accounts trace net borrowing or lending transactions between major **sectors** in the economy. The sectors defined in the accounts are households and unincorporated business, private non-financial business, government, private financial business and the rest of the world.[3] The accounts measure differences between each sector's current income and current expenditure, and thus also capture the difference between each sector's capital formation and its saving. A sector is called a **surplus sector** if its savings exceeds its capital formation, a **deficit sector** if its capital formation exceeds its saving. Surpluses are lent to or invested in other sectors, deficits are financed by raising funds from other sectors.

> **sector** a group of like units for purpose of economic analysis. The financial flow accounts use households and unincorporated businesses, non-financial business, financial business, government and the rest of the world as their principal sectors. A surplus sector's savings exceeds its investment expenditure; a deficit sector's savings falls short of its investment.

The financial flow accounts are constructed using changes between balance sheets. The balance sheets are estimated for each of the economy's major sectors at two successive points in time,[4] so that the changes in each category can be computed. The balance sheets are structured like those shown in Table 5.1, which indicates that the main changes of concern are differences in financial assets, in real assets, in liabilities and in net worth.[5] Table 5.1 indicates by a (+) or a (–) whether an increase in a balance sheet category represents a source (+) or a use (–) of funds. Thus, for example, an increase in a liability represents a source of funds, an increase in an asset represents a use of funds. If the category decreases from one period to the next, the effect is the opposite of the sign shown.

In many developed countries, including the four to be examined below, the funds flow accounts display the pattern displayed in Table 5.2. Households are net suppliers of funds, lending to the rest of the economy and building up financial assets while they do so. Business is the principal user of funds, but in many developed countries government has also been a user of funds. The US government has been a user of funds over most of the 1980s and 1990s, and in the 1990s the governments of the UK and of Germany have also been borrowers. Typically the financial sector lends about as much as it borrows and therefore acts principally as a transmission mechanism.[6] Economies can also be net users or net suppliers of funds in their transactions with other economies.Those economies which invest more funds than they save are net users, while economies which save more than they invest domestically are suppliers.

The effects of funds flows are indicated by four accounting identities. First, Equation 5.1 takes a balance sheet identity, Assets ≡ Liabilities + Net Worth, and restates it in the form used most frequently in financial flow analysis. Equation 5.1 holds for every agent, and for every sector in the economy, as well as for the economy as a whole, in every time period.

Table 5.1 Condensed balance sheets

Assets	Liabilities and net worth
Financial assets (–)	Liabilities (+)
Real assets (–)	Net worth (+)
Total assets	Total liabilities and net worth

Table 5.2 Typical patterns of sources and uses

Sector	Net supplier (+) or net user (–)
Household	+
Business	–
Private financial	Relatively small
Government	+/–
ROW (rest of the world, i.e., other countries)	+/–

$$\text{Assets} \equiv \text{Liabilities} + \text{Net Worth}$$

$$\text{Assets} - \text{Liabilities} = \text{Net Worth} \tag{5.1}$$

Since Assets – Liabilities = Net Worth, it also follows that changes in assets, less changes in liabilities, equal changes in net worth. If an agent, sector, or the economy itself has net savings, its net worth increases. In this case the difference between assets and liabilities increases to reflect the increase in net worth; more savings means more net assets are built up.

Equation 5.2 says that savings is defined as the difference between income and consumption expenditures.

$$\text{Income} - \text{Consumption} \equiv \text{Savings} \tag{5.2}$$

Savings (income not spent) is reflected in balance sheet accounting as an increase in net worth. Since the changes in financial assets for all sectors in an economy must equal the changes in liabilities of all the sectors (for every borrower there must be a lender),[7] it follows that changes in the economy's aggregate balance sheets indicate

$$\text{Savings} = \text{Change in Net Worth}$$

$$= \text{Change in Real Assets} \tag{5.3}$$

$$= \text{Net Investment}$$

The structure of the aggregate balance sheets reflecting these changes is the same as the structure of the sector balance sheets shown in Table 5.1.

The foregoing concepts can be expanded to recognise both the effects of monetary activity and to recognise that capital wears out as it is used. Taking both these features into account, the expanded accounting identity looks like:

$$RA + M + F = S + D + MI + L \tag{5.4}$$

$$\text{Uses of Funds} = \text{Sources of Funds}$$

where RA = change in real assets, before deducting depreciation

M = change in money balances
F = change in financial assets
S = savings
D = depreciation
MI = changes in money supply
L = changes in liabilities and equities issued.

All changes in Equation 5.4 are interpreted as increases. Rewriting (5.4) gives

$$S = (M + F) - (MI + L) + (RA - D) \tag{5.5}$$

When all financial assets and liabilities are added up, the changes in financial assets must equal the changes in liabilities, because for every borrower there is a lender:

$$M + F = MI + L \tag{5.6}$$

Finally, substituting (5.6) in (5.5) gives:

$$S = RA - D;$$

$$\tag{5.7}$$

$$\text{Savings} = \text{Net Investment}$$

The financial flow accounts trace the details of the transactions which equate savings with investment. The accounts thus show how funds flow from an economy's original suppliers to its final users. When both domestic and international transactions are considered, the amount of funds demanded by all sectors equals the amount of funds supplied, because for every borrower there is still a lender. Total savings still equals total investment, but domestic savings may not equal domestic investment.

5.4.2 Financial system growth

The financial systems of the four countries examined in this chapter have all grown rapidly over the period 1950–95, with Japan and Germany posting the most rapid increases. Since the mid-1970s, the financial services sector has grown much faster than economic output in all four countries, but there are also notable differences in the growth rates. Sakakibara and Feldman (1990) find that relative to the US, Japan's financial liabilities have grown rapidly when expressed as a percentage of GNP. One of the factors stimulating this more rapid growth is the high degree of intermediation within the Japanese financial system. Second, the Japanese government has offered advice and counsel to the private financial system, quite often behaving more like a member of the industry than like a regulator. Moreover, the Japanese government has set up institutions to encourage both saving and providing finance to industry. For example, the Postal Savings Bank has long played an important role in collecting the small deposits of workers, thus making funds available for relending. Third, consumers were largely excluded from borrowing until the 1970s (Sakakibara and Feldman 1990). The picture that results from comparing the UK to Japan is similar to the picture developed for the US. Equally, comparisons between the US or the UK on the one hand and Germany on the other show a similar pattern, with more rapid financial system growth taking place in Germany.

5.4.3 Linkages with the rest of the world

There is no particular reason for a country's citizens to borrow exactly as much as they lend at home, and most countries' residents do carry out financial deals both at home and abroad. The financial flow accounts show whether an economy is a net borrower (domestic savings falls short of domestic investment) or a net lender (domestic savings exceeds domestic investment). Most developing economies are importers of capital, or net borrowers. The United Kingdom was a net borrower during its development period, and a net lender during much of the colonial period. Japan has been a net lender of funds throughout the 1980s and 1990s.

An example of these patterns is given in Table 5.3, which shows savings and investment as proportions of national income for each of the four countries during 1994. In that year, savings exceeded investment in Germany and Japan, while savings was less than investment in the US and the UK. Thus, agents in the first two countries were net lenders in world financial markets, in the second two they were borrowers. Since the latter 1980s the United Kingdom and the United States have been net borrowers largely because government deficits have used up a considerable proportion of the funds provided by household savings. As a result, in these countries domestic productive investment (i.e., capital formation) has exceeded the amount that can be financed by the net domestic savings of the private and public sectors combined.

Table 5.3 Domestic savings and investment as percentages of GNP, 1994

	Savings*	*Investment*	*Balance*
Germany	27.3	24.5	2.8
Japan (1991)	31.0	28.9	2.1
United Kingdom	14.4	15.4	−1.0
United States	15.7	17.1	−1.4

Source: International Monetary Fund (1996) *International Financial Statistics Yearbook.*
Note: *Percentage of GNP not spent on consumption.

5.5 INTERPRETING ASSET DATA

The cumulative effects of transactions can be assessed by examining outstanding financial assets. These data provide information regarding who owes whom, the current size of different financial intermediaries, and of different kinds of public market financings.

5.5.1 Household financial assets

Saunders (1994) observes that household financial assets have shown similar dramatic changes in each of Germany, Japan, the UK and the US between 1980 and 1987. As Table 5.4 reports, in all four countries the shares of savings and demand deposits decreased, while the shares of pension and insurance funds increased, that is the holdings show a relative decline of traditional financial intermediation products and a compensating increase in the holdings of either securities themselves or the shares of investment companies.[8] The 1993 US data in Table 5.4 show that similar trends continued until that time. In essence,

Table 5.4 Percentages of household financial assets

	Germany		Japan		UK	
	1980	*1987*	*1980*	*1987*	*1980*	*1987*
Savings deposits	42	37	55	47	22	19
Cash, demand deps	21	20	8	6	10	8
Pension, insurance assets	16	18	24	24	41	47
Securities*	14	18	10	20	20	19
Other	7	7	3	3	7	7
	100	100	100	100	100	100

	US		
	1980	*1987*	*1993*
Savings deposits	20	21	13
Cash, demand deps	4	4	4
Pension, insurance assets	23	24	33
Securities*	22	30	35
Other**	31	21	15
	100	100	100

Sources: For Germany, Japan and UK: Saunders (1994: 67). For US: Federal Reserve System, Statistical Releases, Balance Sheets for the US Economy, 1945–93.
Notes: *Corporate and government securities. **Principally equity in unincorporated business.

householders have increasingly been looking for higher returns than they have traditionally earned on intermediary deposits. The same householders seem to be less concerned by the fact that securities market investments offer both generally higher returns and higher risks.

While Table 5.4 shows that some trends among countries are similar, a 1992 OECD survey summarised in Table 5.5 shows that quite wide variations also remain, such as the 1990 ratio for Germany.

Table 5.5 Household debt/GNP

	1980	*1985*	*1990*
Germany	0.10	0.10	0.11
Japan	0.55	0.61	0.76
United Kingdom	0.40	0.58	0.80
United States	0.62	0.60	0.70

Source: OECD (1992) *Financial Market Trends*.

5.5.2 Corporate finance

In all four countries, the greatest proportion of new business investment is financed internally, that is by using businesses' own savings. Intermediaries typically account for the largest proportion of external financing, and their share is typically very much larger than that provided through securities markets. Even so, significant differences in the countries' emphases on intermediated and market financing can also be observed. First, of the four countries, the US and Japan have the largest equity[9] markets in absolute terms, as shown by the capitalisation data of Table 5.6. The United Kingdom ranks third in absolute terms, but first relative to GNP. The US and Japan also have large stock market capitalisation in relation to GNP, while Germany ranks lowest in both absolute terms and relative to GNP.

Table 5.7 indicates that debt–equity ratios are higher in Germany and Japan than they are in the US or the UK. While the ratios are affected by (i) differences in taxation, (ii) the manner in which pension reserves are set up, and (iii) rates of inflation (Edwards and Fischer 1994), it does not seem likely that these factors account for the entire difference. While comparisons are difficult to make, the differences between the countries with a tradition of universal banking (Japan and Germany) and countries with traditionally greater emphasis on securities market financing (the US and the UK) are due in part to different kinds of financial governance resulting from depending proportionately more on banks in the first case, on securities markets in the second.

Table 5.6 Stock market capitalisation, November 30, 1995 (billions of US$)

	Capitalisation	*As % of GNP*
Germany	580	27
Japan (Tokyo)	3,393	74
United Kingdom	1,329	130
United States (NYSE)	6,254	93

Source: Morgan Stanley Capital International, as published in *The Economist*, December 23, 1995.

Table 5.7 Non-financial companies, debt–equity ratios

	1980	*1985*	*1992*
Germany	1.92	1.72	1.53
Japan	5.16	4.40	3.93
United Kingdom	1.15	1.04	1.07 (1990)
United States	0.42	0.55	1.05

Source: OECD (various issues) *Financial Market Trends*.

5.5.3 Financial intermediaries

We next examine data for the financial sector in greater detail. Table 5.8 uses asset data to examine changes in the relative importance of financial intermediaries, over the period 1960–80, for the four countries. Although historically the percentages of business held by depository and non-depository institutions have differed considerably between countries, within a given country there was little change up until 1980. However, as the US data show, since 1980 depository institutions have lost ground to non-depository institutions, at least

Table 5.8 Changes in relative importance of financial intermediaries

		Percentages of assets held by		
		Depository institutions	Insurance, pension and mutual funds	Other
Germany	1960	84	16	–
	1970	82	18	–
	1980	79	21	–
Japan	1960	88	12	–
	1970	87	13	–
	1980	86	14	–
United	1960	58	36	6
States	1970	58	35	7
	1980	56	37	7
	1990	43	49	8
	1994	35	57	8

Sources: Germany and Japan: OECD (1992) *Financial Market Trends*. United States: James and Houston (1996).

as far as asset data are concerned. On the other hand, the data do not reveal the full picture, because they show only a declining role in banks' (and to a lesser extent other intermediaries') funding of loans. As James and Houston (1996) point out, banks' fee-based services and off-balance sheet transactions have shown rapid growth over the period since 1980, leading these authors to conclude that banks remain as important as before in the sense of still being active in arranging corporate finance, even though they have lost ground in providing the actual funding for the lending activities they arrange.

5.6 SUMMARY

This chapter compared and contrasted principal features of four developed financial systems. It first examined some relations between finance and real economic activity, indicating the nature of the controversy over whether financial systems in and of themselves make an important difference to a country's economic performance. The chapter then discussed how financial flow accounts are constructed, and used the accounts to provide one description of the four systems. This discussion of financial flows also showed how each financial system is linked to the rest of the world. Finally, the chapter provided quantitative descriptions of household assets, financial instruments, and financial intermediaries in a section concerned with long term system change.

REVIEW QUESTIONS

Exercise 1 Suppose a country sometimes lends abroad, sometimes borrows from abroad. Assuming all other features to be equal, when would interest rates likely be higher?

Exercise 2 If a domestic deficit sector raises more funds while nothing else in the economy changes, what might happen to interest rates? Would your answer be affected by the economy's international credit rating? If so, how?

Exercise 3 Even though there is now much international financial activity, it is mostly short term, and domestic savings for most countries over the longer run is still relatively close to domestic investment. Why might this be?

Exercise 4 Do you think the higher debt–equity ratios in Germany and Japan could be evidence that, at least for some companies, governance in those countries involves closer monitoring and control than in the US or the UK? Why or why not?

Exercise 5 Describe how a financial system's flows can be traced, and explain what is most useful about this information.

Exercise 6 What policy instruments can be used to affect financial flows?

Exercise 7 Is the United Kingdom a borrower from or a lender to other countries? Explain what data in the chapter support your answer.

Exercise 8 What data in the chapter indicate that, relative to the US and the UK, Japan and Germany have discouraged consumer credit?

Part II

Concepts

This part continues to develop the theoretical framework, or road map, whose essentials were presented in Part I. The theory now being developed will be applied in the book's remaining three parts. In essence, Part II presents concepts of asset pricing, developed in a relatively simple financial environment, then discusses how these concepts relate to the governance of financial deals in the more complex world of financial practice. Chapter 6 examines the principles of asset pricing, explaining how securities prices are determined in a world of perfectly competitive markets. Chapter 7 continues this discussion. It explains both how risks can be divided using financial instruments, and how these instruments are priced, or valued. Chapter 8, recognising complexities from which the pricing theories of Chapters 6 and 7 abstracted, shows how the three governance mechanisms introduced in Part I are used to administer financial deals in practice. Chapter 9 shows how the ideas of governance can be specialised to study problems of portfolio administration, while Chapter 10 discusses how individual deals' terms are selected with a view to fine tuning governance capabilities. Chapter 11, returning to the concepts of Chapters 6 and 7, discusses trading and intermediary links between the specialised parts of a typical financial system.

By the time the reader has finished Parts I and II he or she will have an understanding of how financial assets are priced, of how they can be used to divide up and transfer risks, and of how financial deals representing these activities are governed. The ideas of governance explain both how deals are done in the perfectly competitive markets usually examined by financial theory, and also how deals are done when the transactions are negotiated with intermediaries. The basic ideas of risk management are also used in explaining how deals are structured in practice, and why they take the forms they do.

6   Principles of asset pricing

6.1	Pricing a payments stream	70
6.1.1	Relative pricing of payments streams	70
6.1.2	Net present value	71
6.1.3	Risk adjusted interest rate	73
6.1.4	Discounted certainty equivalent	74
6.2	Pricing by arbitrage	75
6.2.1	Equilibrium price relations	75
6.2.2	Identical payments streams	76
6.2.3	Risk adjusted probabilities	77
6.3	Returns on risky securities	79
6.3.1	Capital Asset Pricing Model	79
6.3.2	Arbitrage Pricing Theory	81
6.4	Other relations between securities returns	82
6.4.1	Fisher relation	82
6.4.2	Real and nominal rates	85
6.4.3	Index linked bonds	86
6.4.4	Nominal rates and yield curves	87
6.5	Summary	90

LEARNING OBJECTIVES

After reading this chapter you will understand

- how to value future cash flows under certainty and under risk
- how the search for trading profits eliminates arbitrage opportunities, and as a result relates asset prices to each other
- how price relations determined by an absence of arbitrage opportunities can be used to calculate risk adjusted probabilities
- how risk adjusted probabilities can conveniently be used for valuation
- current explanations of how risky securities are priced
- how securities prices allow for inflation
- how yields on bonds of different maturities are related by arbitrage
- how interest rates in different countries are related by arbitrage

---

This chapter first considers how payments streams are priced or valued. To begin, the effect of interest calcuations on the value of riskless payments is examined. The chapter shows that the longer investors must wait to receive a given riskless payment, the greater the premium they require to be paid. If the intended payments are risky, and if investors are risk averse, they demand compensation for taking on the risk as well as for waiting. When the intended payments are risky, interest rates on certainty payments must be adjusted to reflect the premium investors demand for assuming extra risk.

Whether they offer risky or riskless payoffs, financial theory offers two methods of valuing instruments. The first method is based on relations established by active trading or arbitraging between instruments, the second on the factors that, according to financial theory, determine interest rates. The chapter discusses each of these approaches in turn.

6.1 PRICING A PAYMENTS STREAM

A financial asset's value is determined by the amount and the timing of the payments it promises. In examining how financial assets are valued, at least three issues arise. How are the prices of different financial assets related to each other? How are funds to be received in the future valued, relative to funds received now? How can the effects of risk, that is the possibility of not being paid in full, be taken into account?

6.1.1 Relative pricing of payments streams

The simplest way of valuing the payments stream represented by some financial instrument is to price it relative to some other, equivalently risky stream whose price is already known. For example, if two instruments offer the same payments stream, and with the same risk, they should sell at the same price.

That is, relations between similar or closely related instruments are maintained by arbitrage-based trading – trading aimed at realising profit opportunities that present no risk of loss.[1] The principle of pricing by arbitrage defines an equilibrium as a situation in which possibility of any such arbitrage opportunities has already been eliminated. As and when arbitrage opportunities have been eliminated, different instruments offering the same probability distribution of payoffs will have the same value, so long as one instrument can be exchanged for the other without payment of transactions costs.

> **arbitrage** trading undertaken to profit from atypical market relationships, such as buying a low priced security and later selling it at a higher price, or buying a low priced security in one market and simultaneously selling it in another at a higher price. An arbitrage opportunity is an opportunity to trade for some gain, at no risk of loss.

The idea that the absence of arbitrage opportunities permits calculating the value of one instrument in relation to another will be used extensively in the rest of this book, and it is therefore worthwhile illustrating how the principle can be applied. First, consider a situation in which the payoffs are known with certainty. Are there any practical differences between five one-pound coins and a five-pound note? The principle of pricing by arbitrage says that if it is only total buying power that matters, there are no practical differences between the two: the five coins should exchange freely for the note, and vice versa. On the other hand, any impediments to free exchange between coins and note can frustrate the workings of the principle. If you need a one-pound coin to put in a vending machine at midnight, and there is no one around to change the only five-pound note you have, the note is clearly worth less to you at that particular moment in time than five one-pound coins would be.

As a second example, consider prospects with risky payoffs. Suppose you have made a bet with someone which involves paying them $1.00 if a fair coin comes up tails, and their paying you $1.00 if the fair coin comes up heads. Compare this with a second bet, on which you will get $1.00 if the first roll of a balanced die comes up 1, 2 or 3, and will lose $1.00 if the first roll comes up 4, 5 or 6. In either case your companion is assumed to be sure to pay, as are you. The probability of winning (or losing) is then ½, whichever of the two bets you take, and the principle of pricing by arbitrage says that either bet has the same value to you as the other. Each offers exactly the same payoffs with the same probability distribution, and there are no impediments to substituting one bet for the other.

6.1.2 Net present value

How do economic agents place a value today on funds they will receive at some future date? Investors or creditors place a different value on the same amounts when they are received at different times, because investors require to be compensated for waiting. Consider first how investors are compensated for waiting when they are sure to be repaid in full. Suppose that an asset promises to pay $100.00 with certainty, one year from now. What is the asset worth today?

A lender or investor who advances you $100.00 today, to be repaid a year from now, cannot spend those funds herself until you repay her. To compensate, she will usually charge an interest rate, which represents her price for waiting to spend or reinvest the funds. Suppose the person lending you the $100.00 requires to be paid 10 percent per annum on the loan, and that you agree to pay this interest rate. If the $100.00 is to be repaid in a lump sum one year from now, your payment will have to be $110.00 to cover both the sum advanced and the agreed amount of interest. (Since we have assumed the payment is certain to be made, questions of your being unable or unwilling to repay the loan one year from now have been ruled out for the present.)

The effect of charging an interest rate can be expressed either in terms of the amount of funds to be later repaid, or in terms of their value today, that is their present value. The present value of $110.00 to be repaid for certain one year from now at an interest rate of 10 percent is clearly $100.00, the amount you borrow. But suppose you wanted to repay exactly $100.00, principal and interest. How much cash could you get today in exchange for this promise? The present value of $100.00 to be repaid one year from now, when the interest rate is 10 percent, is

$$V_0 = \$100.00 \; / \; 1.10 = \$90.91$$

You can check to see that $90.91(1.10) = $100.00, as it must if the lender is to receive 10 percent on this arrangement.

The principle of pricing by arbitrage is at work even in the foregoing simple example. If interest rates are 10 percent, an instrument promising to pay $110.00 one year from now can be exchanged today for another instrument promising to pay $100.00 immediately, whenever there are no transactions costs to making the exchange. This particular conclusion regarding pricing by arbitrage seems rather trite. However, as the rest of this chapter shows, applications of the principle of pricing by arbitrage are numerous, and their application is usually not as obvious as in the present example. Therefore, it is worthwhile introducing the principle in such a way that its workings are easy to see.

It is also useful to examine how interest rates affect value over more than one period. For instance, suppose you wanted to borrow $100.00 for two years, at 10 percent per annum, and that you agreed to make the repayment in one lump sum at the end of the two years. Your first interest payment is due at the end of the first year. However, since you will actually pay nothing until the end of the second year, most lenders would require you to pay interest on the unpaid interest as well as on the principal. The usual terminology for such a deal says you would pay 10 percent interest, compounded annually. In this case your total payment at the end of two years would be

$$\$100.00 + 2[\$100.00(0.10)] + \$10.00(0.10) =$$

$$\$100.00(1.10)^2 = \$121.00$$

The first term of the first line represents the repayment of principal, the next term the one year interest bills for each of the two successive years. The third term represents the interest on the first year's interest bill, which remains unpaid for one year after the obligation to pay the interest is incurred. The second line compresses the information in the first line to show you the compound interest calculation in the manner it is usually written.

If the arrangement contemplated only a simple rather than a compound interest calculation, it would not incorporate a charge for unpaid interest bills. In this case the third term of the first line in the above calculation would change to zero. However, if you were being charged only simple interest, the lender would probably require you to pay it punctually at the end of the first year, rather than allowing it to go unpaid. To do otherwise would mean the lender lost an earnings opportunity. You should try to use the principle of pricing by arbitrage to explain why the lender will insist on compound interest if you do not plan to pay anything for two years. (In this section the explanation cannot have anything to do with credit risk, because it is assumed you will be certain to make the repayment in full, with interest, as scheduled.)

6.1.3 Risk adjusted interest rate

Now suppose the future payment is risky. That is, the amount that will actually be paid one year from now can be described today only in probabilistic terms. The future payment might, for example, depend on the success of a business venture whose outcome cannot be known exactly. In this case the lender or investor cannot be sure how much will actually be paid. As a result he will require to be compensated, both for waiting and for bearing a risk of not being repaid in full. Consider the risky prospect given by:

$$X = \begin{cases} \$95.00 \text{ with probability } 0.5 \\ \$105.00 \text{ with probability } 0.5 \end{cases} \tag{6.1}$$

Only one of the two possible outcomes of this so-called risky prospect will actually be realised, but at the present time it is not known which of the two possibilities, $95.00 or $105.00, will actually eventuate. Viewed from today's perspective, the outcome one year from now can be described only probabilistically.

Definition (6.1) indicates that the probability of either outcome is 0.5. In this case, the expected value of the risky prospect is defined as

$$E(X) = (0.5)\$95.00 + (0.5)\$105.00 = \$100.00$$

To compensate for the risk of not knowing exactly what the payment will be, the lender or investor can discount the expected value of $100.00 at a rate called a **risk adjusted interest rate**. Since investors are assumed to be risk averse and demand a premium for taking on risks, the risk adjusted interest rate will be higher than the risk free rate.

> **risk adjusted interest rate** an interest rate, higher than the risk free rate when investors are risk averse, that is used to discount expected values of future risky payments.

Suppose a suitable risk adjusted rate for the present example is 12.36 percent. (We show later how this rate might be determined.) In this case the value of the risky prospect is

$$V_0 = E(X) / 1.1236 = \$100.00 / 1.1236 = \$89.00 \qquad (6.2)$$

less than the \$90.91 present value of a riskless payoff of \$100.00. The risk adjusted rate is often compared to the risk free rate, still assumed to be 10.00 percent, by saying that the former incorporates a **risk premium** of 12.36 percent − 10.00 percent = 2.36 percent.

> **risk premium** the difference between the expected interest rate on a transaction and the risk free rate.

6.1.4 Discounted certainty equivalent

A second way of compensating an investor for taking risk is to value the risky payment at an amount less than its expected value, then discount this lower amount at the interest rate used for riskless deals. The method involves determining an amount, to be paid with certainty, that is just large enough to induce the holder of the asset to exchange the title to her risky earnings for a certainty amount, to be paid at the time when the risky earnings would be realised. This value is called, naturally enough, a **certainty equivalent value**.

> **certainty equivalent value** the smallest value, to be paid for certain, that the holder of a risky prospect will accept in exchange for the prospect. The certainty equivalent value will be smaller than the expected value of the risky prospect whenever the investor is risk averse.

Suppose our investor would willingly trade the risky prospect (6.1) for a sure payment of \$97.90, to be received exactly one year from now. Since the \$97.90

will be paid with certainty one year from now, it can be discounted at the risk free rate, still assumed to be 10 percent. Thus the value calculation is

$$V_0 = (E(X) - \pi) \, / \, 1.10 = (\$100.00 - 2.10) \, / \, 1.10$$

$$= \$97.90/1.10 = \$89.00$$

(6.3)

The $2.10 difference between the expected value and the certainty equivalent, denoted by π, is also called a **risk premium**, but in this case the risk premium is expressed in terms of absolute amounts rather than an interest rate as before.

As may be seen by equating the left-hand sides of (6.2) and (6.3), the interest rate risk premium can be determined from the risk premium expressed as an amount, and vice versa. In symbols,

$$E(X) \, / \, (1 + r_f + \rho) = (E(X) - \pi) \, / \, (1 + r_f)$$

where r_f is the riskless rate, ρ is the interest rate risk premium, and π is the risk premium subtracted from the amount of the payment.To eliminate possible confusion, this book will subsequently reserve the term **risk premium** for use with interest rates, unless the contrary is stated explicitly.You should check to see that if you take $E(X) = 100.00$ and $r_f = 0.10$, then, as indicated by the two previous examples, the two sides of the last expression are equal if $\rho = 0.0236$ and $\pi = 2.10$.

6.2 PRICING BY ARBITRAGE

An equilibrium price is a price at which no agent has an incentive to trade. If all instruments in a financial market have attained equilibrium prices, the market itself is said to be in equilibrium. If a financial market is not in equilibrium, agents try to estimate what the eventual equilibrium prices will be. They then seek to earn trading profits by purchasing instruments at prices below that estimate, or by selling instruments at prices above that estimate. Under a wide variety of realistic market conditions, such trading activity can bid low prices up, and high prices down.[2] Equilibrium can obtain only when trading has eliminated all incentives to trade, including all possible arbitrage opportunities.

6.2.1 Equilibrium price relations

At equilibrium agents have no further desire to trade, which means in particular that there are no remaining arbitrage opportunities. As already suggested, the absence of arbitrage opportunities means that securities prices are related to each other in particular ways. That is, the absence of arbitrage opportunities can be used to determine the price of one security relative to a second, so long as the price of the second is known and the payments promised by the two can be related in a known way. You have already seen how pricing by arbitrage can be used in some special cases. It is now time to examine additional applications of the idea.

6.2.2 Identical payments streams

As already pointed out, an arbitrage opportunity is a combination of trades in which there is some chance of making a profit, and no chance of making a loss. Such an opportunity is sometimes called a riskless arbitrage opportunity, because the agent entering it cannot be made worse off.[3] Since rational investors will take up arbitrage opportunities whenever they can be found, pricing by arbitrage becomes a way of pricing one security in relation to the known price of another. To illustrate, if one security promises to pay the amounts specified by the risky prospect X defined in (6.1), and if a second security Y promises exactly twice the amounts specified by the risky prospect X (with each outcome having the same probabilities as in the original case), the second instrument must have a market equilibrium value that is exactly twice that of the original risky prospect. Since the payments from holding 2X are exactly the same as the payments from holding Y, regardless of the outcome that obtains, substituting 2X for Y leaves the assetholder's position unchanged. Since the positions are the same, the value the assetholder places on either of them is also the same.

Pricing by arbitrage extends to more substantial practical problems as well. Suppose, for example, that you have just discovered a gold mine which can be developed for $100.00 spent today, and which you know will produce $125.00 worth of gold one year from now. The $100.00 spent today covers all expenses, and you will get exactly $125.00 back with certainty. Even if you have no money of your own at all, the principle of pricing by arbitrage can be used to show that the discovery is still worth something to you.

Suppose bankers can costlessly verify your statement that the returns from the mining project are certain. Suppose moreover that the going rate on loans whose repayment is certain is 10 percent. In this case you will have no difficulty in arranging a loan to raise $100.00 at an interest rate of 10 percent. One year hence, after paying back $110.00, the loan principal plus interest, the project's yield to you would be

$$\$125.00 - \$100.00(1.10) = \$15.00$$

A sum of $15.00 received with certainty one year from now is worth $15.00/1.10 = $13.63 today, the value of the discovery to you after taking account of the fact that the returns from the project will be realised in a year's time rather than immediately.

The principle of pricing by arbitrage thus says that your discovery is worth something to you even when you do not have your own funds to carry the project out.[4] More importantly, the principle tells you how to calculate your own immediate profit if you were to sell out your entire interest in the mine today. There would be no reason to let a prospective purchaser earn more than 10 percent on her investment, since you have made the discovery and since in a competitive financial market there are plenty of investors willing to put up funds for the going rate of interest. If you want to sell the mine immediately, the principle of pricing by arbitrage tells you to charge

$$P = \$125.00 \ / \ 1.10 - 100.00 = (125.00 - 110.00) \ / \ 1.10$$

$$= \$15.00 \ / \ 1.10 = \$13.63$$

exactly the same value as before. This calculation also shows that, when pricing by arbitrage is possible, two different ways of doing (what amounts to) exactly the same thing will yield the same profit to you, at least so long as both forms of deal are correctly priced.

In addition, the principle of pricing by arbitrage says that when you sell your discovery for what you know it to be worth, the buyer should get just the interest rate, and no more, on her investment. Of course, if you erred in calculating what the mine was worth, and sold it for too little, the new investor would make more than 10 percent. Assuming no errors have been made, the principle says that if an asset is sold at its equilibrium price (i.e., for exactly the present value of the future earnings it represents), the purchaser will earn zero profits on the purchase after taking the market rate of interest into account. In the first of the above examples, the bank gets a 10 percent return on its $100.00 loan. In the second example, the purchaser of the mine puts up $100.00 to develop the mine and pays you $15.00/1.10 = \$13.63 at the same time. She recovers $125.00 one year from now. Since

$$\$125.00 = [\$100.00 + \$15.00 \ / \ 1.10] \ (1.10)$$

$$= [\$100.00 + \$13.63] \ (1.10)$$

it is clear that she earns exactly the going rate of interest on her original investment of $113.63.

6.2.3 Risk adjusted probabilities

The principle of pricing by arbitrage has still further merit because it can be used to organise valuation calculations in an especially convenient way. Instead of using a certainty equivalent to value a risky prospect, suppose we were to take risk premia into account by using quantities called **risk adjusted probabilities**.

---

risk adjusted probability a measure, defined in the absence of arbitrage opportunities, used to value instruments in relation to each other. The measure is used exactly like a probability is used to calculate an expected value. Risk adjusted probabilities are often called an equivalent martingale measure. Valuation using risk adjusted probabilities is sometimes referred to as using a risk-neutral valuation method.

Formally, the procedure is to define a probability distribution of payments whose expected value, when discounted at the risk free rate, equals the instrument's current market value.[5] In the case of (6.1), this means finding a quantity p* which solves

$$\$89.00 = p*(105.00 / 1.10) + (1 - p*)(95.00 / 1.10) \qquad (6.4)$$

To find such a solution, rewrite (6.4) as

$$\$97.90 = p*(105.00) + (1 - p*)(95.00)$$

from which it follows that

$$p* = (\$97.90 - \$95.00) / (105.00 - 95.00)$$

That is, p* = 0.29, and 1-p* = 0.71.

The reasoning can be reversed. Suppose the values of p*, 1-p*, and the riskless rate are all given. Using these data, in the above case it would be correct, because of the way the risk adjusted probabilities were defined, to calculate the value of the firm using calculations that look exactly like discounted expected value calculations.[6] Since the riskless rate in the present example is 10 percent, the calculations would be

$$V_0 = [105.00p* + 95.00(1-p*)] / 1.10$$

Substituting the value of p* into the last line

$$V_0 = \{ 105.00(97.90 - 95.00) / (105.00 - 95.00)$$

$$+ 95.00(105.00 - 97.90) / (105.00 - 95.00)\} / 1.10 =$$

$$(105.00 - 95.00)(97.90) / (105.00 - 95.00)1.10 =$$

$$97.90 / 1.10 = 89.00$$

Of course, the calculations must turn out this way, because in the present case the risk adjusted probabilities were chosen to ensure the result. But as we next show, the risk adjusted probabilities can also be used value instruments other than the ones used to define the probabilities.

One way to verify that risk adjusted probabilities could be used to value different instruments (other validity checks will be presented later) is to recalculate what the firm is worth over and above the $95.00/1.10 the bank will lend it at a riskless interest rate. If the firm does well, there will be $10.00 = $105.00 − 95.00 for shareholders after paying off the bank loan, but if the firm does badly, there will only be $95.00 to pay the bank and nothing will remain for the shareholders. That is, the value of the shareholders' claims is

$$[p*\$10.00 + (1 - p*)\$0.00] / 1.10 = 0.29(\$10.00) / 1.10 = \$2.90 / 1.10$$

To see that the value is consistent with the principle of pricing by arbitrage, recall that the present value assumed for the firm is $89.00, while the present value of the bank loan is $95.00/1.10. Accordingly, pricing by arbitrage indicates the residual value of the firm must be

$$\$89.00 - 95.00 \; / \; 1.10 = [97.90 - 95.00] \; / \; 1.10 = \$2.90 \; / \; 1.10$$

exactly the value determined using the risk adjusted probabilities.

At least in the foregoing example, the risk adjusted probabilities found the same value as did the principle of pricing by arbitrage. It can be shown by more advanced methods (see Huang and Litzenberger 1988) that in an equilibrium with no arbitrage profit opportunities, risk adjusted probabilities always exist and can be used to value any risky asset. Subsequently, this book gives several additional illustrations of how risk adjusted probabilities can be used for valuation purposes.

6.3 RETURNS ON RISKY SECURITIES

Every deal involves an interest rate, which may be stated either implicitly or explicitly. For example, suppose that risky prospect (6.1) represents the proceeds to which the shareholders of a 100 percent equity financed firm are entitled. Suppose also that these shares sell for \$89.00 as before. The expected value of the risk adjusted interest rate on this investment, $E(r_X)$, is determined from

$$\$89.00 = [(1/2)(105.00) + (1/2)(95.00)] \; / \; (1 + E(r_X))$$

that is,

$$E(r_X) = (100.00 - 89.00) \; / \; 89.00 = 12.36\%$$

We have already used the absence of arbitrage opportunities to calculate the risk premium of 2.36 percent on this deal, but we have not yet explained how the risk premium is determined. In the preceding discussion the value of the risk premium was first assumed, and then arbitrage-based calculations were used to verify its size. Neither the assumption of a risk premium's size, nor the verification of calculations based on it, explains how the premium is determined. However, each of the next two theories does explain the existence and size of a risk premium.[7]

6.3.1 Capital Asset Pricing Model

The Capital Asset Pricing Model (CAPM) argues that the 2.36 percent risk premium results from the way investors view risks as well as from the way they require to be compensated for taking risks. The CAPM is an equilibrium theory of how capital assets are priced when investors conform to assumptions specified below. The CAPM argues that since investors can purchase a diversified reference portfolio (called the market portfolio), the risks of individual securities can and should be assessed in terms of their contribution to the risks of that market portfolio. According to the CAPM, this means that the market required rate of return on a given security is

$$E(r_X) = r_f + \beta_X[E(r_M) - r_f] \tag{6.5}$$

where $E(r_X)$ is the expected return on the security in question, r_f is the risk free rate, $E(r_M)$ is the expected return on the market or reference portfolio, and β_X is the volatility of the security in question. Intuitively, β_X measures the sensitivity of changes in the expected return on the security to changes in the expected return on the reference portfolio.

Using the variance of return as a measure of risk, the CAPM establishes formally that

$$\beta_X = COV(r_X, r_M) \, / \, \sigma^2(r_M)$$

where β_X is the market price of risk for asset X, r_X is the rate of return on asset X, r_M is the rate of return on the market portfolio, $COV(r_X, r_M)$ is the covariance of returns on X and M respectively, and $\sigma^2(r_M)$ is the variance of returns on the market portfolio.

In the present example, if we assume that $E(r_M) = 12.00$ percent, and if we continue to assume that the risk free rate is 10 percent, then (6.5) takes the form

$$E(r_X) = 10.00 + \beta(12.00 - 10.00) = 12.36 \qquad (6.6)$$

In (6.6) the 2.36 percent risk premium is the product of the risk measure, β, and the market price of risk, 2 percent. Since $2.36 = \beta(2.00)$, it follows that $\beta = 1.18$. The explanation given by the CAPM is that if the risk free rate of interest is 10 percent, and the rate on the market portfolio is 12 percent, then an instrument with a β of 1.18 will have a market required rate of return equal to 12.36 percent. Similarly, an instrument with a β of 0.75 will have a market required rate of return equal to

$$E(r_X) = 10.00 + (0.75)(12.00 - 10.00) = 11.50\%$$

The principal tenets of the CAPM are:

1   investors require to be compensated for risk, where risk is measured as the variance of a portfolio's return
2   investors assess risk in relation to a reference or market portfolio
3   the market price of risk is determined using a standardised measure of the covariance of the asset's returns with returns on the market portfolio
4   all investors use the same information, capital markets are in equilibrium and any trading incurs no transactions costs.

The equilibrium risk–return relationship defined in (6.5) is often written in a form called the security market line (SML) and drawn as in Figure 6.1. The CAPM argues that if a security offers a risk–return combination which does not plot on the security market line, trading will occur until the anomaly is eliminated. Suppose, for example, a security is underpriced and yields a higher rate of return than other instruments with the same risk. Market agents will buy the underpriced security, bidding up its price until the excess return is eliminated. Similarly, an overpriced security offers too low a return and is subject to selling pressures until its price declines. In other words, if the CAPM correctly

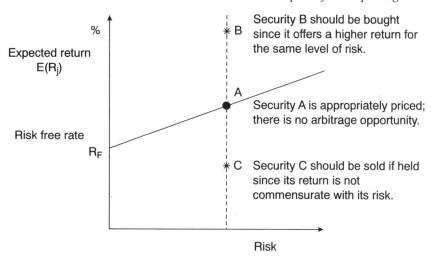

Figure 6.1 The security market line and arbitrage possibilities

describes capital market equilibrium, profit motivated trading will ensure that securities are priced so their risk–return combinations plot on the security market line.[8]

Tests of the CAPM are difficult to conduct, and as a result the tests that have been conducted give somewhat inconclusive results. First, Roll (1977) argues that while the CAPM is testable in principle, it is unlikely that a definitive test can be conducted. Roll demonstrates that the only potentially testable hypothesis of the CAPM is whether the market portfolio is mean-variance efficient, and that for a proper test the market portfolio should contain all assets sold worldwide. Cheng and Grauer (1980) design a test to circumvent the need for identifying a market portfolio, but their rather inconclusive results actually comprise a joint test of the CAPM and of the returns distribution they assume. Stambaugh (1992) shows that changing the proxy for the market portfolio does not much affect the results of tests aimed at validating the CAPM. However, Stambaugh uses only a restricted set of assets in his tests and the results therefore do not address the criticism that the CAPM defines the market portfolio as consisting of world-wide assets (Fabozzi and Modigliani 1992: 145–148).

6.3.2 Arbitrage Pricing Theory

The Arbitrage Pricing Theory (Ross 1976) predicts that the rate of return on a security is related to several risk factors rather than just the single one used in the CAPM.[9] Formally, the APT argues that $E(r_X)$, the expected return on an asset X, is determined as

$$E(r_X) = r_f + \beta_1 F_1 + \beta_2 F_2 + \ldots + \beta_I F_I \tag{6.7}$$

where r_f is the risk free rate, F_i is the risk premium associated with factor i, and β is the sensitivity of the return on the shares in question to the i'th factor; $i = 1, 2, \ldots, I$. Equation 6.7 is established using arbitrage arguments, and is an equilibrium relation like the CAPM. For example, the APT explains the 12.36 percent of the previous example using

$$12.36 = 10.00 + \beta_1 F_1 + \beta_2 F_2 + \ldots + \beta_I F_I$$

If the security's return were dependent only on the first two factors, for instance, some values which might satisfy the equation are

$$12.36 = 10.00 + 1.08(1.00) + 0.64(2.00)$$

In this case $\beta_1 = 1.08$ and $\beta_2 = 0.64$.

Both the CAPM and the APT argue that investors are concerned, not with a security's total risk, but only with those risks which cannot be reduced through diversification. Like the CAPM, the APT argues that the risk of an individual security is measured relative to reference risks, in this case the underlying risk factors. Unlike the CAPM, the APT does not explicitly define the risk factors entering into prices. That is, the CAPM explains that risk is defined in terms of β, but the APT is developed using arguments that do not identify the nature of the risk factors underlying the model. Moreover, while Equation 6.7 indicates there are I risk factors, the arguments on which the APT is based do not actually specify the size of I.

However, empirical tests of the APT help to define the meaning of the risk factors and also suggest that a practical number of risk factors for explaining the prices of marketable securities might be three or four. An empirical study by Chen, Roll and Ross (1980) identifies four risk factors. They are unanticipated changes in each of: an index of industrial production, the spread between high and low grade bonds, interest rates and inflation.

6.4 OTHER RELATIONS BETWEEN SECURITIES RETURNS

This chapter has already shown that many relations between securities prices are determined by arbitrage. To display still more uses of the arbitrage principle, this last section considers the Fisher relation and shows how some relations between bond yields are defined.

6.4.1 Fisher relation

The discussions of the CAPM and the APT in Section 6.3 took the existence of a risk free interest rate for granted. While a risk free interest rate is often assumed for analytical purposes, the student of financial markets should be aware that in practice a risk free investment can almost never be found. First, truly default free instruments are hard to find. However, this is not an overly serious problem, because for many practical purposes the bonds of some governments, as well as instruments guaranteed by some exchanges, can be regarded as essentially default free in the sense that there is a low probability of their not being redeemed in full.

Second and more importantly, even the returns on instruments with low or zero default probabilities are risky, because the future purchasing power of the payments they promise is not known with certainty.[10] It is not difficult to adjust a financial deal for a known rate of inflation, but future changes in purchasing power are difficult to predict in practice, and as a result it can be difficult to determine the future purchasing power represented by a financial deal.

To see how inflation can influence the effective interest rate on a deal, consider first an example of a payment made with certainty. In the absence of inflation, the present value of $100.00 to be paid one year from now is determined using

$$V_0 = \$100.00 \ / \ 1.10 \tag{6.8}$$

Now assume that the future rate of inflation is a certain 5 percent. (The problem of compensating for risky inflation rates is taken up later.) A 5 percent rate of inflation means that one year from now it will take $105.00 to buy a basket of goods that can be bought today for $100.00. To maintain constant purchasing power, a lender or investor must be compensated, not just for the use of funds, but also for the price increases due to inflation.

To take both the interest rate and the rate of inflation into account, the present value calculation (6.8) can be rewritten as

$$V_0 = \$100.00(1.05) \ / \ (1.10)(1.05)$$
$$= \$105.00 \ / \ (1.10)(1.05) \tag{6.9}$$

The idea of (6.9) is to show that maintaining a constant purchase power requires one to take inflation into account. In this case, it is reflected in both the numerator and the denominator of (6.9), so that you can readily see the two factors cancel each other out. That is to say, if inflation were to be 5 percent, the adjustments in the first line of (6.9) would maintain your constant purchasing power. It would do so by (i) increasing the amount you will be paid, and (ii) using a higher interest rate.

In greater detail, the factor of 1.05 in the numerator of the first line of (6.9) takes the rate of inflation into account. It says that to maintain a constant purchasing power one must have more dollars one year from now than today. To compensate for the fact that this loan arrangement pays more dollars one year from now than did the original loan transaction (when we didn't worry about inflation), the same factor is used in the denominator to define a new and higher interest rate. By lending on the new terms, the investor assures herself of getting a 10 percent return on her funds after adjusting for the decline in purchasing power due to inflation. In other words, the calculation is set up to give the same present value as before, but it now takes changes in purchasing power into account in two ways. The amount of funds to be repaid is increased, and so is the interest rate used to determine their present value.

In most cases where lenders want to be compensated for inflation, they combine the two factors in the denominator to give what is called a **nominal rate of interest**. That is, (6.9) is typically written

$$V_0 = \$105.00 \; / \; 1.155 \tag{6.10}$$

The 15.5 percent is the nominal rate of interest, 10 percent is called the **real rate of interest**, and the additional 5.5 percent the **inflation premium**. The equality

$$\text{Nominal Rate} = \text{Real Rate} + \text{Inflation Premium} \tag{6.11}$$

is called the **Fisher relation** or Fisher Effect.[11]

Fisher relation a relation stating that the nominal interest rate on a transaction equals the real interest rate plus a premium intended to account for expected future inflation. Named after the economist Irving Fisher (1867–1947), who first pointed out the effect in the 1930s.

---

inflation premium the percentage by which a nominal rate of interest exceeds a real rate of interest.

As the foregoing discussion has shown, financial markets can adjust readily to future inflation if the inflation rate is known with certainty. However, future inflation can be highly variable, since it depends on such policy choices as the rate of monetary expansion. The Fisher relation does not normally take this risk of predicting inflation into account. Yet possible changes in the rate of inflation can add substantially to the risk faced by borrowers and lenders, and relatively large premia may be required to offset this particular form of risk, particularly when inflation rates are relatively high.

For example, during one year in the 1980s inflation rates in Bolivia were 30,000 percent; prices increased over that year by a factor of 300. If at the beginning of the year a glass of orange juice had cost 1.50 Bolivian currency units, at the end of the year its price would have increased to 450.00 Bolivian currency units. If the inflation had taken place at an even rate every day, the glass of orange juice costing 1.50 Bolivian currency units in the morning of the first day of the year would have cost 2.73 Bolivian currency units the next morning.

In such an environment, even a small percentage error in forecasting the rate of inflation could have devastating consequences for the purchasing power of cash or cash-like financial instruments. In the Bolivian situation forecasting inflation was so risky that very few persons were willing to hold financial instruments of any kind. Those receiving cash hurried to exchange it for real commodities, whenever possible within minutes of receiving the cash. After all, the orange juice example shows that if you were paid in cash one morning and kept the cash until the next, the effect was almost the same as having been paid only half the original amount.

6.4.2 Real and nominal rates

The foregoing discussion of the Fisher relation implies that returns on instruments such as bonds are not riskless. A bond may be default free for all practical purposes, but neither its real nor its nominal return is likely to be riskless. First, real interest rates change unpredictably from one period to the next as underlying economic conditions change. Second, nominal interest rates can change as a result of changes in the expected rate of inflation. Third, unpredictable changes in inflation can disturb the normal pattern predicted by the Fisher relation: a sudden burst of inflation may not immediately be reflected in nominal rates, with the result that realised real rates may be negative for a time before reverting to their normal positive levels. The next example illustrates these effects of inflation on interest rates.

Suppose first of all that an investor buys a three year bond and intends to hold it to maturity. For simplicity, suppose the bond pays no interest over its life, but is redeemable for the lump sum of $1,000.00 at the end of the three years. If it were known there would be no inflation, and that the risk free rate would remain unchanged at 4 percent over each of the next three years, the bond would sell now for $1,000.00/1.04^3 = $889.00. An investor purchasing the bond for $889.00 would earn a real interest rate of 4 percent, compounded annually, if he held it to maturity.

Now suppose that over the three years in question price levels are not expected to increase, but that in fact they do increase by 1 percent per annum, again at a compound rate. The investor who did not anticipate the inflation and paid the purchase price of $889.00 would earn substantially less than a real interest rate of 4 percent on his investment. In terms of purchasing power the investor will only be repaid $1,000.00/1.01^3. Given that the unanticipated inflation was not taken into account, the real interest rate realised on the investment is given by

$$\$889.00(1 + r)^3 = \$1,000.00 / (1.01)^3$$

or

$$[\$1,000.00 / 1.04^3](1 + r)^3 = \$1,000.00 / (1.01)^3$$

That is,

$$(1 + r) = (1.04) / (1.01)$$

which gives a value of $r = 2.9703$ percent.

The preceding example showed that inflation can make a bond's real interest earnings risky. Worse yet, an investor cannot escape the risk of unanticipated changes in inflation by selling an ordinary bond as and when expectations regarding inflation are revised. As soon as the new expectations become known to the market, the bond price changes to reflect them. Thus, in the previous example, suppose the inflation forecast changes from 0 percent to 1 percent later in the day our investor first purchases the bond. When the forecast changes, the price would fall from its previous

$$\$1,000.00 \ / \ (1.04)^3 = \$889.00$$

to

$$\$1,000.00 \ / \ (1.01)^3(1.04)^3 = \$862.85$$

that is by 2.94 percent of its original capital value in a single day! As soon as the market accepts the new forecast, bond prices change to reflect it. But as soon as bond prices change, it is too late for the investor holding the bond to sell it without suffering the capital loss illustrated above.

6.4.3 Index linked bonds

Index linked bonds make it easier for investors to hedge against inflation risk, and at the same time also make it easier to test for the presence of the Fisher relation. Index linked bonds adjust payments of interest and principal by current price level indexes so that the purchasing power of the payments is maintained, at least approximately. Thus, by purchasing index linked bonds investors can assure themselves that their funds will earn something close to the real rate of interest, the degree of closeness depending on how well the index chosen to inflate the bond principal and interest payments reflects the actual impact of inflation experienced by the investor.

> **index linked bond** a bond whose principal and interest payments are increased according to some index measuring the rate of domestic inflation.

Previously, attempts to assess the validity of the Fisher relation were hampered by the difficulty of finding an appropriate proxy for the expected rate of inflation. Bond yields are expressed in nominal terms and it is not usually easy to infer the market expectations of future inflation, and hence the level of real interest rates, from these yields. However, by taking an index linked bond and by assuming that the index used to increase the bond payments mirrors rates of inflation relatively well, the observed rates of return on the indexed bonds are close to the real rates of interest. The data on UK index linked bonds in Table 6.1 give an approximate indication of the Fisher relation for bonds of about a twenty year maturity. Note that the third column, which roughly indicates the market's expectation of the inflation premium, varies from 6.33 percent in January 1993 to 4.27 percent in December.

Table 6.1 Real and nominal UK interest rates, 1993

	Nominal	Index linked	Difference
Jan.	8.66	2.33	6.33
Feb.	8.31	2.17	6.14
Mar.	8.40	2.42	5.98
Apr.	8.48	2.65	5.83
May	8.60	2.88	5.72
Jun.	8.16	2.89	5.27
Jul.	7.77	2.59	5.18
Aug.	7.23	2.38	4.85
Sep.	7.29	2.45	4.84
Oct.	7.14	2.20	4.90
Nov.	6.94	2.04	4.90
Dec.	6.25	1.98	4.27

Source: UK Central Statistical Office (December 1994) *Financial Statistics, Economic Statistics*.
Notes: Nominal rate is on 7.75 percent bonds maturing 2012–15.
        Real rate is on 2.50 percent index linked bond maturing 2016.

Expected rates of inflation can be calculated if the index used to increase the linked bond's interest and principal payments is a good proxy for inflation and if the index linked bond can be compared with another, nominal interest rate bond of about the same risk and same maturity. Studies by Breedon (1995) suggest that, when calculated from these data, inflation expectations are volatile (as suggested by the Table 6.1 data) and are also reasonably good leading indicators of subsequent rates of price level increase.

6.4.4 Nominal rates and yield curves

There are similar risks to establishing the nominal interest earnings on any long term bond that is not held to maturity. Whatever the cause of a change in expected interest rates, the market value of a bond will change immediately to reflect the change in rate expectations. Thus unless the investor intends, when purchasing the bond, to hold it until maturity, she cannot be sure of the interest rate she will earn on the investment.

Moreover, even if a bond is held to maturity, there is still an opportunity risk to take into account. In the previous example a bond purchased for $889.00 will yield 4 percent for certain if held to maturity and there is no inflation. But this will give little comfort to an investor who, having purchased the bond, finds that nominal interest rates are 5 percent because the market has changed its expectations from no inflation to an inflation rate of 1 percent. She will have purchased the bond for a higher price than she would have liked, and as a result will not earn the real 4 percent that subsequent purchasers could earn by buying the bond at a lower price than she had paid.

Recognising the risks of interest rate change, whether due to unanticipated changes in inflation or to some other cause, investors may attempt to compensate by requiring higher returns. If they believe that long term bonds carry greater risks than short term ones, they will demand higher interest rates on the longer term bonds. Thus, for example, in the case of the three year bond just discussed, investors might expect real interest rates to be 4 percent in each year because they forecast no inflation in each of the three next years. However, they might still add increasingly higher risk premiums to the rates to compensate for what they see to be increasingly greater risk that the inflation forecast might change.[12] They might, for example, price the bond using

$$\$1,000.00 \ / \ (1.04)(1.05)(1.06) = \$863.92$$

where the terms 1.04, 1.05 and 1.06 respectively reflect investors' using risk adjusted interest rates of 4 percent, 5 percent and 6 percent in years one, two and three.

In this example investors may be said to use no liquidity premium in the first year, a liquidity premium of 1 percent in the second year, and a liquidity premium of 2 percent in the third year. The average yield to maturity on a three year bond is then

$$[(1.04)(1.05)(1.06)]^{1/3} - 1 = 4.9968\%$$

The principle of pricing by arbitrage will equate the prices of bonds having the same coupons and the same maturities. Trading will also relate the prices of bonds with different maturities, but in this case the relation is not determined by arbitraging in the usual sense, because such types of trading are not riskless. For example, trading between a two and a three year bond means exchanging risks of different types. The return on a two year bond can be calculated with certainty if the investor is sure to hold the two year bond until its maturity.[13] However, the return over the first two years of a three year bond can be calculated only by using an assumption regarding the bond's value at the end of the first two years. If that value changes, the return changes, making it risky.

The information from the above calculation can be used to determine how an investor would value a two year bond at the time of the original purchase, using the same expectations as shown above. A $1,000.00 two year bond would be worth

$$\$1,000.00 \ / \ (1.04)(1.05)$$

and would have an average yield to maturity of

$$[(1.04)(1.05)]^{1/2} - 1 = 4.4988\%$$

The last calculation can be made because the two year bond will be worth a known $1,000.00 at the end of two years.

However, at the end of two years the value of the original three year bond will be determined by the interest and inflation rate expectations in force over the last year of its life. If, for example, at the end of year 2 real rates are still 4 percent but there is an expecation that inflation will be 3 percent, the original three year bond will then have to be discounted in its last year using a factor of $(1.04)(1.03) = 1.0712$ to take account of both the real rate of interest and the expected price level increase. Accordingly, the bond will be worth

$$\$1,000.00 \: / \: (1.04)(1.03) = \$933.53$$

An investor selling the bond at time 2 for the new market price of $933.53 will realise an annual average yield over the two years of her investment equal to

$$(\$933.53 \: / \: \$863.92)^{\frac{1}{2}} - 1 = 3.9507\%$$

This rate is lower than the average annual yield 4.4988 percent, on the bond purchase when no change in expected inflation occurred. The difference, of course, comes from the fact that inflation expectations rose in the last year from 0 percent to 3 percent.

The relations between interest rates on bonds with different terms to maturity are usually displayed using graphs known as yield curves, the most well known of which display the average yields to maturity on government securities relative to the maturities themselves. When calculated in practice, yield curves are determined for coupon bonds rather than for the pure discount bonds used in the above examples. Calculating a yield curve for coupon bonds is only slightly more complex than calculating the yield curve for pure discount bonds, because each of the coupons on a coupon bond can itself be regarded as a pure discount bond, as can the principal payment. Thus in practice the calculations include several terms of the types used in our foregoing examples. An example of the government yield curve, along with a comparable yield curve for corporate securities, is given in Figure 6.2. A given yield curve shows the average

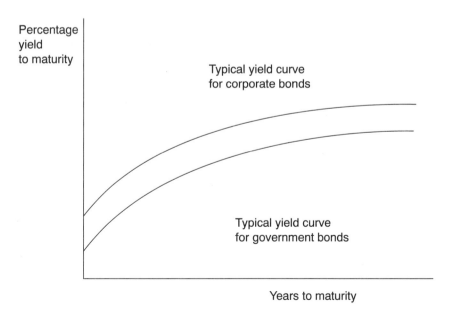

Figure 6.2 Examples of yield curves for government and corporate bonds

interest rates on bonds of comparable default risk but different maturity. The yield curve for government bonds is below the yield for corporate bonds because the latter are regarded by the market as having higher default risk than the former.

Yield curves do not explicitly reflect the differing degrees of risk to which investors in different maturities are exposed. The longer a bond's maturity, the greater the percentage fluctuation in its capital value due to changes in expectations. Table 6.2 compares the prices of a one and a ten year bond when annual rates are expected to be 4 percent in each successive year, to the prices of the same bonds when annual rates are expected to be 5 percent in each successive year. An increase from 4 percent to 5 percent causes the price of the one year bond to fall by $9.15 or 0.95 percent, whereas the price of the ten year bond falls by $61.65 or 9.13 percent.

Table 6.2 Comparisons of changes in bond prices

Interest rates	*$1,000 one year bond*	*$1,000 ten year bond*
4%	961.53	675.56
5%	952.38	613.91
Percentage decline from value at 4% to value at 5%	0.95%	9.13%

6.5 SUMMARY

This chapter introduced principles of asset pricing in a perfectly competitive financial market in which transactions can be made without payment of transactions costs. (An interest rate is not regarded as a transaction cost. Rather, it is the price for waiting to receive funds.) The chapter began by showing how a payments stream is valued under certainty, then examined how the same payments stream is valued under risk. The principles of discounted expected value and of discounted certainty equivalents were shown to be two methods of compensating for risk, methods that if correctly set up lead to the same value for the payments stream.

Second, the chapter considered how pricing by arbitrage can be used to value instruments whose payments streams are related to each other. In particular, the idea of risk adjusted probabilities was used to make the calculations particularly easy.

Third, the chapter discussed how returns on financial instruments are determined and related to each other. It began with returns on securities, discussing both the Capital Asset Pricing Model and the Arbitrage Pricing Theory, both of which determine present values under risk and relate the prices of different instruments.

Returns on other instruments can also be interpreted and determined using the principle of pricing by arbitrage, as shown by the chapter's discussion of the Fisher relation and of bond yields.

REVIEW QUESTIONS

Exercise 1 In the example of section 6.2.1, use the principle of pricing by arbitrage to explain why the lender will insist on compound interest if you do not plan to pay anything for two years. Your explanation cannot have anything to do with credit risk, because it is assumed you will be certain to make the repayment in full, with interest, as scheduled.

Exercise 2 Suppose the risk free interest rate is 8 percent, compounded annually. What is a risk free payment of $150.00, to be made exactly three years from now, worth today?

Exercise 3 Suppose that risky prospect (6.1) is worth $87.00 today. What is the risk adjusted rate of interest? In terms of their willingness to take on risk, what can you say about these investors, relative to the investors willing to pay $89.00 for the prospect?

Exercise 4 If you do not yet think the principle of pricing by arbitrage has practical value, explain how it can help you to evaluate a telephone sales person's pitch offering you, say, a sure 100 percent return (much higher than the current risk free rate) on some investment that he just cannot wait for you to put money into. If it really is a sure thing, why is he offering it to you at such a low price (i.e., at such a high rate of return)? Why doesn't he keep the extra income for himself?

Exercise 5 What are the risk adjusted probabilities if risky prospect (6.1) is worth $87.00 today, and if the riskless rate of interest is 10 percent as before?

Exercise 6 Suppose a project has an expected payoff of $150.00 one year hence, and suppose that it requires an investment today of $100.00. If the rate on the market portfolio is 12 percent, the riskless rate is 8 percent, and the project has a β of 2.50, what is its net present value?

Exercise 7 Suppose that interest rates on twenty year bonds are 12 percent, and that interest rates on one year bonds are 5 percent. The market consensus is that real interest rates should remain roughly constant over the next twenty years. What is the expected long term rate of inflation?

Exercise 8 Suppose that $E(r_M) = 12.00$ percent, and the riskless rate is 10 percent, so that (6.5) takes the form $E(r_X) = 10.00 + \beta(12.00 - 10.00) = 12.36$ percent. What is the value of β? What is the expected return on an instrument with a β of 0.75?

Exercise 9 How does the principle of pricing by arbitrage work when asset payoffs are known with certainty? Try to frame your answer in terms of the following example: are there any practical differences between five one-dollar coins and a five-dollar bill?

Exercise 10 Suppose interest rates are currently 5 percent, compounded annually. What is the value today of a lump sum payment of $1,000 to be made twenty years from now?

Exercise 11 Suppose interest rates contained an inflation adjustment component which raised them from 5 percent to 8 percent. Using this new rate, what happens to the value today of the lump sum payment in Exercise 10?

Exercise 12 Suppose that some project has a β of 1.3 if market financing is used, but a β of only 1.1 if it is financed as a conglomerate subsidiary. On the other hand, setting up the conglomerate investment means incurring today a fixed cost of $300 that is not incurred when market financing is used. Suppose the market rate of return is 10 percent, and the risk free rate is 6 percent. Show that the project's expected cash flows X would have to be large enough to satisfy

$$X/1.112 \leq X/1.104 - \$300.00$$

before considering conglomerate financing. (Hint: compare the present values of the cash flows using discount rates calculated from (6.5).)

Exercise 13 Suppose annual real interest rates are 8 percent and the inflation factor is 10 (i.e., the inflation rate is 1,000 percent per annum). What nominal rate of interest will yield a real rate of 8 percent? Suppose your guess of the inflation rate was wrong by 12 percent. Over what range would the real rate of interest vary?

Exercise 14 If a one year zero coupon bond bears an interest rate of 6 percent, and a three year bond bears a rate of 8 percent, what is the return to maturity on a two year bond of comparable default risk? What assumptions must you make to complete the calculation?

Exercise 15 Suppose you have made a bet with someone which involves paying them $1 if a fair coin comes up tails, and their paying you $1 if the fair coin comes up heads. Compare this with a second bet, on which you will get $1 if the first roll of a balanced die comes up 1, 2 or 3; and will lose $1 if the first roll comes up 4, 5 or 6.

Exercise 16 Suppose you wanted to repay exactly $100.00, principal and interest. If rates are 10 percent, how much cash could you get today in exchange for a promise to pay exactly $100.00, one year from now?

Exercise 17 How is the principle of pricing by arbitrage illustrated by Exercise 16?

Exercise 18 If two instruments both promise to pay $110.00 one year from now, if interest rates are 10 percent and one instrument is worth $100.00 today while the other is worth $99.00, which will people buy? Which will they sell? What would this do to the prices?

Exercise 19 Suppose an investor buys a three year bond and intends to hold it to maturity. For simplicity, suppose the bond pays no interest over its life, but is redeemable for the lump sum of $1,000.00 at the end of the three years. If the risk free rate is 4 percent and no inflation is expected, what is the bond worth today?

Exercise 20 Suppose in Exercise 19 that investors change their minds and now expect price levels to increase by 1 percent per annum, again at a compound rate. What would the investor lose because of this change in expectations?

7   Dividing and pricing risks

7.1   Introduction   95

7.2   Forward contracts   96

   7.2.1   What is a forward contract?   96
   7.2.2   How is a forward contract valued?   99

7.3   Options   100

   7.3.1   What are options contracts?   100
   7.3.2   How are options valued?   103
   7.3.3   Method of riskless hedge   103
   7.3.4   Risk adjusted probabilities and the riskless hedge   104
   7.3.5   Deriving the risk adjusted probabilities from the
             riskless hedge   104
   7.3.6   Put-call parity and a certainty payoff   105
   7.3.7   Put-call parity and risk adjusted probabilities   106
   7.3.8   Put and call with equal values   107

7.4   Debt and equity   108

   7.4.1   How are risks divided with debt and equity?   108
   7.4.2   How are debt and equity valued?   109
   7.4.3   Risky debt   110
   7.4.4   Debt, equity and options   111

7.5   Futures contracts   112

   7.5.1   How do futures contracts differ from forwards?   112
   7.5.2   Relations between futures and forward prices   112

7.6   Summary   115

LEARNING OBJECTIVES

After reading this chapter you will understand

- how the payoffs to risky securities can be divided up using different forms of financial instruments – forward contracts, options, debt and equity, and futures contracts
- how the different instruments discussed in this chapter are conceptually related to each other
- how different contracts can be valued when no arbitrage opportunities exist
- how risk adjusted probabilities can be found
- how risk adjusted probabilities can be used to value different instruments

---

7.1 INTRODUCTION

This chapter explains both how different financial instruments can be used to divide risks, and how these different financial instruments can be valued. The chapter does not intend to make you an expert in writing or valuing derivative securities, but it does intend to show you how the different instruments are constructed from the same building blocks. Once you have been introduced to these building blocks, the chapter explains the basic purposes for using the different contracts, and shows how they can be valued using the principles of pricing by arbitrage. These ideas will then help you understand the instruments' practical uses, which are discussed at later points in the book.

Students of finance should understand both the conceptual similarities among financial instruments and the practical reasons for using the different instruments. This chapter focuses on conceptual similarities, subsequent chapters examine practicalities. In particular, Chapter 9 shows how portfolio administrators can use the ideas of risk management. Chapter 13 examines how derivatives are traded on organised exchanges, and explains that although derivatives are not a new instrument, their use has virtually exploded since the 1970s. The reasons for this sudden increase will also be discussed in Chapter 13.

Securities designed principally for risk management include instruments such as options, forward contracts, and futures contracts. These instruments have the generic name of **derivative securities** because their payoffs depend on the value of the assets against which they are written. Derivatives can be written against almost any kind of asset, but most often they are written against actively traded financial instruments or such commodities as crude oil and gold.

> **derivative securities (derivatives)** securities whose returns depend on the value of some underlying asset against which they are written. For example, a call option on a stock is a derivative security whose value depends on the value of the underlying stock.

Although there are close conceptual relations between derivatives and such instruments as debt and equity, the two classes of instruments are used differently. Debt and equity are used primarily for raising funds from investors. Both debt and equity are used in fund raising because they represent different claims against a firm's earnings, and as a result appeal to different investor groups.[1] Derivatives are primarily used for tailoring and trading risks rather than for raising funds.[2] A derivative instrument does not represent a direct claim against an underlying asset. The derivative's value depends on the value of the underlying asset, but the instrument itself represents a claim on a third party – the issuer of the derivative.

7.2 FORWARD CONTRACTS

Forward and futures contracts are both used to separate the risk of an asset's future price fluctuations from its known, current market value. However, they do so in different, albeit related ways. It is easiest to appreciate the differences between forward and futures contracts after first acquiring some basic ideas about forward contracts and other financial instruments. Thus, forward contracts will be examined first. The chapter then examines options, then debt and equity, and finally futures contracts.

7.2.1 What is a forward contract?

A forward contract is an agreement under which an investor assumes an obligation to trade a specified asset, at a given time, for a given price. Taking a long position in a forward contract means assuming an obligation to purchase a specified asset, at a given time, for a given price. Similarly, taking a short position in a forward contract means assuming an obligation to sell the specified asset, again at a given time and for a given price. The principal purpose of the forward contract is to write an instrument that permits trading in the risk of asset price changes. The price changes in question are those which can occur between the time the forward contract is written and its **delivery date** – the date when the contract specifies the asset must be exchanged. The parties entering a forward contract may or may not have the asset at the time they enter the contract, and they may or may not intend to take possession of the asset on the delivery date. These practical issues will be discussed further in Chapter 13.

> **delivery date** the date the commitments under a forward contract must be carried out.

The gross profits or losses on a forward contract, and consequently the contract's value, depend on the relation between price specified in the contract – called the forward price – and the cash price of the asset on the delivery date. A **long position** in a forward contract conveys an opportunity to profit if on the delivery date the asset's cash price turns out to be more than the forward price specified by the contract. For example, if the holder of a forward contract has agreed to buy an asset for $100.00, and if the asset is actually worth $111.00 on that date, the position permits turning an immediate gross profit of $11.00 by purchasing and reselling the asset. By the same token, having a long position in a forward contract can imply losses if the asset's future cash price turns out to be less than the forward price. For example, if the holder of a forward contract has agreed to buy an asset for $100.00, and if the asset is worth only $91.00 on that date, the position implies an immediate loss of $9.00, because the contract requires paying $9.00 more than the market price for the asset.

> **long position** an investor who owns an asset is said to have a long position in the asset. An investor who has entered a forward contract requiring him to purchase the asset is said to have a long position in the forward contract.

A **short position** is the reverse of a long position. Therefore, the gross profits or losses to a party with a short position in the forward contract are exactly the opposite of those realised by the party with the long position.

> **short position** a short position is the opposite of a long position. An investor who has sold an asset before acquiring it is said to have a short position in the asset. An investor who has entered a forward contract requiring her to sell the asset is said to have a short position in the forward contract.

Now that you have been introduced to the essential mechanics of a forward contract, it is time to re-examine the principal reason for its use. As already noted, the essential purpose of a forward contract is to separate the asset's expected market value from the risk of price change. For example, one might wish to buy an asset at a future point in time, but one might also want to fix the amount that will have to be paid for it. A forward contract would achieve this purpose: taking a long position in a forward contract means fixing the price at which the asset can later be acquired.

Naturally, the contract will also have to be agreeable to the counterparty, who will be assuming the price risk the first party wishes to sell off. How might a contract agreeable to both parties be found? To answer this question, consider the example of the risky prospect X discussed in Chapter 6:

$$X = \begin{array}{l} \$95.00 \text{ with probability } 0.5 \\ \\ \$105.00 \text{ with probability } 0.5 \end{array} \qquad (7.1)$$

Suppose X now represents the distribution of time 1 market values for some asset, and consider a forward contract written today, at time 0, specifying that you will buy the asset at time 1 for $100.00. You do this because you wish to avoid the price risk that you would incur if you waited until time 1 to buy the asset in the marketplace at the then prevailing price. Column F of Table 7.1 shows the gross profits or losses that your long position will create at time 1. By taking the long position in the forward contract you agree, at time zero, to pay $100.00 at time 1 for the asset. This means you will be $5.00 ahead if the asset price turns out to be high, but $5.00 out of pocket if it is low. In essence, Table 7.1 says that a forward contract divides the payoffs to a risky prospect X into a sure payment – the forward price embodied in the contract – and fluctuations about that forward price.

Symbolically, this division of the original risk can be expressed as

$$X \equiv S + (X - S) \equiv S + F$$

where X represents the asset payoffs, S the forward price, and F the gross gains or losses to the long forward position, that is the payoffs to the forward contract.[3] The left-hand column of Table 7.1 displays the different possible values of X, while the two right-hand columns display its division into the sure payment, S, and the fluctuations about it, F. Adding the symbols corresponds to adding across each row of Table 7.1. In effect, the equation summarises the information in the table: the forward contract represents a division of payoffs no matter which value of the asset is actually realised. By entering the forward contract, you can trade the price risk with a counterparty. Will you have to pay the counterparty something to take on the risk? As the next section shows, that depends on the choice of the forward price, which in turn defines the distribution of the price risk.

Table 7.1 Profits or losses on a forward contract with forward price of $100.00 (The forward price is to be paid at time 1)

	X (asset price)	S (forward price)	F (gross gains or losses)
Time 1 high price	105.00	100.00	5.00
Time 1 low price	95.00	100.00	−5.00

7.2.2 How is a forward contract valued?

The forward contract of 7.2.1 specifies you will pay $100.00 for the asset, come what may. In the absence of any arbitrage opportunities, the time zero value of the forward contract must equal the difference between the time zero value of the asset and the time zero value of the sure $100.00 payment, where the latter is represented by the forward price. Suppose, as in Chapter 6, that the asset has a time zero value of $89.00, and that the riskless interest rate is 10 percent. The 10 percent interest rate means a riskless payment of $100.00 has a time zero value of $90.91. Therefore, in the absence of arbitrage opportunities it follows that the payoffs to the forward contract in Table 7.1 must have a time zero value of

$$\$89.00 - \$90.91 = -\$1.91$$

This negative value means that, given the asset price of $89.00 and the riskless rate of 10 percent, a long position in the forward contract[4] is worth $1.91. The value calculations are summarised in Table 7.2.

Forward contracts usually specify a forward price that gives the contract a value of zero at the time it is written. In the present example, the forward price will have to be less than $100.00 if the contract is to have a zero value both to yourself and the counterparty. Since the asset is worth $89.00 today, its certainty equivalent value must be $89.00(1.10) = 97.90 one year from now. If the forward contract stipulates paying this amount for certain one year from now, its present value is $89.00, the same as the current market value of the asset, and the contract itself has a present value of zero. In other words, the contract stipulates paying a time 1 price that merely accounts for the interest between now and time 1, and both parties agree that 10 percent is the market rate of interest. The value calculations are shown in Table 7.3.

Table 7.2 Values of asset and forward contract with a forward price of $100.00 (The forward price is to be paid at time 1)

	X	*S*	*F*
Time 1 high payoffs	105.00	100.00	5.00
Time 1 low payoffs	95.00	100.00	−5.00
Time 0 values	89.00	90.91	−1.91

Table 7.3 Valuing a contract with a forward price of $97.90

	X	*S*	*F*
Time 1 high payoffs	105.00	97.90	7.10
Time 1 low payoffs	95.00	97.90	−2.90
Time 0 values	89.00	89.00	0.00

In this contract your gains are $7.10 if the asset price turns out to be high, and your losses are $2.90 if the asset price turns out to be low. If the underlying asset has a market price today of $89.00, and if the riskless interest rate is 10 percent, the future payments in column F must have a market value of zero at time zero.

The risk adjusted probabilities found in Chapter 6, $p^* = 0.29$ and $1 - p^* = 0.71$, can be used to check that the new forward contract indeed has a present value of zero:

$$(0.29)(7.10) \ / \ 1.10 - (0.71)(2.90) \ / \ 1.10 = 0.00$$

7.3 OPTIONS

> **option** a contract that permits its holder to trade in a security at a fixed price, either on a given date or over a given time interval, should the holder elect to do so. A contract that permits a purchase is known as a call option; one that permits a sale is known as a put option. Options can be written to permit exercise either on a given date or over a given time interval. Instruments which can be exercised only on a given date are called European options, while those which can be exercised at any time within a given interval are called American options.[5]

7.3.1 What are options contracts?

This chapter discusses and values European options; its methods are extended to value American options in Chapter 9. A European call option is an instrument that allows its holder to purchase some underlying asset (usually a security, but options can also be written on such real assets as, say, property) at a fixed purchase price and fixed future point in time, should the holder wish to make the purchase. A European put option is a similar security that allows its owner to sell, should he wish to do so, a specified asset at a fixed price and at a fixed point in time.

Like forwards, options offer a way of dividing up the payoffs to risky prospects. A forward contract requires you to honour a commitment to trade whether asset prices increase or decrease. With options, these possibilities are represented by two contracts – a call and a put – which can be exercised at the discretion of the holder. The holder of the options will exercise them only when it is profitable to do so. A call will be exercised if the underlying instrument's price rises above the call exercise price, a put will be exercised if the underlying instrument's prices fall below its exercise price. As will be shown, the existence of two instruments and the discretionary exercise privilege implies that options permit a finer division of risks than do forwards.

To examine the differences further, recall the prospect (7.1). Since options are very often written against shares, assume for purposes of discussion that the firm in question has issued one share, and that the possible future market values of the share are described by (7.1). Suppose a European call option with an exercise price of $100.00 has been written against the share. The call conveys to its owner the right to purchase the share for $100.00 at time 1. The call will be worth $5.00 at time 1 if the share has a high value, but nothing if the share has a low value. If the share has a high value, the holder will use his option to buy an instrument, with a market value of $105.00, for a payment of $100.00. If the share instead attains the value of $95.00, the option is valueless to the holder, who will discard it. These option payoffs corresponding to the different share values are listed in column C of Table 7.4.

Now consider a put option, also written with an exercise price of $100.00. If you own this option, it allows you to sell the share to someone else for $100.00. Clearly, you would want to do this when the market value of the share was $95.00, but not when it was $105.00. The put option is therefore worth $5.00 to its holder when the share value is low, and zero when the share value is high.

Now consider what the put option is worth to the person who writes or creates it. If you write the put option you lose $5.00 to its holder when the share is worth $95.00, because in that case the holder of the put will require you to buy the share, worth only $95.00, for a contracted price of $100.00. However, you lose nothing when the firm payoffs are $105.00, because in that case the holder of the put discards it without exercise. The gross profits or losses to you, as issuer of the option, are shown in the column headed –P, where the negative sign indicates that the column adopts the viewpoint of an option writer. (Column C, with its implied positive sign, adopts the viewpoint of an option holder.) We can now see how the combination of a call and a short put position give the same payoffs as the previously discussed forward contract. In either row of Table 7.4, the algebraic sum taken across the last two columns equals the corresponding amount in column F of Table 7.1: the call option and the short put position together give exactly the same payoffs as did the forward contract. Recall from (7.1) that, symbolically, it was possible to write

$$X \equiv S + F$$

Since Table 7.4 has indicated that $F \equiv C - P$ (when the forward price equals the common exercise price of the two options), we can rewrite (7.1) as

$$X \equiv S + C - P \tag{7.2}$$

Table 7.4 Options with exercise price of $100.00

	X (firm)	S (certainty payoff)	C (call position)	–P (short put position)
Time 1 high payoffs	105.00	100.00	5.00	0.00
Time 1 low payoffs	95.00	100.00	0.00	–5.00

Next, you can verify (7.2) by noting that, for any row, the sum of the payoffs in columns S, C and –P is exactly equal to the corresponding amount in column X. Thus, in symbolic form, (7.2) says that no matter what the value of the share turns out to be, the payoffs to the three instruments in columns S, C and –P add up to the payoffs in column X. In other words, the payoffs to a risky prospect X can be divided up into the payoffs to a sure thing, the positive payoffs represented by the long call position, and the negative payoffs represented by the short put position. This is the sense in which options permit a finer division of payoffs than does a forward contract.

Since the previous paragraph showed that a forward contract is exactly the same thing as a properly constructed portfolio of a call and a short put, the question of why market agents would use both kinds of instruments arises. A quick answer to the question is that in practice forward contracts and options contracts are not the same, because they trade on different exchanges and possibly at different transactions costs. It is also possible that at a given time one or the other instrument may be available at disequilibrium prices, but you should be able to explain why this will be unlikely in markets with active arbitraging.[6] These practical reasons for preferring one kind of instrument to another will be examined further in Chapter 13. For the present, we continue to develop additional theoretical relations between the instruments used for risk trading.

Note that (7.2) shows there are at least two ways of getting the payoffs in column X of Table 7.4. One way is to hold all the shares issued by the firm – the payoffs in column X. Another way is to hold the instruments in columns S and C while simultaneously issuing the instrument in column –P. This position in three instruments offers a total payoff distribution equal to the payoffs to X.

Another way of expressing relation (7.2) is to note that X can always be written as

$$X \equiv S + \max(X–S, 0) - \max(S–X, 0) = S + C - P$$

The first equality in the last line says you can divide any risky payoff distribution X into a certainty part, a positive part, and a negative part. The second equality says this division can be interpreted as a certainty payoff, the payoff to a long call, and the payoff to a short put position.

Although Table 7.4 conceptually defines an instrument whose payoff S is $100.00 regardless of whether the firm (and consequently the single share it has issued) does well or badly, we know that the firm cannot always generate a payoff amounting to at least $100.00. Thus Table 7.4 needs to be interpreted rather carefully. The table means that if you own the firm (i.e., the payoffs in column X), then you are in the same position as if you held a portfolio of the securities in columns S, C and –P. In other words, owning the whole firm is notionally the same thing as having long position in a sure thing that will pay $100.00, a long position in a call option from which you will profit by $5.00 if the firm does well, and at the same time writing a put option which will cost you $5.00 in payments to others if the firm does badly.

7.3.2 How are options valued?

In the absence of arbitrage opportunities, it follows from (7.2), and is illustrated by the example in Table 7.4, that the value of the payments in column X is equal to the combined values of the payments in columns S, C and –P. If, for example, the time zero market value of the payments in column X is $89.00 as assumed earlier, then the sum of the time zero values of the payments in columns S, C and –P must also be $89.00 in the absence of any arbitrage opportunities. This same insight permits finding values for both the put and the call individually, so long as a portfolio containing the put or the call can be appropriately structured. The next section shows how the structuring is done.

7.3.3 Method of riskless hedge[7]

Options were first valued by constructing a riskless portfolio and using its value to infer the value of an option included in the portfolio. The valuation method, called the method of constructing a riskless hedge, is both of historical interest and helpful to the student looking for alternative ways of deriving option values. The idea underlying the method of the riskless hedge is straightforward, but the calculations can be a little tricky at first sight. Let us begin with the underlying idea, then explore the calculations.

First, if we know the riskless interest rate, we can value a riskless portfolio simply by discounting its payoff at the riskless rate. Now suppose we also know the current (time zero) price of an asset, say a stock, as well as the probability distribution of payoffs to be received from investing in the stock and holding it over some fixed period. (A year is used in the following example.) Then, if we could make up a portfolio consisting of a position in the stock and a call option, taking care to structure the portfolio so that it had riskless payoffs, we would be able to derive the time zero value of the option from values that are already known. In other words, if we make up a portfolio of a stock with a known value and an option with an unknown value, and if the portfolio is riskless so that we know its value also, we can figure out the value of the option.

One way of doing the calculations is to use a combination of a long equity position and a short call position to find a time zero value for the call. (You should be able, at least after working through the exercise, to see that you could also use long positions in both a stock and a put.) The size of the equity position is adjusted to create exactly the negative of payoffs to the short call position shown in Table 7.5. Then, if one knows the value of the equity and the value of the risk free rate, it is possible to value the call as shown next.

The example we now use continues to suppose that X represents the payoffs to a firm financed entirely by equity. As before, there is a difference in call payoffs according to whether the firm does well or badly. Assuming the call is written on the whole of the firm's equity, that the call has an exercise price of $100.00, and that the firm's payoff distribution is still (7.1), the difference in call payoffs is

$$\$5.00 - \$0.00 = \$5.00$$

The difference in payoffs to the entire equity position of one share is

$$\$105.00 - 95.00 = \$10.00$$

Accordingly, the difference in payoffs to a half-share can be used to offset exactly the difference in payoffs to a short call position. That is, the payoff to $X/2 - C$ is a sure \$47.50, as shown in Table 7.5.

Using the principle of pricing by arbitrage, the time zero value of the portfolio $X/2 - C$ must equal $\$89.00/2 - C_0 = 44.50 - C_0$, where C_0 is the time zero value of the call. Also, since $X/2 - C$ represents a certainty payoff of \$47.50 at time 1, it must have a time zero value of $\$47.50/1.10 = \$43.18$. Equating the two expressions,

$$(\$44.50 - C_0) = \$47.50 / (1.10)$$

$$C_0(1.10) = \$44.50(1.10) - \$47.50 = \$48.95 - \$47.50 \qquad (7.3)$$

$$C_0 = [\$48.95 - \$47.50] / 1.10 = \$1.45 / 1.10 = \$1.32$$

As shown in Table 7.5, the time 1 payoffs in each row add to the total time 1 payoffs. Accordingly, by the absence of arbitrage opportunities the time zero values of the equity position, \$44.50, and the short call position, –\$1.32, must add up to the time zero value of the portfolio, \$43.18.

Table 7.5 Valuing the call by the riskless hedge method

	X/2	–C	X/2 – C
Time 1 high payoffs	105.00/2	–5.00	47.50
Time 1 low payoffs	95.00/2	–0.00	47.50
Time 0 values	89.00/2 = 44.50	–1.45/1.10 = –1.32	47.50/1.10 = 43.18

7.3.4 Risk adjusted probabilities and the riskless hedge

Recall that section 7.2.2 used the risk adjusted probability $p^* = 0.29$ to value payoffs realised when the firm does well, and $1 - p^* = 0.71$ to value payoffs realised when the firm does badly. For the payoffs to the call of the previous section, the risk adjusted probability calculation gives a value of

$$C_0 = [(0.29)\$5.00 + (0.71)\$0.00] / 1.10 =$$

$$(0.29)\$5.00 / 1.10 = \$1.45 / 1.10 = \$1.32 \qquad (7.4)$$

the same as before. (The \$1.32 is preceded by a minus sign in Table 7.5 because it represents the value of a short position in the call.)

7.3.5 Deriving the risk adjusted probabilities from the riskless hedge

The reason the risk adjusted probabilities give the same value as the riskless hedge method is that, when rearranged, the numbers in the riskless hedge calculation actually define the risk adjusted probability p*. To verify this observation, notice that (7.4) can be written

$$(\$89.00/2 - C_0)(1.10) = \$105.00 / 2 - \$5.00$$

That is,

$$C_0(1.10) = \$5.00 + \$97.90/2 - \$105.00 / 2$$

$$C_0(1.10) = \$5.00 - [\$105.00 - \$97.90] / 2$$

$$C_0(1.10) = \$5.00\{1 - [\$105.00 - \$97.90] / \$10.00\}$$

$$C_0(1.10) = \$5.00 \{1 - [\$105.00 - \$97.90] / [\$105.00 - \$95.00]\}$$

$$C_0(1.10) = \$5.00 \{[\$97.90 - \$95.00] / [\$105.00 - \$95.00]\}$$

and the expression in the braces of the last line is the value for p* obtained in section 7.2.2.

A symbolic version of the foregoing argument is given in the Appendix to this chapter. It can be shown by advanced methods (see Huang and Litzenberger 1988) that whenever securities prices satisfy an equilibrium characterised by no arbitrage profits, the risk adjusted probability method can be used to relate the equilibrium prices to each other. The risk adjusted probabilities can be derived using hedging arguments as shown, for example, in Cox and Rubinstein (1985). The example just presented verifies the theoretical results by showing that when prices are calculated from each other according to the principle of pricing by the absence of arbitrage opportunities, the risk adjusted probabilities are implicit in the calculation.

7.3.6 Put-call parity and a certainty payoff

Even though our discussion is still at a conceptual level, we intend to put the concepts to practical use. The next example suggests one such practical application. Suppose you own the firm, and want to keep its expected income of $100.00, but without assuming any risk at all. (You realise, of course, that you will have to pay something to induce another party to assume the risk. The principle is the same as buying insurance – you have to pay an insurance company to assume a risk on your behalf.) The key to the practical interpretation is to think of actually trading the options whose payoffs were listed in Table 7.4. Could you add other securities to your holdings of the stock in such a way as to eliminate the risk of changes in the payoffs you would receive? Recall from Table 7.4 that when you wrote a put, you did badly if firm earnings fell. On the other hand, as the owner of a call, you did well when firm earnings rose. So, if you own the firm (or the firm's shares) and want to eliminate the risk of changes in value, one way to do so would involve selling or taking a short position in a call, and buying or taking a long position in a put, as shown in Table 7.6.

Now, your portfolio (in the three right-hand columns) consists of an investment in the firm, a short call position and a long put position. It has exactly

Table 7.6 Devising a portfolio with a certainty payoff: illustration of put-call parity

	S (certainty payoffs)	X (long position in firm or shares of firm)	−C (short call position)	P (long put position)
Time 1 high payoffs to firm	100.00	105.00	−5.00	0.00
Time 1 low payoffs to firm	100.00	95.00	0.00	5.00
Time 0 values	90.91	89.00	−1.32	3.23

the same payoffs of $100.00 whether the firm does well or badly. This relationship between the shares of a firm, the options, and a riskless investment with certainty payoffs is a well-known one in options pricing theory, and is referred to as **put-call parity**. At this point you can see that one interpretation of put-call parity is that it shows how to devise an insurance policy to offload certain kinds of investment risks.

---

put-call parity a relationship in options pricing theory which says that the value of a sure thing can be arranged using a portfolio consisting of a long position in an asset, accompanied by an (appropriately adjusted) short position in a call and a long position in a put. Both options are written against the asset; both have the same exercise price and maturity.

Symbolically, the payoffs defining the put-call parity relation derived above can be expressed as

$$S \equiv X - C + P \tag{7.5}$$

Equation 7.5 is algebraically the same expression as (7.2), but with S rather than X on the left-hand side. Since the two equations are the same, (7.2) and (7.5) show formally that the put-call parity relation uses the same idea of dividing up risks that were used in the earlier discussion.

7.3.7 Put-call parity and risk adjusted probabilities

We can now use the risk adjusted probabilities to verify the put-call parity relationship stated in 7.3.5. For example, the value of the put position in Table 7.6 is

$$(1 - p^*)\$5.00 / 1.10 = 0.71(\$5.00)/1.10 = \$3.55/1.10 = \$3.23$$

Similarly, the value of the short call position in Table 7.6 is

$$(-\$5.00 / 1.10)p^* = (-\$5.00 / 1.10)(0.29) = -\$1.45 / 1.10 = -\$1.32$$

Symbolically, the valuation relations corresponding to the payoffs in (7.3) can be written

$$v(S) \equiv v(X) - v(C) + v(P) \qquad (7.6)$$

where v(X) means 'determine value using the risk adjusted probabilities', and the capital letters S, X, C and P refer to the sure thing, the risky prospect, the short call and the long put positions respectively. Finally, substituting the values obtained above, along with the previously determined value of the firm, into (7.6), we can verify that the left-hand side

$$v(S) = \$100.00 / 1.10 = \$90.91$$

is just equal to the value of the right-hand side,

$$v(X) - v(C) + v(P) = (\$97.90 - 1.45 + 3.55) / 1.10 = \$90.91 \qquad (7.7)$$

Thus, as follows from their construction, the risk adjusted probabilities can be used to verify pricing relations like the (7.7) relation for put-call parity.

7.3.8 Put and call with equal values

If you look at (7.6) carefully, you might guess that there would be a special value of the exercise price S, say S*, such that $v(X) = v(S^*)$, exactly. That is, a call and a put written with exercise price S* would have exactly equal values. Table 7.7 shows how to verify that such an exercise price S* can be found.

The values at the bottoms of columns C and −P can be checked using the method of risk adjusted probabilities. They are given respectively by

$$(0.29)(\$7.10) / 1.10 = \$1.87$$

and

$$-(0.71)(\$2.90) / 1.10 = -\$1.87$$

Conceptually, Table 7.7 shows that the value of a risky prospect such as X can be divided, using options, into the value of a sure thing, the value of an upside potential and the value of a downside risk. Moreover, when the size of the exercise price (equal to the size of the certainty payoff) is chosen to equate the values of the call and the short put position, the value of the upside potential is exactly equal to the value of the downside risk. (The possible payoff on the up side is greater than the payoff on the down side because the market agents valuing the options are assumed to be risk averse.)

Table 7.7 Finding a put and a call with the same value

	X	S*	C	−P
Time 1 high payoffs	105.00	97.90	7.10	0.00
Time 1 low payoffs	95.00	97.90	0.00	−2.90
Time 0 values	89.00	89.00	1.87	−1.87

This same idea is used in writing forward contracts whose time zero value is itself equal to zero. If you go back to Table 7.3, you will see that the forward price which gave the forward contract an originating value of zero is the same as the $97.90 exercise price that equated the value of the put and the call. Since the forward contract can be interpreted as a long call and a short put, the equality of values verifies once again that in the absence of arbitrage opportunities the value of the forward contract must equal the value of a long call and a short put, when the exercise prices of the options are both equal to the forward price specified in the forward contract.

7.4 DEBT AND EQUITY

Risky prospects can also be divided using debt and equity. You might therefore suspect that the payoffs to debt and equity could somehow be related to the payoffs to option contracts, and this section shows how such payoff relations can be established. It then follows, in the absence of arbitrage profits, that the values of debt and equity can also be related to the values of options.

7.4.1 How are risks divided with debt and equity?

Suppose the prospect X defined in (7.1) is now interpreted as a distribution of the cash flows generated by a firm (i.e., the net earnings from its operations). Continue also to assume that the firm will realise one of the values from this distribution, at a time one year from now. Finally, suppose the firm's current market value continues to be $89.00. Recalling the discussion from Chapter 6, suppose that a bank lender (or purchaser of a bond issued by the firm)[8] believes the firm's earnings to be described by the payoff distribution (7.1). If the loan is to be repaid from the the realised cash flow described by (7.1), there is a maximum amount the banker will lend on a risk free basis. Assuming the risk free rate of interest to be 10 percent, that maximal amount is $95.00/1.10. (The $95.00 is the amount of principal and interest to be repaid one year later, while the proceeds are $95.00/1.10 = $86.36, the present value of the $95.00.) By advancing no more than $95.00/1.10, the lender is assured of getting back $95.00 at time 1 whether the firm does well or badly: with this deal the lender is assured of earning 10 percent without risk. A loan for more than $95.00/1.10 could not be always paid in full from the firm's cash flows, because the cash available to make the repayments can be as low as $95.00 if the firm does badly.

Assuming the firm does raise $95.00/1.10 on a risk free basis, consider what happens one year later when the firm's cash flows are realised and the loan becomes due. The promised $95.00 principal and interest will be paid to the lenders, and any cash flows in excess of $95.00 will be available as a return to the firm's shareholders. Symbolically, this division of payoffs into debt and equity can be written $X \equiv D + E$, where X represents the random payoffs, D the payments to debtholders (principal and interest), and E the payments to shareholders, all at time 1. In the present example, the division of payoffs is shown in Table 7.8.

Table 7.8 Payoffs when debt with principal and interest payment of $95.00 is issued

	X (total amount generated by the firm)	D (payoffs to debtholders)	E (returns to owners of the firm's equity)
Time 1 high payoffs	105.00	95.00	10.00
Time 1 low payoffs	95.00	95.00	0.00

The column headings of Table 7.8 indicate the available funds and the amounts paid to the two classes of securityholders under different scenarios. Each of the two main rows represents a scenario, the first showing the payoffs to be received if the firm does well, the second if it does badly. It is clear from the table that the combined payoffs to debt and equity, the sum across a given row, exactly equals the payoffs to the firm as a whole, represented by the corresponding row amount in column X. Note that the payments to the debtholders are the same, whether the firm does well or badly. This means the debt in the current example is riskless. As has already been discussed, the fact that the row payoffs in columns D and E sum to the row payoff in column X means that in the absence of arbitrage opportunities you only have to know two of the columns' time zero values to determine the third.

7.4.2 How are debt and equity valued?

The principle of determining prices in the absence of arbitrage opportunities can be used to value debt and equity, just as it was used to value forwards and options. Continuing to assume the riskless interest rate is 10 percent, the market value of a riskless investment in the firm is $95.00/1.10. Assuming further that the market value of the whole firm continues to be $89.00, it follows from the assumed absence of arbitrage opportunities that the value of the equity in the project must equal the difference between the value of the whole firm and the value of its debt.[9] That is, the equity is worth

$$\$89.00 - \$95.00 / 1.10 =$$

$$[\$97.90 - 95.00] / 1.10 = \$2.90/1.10 = \$2.64$$

Another method for determining the same value was presented earlier: in the Chapter 6 discussion referring to Equation 6.4, it was shown that the risk adjusted probability $p* = 0.29$ could be used to calculate the value of the equity as $(0.29)\$10.00/1.10 = \$2.90/1.10 = \$2.64$.

Since the payoffs to a position that combines all the debt and all the equity are exactly the same as the payoffs to the whole firm, it follows from the assumed absence of arbitrage opportuntities that the value of the debt plus the value of the equity equals the value of the firm. Table 7.9 verifies the following observations. The $89.00 at the bottom of column X is given by assumption, and the value $86.36 at the bottom of column D must be the value

Table 7.9 Valuing debt and equity

	X	D	E
Time 1 high payoffs	105.00	95.00	10.00
Time 1 low payoffs	95.00	95.00	00.00
Time 0 values	97.90/1.10 = 89.00	95.00/1.10 = 86.36	2.90/1.10 = 2.64

of the riskless debt if interest rates are 10 percent. (The debt is riskless because it has the same payoff whether the firm does well or badly.) It can be seen that under either the high or the low payoff scenario, the payoffs to the equity are exactly the same as the payoffs to the whole firm minus the payoffs to the debtholders. It follows that, in the absence of arbitrage opportunities, the value of the equity equals the value of the whole firm less the value of the debt. That is,

$$\$97.90 / 1.10 - \$95.00 / 1.10 = (\$97.90 - 95.00) / 1.10 = \$2.90 / 1.10 = \$2.64$$

7.4.3 Risky debt

Now suppose the firm were to issue debt with a promised repayment of more than \$95.00. It is clear from (7.1) that the firm will not always be able to redeem such a promise in full. For example, suppose the firm issued debt that nominally promised to pay \$99.00 in principal and interest at time 1. Assuming the firm has no other resources, and that there are no costs to defaulting on the promise, the payoffs to the securityholders would be as shown in Table 7.10. In this case the debt is not riskless. The amount that can be repaid is \$99.00 if the firm does well, but in spite of its promise, the firm cannot actually deliver more than \$95.00 if earnings turn out badly.

Since the two possible realised outcomes are assumed to be equally likely in (7.1), the expected value of the time 1 payments to the debtholders is

$$(1/2)(\$99.00) + (1/2)(95.00) = \$97.00$$

In the absence of arbitrage opportunities, the value of the debt must be less than \$97.00 discounted at the risk free rate of 10 percent: discounting an expected value at the riskless rate is not sufficient to adjust for the fact that the debt is risky and cannot always fully be repaid. A higher discount rate must be used because the purchaser of risky debt will require a risk premium as compensation for taking on a prospect that is not a sure thing. To put the matter another

Table 7.10 Payoffs when debt with principal and interest payment of \$99.00 is issued

	X (firm)	D (debt)	E (equity)
Time 1 high payoffs	105.00	99.00	6.00
Time 1 low payoffs	95.00	95.00	0.00

way, the firm cannot become worth more just because it has changed the amount it promises to pay debtholders. Investors look at what the firm can earn, and will value its securities in relation to those earnings, no matter what the nominal promises made by the firm are. The ways the securities' values change will be examined next.

7.4.4 Debt, equity and options

The risky debt whose payoffs are shown in Table 7.10 can be valued by regarding it as a combination of a sure thing and an implicit put option. Table 7.11 shows the two classes of securityholders – debt and equity – while Table 7.12 shows the equivalent positions in terms of options. You will notice that for any row in Table 7.11, the payoffs to the debt are actually equal to the algebraic sum of the payoffs to the sure prospect S and the short put position in Table 7.12. Thus, risky debt can be thought of as representing a combination of riskless promise and an implied short put position, two instruments whose payoffs are separately recognised in Table 7.3. The equivalence of payoffs can be seen by comparing Tables 7.11 and 7.12. In other words, holders of risky debt are in the same position as holders of riskless debt when the latter have also written a put option. This implicit put position represents the risk, borne by the bondholders, that they will not be repaid in full.

The securities in Tables 7.11 and 7.12 can be valued using risk adjusted probabilities. The calculations for Table 7.11 are

$$[(0.29)(99.00) + (0.71)(95.00)] \,/\, 1.10 = \$87.42$$

for the debt, and

$$[(0.29)(6.00)] \,/\, 1.10 = \$1.58$$

Table 7.11 Payoffs when risky debt with principal and interest payment of $99.00 is issued

	X (firm)	D (debt)	E (equity)
Time 1 high payoffs	105.00	99.00	6.00
Time 1 low payoffs	95.00	95.00	0.00
Time 0 values	89.00	87.42	1.58

Table 7.12 Options with exercise price of $99.00

	X (firm)	S (certainty payoff)	C (call position)	–P (short put position)
Time 1 high payoffs	105.00	99.00	6.00	0.00
Time 1 low payoffs	95.00	99.00	0.00	–4.00
Time 0 values	89.00	90.00	1.58	–2.58

for the equity, adding to the $89.00 value for the firm. In the case of Table 7.12, the same kinds of calculations show that the value of the risky debt, $87.42, is just equal to the value of a sure payment of $99.00 less a put with an exercise price of $99.00. Comparison of Tables 7.11 and 7.12 shows that risky debt implicitly creates a short put position which reduces the value of the debt from what it would be if the promise were riskless.

7.5 FUTURES CONTRACTS

This section defines a futures contract, discusses how and why it differs from a forward, and shows how the futures contract can be valued. The problem of valuing a futures contract is more complex than that of valuing a forward, because in the case of futures the possibility of price changes to the contract must be built into the valuation method.

7.5.1 How do futures contracts differ from forwards?

A futures contract is like a forward contract, but with the additional feature that it provides for interim settlement of any realised capital gains or losses. Like forwards, futures contracts can be written against many different kinds of assets. Also like forwards, there can be capital gains or losses on a futures contract. In contrast, the capital gains or losses on a futures contract are realised at the end of each trading period (usually the business day) rather than just on the delivery date as with forwards. When a futures contract is first issued, the usual practice is to specify a futures price that makes the contract's initial value equal to zero. The contract value typically changes each trading day as the value of the underlying asset changes. The change in asset value produces a capital gain or loss for the holder of the futures contract, and at the end of each trading day, this gain or loss must be accounted for to the broker through whom the contract was arranged. After the gain or loss is settled, the futures contract is 'marked to market' by changing the futures price it embodies, so that once again the contract has a value of zero.

The principal reason for settling capital gains or losses each day is to reduce the risk of contract non-performance. There is always a possibility that a forward contract will be defaulted upon by the losing party, either before or at maturity. The default risk of a futures contract is lower, because neither capital gains nor losses are permitted to mount up, but must instead be settled every trading day. This process of realising capital gains or losses and marking the futures contract to market means that valuing the future is more difficult than valuing the corresponding forward contract.

7.5.2 Relations between futures and forward prices

To value a futures contract, one must take into account the possibility that the futures prices embodied in the instrument will be changed as realised capital gains or losses are credited to the parties' trading accounts. Although a complete investigation of the issues in valuation is a complex subject beyond the scope of this text, the following example (i) shows how to compare forward and futures prices, and (ii) illustrates the principal differences between the two types of contracts.[10] As will become evident from the discussion, the principal technical difference between the two is that futures contracts create a cash throwoff from the marking to market process. However, as will also become evident from the discussion, the technical difference is a difference of economic importance only if interest rates are uncertain.

Consider first the cash flows from going long in a forward contract which will remain outstanding over two periods, chosen for simplicity to be of equal length. When we compare the forward and the futures contract, we shall assume the futures contract is revalued only once – at the end of the first period. While we could consider more periods, to do so would mean having to repeat similar calculations without adding further insights to those provided by the two-period example.

Consider the cash flows from a forward and a futures contract, as shown in Table 7.13. In the table, $F_{0,2}$ is the forward price, set at time zero and referring to delivery at time 2. Similarly, $G_{0,2}$ is the futures price, set at time zero and referring to delivery at time 2. In addition, $G_{1,2}$ is the futures price after the contract (still specifying delivery at time 2) has been marked to market at time 1. Finally, P_2 refers to the spot price of the commodity at time 2, and to make the discussion easy we shall assume it to be known at time 0. As is evident from Table 7.13, the main difference between the long positions in the two contracts is the cash throwoff (positive or negative) on the futures contract, which results from its being marked to market at time 1. If the cash throwoff is positive, we assume it can be invested at the then prevailing interest rate, while if it is negative, we assume funds can be borrowed at that rate.

Now suppose the two one-period interest rates are respectively $i_{0,1}$ and $i_{1,2}$. For now, suppose that while $i_{0,1}$ is known for certain at time zero, $i_{1,2}$ can be specified only as a random variable. (Its value will become known at time 1.) The assumed randomness of $i_{1,2}$ means that the values of the cash flows cannot be stated with certainty at time 0. However, since both interest rates are known by time 2, we can easily write the values of the cash flows then as shown in Table 7.14.

Table 7.14 shows why the two contracts have different risks, when they are regarded from the perspective of time 0. With a known spot price at time 2,

Table 7.13 Forward and futures contracts

	Time 0	Time 1	Time 2
Cash flow from forward contract	0	0	$P_2 - F_{0,2}$
Cash flows from futures contract	0	$G_{1,2} - G_{0,2}$	$P_2 - G_{1,2}$

Table 7.14 Values of long position in forward and futures contracts

	Time 2
Cash flow from forward contract	$P_2 - F_{0,2}$
Cash flows from futures contract	$P_2 - G_{1,2} + [G_{1,2} - G_{0,2}](1 + i_{1,2}) =$ $P_2 - G_{0,2} + [G_{1,2} - G_{0,2}] i_{1,2}$

the cash flows from the forward contract can be stated with certainty at time 0. However, the time 0 value of the time 2 cash flows from the futures contract cannot be stated with certainty, because this value depends on an unknown interest rate.

Another way of seeing the effects of the interest rate risk in the futures contract is to compare the forward and the futures prices. Assume the time 0 present value of an uncertain time 2 cash flow can be calculated using a valuation method denoted $v[\cdot]$, while the time 0 present value of a known cash flow at time 2 is $1/(1 + I_{0,2})$. That is, known cash flows are discounted at a riskless rate denoted by $I_{0,2}$; random cash flows are discounted at some (unspecified) discount rate reflected in the use of $v[\cdot]$. The calculations are shown in Table 7.15. Then, since both forward and futures contracts have a present value of zero at time 0, the two expressions in Table 7.15 can be equated to obtain the following relation between the forward and the futures price:

$$\{F_{0,2} / (1 + I_{0,2})\} = \{G_{0,2} / (1 + I_{0,2})\} - v[(G_{1,2} - G_{0,2}) i_{1,2}]$$

The above line shows the relations all expressed in terms of present values, while the next line, which is a more customary expression, shows the values at time 2:

$$F_{0,2} = G_{0,2} - v [(G_{1,2} - G_{0,2}) i_{1,2}] (1 + I_{0,2})$$

From the last line, we can see that the forward price equals the future price minus an adjustment term for the value of the interest earned or owed from marking to market. Depending on relations between interest rates and commodity prices, this last term can be either positive, zero or negative.

Finally, if $i_{1,2}$ is known with certainty, the following arbitrage arguments used by Jarrow and Turnbull (1996: 55–58) show that when there is no interest rate uncertainty the forward price and the futures price must be identical. The purpose of the demonstration is to show that the economic difference between

Table 7.15 Present values of long position in forward and futures contracts

	Time 0
Present value of cash flow from forward contract	$(P_2 - F_{0,2}) / (1 + I_{0,2})$
Present value of cash flows from futures contract	$(P_2 - G_{0,2}) / (1 + I_{0,2}) + v[(G_{1,2} - G_{0,2}) \cdot i_{1,2}]$

a forward and a futures contract arises only when there is interest rate risk. The example involves the following steps.

First, construct a portfolio which has a value of zero by writing n forward contracts and at the same time taking a long position in m futures contracts. Take $n = (1 + I_{0, 2})$ and $m = (1 + i_{0, 1})$. The time 2 value of the forward position is

$$n(P_2 - F_{0, 2}) = (1 + I_{0, 2})(P_2 - F_{0, 2})$$

The cash throwoff from the futures contract position, valued at the end of time 2, is

$$m(G_{1, 2} - G_{0, 2})(1 + i_{1, 2}) = (1 + i_{0, 1})(G_{1, 2} - G_{0, 2})(1 + i_{1, 2})$$

Now, after the marking to market has occurred, the futures contracts again have a value of zero, and so at time 1 it is possible to increase the futures position to $m_1 = m(1 + i_{1, 2})$ without incurring any further cost. This means that the time 2 value of the futures position, including the cash throwoffs (positive or negative), becomes

$$m_1(P_2 - G_{1, 2}) + (1 + i_{0, 1})(G_{1, 2} - G_{0, 2})(1 + i_{1, 2}) =$$
$$m(1 + i_{1, 2})(P_2 - G_{1, 2}) + (1 + i_{0, 1})(G_{1, 2} - G_{0, 2})(1 + i_{1, 2}) =$$
$$(1 + i_{0, 1})(1 + i_{1, 2})(P_2 - G_{1, 2}) + (1 + i_{0, 1})(G_{1, 2} - G_{0, 2})(1 + i_{1, 2}) =$$
$$(1 + i_{0, 1})(1 + i_{1, 2})(P_2 - G_{0, 2}) =$$
$$(1 + I_{0, 2})(P_2 - G_{0, 2})$$

because in a certainty world with no arbitrage possibilities interest rates must satisfy

$$(1 + i_{0, 1})(1 + i_{1, 2}) = (1 + I_{0, 2})$$

But at time 2 the value of the portfolio is

$$-(1 + I_{0, 2})(P_2 - F_{0, 2}) + (1 + I_{0, 2})(P_2 - G_{0, 2}) = 0$$

The portfolio must still have a value of zero because it was created with no resources in a world with no arbitrage opportunities. Finally, after eliminating common terms the last line simplifies to $F_{0, 2} = G_{0, 2}$ showing that a futures and a forward price are identical when interest rates are known with certainty. To repeat the intention of the example, the foregoing reasoning shows that the economic difference between a forward and a futures contract arises only when there is interest rate risk.

7.6 SUMMARY

This chapter considered dividing up and pricing risks, in different ways using different instruments. One of the main purposes of the chapter was to show that apparently different methods of dividing up and pricing risks have the same ideas behind them, thus making it easier to understand the basic nature of activity in a number of different financial markets. The discussions of this chapter emphasise similarities, while the applications discussions in Part III emphasise the institutional differences between instruments as they are used in practice.

Three ways of dividing up and trading risks were examined in the present chapter: the use of debt versus equity, the use of options, and the use of forward and futures contracts. Arbitrage-based methods of pricing these instruments were then examined, and the relations between different instruments' prices explored, illustrating the meaning behind such apparently exotic relationships as put-call parity. The principle of the riskless hedge was developed and used to price an option, and also shown to give the same value as can be calculated using risk adjusted probabilities. Finally, related methods, also based on the assumed absence of arbitrage opportunties, were employed to find the prices of both forward and futures contracts.

REVIEW QUESTIONS

Exercise 1 What payments could the firm make on a debt instrument that promised to pay its holder $105.00 in principal and interest at time 1? Given these payments, what can you say about the value of this instrument? Even though it might be called a debt instrument, does it conform to investors' usual idea of debt? Why or why not?

Exercise 2 The put-call parity relationship in Table 7.4 shows how to arrange a sure payment of $100.00. The same table shows that the earnings of the firm have an expected value of $100.00, but that these payments are risky. Which of the two prospects, the sure thing or the cash flows from the firm, would be worth more, and why? So, when you go from holding the firm to holding the $100.00 certainty payment, would you have to make a net outpayment to acquire the options needed to give you the certain outcomes? Why or why not?

Exercise 3 Use the discussion referring to Table 7.9 to find the value of the equity by using risk adjusted probabilities. The value must turn out to be the same $2.90/1.10 shown above.

Exercise 4 Use the discussion referring to Table 7.5 to show that the value of the call, found using risk adjusted probabilities, must be the same $1.45/1.10 found before.

Exercise 5 Use risk adjusted probabilities to verify the put-call parity relationship stated in section 7.3.6. That is, check each term of the relation $v(S) \equiv v(X) - v(C) + v(P)$ and make sure the values add up.

Exercise 6 Use risk adjusted probabilities to verify that, if the exercise prices of both the call and the put are 97.90, then the call and the put have the same time zero value of $1.87 shown in Table 7.7.

Exercise 7 In Table 7.2 the forward contract has a value of –$2.10/1.10. What does this negative value mean?

Exercise 8 Use the data in Table 7.3 to explain why a forward price of 97.90, the price used to give the call and the put equal values, also gives the forward contract a value of zero.

Exercise 9 Use risk adjusted probabilities to verify that a forward price of 97.90 gives the forward contract a value of zero.

Exercise 10 Consider a financial instrument that pays off one year from now. The two scenarios given below indicate two possible payoffs, only one of which will actually obtain. The payoff amounts are shown in column X along with today's value, which is determined according to the equation

$$p^*(\$110.00 / 1.10) + (1 - p^*)(\$99.00 / 1.10) = \$93.00$$

	X
Good scenario	$110.00
Bad scenario	$99.00
Today's value	$93.00

What is the value of p*?

Exercise 11 Using information from Exercise 10, what is the value of the instrument whose payoffs are listed in column X/2? Next, use the payoffs in the remaining columns to compute the value of a call option using the riskless hedge method. If the call option is written against the payoffs in Exercise 1, what must its exercise price be? Finally, check your calculations of the call value using p*.

	X/2	– C	X/2 – C
Good scenario	$55.00	$ 5.50	49.50
Bad scenario	$49.50	$ 0.00	49.50
Today's value			

Exercise 12 Now use p* from Exercise 10 and the information in the table to verify the put-call parity expression (7.4).

	S	X	–C	P
Good scenario	$103.00	$110.00	–$7.00	$0.00
Bad scenario	$103.00	$99.00	$0.00	$4.00
Today's value		$93.00		

Exercise 13 If the riskless interest rate is 10 percent, complete the entries in the next table in such a way that the payoffs from the forward contract in column F have a value of zero. What is the forward price in this case? (Hint: compute a new risk adjusted probability for this problem.)

	X	S	F
Time 1 high payoffs	$210.00		
Time 1 low payoffs	$180.00		
Time 0 values	$188.00		

APPENDIX

The reason the riskless hedge method gives the same result as the method of risk adjusted probabilities is that the quantities in the calculation using the riskless arbitrage principle can be grouped together to obtain the risk adjusted probability p*. To see this, notice that (7.3) can be written symbolically as

$$(\alpha S_0 - C_0)(1 + r) = \alpha S_u - C_u \tag{A1.1}$$

where $\alpha = (C_u - C_d)/(S_u - S_d)$, S_0 and C_0 are respectively the price of the firm and of the call at time 0, S_u and C_u are respectively the payoff to the firm and the call if the firm does well, S_d and C_d are respectively the payoff to the firm and the call if the firm does badly, and r is the riskless rate of interest.

Rewriting (A1.1),

$$C_0(1 + r) = C_u + \alpha S_0(1 + r) - \alpha S_u;$$

$$C_0(1 + r) = C_u - \alpha[S_u - S_0(1 + r)]; \tag{A1.2}$$

$$C_0(1 + r) = C_u\{1 - \alpha[S_u - S_0(1 + r)] / C_u\}.$$

But since $C_d = 0$ and $\alpha = (C_u - C_d) / (S_u - S_d)$,

$$\alpha / C_u = \alpha / (C_u - C_d) = 1 / (S_u - S_d). \tag{A1.3}$$

Substituting (A1.3) into (A1.2) gives

$$C_0(1 + r) = C_u\{1 - [S_u - S_0(1 + r)] / (S_u - S_d)\};$$

$$C_0(1 + r) = C_u\{[S_0(1 + r) - S_d] / (S_u - S_d)\},$$

and the last line's expression in braces is the value for p* obtained in 2.2.

8 Financial governance

8.1	Introduction	120
8.2	Governance in a perfectly competitive system	120
	8.2.1 Allocative and operational efficiency	121
	8.2.2 Intermediaries in a perfectly competitive market	123
8.3	Governance in practice	124
	8.3.1 Transactions costs	124
	8.3.2 Screening costs	124
	8.3.3 Informational asymmetries	125
8.4	Deal types and attributes	126
	8.4.1 Type S and type N deals	126
	8.4.2 Deal attributes	127
8.5	Capabilities	128
	8.5.1 Market (type M) capabilities	129
	8.5.2 Internal (type H) capabilities	129
	8.5.3 Intermediary (type Y) capabilities	129
8.6	Alignment	130
	8.6.1 Principles	130
	8.6.2 Cost-effectiveness	131
	8.6.3 Dynamic implications	132
8.7	Summary	133

LEARNING OBJECTIVES

After reading this chapter you will understand

- the meaning of allocative and operational efficiency
- how intermediaries create value in imperfectly competitive markets
- why financial governance receives little attention in a perfectly competitive financial system
- the differences between a type S and a type N deal
- how transaction and screening costs affect governance
- how differences in information affect governance
- how markets provide cost-effective governance of type S deals
- how intermediaries and conglomerates provide cost-effective governance of type N deals

8.1 INTRODUCTION

This chapter uses the concepts of governance, introduced in Chapter 3, to broaden the analyses of Chapters 6 and 7. While the conditions assumed in Chapters 6 and 7 help to clarify some important properties of real world financial systems, a practically oriented explanation of financial system activity must also recognise additional complications. This chapter argues that transaction costs, incomplete contracts and illiquid assets are important additional factors in developing practically oriented explanations of how financial deals are governed.

8.2 GOVERNANCE IN A PERFECTLY COMPETITIVE SYSTEM

Governance would be comparatively simple if all financial markets were perfectly competitive. In perfectly competitive markets, numerous transactors take market interest rates as given and enter financial deals without paying any other costs. All agents have the same information, and all strive to earn maximal profits by trading on the basis of their common information. These trading activities determine equilibria in which securities are priced correctly on the basis of publicly available information, a result frequently referred to as the **efficient markets hypothesis**. The efficient markets hypothesis and the absence of arbitrage opportunities are valuable tools for helping to relate securities prices to each other, as Chapters 6 and 7 showed. However, the restrictions of Chapters 6 and 7 need to be relaxed to develop a complete explanation of financial system activity.

efficient markets hypothesis a theory that, in a competitive market equilibrium, all securities prices fully reflect all publicly available information relevant to determining their value.

First, the efficient markets hypothesis has restrictive implications for the meaning of governance. The efficient markets hypothesis implies that all deals done in competitive markets are governed at the same cost. In a competitive equilibrium there is only one type of financial deal – trading under conditions of publicly distributed information. In this environment, no financier's governance expenditures can be any greater than those of the most efficient competitor. Governance methods with different costs could not be used, because under perfect competition only the least cost method can remain viable at equilibrium.

In practice more than one type of deal will be encountered, and more than a single type of governance will be employed. In particular, there are deals in which both parties do not have the same information, as Chaper 3 pointed out. Different types of deals cannot be governed using the same methods, because different attributes require different forms of screening and monitoring. Moreover, different types of governance make different use of scarce resources, and therefore have different costs. At the very least, then, the efficient markets hypothesis needs to be elaborated to recognise the possibility of different types of deals, and of governance methods with different costs. These differences mean that a more complex picture of deals and their governance, and a more complex meaning to efficiency, must be used to describe additional practical details of financial system activity.

8.2.1 Allocative and operational efficiency

A perfectly competitive financial market is efficient in two senses. First, it is **allocatively efficient**: equally risky proposals are funded at the same interest rate. If an allocatively efficient system is not in equilibrium, atypical interest rate differentials signal that profit opportunities are available. As the Chapter 6 and 7 discussions of arbitrage showed, if atypical interest differentials emerge, they will be exploited by trading which continues until the differentials have been eliminated. Trading continues until all arbitrage opportunities have been eliminated because Chapters 6 and 7 assumed there are no transactions costs or other impediments to arbitraging.

> **allocative efficiency** a property of a financial market in which equally risky propositions have equal access to funding at the same market rate of interest.

A financial system is **operationally efficient** if financial services are performed at the lowest possible cost. A perfectly competitive market is operationally efficient by definition, because by assumption all deals can be completed without payment of transactions charges.[1] Perfect competition is also operationally efficient in the deeper sense that agents trading in perfectly competitive markets must either deal at lowest feasible cost or be driven out of business. Under competition, any deal whose costs were above the minimum would also have to yield above-market returns in order to cover the higher costs. But the only way to earn returns over and above their competitive levels is to buy securities at less than their market prices, and this is not possible at a competitive equilibrium. If some market agents do not have costs as low as other market agents, then they will earn less than competitive returns. But since competitive returns are necessary for the survival of a business, the former will then either have to find ways of reducing their costs or be driven out of business. Similarly, if a firm cannot perform its financial services at the lowest possible cost, any securities it sells would have to be overpriced to cover the higher costs. But then no one would buy the securities from such a firm. In order to survive, the firm would have to trim its costs back to the same levels as those of other firms.

---

operational efficiency a property of a financial market in which agents carrying out transactions do so at the lowest possible cost.

To illustrate the importance of allocative and operational efficiency, consider a business person presenting the same loan application to three different intermediaries. Suppose the applications accurately provide the same information to all three intermediaries, and that all three follow the same assessment procedures to arrive at similar conclusions: the loan should be granted. Suppose also, as in Table 8.1, that the interest rate intermediary C proposes to charge the applicant is higher than that proposed by intermediaries A and B. In the example, the rate difference of 2 percent can be attributed to firm C's being operationally inefficient, and therefore having higher costs than firms A and B. If C is to earn the same returns on invested capital as firms A and B, the higher costs must be covered through charging higher interest rates. If the three intermediaries face a competitive market, C is likely to be driven out of business. A and B will survive, and their operational efficiency will also contribute to allocative efficiency, because the two firms provide financing at the lowest feasible interest rates.

Research suggests that most developed countries' government securities markets are allocatively and operationally efficient in the sense just illustrated, albeit to varying degrees in different economies and even in different markets within the same economy. On the one hand, research shows that several countries' public securities markets exhibit a highly developed degree of allocative

Table 8.1 Illustration of efficiency concepts

Intermediary	A	B	C
Loan rate offered	Prime + 1%	Prime + 1%	Prime + 3%

and operational efficiency. On the other, not every financial deal is best governed by market agents. Indeed, the rest of this book contends that deals under uncertainty (i.e., deals which cannot employ complete contracts) are usually governed cost-effectively by intermediaries or even internally. Moreover, deals using these more expensive methods of governance represent an important proportion of financial system activity. In its own way, intermediary and internal governance may be as efficient as market governance, but in these cases the meaning of efficient operations needs to be interpreted more broadly. To see the differences, let us first consider some practical aspects of intermediary activity.

8.2.2 Intermediaries in a perfectly competitive market

In a perfectly competitive financial market, the Capital Asset Pricing Model outlined in Chapter 6 argues that all investors have the same information and can determine the best available combination of risky securities, called the market portfolio. All investors who wish to assume at least some risk will invest funds in the market portfolio, albeit in different proportions according to their attitudes regarding risk. That is, investors with different attitudes toward risk combine holdings of the market portfolio with a riskless security (assumed also to exist) in proportions that reflect their individual attitudes toward risk.

The CAPM introduced in Chapter 6 does not explain how intermediaries, a prominent feature of any financial system, are able to create value. In the perfectly competitive equilibrium of the CAPM any intermediary can buy or sell securities only at prices reflecting their contribution to the risk of the market portfolio; that is, at risk–return combinations plotting on the security market line described in Chapter 6. At equilibrium no intermediary can purchase securities plotting above the security market line, and no intermediary can sell securities plotting below the security market line. But this means that individuals can buy or sell on the same terms as intermediaries, and can create the same diversification possibilities without paying any extra costs to do so. Moreover, intermediaries cannot save on transactions costs because the theory of perfect competition assumes transactions costs are zero. As a result, in the standard form of efficient market setting there is no role for intermediaries to perform.

Nevertheless, theory based on the assumptions of perfectly competitive markets is far from impractical. By showing that intermediaries offer no advantage to investors in a world of perfectly competitive markets, the theory helps narrow the search for ways in which real world intermediaries do create value. It suggests looking to non-market diversification services and transactions costs savings to explain how intermediaries can create value in practice. In the real world, intermediaries create value by taking positions in illiquid assets, by information processing, and by saving on transactions costs. In particular, the ways intermediaries process information greatly affect the relative cost-effectiveness with which they can govern different forms of financial deals.

8.3 GOVERNANCE IN PRACTICE

In practice, doing a deal means incurring transactions and information processing costs. Transactions costs differ according to the deal involved, and the magnitude of these costs affects the way a deal is governed. In the circumstances now being envisioned, deals are still agreed with a view to maximising profits, but the profit calculation takes transactions and information processing costs into account. For example, a market transaction in bonds represents an exchange under risk, based on information publicly available to both parties. But extending funds to finance a new business venture represents an exchange of funds under uncertainty, based on the parties' having different information about the deal. The net profit calculation in the first instance reflects a very small proportion of information gathering and processing costs, while the net profit calculation in the second instance will reflect proportionately larger costs of this type.

8.3.1 Transactions costs

Transactions costs are the non-interest costs of doing a deal. From the client's point of view, the costs include brokerage or loan application fees, as well as the costs of searching for an accommodating financier. For example, the owner of a small business might look long and hard to find someone interested in investing long term capital in his business, and this search imposes costs upon the small business. At the same time, any costs incurred by financiers must be recovered from the charges they levy, and such charges will form a part of total transactions costs that clients must pay as and when they are successful in obtaining financing.

The amount of a financier's transactions charges will depend on the financier's efficiency, and on the information to be acquired and processed. Two parties trading in government bonds may be equally informed as to the risk of the transaction, but the venture investor dealing with the owner of a new company may have very different information about the risks of the deal than does the client. In either kind of deal, financiers charge interest rates and other fees which cover all their costs. Thus the size of the costs absorbed by the client in a given deal depends on the amount and type of information processing the financier must perform.

8.3.2 Screening costs

Screening costs refer to the costs of assessing a financing proposal. Since screening costs usually include a fixed as well as a variable component, the average cost of screening can be expected to decline with increasing numbers of transactions. That is, there are economies of scale to processing the same kinds of information many times: many screenings can be done at a lower unit cost than can a few. In addition, screening costs will be greater, the greater are informational differences between client and financier. Finally, screening costs can likely be reduced as experience is gained and financiers learn how to perform the task of screening more efficiently.

8.3.3 Informational asymmetries

Even after a proposed deal has been screened, the parties to it may still face **informational asymmetries**. First, transactors may differ in their initial capabilities to understand the situation: for example, one may be an uninformed party. Second, the parties may differ in their estimates of the deal's profitability. Third, the parties may have the same information about the deal at the outset, but their ability to keep informed about its progress may differ.

---

informational asymmetry a situation in which two parties do not share the same view of an arrangement's risk, either because they do not have access to the same data or because they interpret them differently.

Informational asymmetries affect a deal's governance. It is much more difficult to reach a satisfactory agreement when financier and client differ greatly over a project's viability than when they share the same view. If the asymmetries in a deal are great enough, it may be possible to do the deal only at non-market interest rates. In other cases it may not be possible to reach agreement at any interest rate. For example, in the early 1980s opinion regarding the value of the troubled Continental Illinois Bank's loan portfolio varied so greatly that counterparties found it difficult to agree on a mutually satisfactory price for the bank's shares.

The potential volume of deals of a given type is determined by the demand for the financial services involved. If client demand means that many deals of a given type are likely to be done, unit screening costs will likely be relatively low, because firms can reap scale economies from performing the same screening task many times. That is, a demand for many deals of the same type means that financiers can spread their fixed costs of learning over a relatively large number of deals.

Even though financiers learn how to do new deals over time, it will not always be possible for clients to obtain financing of a deal, especially a new type. The issue is not just whether the deal is viable in some objective economic sense. Even if that is the case, at any given point in time financiers may believe it is uneconomic to do certain kinds of deals. While financiers are most likely to hold these beliefs for unfamiliar deals, they may sometimes also regard certain classes of familiar deals as unprofitable.

Sometimes profit assessments deter entry to a market. Potential new entrants may not be willing to set up new and more innovative financing arrangements because they see existing financiers as having entrenched advantages that are difficult to overcome. Through learning, the financier who first enters a market can gain a competitive advantage over subsequent entrants, particularly if the skills acquired are in short supply and difficult to communicate.[2] As an example, there are high fixed costs to setting up venture capital firms, because the personnel in a new firm need to learn how to screen prospects, and because any one person can supervise only a limited number of venture investments. Even if the firm has some personnel with screening experience, these skills are acquired principally through experience rather than in a classroom setting. As a result any new employees have to acquire the new skills on the job in much the same way as the now experienced personnel learned. Thus existing firms may not be able to accommodate the entire market's demands for financing, but unless there are enough new projects to cover the fixed costs of setting up a new firm, some demands may go unsatisfied.

8.4 DEAL TYPES AND ATTRIBUTES

Chapter 3 introduced the notion that financial deals can have significantly different attributes, but there are only a few of these significant attributes. Thus whether deals are entered primarily to raise funds or to manage risks, they present financiers with differing combinations from the same common attribute list. Consequently, a deal presents financiers with governance challenges determined by the combination of attributes it possesses. For purposes of discussion, it is convenient to classify the different possible attribute combinations into two polar types, S and N. In practice, most deals' attribute combinations fall somewhere in between the two polar types, but these additional details are best discussed after first considering the main differences.

8.4.1 Type S and type N deals

Standard deals (type S) are familiar to financiers. Their successful conclusion depends primarily on the results of an initial screening. Non-standard (type N) deals are unfamiliar to financiers, have non-standard terms, and greater uncertainty regarding their payoffs. Type N deals require relatively more monitoring, because information about them is usually revealed with the passage of time, and after financing is initially provided. Moreover, if the monitoring is to be effective, type N deals need to provide for adjustment of deal terms or even control of underlying operations as and when monitoring reveals that changes are necessitated.

Type S financings arise either when clients acquire relatively liquid assets,[3] or when collateral with a readily established market value can be used for security. Financiers find it relatively easy to fund purchases of assets with readily determined market values. Type S risk management is similarly standardised. Type S deals present risks rather than uncertainties, and can be formalised using rule-based, complete contracts. For example, a deal which can be classified as a type S risk management deal does not have large fixed information processing costs, and can be agreed after only relatively cursory investigation.

Type N deals involve financing the purchase of illiquid assets when there is no collateral to serve as security. For example, projects whose success rests on the talent and commitment of given individuals present circumstances in which financiers' rewards will depend on highly uncertain future earnings rather than on agreed market values of assets. Type N deals present uncertainties rather than risks. Financiers secure their positions in type N deals through enhanced governance capabilities based on discretionary and incomplete rather than rule-based and complete financing contracts. The ability to exercise continuing supervision, and to control unfavourable outcomes, can be crucial to the success of projects in which financiers' returns depend on earnings rather than on asset value.

Table 8.2 indicates that increase in the degree to which a deal possesses certain attributes will decrease the likelihood that it will be regarded as a routine or type S deal. An increase in the degree to which a deal may be said to possess one of the attributes in Table 8.2 will, other things being equal, contribute to making a financier more likely to treat the deal as one of type N. For example, as information differences between client and financier increase, the deal is more likely to be treated as type N. As a second example, the less liquid the assets whose acquisition is being financed, the more likely the deal is to be treated as type N.

Table 8.2 Attributes and deal types

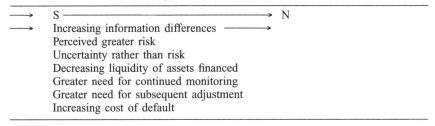

8.4.2 **Deal attributes**

One important deal attribute is the liquidity of the assets being financed. If the underlying assets can readily be traded in secondary markets, financiers have two potential sources of returns. They will recoup their investment with interest if the project being financed turns out well. In a worst case situation where project profits do not materialise, assets can still be sold to recover at least some of the funds initially put up. But if the assets being financed are project specific and therefore illiquid, financiers can expect to recover a return on their investment only by ensuring that, to the greatest possible extent, the project will operate profitably.

A second important deal attribute is whether its payoffs can be described quantitatively, using a probability distribution. If the returns to a deal can usefully be described using a probability distribution, the deal can be called risky. For example, estimating the returns on a typical small business working capital loan is a relatively straightforward task, even after allowing for likely writeoffs.

While a quantitative description of profitability can contribute to asset liquidity, a quantitative description does not ensure asset liquidity. The earnings on some relatively illiquid assets, such as the cash flow from an apartment building, can be reasonably well defined. However, the capital value of the real estate may be very difficult to describe with the same quantitative precision, because such other factors as changes in zoning laws or the possible construction of other projects in the neighbourhood can also affect its value over the longer term.

Asset illiquidity can mean that a deal's payoffs are uncertain, that is the payoffs are so diffuse, or so difficult to attribute to underlying factors, that it is impractical to describe them using a probability distribution.[4] For example, the deal may depend critically on some difficult-to-quantify factor such as the ability of an entrepreneur to respond creatively to unforeseen business challenges. In some cases, it may not even be possible to identify in advance what the critical challenges might eventually prove to be. Consider, for example, how press reports of profitability estimates for the Channel Tunnel project have changed with the passage of time. Even though the project has some ability to recoup cost overruns through higher toll charges, the tunnel assets are highly illiquid, and estimates of project profitability over, say, the first twenty years of operation still vary over an exceptionally wide range. The range of possible profitability depends not only on the specificity of the tunnel assets, but also on the demand for tunnel services, the reactions of competitors, world interest rates and the like. In such cases even sophisticated models of future profit streams depend critically on assumptions that are extremely difficult to render precise.

8.5 CAPABILITIES

Just as deals can be classified using two types, governance capabilities can be classified using three. Financiers have differing combinations of capabilities, which for simplicity are referred to as type M (market), type Y (hybrid) and type H (hierarchy) respectively. Type M financiers have well-developed research and information processing capabilities regarding readily observable short term changes in the deal's likely profitability. Type H financiers have relatively greater capabilities for estimating illiquid assets' capabilities to generate cash flows, as well as for monitoring and controlling the assets' management. Type Y financiers combine some of the capabilities of both type M and type H (Table 8.3).

Table 8.3 Financiers' governance capabilities

⟶	M ⟶ Y ⟶ H ⟶	
⟶	Greater screening capabilities ⟶	
	Greater monitoring capabilities (particularly on a continuing basis)	
	Greater control capabilities (auditing, replacement of key personnel)	
	Greater adjustment capabilities (ability to alter contracts as circumstances change)	

Financiers acting as principals for very short periods of time specialise in market instruments and have less developed type H capabilities than do financiers holding instruments in their portfolios for relatively long periods of time. The trader in government treasury bills and the real estate developer both act as principals, but the widely differing time scales over which they hold assets mean they use different governance structures.

8.5.1 Market (type M) capabilities

Market agents normally entertain deals that require relatively little monitoring after being struck. Market agents usually govern relatively large numbers of individual trades between parties who are unlikely to know each other, and mainly enter deals financing the purchase of assets that have a ready resale value in secondary markets. Market agents reduce transactions costs both by standardising the terms of the deals they agree to take on and by specialising in recurring transactions of the same type.

Market agents can realise scale economies by taking on many deals of the same type. They can also realise scope economics if the same specialised information processing techniques can be used for a number of related types of deals.

8.5.2 Internal (type H) capabilities

Internal governance, such as having the headquarters of a financial conglomerate firm invest in one of its subsidiary companies, offers agents the greatest possibility for dealing with informational asymmetries through intensive initial screening and continued monitoring. Internal governance also provides capabilities for auditing project performance, for changing operating management and for adjusting financing terms if conditions change.

On all these counts, internal financing arrangements offer greater governance capabilities, but at higher administrative costs than would be involved in a market transaction. In cases where the greater capabilities' advantages outweigh the additional administrative costs, internal governance is likely to be chosen.

8.5.3 Intermediary (type Y) capabilities

Financial intermediaries combine the governance capabilities of market agents and of hierarchies, but use the capabilities of hierarchies to a lesser degree. While most intermediaries serve particular classes of clients, they all perform the same functions of borrowing funds, lending or reinvesting them, and managing risks. Intermediaries usually arrange deals by negotiating with individual clients rather than dealing simultaneously with many clients on an arm's length basis, as is characteristic of market transactions.

Even though intermediaries have capabilities to screen more intensively than market agents, not all intermediaries screen all types of deals equally well.

Differential capabilities are one of the factors explaining why intermediaries are likely to specialise, at least to some degree. For example, some intermediaries can offer automated screening of credit card and consumer loan applications, thereby enjoying scale economies not available to intermediaries with smaller volumes of the same type of business. As a second example, expert systems are likely to play an increasingly important role in assessing many types of deals, perhaps even business lending, in future years. Such systems will also exhibit declining average costs, chiefly because they require a large initial investment but have relatively small marginal operating costs. As a result, expert systems will most likely be installed by a relatively small number of large firms. If they can negotiate profitable terms, smaller firms may license the systems' use.

8.6 ALIGNMENT

The alignments of deal attributes against financier capabilities are determined by cost-effectiveness criteria. Thus relative cost-effectiveness indicates how different kinds of deals are likely to be governed. Financiers tend to specialise in the types of deals they take on and alignment choices are at least partly determined by these specialised capabilities. Thus when they are done cost-effectively, type S deals are agreed by agents having type M capabilities, while type N deals are agreed by agents having either type H capabilities (in the most complex cases) or type Y capabilities (in cases of lesser complexity). In the aggregate, the composition and specialised capabilities of financial firms determines the nature of financial system organisation.

8.6.1 Principles

In the case of market governance, the same or similar information about a transaction is at least potentially available to all agents, and market trading usually employs relatively well-established technologies. One of the best known markets is, of course, the secondary market for publicly traded stocks, which exhibits the characteristics just mentioned.

Intermediated deals replace market deals whenever intermediation gives more cost effective governance of the deal attributes in question. The main deal attributes that render intermediation more cost-effective than market transactions are the need for repackaging, for specialised risk screening when the deal originates, and possibly for continuing monitoring. Usually, financial intermediaries both screen and continue to monitor a client's affairs more closely than do investors who purchase securities through securities markets.

Intermediated deals will be arranged when there is a sufficient number of potential deals to permit recovery of the intermediary's setup costs. Where client classes are large, intermediaries are likely to become equally large because operating economies seem to occur over a relatively large range of total assets. Intermediaries realise these operating economies both through selecting the kinds of deals they will entertain and the manner in which they will subsequently govern their portfolios. Intermediaries can sometimes enjoy scope economies by serving several related client classes simultaneously. Finally, some intermediaries are able efficiently to diversify their investment portfolios geographically, thus gaining an operating advantage in terms of risk reduction.

Financiers typically want a much greater say in projects with uncertain returns, as a means of enhancing the deal's safety and profitability. When facing uncertainty, financiers (if they agree to put up any funds at all) will try to discover and manage key profitability features. But since they cannot specify exactly what might be required in advance, financiers will likely write agreements expressed in terms of principles which allow them to respond flexibly in circumstances that cannot initially be specified with much precision. That is, financiers use incomplete contracts when the uncertainties with which they must grapple cannot be specified quantitatively at the time a deal is first agreed.

Contrast a public issue of stock with the arrangements a conglomerate headquarters might strike with one of its subsidiaries. In the first case information is widely shared by many parties; in the second it is not. Moreover, in the second case there are much greater opportunities for continuing supervision of the business subsequent to the financing's being provided. Finally, in contrast to a public securities issue explained in a publicly distributed prospectus, internal governance may be used to keep information about development plans from being revealed to competitors.

8.6.2 Cost-effectiveness

Clients strive to minimise their costs of obtaining funds, but they will not always find the best available deal terms. Particularly if search costs are high, clients may accept one of the first feasible arrangements they can find. Thus, clients can be biased toward exploring familiar rather than unfamiliar sources of funding. Even so, a client may be able to secure several offers of financing. For example, a client seeking external financing will choose, frequently in consultation with one or more financiers, whether to offer securities in a public market place or through private negotiations. The client's eventual choice will depend on the offers' terms, including interest costs, the amount of information requiring to be provided, the parties who will become privy to the information, and the effects of information release on his competitive position.

Financiers will do only deals they perceive to be profitable, and can do deals profitably only if they possess the requisite governance capabilities. Financiers strive to maximise each deal's profitability, subject to governing its risks or uncertainties. For example, bankers will define the classes of deals they can conduct profitably, given their current or expected future capabilities. They might, for instance, specialise in business working capital loans but rule out merger and acquisition financing on the grounds that they had little expertise in the latter field.

Type M governance is generally cheaper than type H (cf. Riordan and Williamson 1985, Williamson 1987 and Garvey 1993). Symbolically,

C(SM) < C(SH), where C(SM) is the cost of governing standard deals with market capabilities and C(SH) is the cost of governing them with hierarchical capabilities. In governing standard deals there is little room to cover the extra resource costs of hierarchical governance, and the contributions of risk reduction effects to profitability are similarly small. It follows that V(SM) > V(SH), where V is the value to the financier of doing the deal. (Value is expected future earnings discounted at a rate adjusted to reflect the risk involved.)

Nevertheless, type H governance can be a cost-effective alternative to type M if the benefits of its monitoring, control and adjustment capabilities exceed the information and coordination costs involved. Type H governance is especially likely to be cost-effective when the financing environment is uncertain. In such cases, V(NH) > V(NM) even though C(NH) > C(NM), because the reduced risk or increased return from hierarchical governance more than compensates for the greater cost of acquiring the extra governance capabilities.

There will usually be a least cost governance structure for each type of deal, and because of competitive pressures that structure is likely to emerge as the dominant way of doing deals of a given type. When financiers align their capabilities against the deals they will accept, they consider not only such attributes as the informational conditions under which deals will be done, but also the frequency with which typical deals will likely arise. Financiers can earn above normal profits on appropriately governed type N deals.[5] The risk adjusted rate of return on type N deals can exceed that on type S deals, because the markets in which type N deals are agreed are less competitive than those for type S. In summary, the profit maximising combinations are NH and SM.

8.6.3 Dynamic implications

When learning by doing is important to screening deals economically, the institutions initially present have a profitability advantage relative to new entrants. This fact may explain the concentration of foreign investment in some parts of a small, underdeveloped economy. It may be that for some kinds of deals only financiers from developed economies have the capabilities to assess the deals properly, because at the given stage of development the number of domestic deals is too small to allow domestic financiers profitably to acquire the requisite capabilities. For example, if the capabilities are acquired on a learning by doing basis, they would likely first be developed first in a larger economy.

Merton (1992) argues that with experience some type N deals become standardised and are then handled so efficiently they can be regarded as type S. In Merton's phrasing, type S and type N deals can be dynamically complementary. The meaning of dynamic complementarity is that deals which are originally type N become standardised over time, and possibly also become better understood by a wider spectrum of financiers. If they become sufficiently routine, it may eventually prove possible to treat some of these deals as type S, in which case the original type N deal is dynamically complementary to the eventual emergence of the type S deal.

However, dynamic complementarity need not always result. Small type N deals subject to fixed costs are never likely to be traded actively on their own, and will thus remain static complements to type S deals. Similarly some uncertain type N deals, especially those secured only by illiquid assets, can never become merely risky and thus evolve into type S deals. Finally, even though a large number of type N deals may be securitised, and securities written against portfolios of small type N deals may be traded actively, the screening and administration of individual type N deals is not a capability that market agents are likely to acquire, even after becoming familiar with the nature of the deals. These possibilities are all discussed further at various points in the applications chapters of this book, Chapters 12 through 20.

8.7 SUMMARY

This chapter examined financial governance. It began with a description of a financial system in the theoretical world of perfect competition, then examined how financial transactions are organised in practice. The chapter showed that while theory provides a useful road map, real world complications of transaction costs, information processing costs, and informational asymmetries need to be recognised in order to explain fully why a financial system takes its manifest form.

The chapter argued that deals differ chiefly in their informational attributes, and that financiers possess a continuum of capabilities for governing these attributes. For discussion purposes, the continuum is usefully categorised in terms of markets, intermediaries, and internal governance. Alignment means that financiers with specialised capabilities do only certain kinds of deals, principally with the intention of governing them cost-effectively. The aggregate result is that a financial system contains a multiplicity of different financial arrangements, each with its own competitive advantage. Apart from market transacting, the important features of a financial system are in large part those institutional arrangements developed to govern type N deals.

REVIEW QUESTIONS

Exercise 1 Suppose you could choose between marketing a new product in a highly competitive market or in a developing market that is almost surely uncompetitive, for at least the next few years. What benefits would there be to choosing the second? What costs?

Exercise 2 Suggest three ways in which a bank can perform services of value to its customers. Would those services be of value in a perfectly competitive market? Why or why not?

Exercise 3 When a bank lends money to a business, one of the conditions of the loan contract is usually that the client provide the bank with financial statements at regular intervals. How do these statements help resolve informational asymmetries? If the bank had a seat on the company's board of directors, would it likely receive more or less continuing information than it would get from financial statements? Which of the two methods of monitoring (statements or board participation) would be cheaper? Under what circumstances would the more expensive one be the more desirable?

Exercise 4 Give examples of a type S and a type N deal. Compare and contrast the two in as much detail as you can.

Exercise 5 Classify each of the following financiers in terms of type M, Y or H capabilities. Securities traders. Bank lenders. Venture capital firms. Life insurance companies in their function of writing policies. Real estate agents. Real estate developers.

Exercise 6 Explain why a venture capitalist is likely to be better than a foreign exchange trader at predicting the likely pitfalls in the growth patterns of a new small business.

Exercise 7 What is a complete contract? Does a perfectly competitive world permit complete contracting?

Exercise 8 How do informational asymmetries affect the way a deal is governed? Use an example to illustrate your answer.

Exercise 9 Do you think the principle of pricing by arbitrage is useful if trading incurs transactions costs? Why or why not?

Exercise 10 Explain how standardising the terms of trade and guaranteeing the creditworthiness of instruments traded affected the options market.

Exercise 11 Give an example of a deal that can be governed cost-effectively as a market transaction. Give a contrasting example of a deal that would, in your opinion, require hierarchical governance. List what you regard as the crucial differences in the deals' attributes.

Exercise 12 Do informational asymmetries matter if government securities are available for use as collateral? Why or why not?

Exercise 13 Substitution of a highly risky for a less risky project is an example of moral hazard in debt financing. Explain how you would offset this particular difficulty when arranging a long term loan to a corporation.

Exercise 14 Some observers feel that financial holding companies mainly offer possibilities for conflict of interest and self dealing. Do you think financial holding companies might also offer advantages? If so, what, and why?

9 Portfolio governance

9.1	Portfolios of marketable securities	137
	9.1.1 Diversification	138
	9.1.2 Dynamic hedging: theory	141
	9.1.3 Synthetic portfolios	143
	9.1.4 Portfolio insurance: practice	144
9.2	Portfolios of non-marketable securities	144
	9.2.1 Market risk and default risk	145
	9.2.2 Governance	146
	9.2.3 Diversification	146
	9.2.4 Securitisation	147
9.3	Managing closely held investments	148
	9.3.1 Incomplete contracting	148
	9.3.2 Governance responses	149
9.4	Managing interest rate risk	149
	9.4.1 Asset-liability matching	150
	9.4.2 Interest rate swaps	150
	9.4.3 Interest rate futures	152
	9.4.4 Other risk management possibilities	153
9.5	Summary	154

LEARNING OBJECTIVES

After reading this chapter you will understand

- how portfolios of marketable securities are managed
- the importance of diversification for reducing risk
- how derivative securities are used to tailor portfolio risks
- how and why managing non-marketable securities portfolios differs from managing their marketable securities counterparts
- the difference between market risk and default risk
- some circumstances under which different risk management tools – asset-liability matching, interest rate swaps, interest rate futures – are likely to prove cost-effective

---

This chapter shows how the principles developed in Chapters 6 through 8 can be applied to the governance of securities portfolios. The present chapter first recognises that the tasks of portfolio governance depend on the kind of portfolio being held: in particular, governance tasks differ according to the degree to which the portfolio contains liquid securities. A relatively liquid portfolio (i.e., one which principally contains marketable securities) presents the governance tasks of acquiring securities to achieve desirable risk–return tradeoffs, monitoring their performance, and selling them if their performance does not live up to the manager's original expectations. A relatively illiquid portfolio (i.e., one composed mainly of non-marketable instruments) poses different governance tasks, principally because it is not possible to trade illiquid securities whose performance may prove to be unsatisfactory subsequent to their having been included in the portfolio.

Governance tasks also differ according to whether illiquid instruments are held as assets or as liabilities. Thus, governance of an insurance company with relatively large proportions of liquid assets and of illiquid liabilities differs considerably from governance of a bank with relatively large proportions of illiquid assets and liquid liabilities.[1] A major concern in an insurance company is assessing the probability distributions of the liabilities it writes, while a major concern of a bank is securing the risk of the loans it makes. Banks can face short term funding problems, while insurance companies are much less likely to encounter such a situation.

This chapter mainly discusses acquiring and governing asset positions. Thus for present purposes, portfolio governance means screening and purchasing assets, funding their acquisition, and supervising the resulting holdings. Issues related to managing liabilities will be considered further in Chapters 16 through 18.

For portfolios of marketable assets, governance principally involves selecting, purchasing and trading desirable investments to generate a target level of income while minimising risk. The main tasks are monitoring financial data, identifying which securities should be bought or sold, and determining the price and timing of the transactions. Since almost all marketable securities are relatively liquid,[2] investments proving to be unsatisfactory can usually be sold in the marketplace, albeit at a loss, when their performance does not meet expectations.

For portfolios of non-marketable assets, governance poses all the above tasks except active trading, which is supplanted by a need for relatively more intense monitoring than takes place with marketable securities. There is also a greater need for control and adjustment: if the monitoring indicates potential difficulty, it may be necessary to control operations and adjust financing terms, either to avoid impairing the investment's rate of return or to reduce its risk. Governing illiquid assets also includes planning how to survive periods when the financier is pressed for liquidity, but the assets held can be sold only at distress prices.

9.1 PORTFOLIOS OF MARKETABLE SECURITIES

Governance of marketable securities portfolios initially involves developing and screening a list of candidate securities from which the portfolio will be assembled. Almost all managers will select a diversified portfolio in an attempt to obtain as favourable a risk–return tradeoff as can be devised. After purchasing the selected securities, the portfolio manager will continue to monitor their expected contributions to portfolio earnings and risk, tasks which involve forecasting expected earnings and changes in earnings risk. The manager must also reinvest funds deriving from security sales, dividend receipts, and maturing securities. Finally, governance involves tailoring the resulting portfolio's risk and return by using such risk management tools as derivative securities.

The portfolio manager will monitor the performance of the acquired securities with a view to detecting changes in the relations between expected earnings and their risks or uncertainties. Adjustments to unfavourable changes are normally effected by selling the securities. Selling marketable securities is usually a straightforward task, and therefore most portfolio investors do not participate actively in managing the firms whose securities they hold. For example, the manager of a North American mutual fund will not normally acquire any capability to adjust contract terms. However, there can be exceptions when the investments are sufficiently large, as discussed in the next paragraph.

Problems of illiquidity are relatively rare, but there are at least two circumstances in which they can arise. First, a particular security may suddenly become wholly unsaleable, say because the issuing firm goes bankrupt without much advance warning. Second, when individual investments are relatively large, it may not be possible to sell out a position quickly, simply because sale of a large block of securities can be interpreted by the marketplace as unfavourable news. In such cases, portfolio managers may seek to play an active role in the operations of the companies whose securities they hold. When they do so, these managers use procedures similar to those discussed in section 9.3.

9.1.1 Diversification

Portfolio theory studies managing asset portfolios under risk. The principal management problems addressed by portfolio theory are estimating probability distributions of returns on individual securities and determining how different combinations of securities will affect portfolio risk.[3] Defining portfolio risk as the variance of its return, and assuming that investors prefer the smallest attainable variance for any given mean return, the theory argues that risk can normally be reduced, relative to return, by selecting a diversified securities portfolio. Reducing risk through diversification is not just a matter of acquiring many securities, but a matter of judiciously combining securities with different statistical characteristics so as to achieve a given level of expected earnings at the lowest attainable risk.[4] As Chapter 6 indicated, portfolio theory shows that portfolios of securities whose returns are not perfectly correlated can exhibit a lower risk–return tradeoff than the component securities.

To see how diversification can change the risk–return tradeoff, consider a portfolio of two securities. Table 9.1 shows the joint probabilities with which the returns on two securities might be realised. Empty cells mean the probability of the two events occurring is zero. For example, in Table 9.1 the joint outcome $r_X = 6$ percent, $r_Y = 3$ percent is assumed not to occur.

The expected return on either security in Table 9.1 is given by the sum of the outcomes multiplied by their probabilities. Thus

$$E(r_X) = (1/3)(0.03) + (1/3)(0.06) + (1/3)(0.09) = 0.06$$

and similarly $E(r_Y) = 0.06$ also. The standard deviation of returns, and its square the variance, are both measures of how 'spread out' returns can be – the greater the spread, the greater the standard deviation and the greater the variance. It is probably easiest to remember the calculation of the variance, which is given by the square of the difference between outcomes and their expected value:

$$VAR(r_X) = \sigma^2(r_X) = E[r_X - E(r_X)]^2$$

Standard deviation is the square root of the preceding expression. For example,

$$\sigma^2(r_X) = E[r_X - E(r_X)]^2$$
$$= (1/3)[0.03 - 0.06]^2 + (1/3)[0.06 - 0.06]^2 + (1/3)[0.09 - 0.06]^2 =$$
$$(2/3)(0.03)^2 = 0.0006$$

The standard deviation of return is $\sigma(r_X) = (0.0006)^{1/2}$, and for this example $\sigma(r_Y) = (0.0006)^{1/2}$ also.

Table 9.1 Returns on perfectly positively correlated securities

r_X / r_Y	3%	6%	9%
3%	1/3		
6%		1/3	
9%			1/3

Since both securities offer the same expected return of 0.06, any portfolio combining the two securities will also have an expected return of 0.06. For example, a portfolio assembled by investing half the available funds in each of the two securities has an expected return equal to

$$E(r_X / 2 + r_Y / 2) = 0.06$$

The variance of return for a portfolio composed of two risky securities, X and Y, is determined by the following formula

$$\sigma^2 (w_X r_X + w_Y r_Y) = (w_X)^2 \sigma^2 (r_X) + w_X w_Y \; 2 \; COV \; (r_X, r_Y) + (w_Y)^2 \sigma^2 (r_Y)$$

where: $\sigma^2 (r_Z)$ is the variance of return on any security Z, w_X is the proportion of funds invested in security X, $w_Y = 1 - w_X$ the proportion invested in security Y, and COV (r_X, r_Y), known as the covariance term, is a measure of association between the two securities' returns.

The covariance term is defined as

$$COV(r_X, r_Y) = E(r_X \cdot r_Y) - E(r_X)E(r_Y)$$

and in the present example is equal to

$$0.0042 - 0.0036 = 0.0006$$

The correlation (in effect, standardised covariance) between securities returns is

$$CORR(r_X, r_Y) = COV(r_X, r_Y)/\sigma(r_X)\sigma(r_Y)$$

and in the present example is equal to

$$0.0006/(0.0006)^{\frac{1}{2}} \; (0.0006)^{\frac{1}{2}} = 0.0006/0.0006 = 1.0000$$

By definition, correlation must lie between -1 and 1. When the correlation between securities returns equals 1 (or -1), the securities are said to be perfectly positively (or negatively) correlated. When correlation lies strictly between -1 and 1, securities returns are said to be imperfectly correlated.

In the foregoing example the securities are perfectly positively correlated, as just shown. In this case, when equal proportions are invested in the two securities the variance of portfolio return is

$$\sigma^2(r_X / 2 + r_Y / 2) = \sigma^2(r_X) / 4 + 2COV(r_X, r_Y) / 4 + \sigma^2(r_Y) / 4$$
$$= 0.0006 \qquad (9.1)$$

The example illustrates that when two securities have perfectly positively correlated returns, assembling a portfolio made up of equal proportions of them does not affect the variance of return.

Suppose, however, that Table 9.1 was amended so that the joint probabilities in each cell were equal to 1/9. That is, any combination of returns on security X and security Y have the same probability of 1/9. In this case the expected return on portfolio composed of equal proportions of securities X and Y would still be 6 percent, and you can check to see that $\sigma^2(r_X) = \sigma^2(r_Y) = 0.0006$ as before. However, the variance of the portfolio return is reduced, because the covariance term is affected by the assumption of statistical independence. When r_X and r_Y are statistically independent, $COV(r_X, r_Y) = 0$, and (9.1) becomes

$$\sigma^2(r_X / 2 + r_Y / 2) = \sigma^2(r_X) / 4 + 0 + \sigma^2(r_Y) / 4 = 0.0003 \quad (9.2)$$

The example illustrates that risk is reduced by combining securities whose returns have zero covariance and hence zero correlation. The principle extends to combining securities whose returns are imperfectly correlated, whether positively or negatively. In particular, if the securities are perfectly negatively correlated, a portfolio whose returns have zero standard deviation can be constructed. That is, a portfolio with a riskless return can be found.

In theory, the number of different securities needed to diversify portfolio risk is determined by cost-benefit analysis. Including more securities in a portfolio can reduce risk if their returns are not perfectly positively correlated, but investing in larger numbers of securities also means incurring proportionately larger transactions costs. Nevertheless, since both costs and benefits are relatively easy to define, a theoretically optimal balancing of risk and return can be attained by equating marginal changes in portfolio risk to the marginal costs of the additional securities transactions.

In the absence of transactions costs, a portfolio manager can find a point on the capital market line (see Chapter 7) simply by holding a relatively large number of randomly selected assets, since in this case the diversifiable risk component of individual securities' returns will be eliminated. This idea has practical importance for two reasons. First, at least some mutual funds can perform securities selection and portfolio adjustment procedures at relatively low marginal costs. Second, mutual funds' share of total financial asset holdings has risen dramatically since the early 1980s.

Search costs are largely independent of the amounts invested after the search has been carried out. Since portfolio managers spread their search costs over whatever amounts they invest, the same unit search costs do not reduce expected return on a large portfolio as much as on a small one. Similarly, the costs of monitoring securities holdings are also largely fixed, and therefore unit costs of monitoring tend to be smaller for larger portfolios. Both these factors help explain why investment portfolios tend to be relatively large. However, managers of larger portfolios also face certain disadvantages, including the problem of finding a sufficient number of suitable securities. It is cost-effective to place large amounts of funds only in relatively large securities issues, because a large investment in a small issue can sometimes create adverse price effects, both when securities are purchased and when they are sold.

For smaller investment portfolios, determining an appropriate degree of diversification takes on a somewhat different complexion. In a small investment portfolio, only a few securities can be purchased cost-effectively. While most authorities suggest that a portfolio of fifteen to twenty securities are sufficient to give a risk–return combination close to that of the market portfolio, small investors may not find it cost-effective to acquire even this number. First, investment possibilities are limited by the financier's knowledge: financiers cannot invest in securities of which they are unaware. Moreover, expanding the financier's knowledge to finding new securities means incurring search costs, and at any given time a financier may not believe that additional search costs could be recovered through finding profitable new investments. Second and as already pointed out, when the amounts invested are relatively small transactions costs are proportionately large, limiting the cost-effective number of investments.

9.1.2 Dynamic hedging: theory

The options and futures contracts introduced in Chapter 7 are frequently used by managers to tailor the return–risk tradeoffs of portfolios they have assembled.[5] They use options rather than the underlying securities mainly because derivatives can offer ways of tailoring portfolio risk at relatively low transactions costs. One such use of derivatives is known as dynamic hedging, a process of trading derivatives to insure against declines in value.

To illustrate the ideas behind dynamic hedging (further practical application will be examined in Chapter 13), suppose a financial institution holds a single stock currently trading for $100.00. The institution wishes to ensure that the value of the portfolio will not fall below $100.00 two periods hence, and is willing to enter transactions now, at time zero, and again at time 1 to ensure this outcome. Of course, obtaining this insurance will not be costless, and one of the tasks of the portfolio manager is to balance the cost of the insurance against the risk reduction achieved. The present example shows how the tradeoff can be assessed after estimating the statistical process followed by the stock price.

Suppose the stock can either rise or fall in value by a multiplicative factor of 1.10 in each of the two periods, that either event is equally likely, and that the time zero stock price is $100.00. At the end of two periods the stock will be sold for cash. To make computations simple, suppose (i) that risk adjusted probabilities can be used for valuation purposes, and (ii) that interest rates are zero.

The next calculation uses methods of risk adjusted probabilities first introduced in section 6.2. Given that the stock is worth $100.00 today, Table 9.2 shows that the stock can assume one of the values $110.00 or $90.91 one period hence, and one of the values $121.00, $100.00 or $82.64 at the end of time 2.

Table 9.2 Attainable stock prices

Time 0	Time 1	Time 2
100.00	110.00	121.00
	90.91	100.00
		82.64

Next, by assuming the absence of arbitrage opportunities, it can be shown that in either period 1 or 2 an upward movement of the stock can be valued using the risk adjusted probability

$$p^* = (1.00 - 1.10^{-1}) / (1.10 - 1.10^{-1}) = 0.4762$$

Similarly, a downward movement of the stock price can be valued using $1 - p^* = 0.5238$. Moreover, two successive upward movements can be valued using $(p^*)^2$, two successive downward movements using $(1 - p^*)^2$, and either combination of an upward and a downward movement using $p^*(1 - p^*)$.

At time zero, the insurance can be arranged by purchasing a European put to expire two periods hence. The combination of stock and a put with a strike price of $100.00 has the time 2 payoffs shown in Table 9.3. The scenario uu means the stock increases in price both periods, the scenarios ud and du refer respectively to an increase followed by a decrease or a decrease followed by an increase, and dd means the stock decreases in price both periods. The last line of Table 9.3 states that the cost of insuring against capital losses is the purchase price of the put. Using the risk adjusted probability, this purchase price is

$$(1 - p^*)^2 \$17.36 = 0.5238^2(\$17.36) = \$4.76$$

Now consider the portfolio values at the intervening time 1, when the stock price can either be $110.00 or $90.91. If the stock price reaches $110.00 at time 1, the portfolio cannot fall below $100.00 by time 2, and the holder of the originally purchased put might think of selling it to reduce insurance costs. But making a sale implies finding a willing buyer, and the put cannot be sold for a positive price to anyone having the same price expectations as used in the analysis. Under these expectations the put is worthless if the price has reached $110.00 at time 1, because in that event it will not be possible for the price to fall below $100.00 by time 2. On the other hand if the time 1 price is $90.91, the investor should continue to hold the put purchased at time zero, and will exercise it at time 2 if the price falls again to $82.64. If the investor holds the put at time 1 and the price rises to $100.00 at time 2, the put will then be worth exactly zero.

In the present example, once the problem has been stated and none of the parameters or the amount of insurance required changes, the original put purchase provides the desired insurance of time 2 portfolio value. If as assumed in the foregoing example, expectations do not change and the only purpose is to insure the portfolio's capital value at a fixed point in time, the same hedge

Table 9.3 Insured portfolio

Time 2 scenarios	Probability	Stock	Put	Portfolio
Scenario uu	$(p^*)^2$	$121.00	$0.00	$121.00
Scenario ud or du	$2p^*(1 - p^*)$	$100.00	$0.00	$100.00
Scenario dd	$(1 - p^*)^2$	$82.64	$17.36	$100.00
Time 0 value		$100.00	$4.76	$104.76

can be maintained without change (Huang and Litzenberger 1988). That is, the present example indicates the need for readjustment arises if expectations were to change from one period to the next. However, the need for readjustment could arise even with fixed expectations if for some reason the investor wished to change the amount of insurance.

9.1.3 Synthetic portfolios

The put-call parity relationship developed in Chapter 7 can be used both to illustrate the concept behind the hedge just discussed and to suggest a second way of devising the same insured portfolio. Recall from (7.6) that put-call parity states that the value of a certainty payment equal to the exercise price of a put and a call equals the value of the security, less the value of the call, plus the value of the put:

$$v(S) \equiv v(X) - v(C) + v(P) \tag{9.3}$$

Rearranging (9.3),

$$v(X) + v(P) \equiv v(S) + v(C); \tag{9.4}$$

an insured portfolio can be created by purchasing either the combination of the stock and a put, as in the above example, or the combination of an asset with a certainty payoff of S and a call. In practice the second alternative may be cheaper, because treasury bills are a good proxy for a sure asset and typically sell for relatively low commissions. Similarly, call options may sell for lower transactions costs than would the stock itself. The right-hand side of (9.4) gives the values of what is normally called a **synthetic insured portfolio**, an example of which is given in Table 9.4.

---

synthetic insured portfolio a portfolio composed of proxies for riskless securities, such as treasury bills, and derivatives such as stock index futures, intended to emulate the risk–return performance of a diversified stock portfolio.

Since a comparison of Tables 9.3 and 9.4 shows that the payoffs to the two portfolios are the same in every scenario, you know that if there are no arbitrage opportunities the two portfolios should have the same value at equilibrium

Table 9.4 Synthetic insured portfolio

Time 2 scenarios	Sure asset	Call	Portfolio
Scenario uu	$100.00	$21.00	$121.00
Scenario ud or du	$100.00	$0.00	$100.00
Scenario dd	$100.00	$0.00	$100.00
Time 0 value	$100.00	$4.76	$104.76

in perfectly competitive markets. In practice, if the two possibilities were available at different prices, or if they involved different transactions costs, you would choose the cheaper, thus helping to bring about the price relationships predicted by the absence of arbitrage opportunities.

9.1.4 Porfolio insurance: practice

In practice, a portfolio manager will usually employ derivatives such as stock index futures to insure a portfolio. Index futures are used in place of the puts discussed above because the markets in which index futures are traded are larger, subject to fewer limits, have longer maturities, and are cheaper than trading in puts (Fabozzi and Modigliani 1992: 318). On the other hand, synthetic portfolios based on index derivatives create only approximately the same income–risk tradeoffs as actual securities portfolios. The theoretical advantages of insured portfolios can be only approximately realised in practice because it is not always possible to trade instantaneously at market prices. Moreover, portfolio insurance schemes work better under normal trading conditions than when markets are unusually turbulent. When securities markets exhibit rapid price change and atypically high trading volumes, market prices for options and futures can deviate substantially from their theoretically predicted values, making it difficult or impossible to trade quickly at or near theoretical values.

Nevertheless, the more efficient markets become, the smaller the deviations between actual and theoretical prices are likely to be. In an increasingly efficient market, arbitrage works increasingly well and increasingly faster. Hence, if current impediments to efficient market trading are removed or lessened, portfolio insurance schemes' actual performance will more closely approximate their theoretical predictions. In the future some of the impediments – constraints on trading capacity, slow settlement procedures, and separate settlement procedures for each exchange – are likely to be ameliorated as exchanges expand their capacity to handle high volumes of trading and as they change settlement procedures and inter-exchange arrangements.

The theory underlying portfolio insurance does not address the problem of managing a portfolio whose risks change unpredictably subsequent to the assets' acquisition. For example, prior to the stock market declines of October 19, 1987 advocates of portfolio insurance did not always contemplate situations in which turbulent market conditions would impede trading securities at or near their theoretical values, and therefore had not worked out contingency plans to deal with such situations.

9.2 PORTFOLIOS OF NON-MARKETABLE SECURITIES

Managing portfolios of non-marketable securities includes all the governance tasks associated with marketable securities portfolios, except those involving active trading. Instead of active trading, managing non-marketable assets involves monitoring accompanied by processes of adjusting the issuing firms' operations when securities return distributions appear to be changing in an unsatisfactory way. Since many of the largest portfolios of non-marketable securities are assembled by intermediaries, this section emphasises the intermediary perspective on governance.

9.2.1 Market risk and default risk

The problems of managing portfolios of illiquid assets can be introduced by drawing a practical distinction between **market risk** and **default risk**. Market risk refers to being able to trade at or near a given price, that is to the possibility of declines in securities value. Default risk refers to the possibility of suffering losses through inability to pay, that is to the possibility of losing the entire investment. The two categories are not sharply distinguished, but reflect a difference of degree that is associated with the liquidity of the security in question.

A distinction between market risk and default risk is largely unnecessary when discussing marketable securities,[6] because any changes in default risk are reflected quickly in market prices. Losses through changes in the prices of marketable securities are commonplace, but losses through default are less common.[7] On the other hand, when securities are illiquid there is no reliable market price to reflect changes in payoff distributions. Indeed, the loans or investments held by intermediaries are typically recorded at their nominal values unless and until it appears they are likely to default, at which time they are sharply reduced in value or even written off entirely.

> **market risk** the risk of fluctuations in market price due to changes in demand–supply conditions.

Governing market risk demands trading capabilities, while governing default risk requires capabilities for valuing and where possible influencing future earnings prospects. Financiers do not usually possess both types of capability. For example, investment bankers are usually skilled at assessing market but not default risk, while commercial bankers are skilled at assessing default but not market risk. When investment bankers use their own capital to take longer term positions in shares, they can assume default risks with which they are unfamiliar. In the 1980s, substantial losses were sometimes incurred by investment bankers taking what they expected to be temporary share positions. These investment bankers agreed to take the positions to improve their chances of gaining merger and acquisition business, which usually brought very lucrative fees. In arranging a merger, the acquiring company needs funds to pay for the shares of the target company. Temporary or bridging finance may be provided by an investment banker, in anticipation of a subsequent longer term financing that would redeem the investment banker's investment. However, as and when raising the longer term financing proved difficult, the investment bankers in effect became longer term investors in the firm. They did not always realise that the governance structures appropriate for managing market risk are not appropriate for performing the screening, monitoring and subsequent adjustment tasks of managing default risk over the longer term.

9.2.2 Governance

In practice, the largest portfolios of non-marketable assets are created by banks and other intermediaries as a result of their lending operations. Like portfolio investors, lending intermediaries acquire assets to generate income. However, unlike portfolio investors, lending intermediaries usually intend to hold their assets until the deal is paid off, largely because their assets are illiquid and difficult to trade.[8]

To illustrate the governance issues involved, consider the differences between a government bond and a residential mortgage loan. A bond whose return is evolving unfavourably can usually be sold, albeit at a capital loss, and the proceeds reinvested. On the other hand, a mortgage loan is less liquid and also presents a wider possible range of risks. With regard to liquidity, after origination a mortgage loan presenting repayment difficulties cannot generally be sold off, but will rather present collection problems or problems of realising against the mortgage security. With regard to range of risks, two mortgage loans will typically differ more from each other than will two government bonds. Hence in comparison to government bonds, mortgage loans both require a different kind of initial screening and more intensive monitoring after they have been placed on the books.

9.2.3 Diversification

Even though they acquire impressive proportions of individually non-marketable assets, intermediaries still work to assemble diversified portfolios. In particular, a portfolio of statistically independent loans has a lower proportional default and income risk than the individual loans in the portfolio. Intermediaries mainly place their funds in small loans of heterogeneous quality, most of which they hold until maturity. Since few intermediary assets are sold (although increasingly larger amounts are now securitised as will be discussed in section 9.2.4), the aggregate risk of a lending intermediary's portfolio is influenced primarily by the screening processes used when the loans are first made.

Intermediaries assess earnings and default risk simultaneously, but govern the two differently. They manage earnings risk both by setting the terms of invidivual deals and by using derivatives to affect returns at the portfolio level. At the level of the individual deal, the negotiations typically involve such issues as requiring the interest rate on a loan to be fixed or floating. At the portfolio level management uses internal hedging, interest swaps and futures contracts. Banks and other lending intermediaries manage default risk mainly through monitoring and adjustment of individual loan contracts. They diversify some of their non-marketable risks by limiting the amounts they will invest in different asset categories. If they did not use such limits, intermediaries could create overly specialised portfolios with default risks large enough to threaten their survival. For example, some (particularly regional) intermediaries specialise in real estate lending within a given region, and can face severe solvency problems if real estate values decline. Similarly, insurance companies diversify non-market liabilities by limiting the amounts of insurance they will write against different loss categories. Intermediaries also have another traditional defence against overspecialisation – that of syndicating larger loans. In effect, syndication means selling portions of loans, when they are first made, to other intermediaries. This tactic is not available in the cases of small individual loans which cannot economically be divided and resold in the same way as larger loans because of fixed transactions costs.

9.2.4 Securitisation

Since the 1980s intermediaries have made increasing use of a transaction called **asset securitisation**. Securitisation involves selling claims against a portfolio of specialised and almost always relatively illiquid loans. Securitisation both releases funds that have been tied up in illiquid assets and, depending on the terms of the securitisation instruments, can help to diversify the effects of bearing non-marketable risks. One effect of securitisation is that intermediaries whose deposit gathering activities have been growing less rapidly than formerly have been able to replace some of their deposit funds with funds borrowed from such other institutions as mutual funds, whose market shares of savings have been growing rapidly in recent years. The normal buyers of the new securities are financial institutions with a need for long term, specialised investments.

> **asset securitisation** the practice of issuing new securities, designed to appeal to investors, against an asset portfolio of illiquid securities.

When an intermediary securitises some of its assets, the nature of the risks remaining on its books depends on the nature of the claims sold. If the assets are securitised by issuing equity, the deal represents a transfer of default risk to the buyer. By this method, an intermediary can diversify against the risks of overspecialisation. For example, an intermediary with a large proportion of real estate loans in its portfolio might be able to package the loans and sell equity claims against them, transferring both earnings and default risks to purchasers of the equity. On the other hand if the intermediary uses a debt instrument for securitisation, the default risk of the original loans remains on its own books. In this case it has improved its liquidity, but has not changed the default risk it has assumed. Securitisation using debt instruments does not, therefore, help to diversify risks that have previously been created by overspecialisation.

Securitisation has been highly successful in the United States, and is spreading rapidly to other countries. Its degree of success has led some authors to suggest that 'securitisation may eventually replace the traditional system' of financing through intermediaries (Fabozzi and Modigliani 1992: 601). The view of these authors is buttressed by the fact that some banks now sell loans directly. For example, both credit card receivables and – in the United States – portfolios of FNMA mortgages (mortgages conforming to the standards of the Federal National Mortgage Association) have been sold outright. Both these kinds of transactions suggest that the special characteristics of banks and of bank loans are possibly being attenuated, as does the 1996 example of National Westminster Bank's $5 billion securitisation of large UK corporate loans.

However, from the perspective of this book it is important not to overemphasise such developments. Securitisation does allow banks or other intermediaries to resell or to institutionalise the financing of some of the assets they previously funded on their own. However, the instruments used in securitising the portfolio are sold to institutional investors whose willingness to purchase the instruments depends on their confidence in the bank's performing its screening and monitoring functions. That is, confidence in screening and monitoring processes is in effect a prerequisite to successful securitisation.[9] Obviously, screening determines the quality of the portfolio to be securitised. Moreover, if the loans are not sold outright, banks continue to monitor the individual transactions in the securitised portfolio. If the loans are sold outright, the monitoring functions are still performed, but now by the acquiring institution rather than the originating bank. Securitisation is not a substitute for screening and monitoring, and therefore securitisation is no more a threat to these bank-like activities than is reinsurance a threat to the insurance company selling policies to the public.[10]

9.3 MANAGING CLOSELY HELD INVESTMENTS

Some financial holding companies assemble specialised asset portfolios. They usually make relatively small numbers of investments, which are both large and relatively illiquid. Even when they purchase public issues of securities, financial holding companies are likely to acquire control blocks. Managing closely held investments mainly involves devising governance capabilities to administer these attributes, especially the investments' lack of liquidity. The requisite capabilities include monitoring the evolution of the subject firms' businesses, deciding when adjustments to operations are needed, and choosing ways to effect the adjustments.

9.3.1 Incomplete contracting

Financiers who specialise in administering large, closely held investments often invest under uncertainty, in which case the financiers' contracts with their clients are incomplete. For example, financing a new venture, especially if it uses unproven technology, may present a spectrum of both financing and operating problems that were unanticipated when the original financing was arranged. Contract incompleteness calls for a governance structure that permits making flexible responses to changing conditions. Holding a control block is one way of dealing with the incompleteness, since it permits exercising a relatively intensive form of monitoring and adjustment capabilities.

However, even a control position will not always provide the flexibility necessary to adjust to unforeseen contingencies. For example, an effective control position might be upset by a takeover bid from a third party who acquires a sufficient number of voting shares. In order to guard against such a possibility, the financier should have at least a contingency plan for the actions to be taken if a third party were to begin assembling shares in anticipation of a possible takeover bid.

9.3.2 Governance responses

The managers of large, closely held investments can experiment with unfamiliar forms of financing if they have the capability to effect subsequent contract adjustments. For example, a conglomerate financier might invest in a new kind of asset with returns that seem unrelated to those of other investments, and thus gain information as to whether additional investments of the new type could be profitable over the long run. A conglomerate financier is in a better position to experiment than is a market agent, because it is less risky to experiment using a high capability governance structure with a capacity for adjusting to originally unforeseen events. Flexible governance structures could be used with marketable securities, but they would probably not be cost-effective, because marketable securities are relatively liquid, and capabilities to adjust operations are therefore not normally needed.[11]

Hybrid or hierarchical governance is likely to be more costly than market governance, and these cost effects should be recognised in assessing financial system efficiency. For example, consider the differences between a deal using a cheap, low capability governance structure, and a second using an expensive, high capability governance structure. Suppose that once the costs of the differing governance structures are recognised, the estimated risks and returns from the two transactions are the same from the perspective of the investors. Even though investors obtain the same risk and return, the effective interest rates paid by the two clients would have to differ, since in each case the governance structure's costs must be covered, and in the second case governance is assumed to be more costly. It would be easy, in such a case, to compare the clients' effective interest rates with the risk–return earnings profiles of the two financiers and conclude that the system was either operationally or allocatively inefficient. But given the circumstances assumed, neither conclusion would be correct.

9.4 MANAGING INTEREST RATE RISK

Portfolio managers' efforts to generate the best attainable risk–return combinations involve both choosing a diversified portfolio of securities and using special techniques to affect aggregate incomes. For portfolios of marketable securities, these special techniques principally involve using derivatives, as discussed in Chapter 7 and earlier in section 9.1.2. For portfolios of non-marketable securities, additional techniques such as asset-liability matching, and arranging swap transactions, are also employed.

9.4.1 Asset-liability matching

The income risks now being discussed are sometimes assessed in relation to a portfolio of both assets and liabilities, while those discussed at the beginning of the chapter are usually employed in managing income from assets. Income risk can be reduced if a portfolio is financed with liabilities whose costs are positively correlated through time with the assets' revenue stream.[12] If there is a perfect positive correlation the resulting income stream will be riskless, because in this case net revenue has perfectly negatively correlated components, the fluctuations in which offset each other. Chapter 15 models and analyses this kind of transaction, which is often referred to as **asset-liability matching**.

---

asset-liability matching borrowing and lending on the same interest rate terms (assessed with respect to the points in time at which rates can be adjusted). For example, a bank may finance floating rate loans using floating rate deposits. Asset-liability matching is internal to the intermediary in the sense that it is arranged on its own books and does not involve any trading of assets or liabilities or of interest rate patterns.

Asset-liability matching means borrowing and lending on the same interest rate terms (assessed with respect to the points in time at which rates can be adjusted), and is arranged without recourse to market trading of assets or liabilities. For example, intermediaries use asset-liability matching when a floating rate loan is funded by floating rate deposits. Such practices are now commonplace in both domestic and international banking transactions. If asset-liability matching is to be completely effective, the amounts of assets and liabilities having the same interest terms must be equal. If the amounts are unequal, say because of differing market conditions on the asset and on the liability side of the balance sheet, other means of managing risks such as trading derivative securities or using interest rate swaps must be found. In some cases intermediaries assume the remaining risks, particularly if they believe a short term trend in interest rates will work in their favour.

9.4.2 Interest rate swaps

Income risks can be hedged externally using instruments called **interest rate swaps**.

> **interest rate swap** an arrangement whereby one economic agent, usually a financial institution, exchanges a pattern of interest rates with a counterparty, usually another financial institution. For example, a United States bank might exchange a pattern of floating interest rate costs with a Japanese bank in exchange for receiving the Japanese bank's fixed rate costs. Both parties enter swap transactions with a view to reducing their earnings risks, usually as measured in an accounting sense.

To understand the logic of a swap, consider two future patterns of interest earnings, both as they appear from the perspective of time 0. Suppose Bank A has fixed rate loans and floating rate deposits, both in the amount of $100.00, while Bank B has floating rate loans and fixed rate deposits, also both in the amount of $100.00. Suppose the average deposit rate is 6 percent, while the average loan rate is 10 percent. The fixed rate arrangements remain at these levels for the two periods, but the floating interest rates change randomly as time passes. Suppose, to keep the example simple, that floating interest rates can be either high or low in each of the two periods, but never equal the average exactly. The floating rates are assumed to be 1 percent above the average if they are high, 1 percent below the average if low. The two floating rates, on the deposits of Bank A and on the loans of Bank B, and deposit costs are assumed to be perfectly correlated, being high together or low together. The earnings on the two banks' portfolios, when interest rates follow the patterns indicated, are shown in Table 9.5. Assuming for simplicity that all rate scenarios are equally likely, average net earnings are $4.00 per period for either bank. Inspection of Table 9.5 also shows that when one bank's net earnings are low the other's are high, and vice versa. Clearly, if Bank A were to pay Bank B $1.00 when the earnings of Bank A were high, and if Bank B were to pay Bank A when the earnings of Bank B were high, both could report steady earnings of $4.00 in each time period, regardless of the scenario which obtained.

Such an arrangement to stabilise earnings can be struck if Bank A swaps its fixed loan earnings for the floating rate loan earnings of Bank B, as shown in Table 9.6.[13] Under the swap now being discussed Bank B will pay Bank A if the loan interest rate is high, and Bank A will pay Bank B if the loan interest

Table 9.5 Net earnings of two banks, before swap

Rate scenario (time 1, time 2)	Bank A		Bank B	
	Time 1	Time 2	Time 1	Time 2
High, high	$3.00	$3.00	$5.00	$5.00
High, low	$3.00	$5.00	$5.00	$3.00
Low, high	$5.00	$3.00	$3.00	$5.00
Low, low	$5.00	$5.00	$3.00	$3.00

Table 9.6 Swap payments from Bank B to Bank A (+), from Bank A to Bank B (−)

Rate scenario	Time 1	Time 2
High, high	$1.00	$1.00
High, low	$1.00	−$1.00
Low, high	−$1.00	$1.00
Low, low	−$1.00	−$1.00

rate is low. Note that if the four scenarios are equally likely, the expected value of the payments in either direction is zero, so that one bank would not gain an advantage for which a compensating payment was required. The advantage of the swap is that it stabilises the net interest earnings of both institutions. As the example indicates, an interest rate swap makes use of both reference interest rates and a reference amount, the latter being called the notional principal.

A swap contract can be interpreted as a package of forward contracts of different maturities. Consider the payment position of Bank A at time 1, which involves receipts when its interest revenues are high, and payments when its interest revenues are low. By interpreting the net revenues of Bank A as the cash price of an asset, and supposing A has a long position in a forward contract to buy the asset at a forward price of $4.00, the time 1 payments in Table 9.6 are seen to be exactly the profit or loss on the one-period forward contract. Similarly, the payments to Bank A at time 2 are exactly the profit or loss on a two-period forward contract written on the same terms. In other words, a swap contract can be interpreted as a package of forward contracts, each of which has a maturity equal to one of the times a payment is contracted under the swap.

Since swaps are not guaranteed by an exchange, they carry a default risk. For example, under scenario HL, Bank A would have no incentive to default at time 1, but would before making the required time 2 payment to Bank B. In the present instance, valuing the swap according to its expected value has ignored any possibility of default in either direction. As will be discussed more extensively in Chapter 13, swaps can be arranged either through private negotiations or in what has evolved into a very active marketplace.[14] If, for example, one intermediary has floating rate assets financed by fixed rate liabilities, while another has fixed rate assets financed by floating rate liabilites, an exchange of their interest costs can stabilise the interest incomes of both.

9.4.3 Interest rate futures

Financial intermediaries and other agents also sell off risks in markets such as the interest futures markets. The most common transactions of this type usually hedge the risk of individual deals, such as a fixed rate loan funded by floating rate deposits. As a management technique for dealing with earnings risks, hedging through interest rate futures can only be effected for maturities up to about a year, and for relatively small amounts of funds. It is possible to use futures contracts to hedge risks on transactions in hundreds of millions of dollars, but not in tens of billions of dollars.

As an example, a financier can sell the interest rate risk of a fixed rate loan by balancing expected interest gains or losses against capital losses or gains on interest rate futures. Treasury bills have market values which are negatively correlated with changes in interest rates. Similarly, futures contracts written against treasury bills have payments streams that are negatively correlated with interest rates. Thus, a short position in treasury bill futures has earnings that rise as interest rates rise, and fall as rates fall. Hence the combination of a fixed rate loan and a short futures position (if the latter is of an appropriate size) behaves like a floating rate loan. If the arrangement is funded by floating rate deposits, the effect on the intermediary is that of matching a floating rate loan with a floating rate deposit, creating a position which is hedged against interest rate change.

Interest rate options, and options on futures contracts, can also be used to hedge interest rate risks. At present in the US, the contracts traded include Treasury Bill futures, Treasury Bond and Note futures, Eurodollar CD futures, and futures on the Bond Buyer municipal bond index. The instruments are also used by financial institutions for such other purposes as creating synthetic put options, enhancing returns when futures are mispriced, and pursuing still other investment strategies. Options on futures contracts, and especially over the counter options on futures contracts, are a preferred vehicle for implementing some investment strategies (Fabozzi and Modigliani 1992: 632).

9.4.4 Other risk management possibilities

Financial institutions use many different kinds of conditional commitments, both for their own portfolio management purposes and in their dealings with clients. Interest rate agreements are widely used to hedge both short term domestic and foreign currency denominated interest rate risk. Such agreements provide that one party will compensate the other, in exchange for an up front premium, if a reference rate differs from a predetermined level called the strike rate. If payment is to be made when the reference rate exceeds the strike rate, the contract is called a cap, and if payment is to be made when the reference falls below the strike rate, it is called a floor. A collar is a combination of a cap and a floor. Still other, more exotic instruments can also be found. They include options on swap contracts (swaptions), on caps (captions) and on floors (flotions). At the present time, these and other agreements can usually be arranged either with investment bankers or with banks.

All the foregoing arrangements are used to divide up and trade risk, to provide one party with a form of insurance. For example, a corporate treasurer can use an interest rate cap to fix the maximum interest cost, while a collar can be used to maintain interest costs within a given band, say current prime plus or minus 2 percent. Naturally, the selling bank or investment banker charges a fee for such a product. Determining the actual payments under a contract, and valuing them appropriately, are important to determining the contracts' profitability to the institutions writing them.

9.5 SUMMARY

This chapter examined the tasks of managing asset portfolios. Managing a portfolio of marketable securities principally involves selecting investment targets and trading assets to generate a target level of income while reducing risk as much as possible. These tasks are addressed through diversification and the use of options, futures and dynamic portfolio restructuring.

Managing portfolios of non-marketable securities principally involves screening new acquisitions, effecting adjustments where necessary, and influencing the income pattern of the aggregate portfolio. All these tasks must be performed without relying on active trading to any significant extent. Loans or investments are characterised by intermediate degrees of asset illiquidity, and higher capability governance structures are needed for monitoring and adjustment purposes.

Problems of asset illiquidity are greatest in portfolios of large, closely held investments. The implications of asset illiquidity for incomplete contracting, and the governance responses to incomplete contracting, were both discussed. The chapter pointed out that a financial conglomerate can represent an effective governance structure for managing illiquid assets under uncertainty. While such governance structures are relatively high cost ones, they also have high capability to effect the kinds of adjustments often needed in a situation of incomplete contracting.

REVIEW QUESTIONS

Exercise 1 Rewrite Table 9.1 so that the three probabilities of 1/3 are on the diagonal from the lower left to the upper right hand corner. All other cells have zero probability. Show that the change makes the correlation between r_X and r_Y equal to minus 1.

Exercise 2 Using the assumptions of Exercise 1, compute the variance of a portfolio made up of equal proportions of securities X and Y. Explain intuitively why this portfolio has a variance equal to zero.

Exercise 3 Use risk adjusted probabilities to show that the value of the call in Table 9.4 is $4.76.

Exercise 4 Use a table like Table 7.8 to show the details of the put-call parity relationship for a one-period call and a one-period put written at time zero, and with an exercise price of $100.00 against the stock whose price behaviour is modelled in Table 9.4.

Exercise 5 Would you be more concerned with market risk or with default risk if you managed a portfolio of government bonds? What if the portfolio you managed consisted of equity investments in small growing companies (i.e., venture investments)?

Exercise 6 Some authors believe that securitisation means the end of banks. What contrary arguments can be offered?

Exercise 7 Explain how funding a floating rate loan by using floating rate deposits is an example of asset-liability matching. What risks are reduced by this form of matching?

Exercise 8 In what ways are swaps and asset-liability matching similar? (Hint: suppose two banks using a swap were to merge.)

Exercise 9 Under what circumstances would an intermediary use the interest futures markets rather than traditional matching techniques?

Exercise 10 Do interest rate swaps offer an alternative to floating rate lending? Why or why not?

Exercise 11 Even though the principles of diversification were developed under risk, they can be used to help offset uncertainties as well. For example, the returns from many property development projects are probably uncertain. If you managed such a property development company, how would you attempt to diversify the uncertainties your company might face?

Exercise 12 Property developers often encounter financial difficulties because their assets are largely illiquid and financed by relatively heavy debt burdens. The problems are compounded by differences in asset valuations: holders of the debt often place much lower values on property than do developers. Suggest some ways of managing a portfolio of development projects that would offset some of the difficulties.

Exercise 13 The management suggestions you made in Exercise 12 are probably not unknown to most developers, and yet they might be quite unwilling to implement your advice. Assuming they regard your advice as conceptually sound, why do you think this might be?

Exercise 14 Why might it be difficult for financiers to become highly skilled at evaluating both market risk and default risk?

Exercise 15 Explain how the enhanced monitoring and control capabilities possessed by a conglomerate permit it to enter incomplete contracts with its subsidiaries.

Exercise 16 Interest rate risk can be hedged both with swaps and in the futures markets. Why do you think both alternatives have developed? Do you regard them as competitive or complementary?

10 Deals' terms

10.1	Principles		157
	10.1.1	Informational conditions	157
	10.1.2	Information and contract types	158
10.2	Complete contracts		159
	10.2.1	Contracts with information exchange	159
	10.2.2	Third party information	159
	10.2.3	Contingency planning	160
10.3	Incomplete contracts		160
	10.3.1	Uncertainty and governance	160
	10.3.2	Subsequent adjustment	161
	10.3.3	Bypassing uncertainty	162
10.4	Informational differences		162
	10.4.1	How do informational differences occur?	162
	10.4.2	Moral hazard and adverse selection	163
	10.4.3	Market failure and credit rationing	164
	10.4.4	Managing informational differences	165
	10.4.5	Preferences for particular instruments	165
10.5	Other deal terms		166
	10.5.1	Effective interest rate	166
	10.5.2	Interest rates and risk	167
	10.5.3	Tax effects	167
10.6	Summary		168

LEARNING OBJECTIVES

After reading this chapter you will understand

- how the terms of individual deals are set to aid their governance
- why the terms of type S deals are usually complete contracts
- why the terms of type N deals are usually incomplete contracts
- why informational differences lead to problems of moral hazard and adverse selection
- how particular instruments help manage informational differences
- the importance of taxes in determining effective interest rates

---

When considering proposals from a given class of client, financiers usually offer each applicant a common set of terms. If they find a particular applicant's proposal generally acceptable, financiers will usually state common terms and outline additional specific terms. These specific deal terms, some of which may be negotiated with an individual client, are intended to enhance the financier's ability to govern the deal's unique attributes. As one instance, the kind of information available affects both the financier's estimate of the deal's return distribution and the kinds of reports the financier will require the client to file during the course of the financing arrangement. A retail client borrowing against accounts receivable might, for example, be asked to submit quarterly statements of accounts receivable outstanding. If negotiations regarding terms can be completed to the satisfaction of both parties, the funds sought will be advanced.

10.1 PRINCIPLES

Chapter 8 argued that a type N deal can be administered more cost-effectively by type H than by type M governance. The particular terms of such a type N deal specify such things as how the monitoring would be carried out. For example, a bank might require a borrowing client to submit quarterly financial statements which would aid the bank in assessing the progress of the business and updating its estimates of the loan's profitability and safety.

10.1.1 Informational conditions

Informational conditions are particularly important deal attributes. When financiers take on familiar deals, and believe they have the same deal information as their clients, the financiers usually treat the deal routinely. If the financiers have less information than their clients, they will try to determine whether it is cost-effective to obtain additional details. If financiers think it would be, they may incorporate their requests in the terms of the deal. If the information is not immediately available, financiers will stipulate the monitoring arrangements by which it will later be provided.

As an example of the differences, the purchaser of a government treasury bill has considerable information about the issuer's credit rating and the market interest rate on the bill. Indeed, the purchaser has access to all potentially relevant information regarding this type of deal at the time the purchase is made. On the other hand, the venture capitalist making an investment in a firm has much less precise information, particularly when the firm's principal asset is the talent of its owner-manager. Moreover, the venture capitalist is likely to learn more about the firm's potential profitability during the period of any financing than will the purchaser of a treasury bill.

10.1.2 Information and contract types

Governance structures differ according to whether a deal is consummated under risk or under uncertainty, as indicated in Figure 10.1. As compared to governance under risk, the details of governance procedures under uncertainty are less completely specified when the deal is first negotiated, but provide for more intensive monitoring and for greater flexibility of adjustment as information becomes available. The extra monitoring effort, and the provision for adjustment, mean the procedures will be more costly than their counterparts for governing deals under risk, but also mean that the financiers regard it as worthwhile to incur the extra cost. Since financiers have to cover their costs from the client, the client presenting a deal under uncertainty can expect to pay a higher effective interest rate than the client presenting a deal under risk.

Financiers see relatively little need for monitoring, or for the contract adjustments to which monitoring can lead, if they can stipulate all important contingencies in advance. In such cases financiers are likely to use complete contracting, meaning that all of a deal's important terms can be and are specified in advance. Incomplete contracting means that financiers believe there is a chance that initially unforeseen contingencies might arise during the course of the arrangement. To detect whether such contingencies occur, financiers need

Informational attribute	Governance structure
Risk	Complete contract. Rule based; little or no provision for monitoring and subsequent control.
Uncertainty	Incomplete contract. Structure allows for discretionary governance. Details of monitoring and control are typically negotiated.

Figure 10.1 Deal attributes and governance structures

to monitor the client's activities. If an unforeseen contingency does occur financiers may have to make contract adjustments, but since the contingencies cannot be foreseen, the necessary adjustments cannot usually be specified in advance. For this reason, incomplete contracts are usually expressed in terms of the principles to be invoked in making adjustments as and when the need for changing contract terms becomes apparent.

10.2 COMPLETE CONTRACTS

This section describes some details of the kinds of complete contracts entered by financier and client in arranging risky deals.

10.2.1 Contracts with information exchange

Whatever type of deal that agents enter, they seek to benefit from it. For example, clients will provide financiers with more information if they can reduce financing charges by more than it costs them to provide the information. Equally, the riskier the deal, the more anxious financiers will be to exercise their capabilities to control or reduce the risk.[1] For example, financiers might use the terms of a debt issue to encourage clients to reveal truthfully any pertinent insider knowledge they might have. Ross (1977) shows that the optimal contract for maximising a risk-neutral entrepreneur's expected return, given a minimum expected return to lenders, is debt with a fixed face value and a bankruptcy penalty. The penalty, borne by management, at least equals any shortfall in the debt payment. The arrangement works if management have resources to pay any bankruptcy penalties. Such a situation is not, however, typical of an entrepreneur who has invested all available assets in a firm. If the firm were to go bankrupt, the entrepreneur might well not have any resources remaining to pay bankruptcy penalties.

Financing arrangements can sometimes be struck even though the parties differ in their estimates of a deal's payoffs. For example, financier and client might disagree on the range of a payoff distribution, but they might be able to agree on a lowest possible outcome, and hence on the amount of financing that both could regard as riskless. (Chapter 7 gave examples of riskless debt.) Similarly, by using combinations of securities attractive to optimists and others attractive to pessimists, it may be possible to obtain agreement on the value of the combination even if financier and client cannot agree on the value of the individual securities making it up.

10.2.2 Third party information

Not all deal information must be provided by management. When a third party can realise cost advantages to information production, say by operating a rating service, financiers may simply purchase the information from the third party. For example, in North America companies like Moody's and Standard and Poor's monitor the creditworthiness of public companies' debt issues and keep the investing public informed of their debt ratings. The companies being rated find it advantageous to pay the agencies for producing the ratings, because the information then makes it easier or less costly for the companies to obtain financing.

In the United States, information is also produced by municipal bond insuring agencies, which covered approximately 25 percent of all new municipal issues in 1990 (Fabozzi, Modigliani and Ferri 1994: 345–346). Benson (1979) argues that by producing information and then finding clients particularly interested in purchasing insured bonds, underwriters can reduce financing costs below those that would be paid if buyers produced the information individually. In these cases, even though the information is collected and used privately by the insurers, other members of the investing public may interpret the existence of the insurance as a signal regarding the issuing municipality's creditworthiness.

Sometimes signalling can be almost incidental to a deal. Fama (1985) argues that firms may use short term bank borrowing as a signal: a bank's willingness to extend short term financing may be regarded by other financiers as information about the firm's quality, and hence may reduce the firm's cost of signalling.

10.2.3 Contingency planning

Some financiers recognise that gradual revelation of information can be used to their advantage. If the contingencies revealed by information can be stated in advance, they can be planned for in writing the original, complete contract. This kind of contingency planning can prove especially useful in financings involving repeated negotiations. For instance, John and Nachman (1985) find that when a firm has repeatedly to return to the market for financing, it faces an incentive to consider the effects of its actions on both current and future securities prices. A firm in this position would try to avoid defaulting on a debt issue if the default were likely to depress the price at which it could sell additional debt.

10.3 INCOMPLETE CONTRACTS

Under uncertainty, making quantitative estimates of payoff distributions is either not possible or overly costly. The parties to the deal recognise that originally unforeseeable contingencies may arise and affect the deal's outcome. It is not possible to know exactly how the client's business will evolve, and therefore deals' terms must allow for actions that cannot be specified exactly in the original contract. To do such deals, financiers write contracts that will allow for adjustments should an originally unforeseen contingency arise.

10.3.1 Uncertainty and governance

Uncertainty regarding payoffs can arise as a result of the actions of clients, of third parties, or of changes in the economic environment. Whenever possible,

financiers may try to offset the possible adverse effects of uncertainty by negotiating with the parties contributing to it. For example, in natural gas pipeline
construction, financiers may request their clients to obtain an advance ruling
from the regulatory authorities, permitting the pipeline company to pass on any
construction cost increases to consumers by increasing the cost of gas. The
advance ruling has the effect of reducing the uncertainty that the project will
be able to turn a profit.

Financiers may also attempt to glean information from management actions.
For example, management's willingness to join an endeavour likely evinces
belief in the project's success, particularly if management invest funds of their
own. On the other hand, resignation of key personnel from a firm could well
indicate their lack of faith in its future prospects.

Rating agencies are unlikely to play prominent information production roles
under uncertainty, since their main function is to refine estimates of risks at
relatively low cost. However, consultants or other experts sometimes perform a
function analogous to that of rating agencies: observers with specialised knowledge may be able to determine key implications of a deal's uncertainties.
Sometimes the experts are the financiers themselves. For example, financiers
might offer clients estimates of a product's likely sales, and this information
could in turn affect the client's product offerings.

10.3.2 Subsequent adjustment

Incomplete contracts create interdependence between financier and client. For
a deal to reach a successful conclusion, financier and client depend on each
other's willingness to reveal information and to cooperate more fully than is
usual with a complete contract. This interdependence is often reflected in
contract terms which provide for greater flexibility in governance as and when
originally unforeseen events come to be realised. Such arrangements include
using equity in place of debt, or a seat on the board of directors in place of
such legal obligations as maintaining a given working capital ratio.

Adjustment capabilities can benefit both financier and client. They allow
financiers to learn more about the key profitability features of a deal and to
manage those features more effectively. They may also allow clients to learn
how to operate the firm more profitably, or to enhance the probability of its
long run survival. For example, some developing countries have found their
financiers willing to accept equity in exchange for their previously issued debt.
The country obtains the advantage of more flexible repayment terms, while
the financier may find the value of the existing investment increased. From the
client's perspective, equity financing eliminates the technical possibility of
default and its attendant renegotiation costs, an important consideration when
debt carries fixed interest payments which might become too great for the
obligant to bear. Debt renegotiation subsequent to a default can be cumbersome
and lengthy because it can mean obtaining agreement from a relatively large
number of lenders who may well not agree on the best course to pursue.

A given set of terms will likely offer net benefits in some kinds of deals but not in others. A contract that does not provide for unforeseeable contingencies can be finely tuned to work perfectly under one set of circumstances, but can work badly if circumstances change. A more flexible contract that contains provisions for unforeseeable contingencies may not work perfectly under any set of circumstances, but there may be many different circumstances under which it works relatively well.

10.3.3 Bypassing uncertainty

One obvious way of dealing with uncertainty is to pass its effects on to another party, say the client. For example, a few Japanese banks, concerned in the later 1980s about the possibility of eventual peaking in Japanese real estate prices, were able to securitise some of their property loans using equity instruments. This device passed the risk of capital loss on to the purchasers of the equities. Of course, it also passed on to the purchasers any possibility of capital gains, and it seems likely that the sellers placed a lower expected value on such possible capital gains than did the purchasers.

Just as they can be used to bypass risks, guarantees or collateral can be used to bypass a deal's uncertainties. For example, export credit insurance is often provided by exporters' governments. Shipments of goods may be insured against events which neither the financier nor the client can control, such as losses from acts of war. Similarly, clients can be bonded so that financiers are insured against various developments or actions that might be inimical to financiers' interests. In some cases, financings are insured against such eventualities as death of key management personnel. After providing for these kinds of risks, the deal may be similar to those of financing inventories for domestic sale.

The parties to a deal do not always recognise that their agreement constitutes an incomplete contract. For example, when a deal is first arranged, financiers might not realise that certain possible outcomes have gone unrecognised in the contract's conditions. Should the incompleteness later be recognised, financiers will then try to devise adjustments, but they will be in a weaker position than if they had originally foreseen the need for adjustments.

10.4 INFORMATIONAL DIFFERENCES

Managing informational asymmetries is relatively easy under risk, since the costs of acquiring additional information can be assessed quantitatively. Under uncertainty only a qualitative assessment is generally possible, and management of any asymmetries essentially becomes an exercise in judgment.

10.4.1 How do informational differences occur?

Informational differences usually occur in deals which do not receive intensive study by a number of agents. However, one survey (Donaldson 1980) found that informational differences can impede even large public market transactions if the corporation involved is changing the nature of its business. Even in routine public market transactions, information is not always obtained at the same time by all parties. In Canada as well as in the United States, stock market trading activity by corporate officers and market specialists based on inside information has been shown to yield abnormal risk adjusted returns (Hatch and Robinson 1989). Whatever the likelihood of informational differences in public market transactions, they are even more likely to occur in private markets or in inter-mediated transactions. For example, financiers are well aware that some clients will provide biased information in attempts to improve financing terms. As the next sections show, there are also a number of other consequences of informational differences.

10.4.2 Moral hazard and adverse selection

One consequence of informational differences is known as **moral hazard**, a phenomenon which affects relations between a financier and an individual client. For example, if the financier does not take precautions to prevent its happening, a client may use the proceeds of a debt issue to finance a riskier investment than originally proposed. The shareholders of the firm receive any benefits from such a substitution, but debtholders bear any increased risk. Moral hazard can also present qualitative difficulties for the financier. For example, management may put less effort into making a project succeed than it appeared they would when seeking financing, and yet it is difficult for the financier to place any quantitative importance on such a change.

> **moral hazard** the possibility that client behaviour will change as a result of the deal being arranged.

A second consequence of informational differences is **adverse selection**, a phenomenon which affects relations between a financier and a group of indistinguishable clients considered as members of a pool. Adverse selection can increase expected losses by discouraging the best credit risks while attracting lower quality ones. If the terms announced by financiers for taking on clients from a pool of risks are unattractive to the lowest risk potential clients, these clients will turn to other financing sources, increasing the average risk of the client pool. The effect is exacerbated if more high risk clients are attracted to the pool by the financiers' terms. Just as moral hazard can present qualitative management problems, so can adverse selection. For example, a financier who treats clients as if they are all honest may attract a group of dishonest clients. A bank manager newly appointed to an area and who is unfamiliar with the new client population may well encounter this kind of difficulty.

adverse selection the possibility that a risk pool will change because of the terms offered to clients whose differing risks cannot readily be distinguished by screening.

10.4.3 Market failure and credit rationing

Information differences can lead to still other management problems, including market failure and credit rationing equilibria. Consider each in turn. **Market failure** is caused by a combination of informational asymmetries and adverse selection. For example, if the newly appointed bank manager of the previous paragraph cannot distinguish good from bad clients, she may decide that it is profitable only to lend against collateral, in which case the market for unsecured loans in her business area can be said to have failed. As another example, it may be difficult to resell the shares of a small business at a price reflecting its value as a going concern, because the purchaser cannot verify the information on which a going concern value is based.

market failure a situation in which economically viable deals cannot be agreed, usually because of informational differences between financier and client which mean that the quality of the deal cannot accurately be assessed by the financier.

While it is commonly believed that changes in interest rates will always equate supply with demand, in some circumstances a **credit rationing equilibrium** can arise. A credit rationing equilibrium, which refers to a situation in which only some potential clients can raise funds at market rates of interest, can result when intermediaries make decisions on the basis of both interest rate and average risk. If increases in interest rates mean that clients take on more risk while still demanding the same amounts of funds, financiers might be made worse off by raising interest rates, because they would then supply the same amount of funds to do riskier deals (Stiglitz and Weiss 1981). In these circumstances there is no reason for a previously existing excess demand to be eliminated by an interest rate increase. Similarly, if financiers lower the rates they charge, the risks actually taken on may decline more slowly than the rate reduction warrants. Accordingly, a form of credit rationing must be used if financiers are to deal adequately with the combination of risks and potential returns they face.

credit rationing equilibrium an equilibrium situation in which not all clients of a given class can obtain financing, even though all present the same risks.

10.4.4 Managing informational differences

Financiers recognise and attempt to manage the difficulties arising from informational differences by appropriately fine tuning the terms of each deal. For
example, most financiers attempt to counter informational bias by verifying the
reports that clients provide. In addition, some financiers propose deal terms that
encourage the client to report information in an unbiased way. To offset the
workings of moral hazard, financiers monitor client activities and impose
sanctions if contract terms are violated. For example, suppose a client proposes
to buy a specific piece of equipment with the funds she is seeking. Then the
financier agreeing to the proposal may supervise the disposition of the funds,
paying them out to a supplier indicated in the original financing proposal.

Monitoring is used to detect both adverse developments and violations of
contract terms. Thus monitoring enhances the safety of a financial arrangement
by presenting a potential for discovery which can discourage clients from taking
damaging actions. The principal benefit to monitoring is that financiers gain
greater capability to offset possible losses. The principal costs of monitoring
are those of setting up and operating the monitoring mechanism, and those of
taking corrective action when it is needed.

When they cannot clearly ascertain the outcomes of a deal in advance,
financiers rely on their ability to learn and to adapt. The benefits of learning
and adaptation include the possibility of discovering new profitable ways of
doing business, while the costs include mistakenly entering transactions which
prove to be unprofitable because their true nature was not originally recognised.
In practice, financial firms both experiment with new lines of business and
terminate attempts which do not work out as profitably as originally anticipated.
The fact that financiers do try new lines of business suggests that financial
managers regard experiments as useful learning devices. The fact that financiers
sometimes terminate unsuccessful lines suggests their experiments do not always
confirm the obvious.

10.4.5 Preferences for particular instruments

When management's and financiers' estimates of future cash flows differ, the
values that financiers place on securities are based on their own risk and earnings
estimates. Any difference in valuation can mean that, in management's view, the
firm's securities are not priced to yield market required rates of return in relation
to the risk involved. For example, if the purchasers of shares are relatively
pessimistic of the firm's prospects, they may place a lower value on the shares
than does management. In such a case management would prefer financing with
debt if they find it easier to agree with financiers on a value for the debt. If both
management and financiers were to regard the debt as essentially riskless, they
would place the same value on it.

Similarly, financiers and management may find it easier to agree on the value
of short term as opposed to long term debt, and may thus prefer to use the

former. Financiers may demand a lower risk premium on short term instruments because they have more confidence in their short term forecasts, and clients may choose short term financing because they are attracted by the lower risk premium.

10.5 OTHER DEAL TERMS

Other deal terms include its interest rate and its tax status.

10.5.1 Effective interest rate

A deal's interest rate is the most important factor determining a financier's return. The financier's expected returns are, of course, affected by the possibility of default, which might occur either because the project generates insufficient returns or because the client is dishonest. That is, financiers need to assess the quality of both the project and its management. With an honest client, the possibility of default depends primarily on the client's ability to generate earnings to redeem the investment. Assessing the costs of default means estimating whether the financier is likely to recover both the funds initially extended and a return on them commensurate with the risk or uncertainty of the arrangement.

To see how default risk differs among transactions, consider two money market instruments – commercial paper and bankers' acceptances – whose details will be discussed further in Chapter 12. For the present discussion it suffices to note that the purchaser of **commercial paper** assumes the risk the issuer will be unable to pay, while the purchaser of a **bankers' acceptance** has a bank guarantee against issuer default. Corporations that are well known as good credit risks to their bankers, but not to the markets at large, may find bankers' acceptances a lower cost source of funding than they would find commercial paper. In effect, such corporations are relying on the bank's credit rating, which is presumably higher than the corporation's.

---

commercial paper money market instrument issued by a corporation and sold in the market for the purpose of raising short term funds.

---

bankers' acceptance money market instrument similar to commercial paper except that its redemption is guaranteed by a bank.

To see why agreement on risk can lower an interest rate, consider how an effective interest rate is related to default risk. For example, suppose a loan will be repaid in full at the end of one year with 10 percent interest if the borrowing firm does not fail. If the firm does fail, an event that occurs with probability 0.01, the financier gets nothing. Then for each dollar invested, the financier expects to recover $(0.99)(1.10)$, and the effective annual interest rate is

$$(0.99)(1.10) - 1.00 = 0.089 \text{ or } 8.9\%$$

In the case of a choice between bankers' acceptances and commercial paper, if the corporation's bank estimates the corporation's default risk is lower than do the market agents who buy commercial paper, the effective rate on the bankers' acceptance will be lower. It may remain lower even after the bank's charges for guaranteeing the paper are taken into account.

The usual methods of assessing and managing default possibilities involve initial screening and, where it is cost-effective, continued monitoring over the term of the arrangement. The greater the likelihood of default, the more intensive the initial investigation and the greater the need for continued monitoring. Default possibilities are sometimes assessed on a project basis, since cash flows from a project can sometimes be forecast more easily than for the firm as a whole. Project financing has long been used by banks, but became particularly popular in the late 1980s as a means of enhancing their governance of large, high risk ventures.

10.5.2 Interest rates and risk

Loan or investment transactions present opportunity costs regardless of the nature of the interest rate arrangement. Financiers incur opportunity costs if they offer fixed rate financing and rates increase after the financing has been arranged, and they also incur opportunity costs if they make floating rate loans and interest rates subsequently fall. In addition, financiers are exposed to a risk of not recovering the purchasing power of their investment if price levels and consequently future interest rates cannot correctly be forecast. First, even on a short term fixed rate loan a financier will not recover purchasing power in full if the loan carries an interest rate that is lower than market rates over its term. Second, on a longer term loan unexpected increases in interest rates can imply large declines in the market value of the instrument involved, subjecting the owner to capital losses if the instrument must be traded.

10.5.3 Tax effects

Taxes affect most financial arrangements. As one illustration, consider how bond issuers tailor the terms of their offerings to minimise the impact of taxation on financing costs. Reported interest rates on long term bonds are calculated assuming the bonds will be held to maturity. But the relevant data for investors are the after tax yield they receive over the period a bond is held. These returns may be received either as interest or as capital gains, and depending on which is the case, the tax treatment of the revenues will differ. The particulars of the tax treatment of interest income and capital gains differ from one country to another.

The zero coupon bond is a way of reducing the cost of funds for corporations able to borrow from other non-financial firms, because capital gains received by non-financial corporations may be taxed at lower rates than gains received by financial intermediaries. Stripped bonds are created when an investment dealer or other agent removes the interest coupons from a bond, selling the components separately. For individual investors, the appeal of stripped bonds has been reduced since the tax authorities in some countries began to treat the increase in bond value as interest income for tax purposes.

In the United States, interest paid on municipal bonds is not taxable as income in the hands of recipients, with the result that reported yields on these securities are about half the yields on securities (of similar risk) whose interest payments are taxable in the hands of the recipient.

10.6 SUMMARY

This chapter discussed fine tuning deals' terms. First, the chapter considered the importance of differing informational conditions, showing how transactions under risk are associated with complete contracting, while those under uncertainty are more closely related to incomplete contracting. Informational differences are managed by choices of governance structures and deals' terms.

Under uncertainty, contracts are usually incomplete, and the effects of incompleteness are usually managed through subsequent adjustments. Adjustments can deal either with changes in the economic environment outside the control of interested participants or with direct reactions of clients or interested third parties.

Contract terms are designed to help detect any bias in client-provided information, and to help offset the effects of moral hazard and adverse selection. Monitoring is also used for the same purpose.

REVIEW QUESTIONS

Exercise 1 Suppose a bank makes a working capital loan against accounts receivable, and that the receivables are assigned to the bank as security. What kinds of information regarding the receivables would the bank likely require the client to submit periodically?

Exercise 2 In some cases, the accounts receivable loan of Exercise 1 can be regarded as a deal implemented with a complete contract. List two or three complications that, in your opinion, could make the contract incomplete.

Exercise 3 Why might financiers buy information rather than work it up themselves?

Exercise 4 Suppose a venture capital investor has a seat on the board of a small company which the investor is financing. Suppose that the board receives information that the company president is spending all of the time on product innovation but that sales are suffering. What kinds of corrective action might the venture investor recommend?

Exercise 5 Classify each of the following difficulties as stemming either from moral hazard or from adverse selection. A client takes the proceeds of a business loan and uses the funds to go on vacation. Clients approach the financier with stories of how they have been badly treated by other financiers. A capital expenditure loan is used to pay off trade suppliers. People in ill health do not declare their medical problems on their insurance applications.

Exercise 6 What happens to the effective interest rate in the example of section 10.5.1 if the default probability rises from 0.01 to 0.02? To 0.05? What does this tell you about why banks typically avoid riskier deals?

Exercise 7 Suppose you are a banker who likes to lend at floating rates, and that you have a client who likes to borrow at fixed rates. What can you do for the client? Would the arrangement you come up with cost the client the same as your standard floating rate loan? Why or why not?

Exercise 8 Suppose you had to make a one year loan in a country where the rate of inflation was expected to be about 100 percent over the next year. How would you structure the loan arrangement to take care of the risk in charging an incorrect nominal rate?

Exercise 9 Suppose the interest on loans to farmers was not taxable in the hands of the lender. Would this make farm loans cheaper to farmers? Why or why not?

11 Market trading and intermediation

11.1	Types of markets		171
	11.1.1	Primary and secondary trading	172
	11.1.2	Public and private markets	172
	11.1.3	Dealers and brokers	174
11.2	Links between markets		175
	11.2.1	Securities trading	176
	11.2.2	Intermediation	177
11.3	Segmentation and externalities		178
	11.3.1	Causes of segmentation	179
	11.3.2	Allocative inefficiencies	179
	11.3.3	Consequences of segmentation	180
	11.3.4	Financial system externalities	181
11.4	Other relations		182
	11.4.1	Short term linkages	182
	11.4.2	Complementary governance	183
	11.4.3	Innovation and adaptation	184
11.5	Summary		185

LEARNING OBJECTIVES

After reading this chapter you will understand

- how securities markets trading produces information regarding securities value
- why some new securities issues are sold in public markets, others in private markets
- the economically important differences between dealers and brokers
- how and why some financial markets are linked by arbitraging and other forms of trading
- how and why other financial markets are linked by the operations of financial intermediaries
- why some markets remain segmented

As Chapters 8 through 10 explained, financiers accept the kinds of deals on which they can turn a profit. Deals can be maximally profitable only if they are governed as cost-effectively as possible. In operations characterised by scale economies, scope economies, or both, financiers can often reduce the unit costs of deals by specialising their activities. The resulting specialisation means the financial system is made up of particular kinds of markets and particular kinds of intermediaries. Specialisation does not mean that the parts of a financial system normally develop in isolation from each other. Typically, in a well-functioning financial system the interest rates on specialised deals are related, either by securities trading, the most important type of which is arbitraging,[1] or by intermediation. It is only when these two kinds of linkages are impaired that some parts of the financial system are segmented.

Segmentation occurs because linkages are inhibited – by high transactions costs, by differing expectations, and by lack of knowledge. But segmentation often contains the seeds of its own destruction: the very impediments that create segmentation can present profit opportunities to financiers who can find ways of overcoming them. For example, the junk bond market evolved as a way of mobilising institutional funds for investment in high risk bonds, as Chapter 12 will explain further. If new forms of transactions can be developed, funds can be moved from low yield opportunities to higher yield ones without a commensurate increase in risk. As and when these opportunities are discovered agents will profit, and existing forms of segmentation will weaken or disappear. In cases where the impediments cannot be overcome, markets remain segmented and interest differentials persist.

11.1 TYPES OF MARKETS

Specialised financial markets perform specialised economic roles, and the manner in which different markets are organised reflects these underlying economic differences. Economically significant differences among deals include whether they are primary or secondary market transactions and whether they are public or private market transactions. Thus, the markets in which primary deals are effected operate differently from those which specialise in secondary trading. Similarly, the brokers and the dealers in these markets play different facilitative roles.

11.1.1 Primary and secondary trading

Primary market agents are concerned mainly with raising new funds, and depend on an effective distribution network to do so successfully. Firms which are successful in capturing primary issue business are those which can effectively manage the costs of searching for securities purchasers. Secondary market agents are concerned mainly with effecting trades at or near existing market prices, functions which depend largely on the agents' ability to find counterparties quickly and relatively cheaply. Successful secondary market firms are those which can find counterparties readily and still manage their trading costs effectively.

Securities firms frequently combine their underwriting (primary market) and trading (secondary market) activity. The combination allows them to realise scope economies deriving largely from the two functions' using a common research department and a common securities sales staff. Nevertheless, the underwriting and trading functions are often organised as separate profit units within the same firm. Each activity requires its own expertise, its own forms of management, and its own incentive structure.

11.1.2 Public and private markets

Primary **public market** issues of securities are sold to large numbers of purchasers who have potentially equal access to public information regarding the issuing firms. Underwriters usually distribute information about new public issues as widely as possible, both to attract investors and to comply with disclosure regulations. In contrast, primary **private market** issues are sold to a smaller number of possible investors. The information produced for analysing and selling private issues is not usually released to the public at large. There is no particular need to inform a wide group of potential investors since private market issues are usually sold to relatively small numbers of sophisticated parties. In addition, such deals are not usually subject to the same disclosure regulations as public issues.

> **public markets** securities markets in which large well-known issues are both floated for the first time and traded after their original flotation. Information about the nature of public market securities is usually widely and relatively evenly distributed. The New York Stock Exchange and the London Stock Exchange are examples of public markets.

private markets markets in which securities are traded between a small number of parties on the basis of information developed in their negotiations with each other. Thus information about private market transactions is usually less widely distributed than it is for public market transactions. A negotiated sale of company debt to a pension fund which buys the whole issue is an example of a private market transaction.

With regard to primary issues, public and private markets differ in the screening arrangements they employ. Assessing the underwriting risks of a public market issue usually involves determining whether a sufficient number of securities purchasers can be attracted to the new issue, and setting a price at which they are likely to be attracted. For example, if a bond issuer is widely known to a large prospective group of purchasers, it is quite likely that a public issue will prove successful at raising the needed funds at or near market rates of interest. On the other hand, the underwriting risk of a private market issue is usually more closely related to its investment risk, because the underwriter needs to find particular clients who will be willing to buy and hold the issue. Thus private issues permit more intensive screening, but possibly require longer negotiations, than their public market counterparts. For example, a less well known firm will be more likely to use a private rather than a public issue because the deal can be examined in detail by one or a few prospective buyers.

Many securities firms underwrite both public and private market transactions, but often have different specialist groups within the firm to attend to the two separate functions. When they can do so, clients choose between public and private market deals on the basis of cost and funding availability. The costs of a public market issue are mainly placement costs, including underwriting commissions, and the costs of information distribution. In addition, using a public issue means the securities will subsequently trade in the secondary market, and if this trading is active, it will price new information about the issuing firm. The possibility of subsequent secondary market trading enhances the issue's liquidity, and can therefore make it easier to sell the securities in the first place.

The disclosure requirements governing primary public issues are satisfied by issuing a prospectus which attempts to ensure that all potential buyers have the same relevant information concerning the deal. Typically, disclosure regulations require that the prospectus stipulate the securities' terms and state how the funds raised will be put to work. The prospectus usually indicates key information about the issuing firm's business plans. Meeting disclosure requirements usually involves a relatively large fixed cost, and public issues are therefore only economic if they exceed a certain minimum size. Private market deals are not subject to disclosure requirements, and therefore fixed issue costs are typically lower.

Some clients also prefer private issues as a way of simultaneously revealing more information to financiers, less to competitors. First, financiers can utilise more intensive forms of screening than is possible with public issues, because with a private issue financiers can enter individual, detailed negotiations with the client. Second, since only there is less chance of business plans becoming public knowledge and being used to advantage by competitors.

11.1.3 Dealers and brokers

The economic function of a **broker** is to find a counterparty for a deal; that is, to provide an information service. A **dealer**'s function is to provide immediacy of transaction services by taking an inventory position in the securities being traded. A broker's competitive advantage rests on an ability to find counterparties quickly, while a dealer's competitive advantage rests on an ability to provide quick trading at close to market prices.

> **brokers** securities firms that act as agents of others in buying and selling such items as financial instruments. Brokers, unlike dealers, do not trade on their own account. Rather, they act only to arrange transactions between parties.

> **dealers** securities firms that trade on their own account, taking securities purchases into inventory, selling securities out of inventory.

The main economic difference between deals handled by brokers and those consummated by dealers lies in the transaction's inventory risk as judged in relation to its expected profitability. The ratio of inventory risk to expected trading profits is smaller for transactions handled by dealers than it is for transactions handled by brokers. For example, government bonds have a relatively low inventory risk (over the length of time the dealer typically holds the bond in inventory) relative to trading commissions, even though the latter are also low on a per unit basis. On the other hand, since a residential property has a relatively high inventory risk in relation to typical real estate commissions, houses are almost always handled by (real estate) brokers rather than by dealers.

A major securities firm may act as a broker in trading some securities and as a dealer in trading others. The two functions are combined within the same firm when there are scope economies to performing the two functions. The securities handled by dealers are a relatively homogeneous and actively traded class of instruments, while the securities handled by brokers tend to trade less actively and to be more heterogeneous in quality. Markets with a preponderance of brokered transactions can exhibit more segmentation than markets with a preponderance of dealer transactions, largely because there may be less active trading when the market agents do not take inventory positions. However, if brokered markets are sufficiently active, these potential segmentation problems may not arise.

The economic difference between brokers and dealers is well illustrated by foreign exchange trading. Under normal conditions, foreign exchange traders act as dealers in forward contracts. Under unusual conditions, say when traders believe a country's currency to be under such pressure that a sharp decline in market prices might be imminent, the ratio of inventory risk to normal commission increases. Traders initially respond to the increased risk by widening their **bid-ask spreads** on forward foreign exchange contracts. If the uncertainty continues to increase, traders become unwilling to take positions in forward (and sometimes even in spot) contracts. In extreme circumstances, they may be willing to trade only on a brokered basis. If the risk is later reduced to a level the traders regard as normal, they will resume active dealing.[2]

---

bid-ask spread the difference between the price a dealer will pay to buy a security (the bid) and the price the dealer charges (the ask) when selling it. The difference covers the dealer's operating expenses and any profits to the transaction.

11.2 LINKS BETWEEN MARKETS

Markets exhibit both superficial and fundamental differences. Much popular discussion emphasises superficial differences at the cost of paying too little attention to more significant differences in economic function. For example, many discussions of money markets devote considerable attention to such matters as the differences between such instruments as **commercial paper** and **finance company paper**. But, the name of the financial instrument is less important than its economic characteristics. Commercial and finance company paper are both highly standardised short term investments about which opinion regarding quality differs minutely, if at all. Since the money market is principally a market for reallocating highly liquid funds on a short term basis, money market instruments of all types differ little in their fundamental economic characteristics.

---

finance company paper a short term promissory note, issued in a large amount and sold in the money market on a discount basis by a highly creditworthy financial corporation, such as an automobile finance company.

In contrast to the money markets, the secondary market for the loan portfolio of a failing bank is an example of a market which is inactive. In such a market, detailed negotiations may become a necessary prerequisite to trading, mainly because market agents may have very large differences of opinion regarding the value of any securities offered for trade. Deals in such a market present a high degree of uncertainty. The instrument to be traded is illiquid, and market prices on related transactions are not always kept in line by arbitrage. There will likely be few potential purchasers, and transactions are likely to be infrequent. For all these reasons, this particular market is functionally different from the money market.

11.2.1 Securities trading

The **efficient markets hypothesis** introduced in Chapter 8 holds that when markets are perfectly competitive and trading is not impeded by transactions costs or institutional practices, securities will have equilibrium prices that fully reflect all publicly available information. The only real difference between instruments traded in efficient markets is in their risk–return characteristics.

In practice markets exhibit a number of economically important differences. The principal differences are volume and frequency of trading, the degree to which agents doing deals either have or will be able to acquire the same information, whether or not the instruments used are written according to an agreed standard, whether or not the instruments are guaranteed by a third party, and whether or not the arrangement can be said to represent a complete contract. All these differences can affect the degree to which prices will reflect available information. For example, even if the market for a certain class of business loans is served by many competing banks, a business may not know whether it is obtaining a loan at a competitive interest rate. The business is likely to have negotiated with only one or possibly a few banks, and the information exchanged in the negotiations is private rather than public. As a second example, a new type of derivative may present pricing problems that have not previously been solved, and as a result the financiers doing the deal may not, at least initially, have the technical knowledge to determine a competitive price or interest rate for it. Finally if markets are less than perfectly competitive, or if transactions costs are relatively high, arbitrage-based trading can be impeded and realised prices may deviate from the kinds of patterns discussed in Chapters 6 and 7.

Market trading is most active when deal terms are standardised and when agents have ready access to the same information. As Chapter 7 showed, prices or interest rates on instruments which are close substitutes are likely to be very closely related whenever there is active trading. In such cases the markets are said to be linked. The commercial and finance company paper of the previous section are close substitutes which trade in active and closely linked markets. It follows that the interest rates on these two instruments would normally be kept closely in line with each other. Any persistent differences between them would be attributable to a market consensus regarding differences in the instruments' risk.

Positive transactions costs do not necessarily destroy arbitraging relationships, although they are likely to modify the patterns that would result from costless arbitrage. For example, much effort has been devoted to testing derivative securities pricing theories, and when transactions costs have been taken into account the theories give relatively good predictions of prices for the most actively traded derivatives. 'The empirical evidence on the pricing efficiency of the stock options market suggests that, after considering transactions costs, the market appears to be efficient' (Fabozzi and Modigliani 1992: 291). Nevertheless, if transactions costs become sufficiently high price relationships can be destroyed. For example, derivatives trading in relatively thin markets will not necessarily conform to the relations predicted by a pricing theory which assumes highly active and highly competitive markets.

Transactions costs are not the only impediment to attaining an equilibrium in which no arbitrage profits can be made. Trading can be impeded if agents do not have access to the same information.Trading in a given market will be more costly if the instruments are not all written according to an agreed standard. Trading can be hampered if the counterparties are unknown to each other and the instruments are not guaranteed by a third party. Finally, instruments representing incomplete contracts are much more difficult to trade than instruments representing complete contracts.

There is usually active trading, including arbitrage, among instruments that are close substitutes. However, trading among complementary securities is usually less active. For example, there is usually active arbitraging among different money market instruments, as well as among government securities of different maturities, but relatively little or no trading between government and corporate securities of similar maturities. Corporate securities are less liquid than governments, and there is usually less information regarding the creditworthiness of the corporations involved. Accordingly, interest rates on government and corporate securities markets are less closely related than interest rates on government securities of different maturities.

11.2.2 Intermediation

Whether trading between different financial markets is strong and active, or weak and impaired, another linkage also exists. Intermediaries' fund allocation procedures complement the effects of trading, keeping interest rates on different securities closer than they would otherwise be. Intermediaries raise funds in markets where they are relatively cheap, and reallocate the funds among competing investments as different profit opportunities arise, thus helping to drive risk–return relationships toward equilibrium levels. Trading is not well suited for transactions in which pooling of funds or information processing functions yield scale economies, but financial intermediaries can often perform such functions profitably. For example, intermediaries such as mutual funds pool the funds of many small savers and invest the funds on the basis of research information about investments that small savers could not gather on their own for the same unit costs.

As one instance of how intermediaries link markets, there is no direct trading between US Savings Bonds and residential mortgages, but savers will allocate their funds between US Savings Bonds and term deposits on the basis of relative interest rates. Hence if rates on US Savings Bonds rise, so must rates on term deposits if deposit intermediaries are to compete effectively for the funds. But a large proportion of term deposits is reinvested in mortgages, and in order to preserve their profit margins intermediaries will increase rates on mortgages as their deposit costs increase. Thus the fact that intermediary deposits compete with US Savings Bonds is sufficient to link the saving bond and mortgage markets, albeit indirectly.

11.3 SEGMENTATION AND EXTERNALITIES

When illiquidity, lack of information, and lack of technical knowledge inhibit the linkages just described, the resulting separation of financial markets is referred to as **segmentation**. Segmentation presents the possibility of carrying out the same transaction at different interest rates in different markets (after duly adjusting for such differences as risk, tax rates and maturity). That is, segmentation is indicated when instruments representing the same risk trade persistently at different rates of interest in different markets and the apparent anomalies cannot be explained on the basis of such institutional features as differing tax treatment or differing degrees of liquidity. A conclusion of segmentation should be reached with some care, however, since not every interest rate difference is evidence of it. For example, an interest rate may appear to be out of line if a reported figure is not properly adjusted to reflect differences in tax treatment. US municipal bonds appear to offer lower rates of return than comparably risky corporate bonds, but the bond interest on municipals is not treated as taxable income in the hands of the recipient, and when this is recognised the interest rates on the two instruments are usually comparable.

---

segmentation the partial separation of financial markets resulting in the same arrangements being available on different terms, especially different interest rates, in different markets.

Segmentation occurs if neither arbitrageurs nor intermediaries detect profit opportunities to linking markets. Either the existing opportunities are not perceived or financiers do not have the technical knowledge to eliminate them. Weak, transient forms of segmentation can be found in almost every financial market. In North America, they include situations in which the shares of small firms do not exhibit the same risk–return relationships as do the publicly traded shares of larger firms, although the evidence on this point is still regarded as controversial.

Strong and persistent examples of segmentation are difficult to find in sophisticated, highly developed economies, but segmentation can be of great importance in less developed countries. Some Asian financial markets exhibited a very strong form of segmentation prior to the 1970s when it was not possible to raise funds for agricultural projects yielding annual returns in excess of 40 percent, while export businesses yielding returns of less than 6 percent were readily able to obtain financing. The main reasons for this segmentation are attributed by McKinnon (1973) to a combination of inadequate geographical diffusion of financial services, and political conditions that enabled well-connected exporters to obtain funds more easily than could agricultural borrowers. Governance considerations strengthened the effects of segmentation. It was more difficult for banks to obtain credit information about rural borrowers than about well-known exporters, and the assets of the latter were usually more liquid than those of the former. For all of the foregoing reasons, potential agricultural investment projects faced more severe credit limitations than did such other businesses as the export trade.

11.3.1 Causes of segmentation

The chief causes of segmentation are transactions costs and informational differences among the parties to a transaction. Persistent segmentation is primarily due to an insufficient degree of trading or intermediation activity. Segmentation can also occur if a market is relatively small and financiers cannot serve it profitably at equilibrium interest rates, because they cannot spread the fixed costs of entering the market over a sufficiently large volume of deals. For example, if a market is small and if screening transactions is subject to scale economies, intermediaries may not find it profitable to develop the capability. Since new forms of transacting will develop quickly if they are seen to be profitable, segmentation can be attributed to a lack of profit opportunities. In some cases, transactions costs remain high enough to frustrate profitability because financiers lack the technical knowledge to reduce them. To the extent segmentation arises from not understanding how to use available technologies profitably, its effects may be mitigated by learning, although the process can be lengthy.

Regulation can contribute to segmentation, at least temporarily, by restricting the kinds of business that are permitted.[3] However, financiers are likely to find ways of circumventing regulations which attempt to limit profitable opportunities. The 1972 Winnipeg Agreement, which placed interest maxima on Canadian-dollar certificates of deposit (CDs) with one year or less to maturity, provides an example. Canadian banks seeking to raise deposits that would be used to fund profitable new loans circumvented the agreement by issuing 366 day CDs and CDs in US currency, neither of which was restricted by the agreeement.

11.3.2 Allocative inefficiencies

Segmentation creates a problem of allocative inefficiency. The prices of securities traded in allocatively efficient markets are closely related to each other, and have risk–return combinations which plot on or near the security market line. The same is not usually true of the less actively traded, smaller or **neglected shares**. Neglected shares is a term used to refer to shares whose **price–earnings ratios** are judged to be atypically low, given the degree of risk the share represents. Most neglected shares are issued by relatively small companies, and their low price–earnings ratios reflect a kind of market segmentation. The segmentation itself results from informational asymmetries stemming from a lack of institutional research, the lack reflecting both the typically small size of an issue and the infrequent trading in it (Arbel and Strebel 1983). Since it is uneconomic for most larger institutions to conduct research on small companies, the neglected share phenomenon is likely to persist, as discussed further in Chapter 12.

> **neglected shares** a term used to refer to shares whose **price–earnings ratios** are judged to be atypically low, given the degree of risk the share represents. Most neglected shares are issued by relatively small companies, and their low price–earnings ratios reflect a kind of market segmentation.

> **price–earnings ratio** a share will trade in the market at a price which is some multiple of its current earnings per share. For example, if a bank has current earnings per share of $5.00, its stock might trade at $30.00, in which case the price–earnings ratio would be 6. The share would also be said to trade at a multiple of six times earnings. A low price–earnings ratio may be taken by the market as an indication that a share's price is less than its expected earnings would warrant. Clearly, there is room for difference of interpretation since the price–earnings ratio is determined by current earnings, and since different analysts might well differ in their forecasts of the relation between current and future earnings.

11.3.3 Consequences of segmentation

Segmentation can present profit opportunities if ways can be found profitably to transfer funds from markets where they can be raised at relatively low costs to those markets where returns are relatively high (in relation to the risks involved). The new profit opportunities may be exploited by designing new securities issues, or through devising new kinds of intermediated or arbitraging transactions. The opportunities may have existed for some time without being perceived as profitable, or they might actually be new. New opportunities can stem either from new sources of information or from technological change that increases a transaction's net revenue. As and when they can exploit such opportunities, innovative agents are likely to earn above normal rates of return, at least temporarily. The innovators' actions are quite likely to be emulated by other financial agents, attracting competition. Should competition increase sufficiently, the original market segmentation will be ameliorated or even eliminated. The above-normal rates of return will persist only until the new business becomes competitive.

While financiers obviously have to detect the new opportunities before they can determine how to exploit them, the process is likely to eliminate segmentation as time passes. Financiers may learn to use new technologies, or to develop new forms of transaction information. For example, banks which traditionally handled only working capital loans had to learn new screening methods to assess and make cash flow loans. Should it not be possible to realise profits on private transactions between segmented markets, the segmentation will likely persist unless and until legislative action is taken to deal with it. However, as Chapter 19 points out, public sector intervention to deal with segmentation is rarely justified, and even when it is the form of intervention must be carefully designed to ensure its effectiveness.

11.3.4 Financial system externalities

A financial system's performance can be assessed from either a private or a societal point of view. The criteria of private cost and benefit are used to assess the private value of economic activity. The notion of a private optimum is interpreted to mean that the activity is pursued to the point at which privately determined marginal costs, as reflected in the prices of resources employed, rise to the point where they are just equal to privately determined marginal benefits,[4] as reflected in the prices charged for the activity's output. The criteria of social costs and benefits are used to reflect society's (possibly differing) assessment of the same activity. The notion of a social optimum is interpreted to mean that an activity is pursued until marginal social costs rise to the point that they just equal marginal social benefits.

It will not always be the case that marginal social benefits equal marginal social costs at the level of activity for which marginal private benefits equal marginal private costs. The term **externality** refers to the impact of an economic activity whose market prices, based on calculations of private cost and private benefit, do not fully reflect the activity's balance of social benefits and social costs.[5] For example, when the prices of goods or services are determined by market forces, the costs of resources used by firms may not fully reflect their social costs. Similarly, when goods or services are sold at market-determined prices, the private revenues firms realised may not equal the social value of the goods produced.

---

externality third party effect not reflected in the market price charged on a transaction. In the case of a financial system externality, the term refers to a third party effect not reflected in the interest rate charged on a financial arrangement.

While externalities are not ubiquitous, and while they are not always significant even when they do occur, there are some circumstances in which they can be important enough to merit remedial attention. In financial markets the most important instances of this type occur when social benefits go unrealised because the quantities of funds employed in particular kinds of deals are not large enough to yield the maximum available benefits to society. In these instances the amounts of funds exchanged are smaller than is socially optimal because it is unprofitable for private sector firms to consummate a socially optimal quantity of such deals.[6]

In developed economics it is not usually easy to find instances where externalities are present. Moreover even when externalities are present it may not be possible to find cost-effective ways of securing the social benefits that are currently being forgone. However, export credit insurance which has made possible larger export shipments offers one example of a situation where society may have benefited from intervention. Social benefits may well stem from the jobs created by expanding export-oriented businesses, but it is sometimes difficult or costly for an exporting firm to insure against default losses on international shipments made on credit. Exporters may need the credit to secure the business, but private sector insurance companies may regard it uneconomic to write the insurance. As Chapter 19 discusses, in these circumstances it may be desirable to use public sector intervention to increase the amount of insurance provided, because without it social benefits would be forgone.

11.4 OTHER RELATIONS

The interest rates on deals done in one part of the financial system are related to those on deals done in other parts. Relations among interest rates (after adjusting for any differences in their risk) on different deals are maintained by market forces, whose workings are reflected chiefly by changing patterns of funds flows among different parts of the system.

11.4.1 Short term linkages

Interest rates on securities that are close substitutes are related by arbitrage-based trading and by intermediary allocations. Both actions work to alter the prevailing pattern of financial flows as atypical interest rate differentials emerge. For example, suppose a given instrument currently offers a higher rate than do close substitutes. Then arbitrageurs, intermediaries or both will direct additional funds to purchasing the instrument, tending to raise its price and remove the emerging interest differential. If the differential is smaller than normal, the reverse will occur.

Both the magnitudes and the **interest elasticities** of the funds flows linking various sub-markets will depend on the profitability of arbitraging or intermediation activities. If neither form of activity is perceived as profitable, linking flows will be relatively small and respond sluggishly to atypical interest rate differentials, that is the flows will be interest inelastic. In extreme cases there may be no flow response at all, and markets will remain segmented. The variation in price–earnings ratios of shares with apparently equal risks offers an example. For example, price–earnings ratios in Japanese stock markets during the late 1980s were much higher than in the New York or London markets. While a number of factors contributed to this international difference in price–earnings ratios, one of them appeared to be a lack of securities market trading between Japan and other countries.[7]

---

interest elasticity a measure of the proportional change in the quantity of a transaction type that is attributable to a proportional change in the transaction's interest rate.

When the economics of a group of deals changes, the size and **interest elasticity** of linking flows will also change. In a developing financial system, the linking flows usually become larger, and more interest elastic, as the system develops. However, the time scale of these adjustments can differ importantly across the financial system. Interest rate or securities price responses to announcements through standard channels are rapid, but changes in practice regarding, say, the processing of small businesses' applications for credit can be much slower. Interest rate anomalies can persist for relatively long periods of time if their elimination would involve changing existing practices or establishing new forms of deals.

11.4.2 Complementary governance

Some deals use a combination of governance mechanisms. For example, the lead bank in a syndicated loan arrangement usually sells participations to other banks through private market negotiations. Typically, the purchasing banks do not screen the loan as intensively as the lead bank; sometimes, they may not screen it all. The loan governance that they would typically exercise is largely delegated to the syndicate's lead bank. To the extent that information production incurs fixed costs, this practice reduces the total costs of developing the information.

Asset securitisation combines both intermediation and market activity. Intermediary governance is involved in the original screening of the loans. Market governance is used when the new securities issued by the intermediary are sold to other financial institutions. The combination of governance methods represents a technological change in that intermediaries have become more nearly precise about which of their activities represent relatively important ways of adding value – screening and portfolio assembly – and which are less important – the process of raising funds to invest in the portfolio. Securitisation is still growing in popularity and its evolution toward a standard form of practice seems likely to continue for some time. It will likely remain popular so long as no large losses are incurred by buyers of the securities, but the regular recurrence of financial market cycles suggests that in any given market securitisation will eventually become so competitive that new securities issues will not always be rigorously screened by their institutional purchasers. At this point transaction losses will likely mount until there is a resulting cutback in the amount of securitisation taking place. Another potential problem is that originating banks capable of selling off default risks may pursue their screening activities less rigorously, thus contributing to the weakness of the securitised portfolio.

Reinsurance represents still another combination of intermediated and market transactions. In reinsurance transactions, intermediaries (insurance firms) originate insurance liabilities, which they then exchange (partially or wholly) through the reinsurance markets. The reinsurance markets are thus a sort of wholesale market in which relatively large liabilities are traded.

Finally, governance methods are combined when both internal and external financing is used. It has long been standard practice for financiers to invest funds in many kinds of projects only if the project's owners do so also. Perhaps the best known instance is the financial market's willingness to buy corporate debt only if the issuer has a sufficiently large amount of equity investment. The equity investment is intended to share the risks, to manage adverse incentives, and to obtain additional information about how project owners view the risks.

11.4.3 Innovation and adaptation

Financial system organisation adapts to economic change: new financial firms or markets evolve in response to changes in supply or demand conditions. For example, an increase in the number of high-technology firms seeking venture financing might encourage new venture capital firms to enter the business. The new entrants premise their entry decision on expected future profits, but may be unable to describe the profit opportunities in quantitative terms. Thus financial system change, while intendedly rational and based on anticipated net benefits of some kind, cannot be described completely without recognising how financiers attempt to take uncertainty into account.

In essence, financiers attempt to take uncertainty into account through experiments intended to help them understand the nature of new opportunities. Financiers differ in their abilities to estimate probabilities, to discern alternatives, to execute plans, and to adapt to change. Thus some financiers will experiment while others will not; both may be acting rationally according to their own assessments of uncertainty and their ability to cope with it. For example, some merchant bankers actively seek to arrange **leveraged buyouts**, including arranging **bridging finance** for mergers and acquisitions. They hope to be able to earn profits by doing the business, but will also acknowledge that for some types of deals there is little quantitative evidence to support the case for profitability.

leveraged buyout a takeover bid based on using substantial amounts of debt to finance the purchase of the target company's shares.

bridging finance the temporary financing provided to fund the purchase of the target company's shares until more permanent debt or equity financing can be arranged.

11.5 SUMMARY

This chapter discussed relations between markets, and some of the factors that inhibit these relations. It began by pointing out that specialised financial markets can exhibit important economic differences. Nevertheless, the interest rates in different specialised markets are linked by both trading and intermediation. These linking activities create the kinds of price patterns exhibited by the term structure, securities pricing theory, derivative securities pricing, and other financial market relations. However, despite the presence of well-known relationships, not all interest rates are closely linked. That is, financial systems also exhibit segmentation. The chapter explored the causes and consequences of segmentation, and discussed conditions under which profit-seeking activity tends to eliminate it. The chapter also discussed complementary governance as found, for example, in securitisation. Finally, some features of financial system adaptation were discussed.

REVIEW QUESTIONS

Exercise 1 Which two of the following three market transactions are fundamentally similar? Trading treasury bills. Making a venture investment. Conglomerate financing of a subsidiary.

Exercise 2 Why would informational differences inhibit arbitraging?

Exercise 3 Some intermediaries switch between investing in government bonds and in loans or mortgages. Is this an example of linking activity? Why or why not?

Exercise 4 Are neglected stocks an example of market segmentation? Why or why not?

Exercise 5 Suppose employment prospects might pick up if business could obtain more equity financing. Is this an example of an externality?

Exercise 6 Why do shares trade in a different market from treasury bills?

Exercise 7 Trading in the treasury bill market determines interest rates which can be used as proxies to a risk free rate. In what way do these rates affect share markets? (Hint: use the risk adjusted probabilities introduced in Chapters 6 and 7.)

Exercise 8 Based on your answer to Exercise 7, suppose interest rates rose sharply. Other things remaining unchanged, would you expect share prices to fall? Why or why not?

Exercise 9 It is possible to find instances of increases in interest rates followed almost immediately by increases in share prices. Why might this occur? Does it deny the linkage you established in Exercises 7 and 8?

Exercise 10 Some of the investment banking firms trading in derivatives are beginning to find their ability to take positions hampered by a lack of capital. Use the idea of asset securitisation to argue how they might overcome some effects of not having enough capital.

Exercise 11 Between what kinds of markets would you expect to find intermediary rather than trading links? Give two examples of intermediary links.

Exercise 12 Give an example of market segmentation. What would be needed, in your opinion, for you to be able to profit from removing the segmentation?

Exercise 13 Does market segmentation normally persist? Why or why not?

Exercise 14 Give an example of a situation in which the economy would benefit from more credit being provided.

Part III

Financial markets

This part uses the ideas of Part I and Part II to examine important economic similarities and differences among a financial system's principal markets. You have already learned that the economically important characteristics are not always the most frequently described features of markets. This part examines details of these functional differences as manifest in the most important kinds of financial markets. Chapter 12 examines domestic financial markets, Chapter 13 markets for risk trading and Chapter 14 examines international financial markets.

12 Domestic financial markets

12.1	Economics of financial markets		190
	12.1.1	Economics of market operations	190
	12.1.2	Economics of financial firms' operations	191
	12.1.3	Economics of information production	192
	12.1.4	Markets and efficiency	193
	12.1.5	Exchanges, networks and electronic trading	193
	12.1.6	Trends	194
12.2	Money market		195
	12.2.1	Types of transactions	195
	12.2.2	US treasury bills	196
	12.2.3	Commercial paper	196
	12.2.4	Bankers' acceptances	197
	12.2.5	Negotiable CDs	197
	12.2.6	Repurchase agreements	198
	12.2.7	Federal Funds market	198
12.3	Equity markets		198
	12.3.1	Importance and functions	199
	12.3.2	Institutional trading	200
	12.3.3	Small firm and neglected firm effects	203
12.4	Bond markets		203
	12.4.1	Differences between stocks and bonds	204
	12.4.2	Importance and functions	205
	12.4.3	Determinants of interest rate spreads	206
	12.4.4	High yield bonds	207
12.5	Mortgage markets		208
	12.5.1	Importance and functions	208
	12.5.2	Innovations	208
	12.5.3	Secondary markets	209
12.6	Summary		211

LEARNING OBJECTIVES

After reading this chapter you will understand

- why some financial markets witness a great deal of arbitraging activity, while others are much less active
- the nature of money markets and the instruments traded in them
- the nature of equity markets and the trading that they facilitate
- some of the differences between retail and institutional trading
- the principal differences between equities and bonds
- the nature of bond markets
- the main characteristics of mortgage markets, and the reasons individual mortgages do not trade actively
- how securitisation facilitates trading blocks of mortgages

12.1 ECONOMICS OF FINANCIAL MARKETS

The chapter discusses significant economic differences among the major domestic markets. Its purpose is not to develop a fully comprehensive list of traded securities, but to help you understand major features of the transactions carried out in four major types of domestic markets. The four types found in most developed financial systems are the money markets, the equity or stock markets, the bond markets and the mortgage markets. To discuss these markets' features, the chapter mainly uses examples from the United States. One reason for focusing on US transactions is that they are representive of most countries' domestic financial market activity. A second reason is that some of the US markets discussed are more fully developed than their counterparts in other countries, and thus serve as examples of the directions in which other countries' markets are likely to evolve.

Domestic financial markets facilitate both primary and secondary market activity. The most significant features of primary market activity, the considerations involved in arranging a deal, were discussed in Part II. Accordingly, this chapter focuses principally on secondary market trading and on market organisation. The next three sub-sections explain that domestic financial markets' specialised forms are determined chiefly by the economics of market operations, the economics of the firms operating in these markets, and the economics of information production.

12.1.1 Economics of market operations

Financial markets emerge because market agents profit from executing trades. Financial markets perform the valuable economic function of creating a central meeting place whose existence minimises the difficulty of finding a counterparty.

That is, a functioning marketplace makes it less time consuming and therefore less costly for potential buyers to find potential sellers, or vice versa. The more prominent the market, and the greater the variety of instruments traded in it, the lower search costs become, because larger markets attract greater numbers of potential counterparties.

If search costs are important in relation to the size of a transaction, the existence of a central meeting place gives its organisers a competitive advantage. So long as the market's members do not charge trading commissions that exceed search costs, parties seeking to trade will use the market's facilities. The bigger the market, the easier it will be to trade, and the more trades the market will attract. Market operating economics create a second tendency for a market to increase in size. The profits earned by a market's organisers increase with trading volume because trading members can either charge their clients trading commissions or profit on the difference between bid and ask prices even if commissions are not explicitly levied. At the same time, the costs of market operations are usually shared proportionately by the market's members. These costs usually have a fixed component so that members' unit trading costs fall with volume. In addition, operating costs can be further reduced if market agents standardise the terms of the instruments they will trade.

The market operating economics just discussed mean that established markets tend to be both large and specialised in form. But this means in turn that transactions which occur only in small volumes and require individual attention will be less easy, and more costly, to carry out. In some cases certain transactions cannot be consummated at all, a phenomenon known as market failure. Market failure occurs when any demand for a product or service cannot profitably be provided by suppliers, and as a result no suppliers attempt to serve the market.

12.1.2 Economics of financial firms' operations

Like the characteristics of financial markets, the size and nature of firms trading in the markets is determined by the firms' operating economics. Since banks and other intermediaries will be studied in Part IV, the economics of securities firms which carry out a large proportion of financial market trading will be discussed here.

Securities firms exhibit two dominant forms of organisation: either large and multipurpose, or small and specialised. Larger firms emerge because they can realise scale and scope economies through increasing the amounts and types of activities they conduct. Securities firms can realise scale economies in performing their research functions, as well as in their data processing and accounting activities. They can realise scope economies through combining such activities as underwriting on the one hand, and arranging mergers and acquisitions on the other. Large firms can also obtain benefits from diversification. For example, by combining retail and corporate sales, large firms may be able to improve the return–risk ratio of their earnings stream.

Many of the mergers of securities firms throughout the world can be explained principally in terms of the operating economics just outlined. Since the later 1980s, there has also been a worldwide trend toward combining commercial banks and securities firms. Banks' acquisitions of securities firms probably reflect the banks' hopes of penetrating new markets, of providing their corporate clients with a wider range of services, of realising scope economies in performing such activities as securitisation, and of reducing profit risk through diversification. Some other acquisitions appear to be based on the need for larger amounts of capital to fund underwriting and merger and acquisition activities. For example, a relatively large capital base can give a securities firm a competitive advantage in acting as lead underwriter for a new issue, or in arranging a **bought deal**.

> **bought deal** an outright purchase of a new issue of securities, which are then distributed from inventory by the securities firm arranging the deal.

12.1.3 Economics of information production

Securities firms develop research information used both for their own trading purposes and for selling to clients. The cost of producing research information probably has a fixed component, meaning that information production is subject to scale economies. The more deals of the same type for which information is produced, the lower its unit cost of production. In addition, the same information can often be sold to more than one client, increasing the revenue obtained from its production.

Research information affects the market value of securities, but not all traded securities receive the same degree of research attention. The amount of research conducted, and the revenue which can be derived from selling the research results, depend on both the kinds of securities traded and the clientele who would likely make use of the information. Information regarding traded instruments is produced only if its value at least equals its cost. The value of a particular kind of information may be less than its cost either because the information cannot be sold to produce much revenue or because the information can only be produced at relatively high cost. Value will be greater than cost in markets where securities information has a degree of heterogeneity and a number of trading agents who will benefit from reducing the heterogeneity.

Of the markets considered in this chapter, the most homogeneous instruments are traded on the money markets, while the most heterogeneous are originated in the primary mortgage markets. In markets such as the money markets, there is little uncertainty regarding the value of a particular instrument and additional research is unlikely to produce enough revenue to make its production profitable.

In markets where there is little trading, information might have large potential value for a few purchasers, but with just a few sales it is not always possible to recover the cost of producing the information. Most research capable of earning profits for its producers seems to be information about securities that are actively traded and about whose value there is some uncertainty which can profitably be dispelled by research.

12.1.4 Markets and efficiency

The larger securities markets are operationally efficient. Research on stock exchange operations shows that exchanges exhibit operating economies of scale (Tinic and West 1974). Other studies, by showing that typical transactions costs are greater in national markets with smaller volumes of activity, indirectly confirm that smaller exchanges have higher unit operating costs. For example, the transactions costs on a US$500,000 trade in the Australian national market are 0.80 percent, while on the UK and US national markets they are respectively 0.50 percent and 0.20 percent (Brinson and Carr 1989).

The larger and more active secondary securities markets are also allocatively efficient. They are capable of conducting both small or retail trades and large institutional trades at very nearly the same market prices. Since about 1960, financial institutions have accounted for increasingly larger proportions of securities trading, and from time to time observers have expressed concern as to whether the larger individual trades of institutions are compatible with retail trading in the same market. However, the most active securities markets can handle both institutional and retail trading without loss of allocative efficiency. For example, large institutions' trading does not appear to influence stock price variability (cf. Gemmill 1996).

12.1.5 Exchanges, networks and electronic trading

Securities are traded both on the organised stock exchanges and in the **over-the-counter (OTC) markets**. The two types of markets differ in their formal organisation, but currently the most fundamental difference between the stock exchanges and the OTC markets is that the former have specific locations while the latter operate as geographically dispersed networks. Most stock exchanges have a number of dealers, who compete to take positions in any stock or stocks they wish.[1] An OTC market may have either dealers or brokers in a given stock, depending on whether or not the stock is actively traded. The existence of dealers in OTC markets depends on the inventory risk–trading commission ratio for a typical transaction, as discussed in Chapter 11. The rapid growth of network trading indicates that electronic marketplaces can now provide strong competition for organised stock exchanges. Brokers who have bid and ask information from all network participants can sometimes effect trades quickly at or near market prices, even if the network has no established dealers in the stock.

> **over-the-counter (OTC) markets** markets for trading securities other than those listed on stock exchanges. In the OTC markets most transactions are carried out between clients and brokers over the telephone as opposed to a physical location like a stock exchange. Some OTC markets, such as NASDAQ (National Association of Securities Dealers Automated Quotation service) in the US, have trades, especially in the larger issues, conducted by dealers as well as by brokers.

Electronic equipment is coming into increasing use on both the organised exchanges and in the OTC markets. At first electronic equipment was used mainly for communications purposes, but it is increasingly being used for consummating the actual trading activity as well. For example, the OTC markets were traditionally based on telephone communication, but computer-based communication is increasingly and rapidly replacing the telephone. In both exchange and OTC trading, electronic access to a market is now available wherever the appropriate computer terminals are located. Some terminals are equipped to carry out trades, while others merely provide a price quotation service. Eventually, many investors may trade mainly from their homes or offices. In some markets, computer programs now match and consummate orders as well as serving as communications devices. Both uses of electronic equipment can be expected to continue to increase.

12.1.6 Trends

Since the 1960s the most important significant change in the secondary markets for shares has been the institutionalisation of investment. The emergence of institutional trading, the increasing competition brought by changing technology, along with pressure from regulatory authorities, has led to the elimination of fixed minimum commissions on major stock exchanges throughout the developed world.

At the same time, markets have become more integrated internationally, leading to greater international competition for the business of trading shares. For example, stock markets are increasingly linked both within and between countries, allowing members of one exchange automatically to route orders for cross-listed stocks to any other exchange on which the stocks trade. A trend toward 24-hour trading is also growing. As one example, Shearson Lehman/Amex has London offices which trade in stocks listed on major American exchanges. In 1986, the London International Stock Exchange opened a 24-hour trading market in both British and international equities, and many other securities markets have since made similar moves.

12.2 MONEY MARKET

The economic roles played by specialised domestic markets can be further explained by examining four main types of markets in greater detail. The most active and most highly integrated of the four markets, the **money market**, is a specialised market for trading short term, highly liquid instruments. Apart from a few minor exceptions, the similarities between the instruments traded in the money markets are economically more significant than their differences. Money market instruments conform to standard terms and are originated by very well-known credit risks such as a country's principal government or its largest corporations. The main participants in money market transactions are businesses, financial institutions, investment dealers and governments. These groups use the money markets chiefly for purposes of managing their cash flows over the short term.

---

money market   market for trading highly liquid, short term securities of high quality.

The money markets in most countries have a relatively small number of dealers who are well known to each other and who trade with each other over the telephone or using computer networks. In most developed economies the money markets are operationally and allocatively efficient. Interest rates on the different instruments traded are closely related by trading, much of it taking the form of arbitrage. The governance capabilities used for money market transactions are relatively minimal. A higher degree of governance capability would not prove cost-effective because of the nature of the instruments traded and the typically short term over which they are held.

The example of the US money market will be used to provide further details of typical activity. The US money market is probably the world's most highly developed, although those of Germany, Japan, the UK and many other developed countries are very similar in nature. The US money market plays several important roles. Open market purchases or sales of government treasury bills, the most prominent money market instrument, are the principal transaction used by the Federal Reserve System to implement domestic monetary policy. Second, the money market provides both government and large corporations with short term funds to finance their working capital needs. Third, since money market instruments are liquid and offer competitive interest rates, they are used to invest temporarily surplus funds.

12.2.1 Types of transactions

Money market deals are all close substitutes when regarded from the perspective of the entire financial system. All such deals involve trading short term instruments issued in large principal amounts. The instruments nearly all have maturities ranging from 1 to 180 days, although some instruments may extend for as long as a year.[2] Money market instruments either represent the obligations of highly creditworthy issuers or (in the case of bankers' acceptances) are guaranteed by them. They are usually issued in bearer form and sold on a discount basis. The instruments are all highly liquid and many are traded a number of times prior to maturity. Since there is active arbitrage between instruments, any persistent interest differentials can usually be explained by differences in the instruments' risks, their liquidity or their tax status.

US money market transactions involve US treasury bills, commercial paper, bankers' acceptances, negotiable certificates of deposit, repurchase agreements and federal funds. All these transactions are domestic: short term foreign currency instruments are usually regarded as trading in the foreign exchange markets discussed in Chapter 13.

12.2.2 US treasury bills

US treasury securities issued at a discount and having one year or less to maturity are called treasury bills. New issues of the bills are sold at auctions organised by the US Department of the Treasury, and subsequent secondary market sales of the bills are conducted by banks and investment banking firms called money market dealers. The auctions are held at regular intervals and amounts of the issue are awarded to the highest bidders. In the event of tied bids, amounts are allocated proportionally. The treasury uses a maximum or stop yield to determine the lowest price at which it will sell a given issue of bills. The US Federal Reserve System may bid for a part of any issue, and those bids are deducted from the issue before it is offered to the money market dealers. Treasury bills represent the greatest volume of money market trading, and are also the most liquid of the money market instruments.

12.2.3 Commercial paper

Commercial paper is issued to fund short term cash needs of non-financial corporations, financial corporations, municipalities or state governments. For entities with strong credit ratings, commercial paper and bankers' acceptances are alternatives to borrowing directly from banks. The choices are made on the basis of cost to the borrower. For entities with sufficiently high credit ratings, commercial paper will frequently be the most cost-effective form of raising short term funds. Commercial paper is also sometimes used by corporations as a form of bridge financing (i.e., for raising funds temporarily). In such cases the commercial paper issue will later be replaced by a longer term bond issue.

Since the US Securities and Exchange Commission (SEC) requires registration of paper with more than 270 days to maturity, and since complying with registration requirements is costly, most US issues are for maturities of 270 days or less. Some issuers of commercial paper use direct placements rather than selling the issue through a money market dealer; about 40 percent of all issues are now direct. The emergence of direct issues has dramatically reduced the fees formerly charged by money market dealers.

Commercial paper is a close, but not a perfect, substitute for a treasury bill. Thus interest rates on the two instruments follow the same pattern, but there is a positive spread between them. Part of the spread is due to differing liquidity, because, unlike treasury bills, there is relatively little secondary market activity in issues of commercial paper. Second and more importantly, the default risk on commercial paper is that of the issuing corporation. Since issuing corporations do not have the credit standing of the US government, rates on commercial paper are higher than on treasury bills. The size of the spread depends on the credit rating of the issuing corporation.

12.2.4 Bankers' acceptances

A bankers' acceptance is a short term promissory note issued and sold by a corporation on the strength of a bank guarantee. The guarantee, evidenced by a stamp on the instrument indicating the acceptance and the name of the bank guaranteeing payment of the instrument at maturity, enhances the marketability of the promissory note by substituting the credit rating of the accepting bank for that of the issuing corporation. That is, the default risk on a bankers' acceptance is that of the accepting bank, and spreads between rates on treasury bills and bankers' acceptances depend largely on the market's estimate of the bank's default risk. Bankers' acceptances are used in foreign trade, where they may be more acceptable to an exporter than the unguaranteed note of a foreign importer, and in raising funds domestically, when a corporation's credit standing is not widely known. Both investment bankers and commercial banks usually act as dealers in the secondary markets for bankers' acceptances.

12.2.5 Negotiable CDs

Negotiable certificates of deposit (CDs) are issued by banks or other depository institutions and payable to the bearer. Thus an original depositor of funds who needs cash before a negotiable CD comes due can sell it in the money market rather than pay the issuing institution a penalty to redeem it. Negotiable CDs were first issued in the 1960s and, because they offer deposit returns without the inconvenience of having to wait until maturity to realise the funds, greatly helped banks to raise additional money market funds. CDs are now issued on both fixed and floating rate terms, and within foreign as well as domestic money markets. For example, EuroCDs are US dollar CDs issued mainly in London by US, European, Japanese and Canadian banks. The default risk on CDs is determined by the perceived creditworthiness of the issuing bank.

Most negotiable CDs are attractive to banks, because they carry low or zero reserve requirements. Thus little or none of the funds raised through issuing negotiable CDs needs to be held as cash or low yield government securities, leaving all or nearly all of the funds raised available for investing in higher yield assets. On the other hand, in many jurisdictions negotiable CDs are not covered by deposit insurance, and thus present a credit risk to their holders that insured bank deposits do not present. To compensate for the credit risk, the yield on an uninsured negotiable CD would be higher than a yield on a similar insured negotiable CD, if such an instrument were available in the same market. Similarly, a negotiable CD would be less risky to its holder than a non-negotiable CD whose terms (including the provision of insurance) were otherwise the same. In this case, at time of issue the negotiable CD could be expected to offer a lower effective rate than its non-negotiable counterpart.

12.2.6 Repurchase agreements

A repurchase agreement is the sale of a security accompanied by a commitment from the seller to buy the security back at a specified price and on a specified date. A repurchase agreement is very similar to a collateralised loan, where the security serves as the collateral. Many different money market instruments may be used in repurchase agreements, but in most countries the principal activity is in government bonds.

Repurchase agreements are generally used by money market dealers for inventory financing purposes. The default risk on a repurchase agreement is not strictly that the seller will fail. Rather, it is that the seller will fail and the buyer of the securities will take some loss because in the event the seller defaults, proceeds from resale of the securities will not cover the amount originally paid to the defaulting seller.

12.2.7 Federal Funds market

Repurchase agreements principally help money market dealers, including banks, manage their inventory financing problems. The Federal Funds market further helps banks manage their cash reserve positions. As its name implies, the Federal Funds market is a market in which banks can lend or borrow reserve funds. The major money center banks are the typical users of Federal Funds, while banks in other centers are suppliers. The default risk in the Federal Funds market is that of the borrowing bank.

12.3 EQUITY MARKETS

The shares of public companies are traded in two principal types of equity markets: the organised exchanges and the OTC markets. Stock trading, whether on the exchanges or in the OTC markets, can be categorised as either retail or wholesale trading. Individuals and their agents trade relatively small amounts per transaction in the retail end of the market; financial institutions trade relatively large amounts in the wholesale end. In addition to the stock exchanges and OTC markets already mentioned,[3] the US has two other markets for institutional trading, known as the **third** and **fourth markets**.[4] Each of these types of markets is discussed in turn.

12.3.1 Importance and functions

Stock exchanges were the original public marketplaces for securities trading. Stock exchanges, organisations whose operating costs are borne by their members, originally emerged as a prominent place to locate counterparties. To promote its business, stock exchange rules require members to use the exchange's facilities when trading listed stocks. Before commissions on trades became negotiable, members were also required to charge their clients minimum commissions. The development of institutional trading in the US, and the minimum commission rules in force in that country prior to 1975, contributed to the development of the third and fourth markets, as will be discussed further below.

Most equity markets have designated dealers known as market makers, whose primary function is to promote secondary market trading. Market makers agree to fill any buy or sell orders submitted at current market prices, whether or not they know of a counterparty for the trade. In other words, one of the principal functions of a market maker is to provide liquidity. US stock exchanges normally have only one market maker (called a specialist) for a given share. Specialists are required by the rules of the exchange to complete orders by taking inventory positions in the stock or stocks for which they act as a market maker. On exchanges in other countries, and in the OTC markets of the US, market agents themselves determine, through competing with each other for the business, whether they wish to act as dealers.[5]

Large exchanges create active secondary markets which both improve the liquidity of the shares traded and value new information regarding the firms issuing the shares. Firms usually prefer to list their shares on the largest and most active exchange for which they can qualify. Information is usually capitalised very quickly on an active exchange, and the shares of large companies usually trade at relatively favourable prices in such an environment. However, listing requirements are also at their most rigorous on the largest and most active exchanges, reflecting attempts by the market's organisers to define minimum quality standards for the securities they will trade. Such standards reduce investors' screening costs, and thus increase trading activity and consequently the income of the exchange's members.

Shares floated in primary issues are usually not sold on North American exchanges, but are marketed separately in off-exchange transactions. The practice of floating new issues off-exchange was established to avoid the possibility that the issues' underwriters might try to manipulate secondary market prices during the flotation process, but it is not a practice that is generally maintained in the rest of the world.

Many stock exchanges, as well as futures exchanges and options exchanges in both the US and other countries, use a method of trading known as **open outcry**. Traders wishing to buy or sell exchange-listed instruments gather around a post on the exchange floor, shouting out and otherwise signalling the kinds of orders they wish to complete. In many markets screen trading and electronic trading systems are increasingly replacing open outcry methods, a change to which many proponents of open outcry methods are fiercely opposed. Supporters of the open outcry methods claim that the new screen trading is inferior to their older method, but the continuing adoption of computerised trading systems suggests that objections to the newer methods are being surmounted success-fully. Eventually, all markets are likely to be organised around computer networks, in which case open outcry methods will disappear completely.

---

open outcry a method of trading assets in which interested parties gather around a trading post to signal the terms on which they are willing to buy or sell. Much of the trading activity is carried out using hand and eye signals, often accompanied by a good deal of shouted commu-nication.

The original function of the OTC markets was to trade the stocks of compa-nies unable to meet the listing requirements of the exchanges. Other securities, such as bonds, are also traded in the OTC markets of the United States,[6] as will be discussed below. The main OTC market in the US now uses an elec-tronic price quotation service known as NASDAQ (National Association of Securities Dealers Automatic Quotation service). NASDAQ prices are quoted by dealers, and brokers can negotiate with dealers on behalf of customers. While many OTC deals are still done over the telephone, NASDAQ also uses screen-based trading systems. NASDAQ provides strong competition for exchange trading, and a substantial proportion of listed stocks are now traded on NASDAQ as well. Some companies have even cancelled their exchange listings, and now trade their shares exclusively in the OTC market.

12.3.2 Institutional trading

Since the 1960s, institutions have become the major participants in the securi-ties markets, and market operations have evolved to accommodate institutional trading needs. Much institutional trading takes place in the so-called **upstairs market**, a network of telephone and computer links between the principal traders. Independent systems such as INSTINET (a system for executing large institutional trades) and POSIT (portfolio system for institutional investors) carry out stock trading directly between institutions without using any inter-vening third party. While many OTC deals are still done over the telephone, INSTINET offers screen-based dealing systems with updated market informa-tion, automatic execution of deals up to 1,000 shares, and on-screen negotiation for larger deals. INSTINET presently quotes over 1,700 listed stocks, over 3,000 OTC stocks, and also some stock and currency options.

> **upstairs market** a network of trading arrangements between major securities firms and institutional investors, communicating with each other by telephone and electronic display systems, designed to facilitate trading in large amounts of individual shares or simultaneous trading in large numbers of different shares.

Institutions typically trade in large amounts and in large numbers of shares. Many of their transactions are **block trades** in which 10,000 or more shares are exchanged in a single deal. The **third markets** and **fourth markets** are specialised facilities in which institutions trade blocks among themselves. Third market trading is usually effected by dealers known as **position houses**, while fourth market trading is usually carried out directly between institutions, often with the help of an agent acting as a broker to find counterparties. The third and fourth markets compete both with each other and with the stock exchanges for institutional trades. The third market poses a particular threat because it facilitates institutional trades conducted after exchange closing hours and when trading in a given stock has been suspended by an exchange.

> **block trades** trades in large numbers of shares, usually defined as single trades of 10,000 or more shares.

> **third market** a specialised facility in which institutions trade large blocks of stock between themselves through dealers known as position houses.

> **fourth market** a broker facility used for inter-institutional trading of large blocks of stock.

> **position house (block positioner)** wholesale dealer in securities, specialising in institutional trading of large amounts.

The position houses which normally handle block trades emerged in the late 1960s and early 1970s. Position houses were not exchange members and were therefore able to waive the minimum commissions that exchange members were then required to levy, even on very large trades. The position houses instead profited on the spreads at which they bought and sold shares for their institutional clients. Minimum commissions were abolished in the US in 1975, but position houses have continued to flourish despite this change. Part of the position houses' current competitive strength derives from the fact that a stock exchange specialist's capital is not always sufficient to finance a block trade. The typically greater capital of a position house means it can more readily take some or all of a block into its inventory, and may therefore be able to offer faster execution at or near the prevailing market price.

The price of a block traded in the upstairs market can differ from the current exchange price for the same shares. For example, while a specialist on a US stock exchange usually takes any amount offered to her (up to a certain prespec- ified limit) at the buying (selling) price she posts, a dealer in the upstairs market will typically negotiate the price at which a block is purchased or sold. However, any such price differences normally persist for only a very short time. As would be expected in an allocatively efficient market, if the exchange prices estab- lished by the specialist and the prices at which institutions trade differ, arbitrage will occur until they are brought back into line.

The block positioners currently operating in the US upstairs market claim to smooth out price fluctuations that would otherwise occur when relatively large amounts of shares are traded. Indeed, market makers are said to prefer dealing in cities such as New York and London where institutional arrangements make it easier to negotiate without revealing the extent of their intentions (Fabozzi *et al.* 1994: 393–394). Indeed, dealers on the London Stock Exchange who specialise in executing institutional trades claim it can be to their disadvantage to reveal the full size of an order. According to Gemmill (1996), London dealers are 'vehement' in their desire to delay the publication of prices for block trades, arguing that it is not in the London marketmakers' interest to encourage the development of a US-like upstairs (auction) market.

However, the importance of this argument is called into question by Gemmill's study of trading data from the London Stock Exchange. Gemmill finds that 'delaying publication does not affect the time taken by prices to reach a new level, which is rapid under all regimes. Spreads differ across years, but their size relates more closely to market volatility than to speed of publication' (1996: 1765). Moreover, the different forms of organising the larger institutional trades do not appear to have significant effects on the markets' allocative efficiency: 'the different market structures – upstairs trading of blocks on the New York Stock Exchange and competitive dealership on the London Stock Exchange – lead to surprisingly similar outcomes' (Gemmill 1996: 1788)

Larger institutions also trade simultaneously in large numbers of different shares, an activity known as **program trading**. Program trading is used to implement investment strategies, such as creating index portfolios, and to perform index arbitraging between the stock and stock index futures markets. Program trading originally came into favour for theoretical reasons. In an allocatively efficient market, theory suggests it will be difficult for portfolio managers to outperform the investment returns on an index portfolio. Studies of portfolio performance confirm the theoretical predictions. For example, when well-diversified portfolios' returns are adjusted for risk and for transactions costs, they do not generally outperform the market (Malkiel 1995).[7]

---

program trading using computers for automated portfolio trading. Usually large numbers of stocks are traded both simultaneously and frequently.

Although it has frequently been suggested that program trading can contribute to volatility, both theory and research question the observation. On a theoretical basis, if program trading were to create predictable price differences between the stock and derivatives markets, it is highly likely that arbitraging would spring up and eliminate the patterns. If this kind of arbitraging were to damp the possibility of cycles or of emerging price differences, volatility should not increase. For example, Santoni (1987) finds little or no evidence of volatility increases from program trading. On the other hand, since program trading largely involves synthetic portfolios, there is a possibility that it might inhibit information-based trading in the underlying securities, thus reducing information-based trading and possibly increasing volatility (Grossman 1988a, 1988b). Again however, if such effects were systematic, it might be expected that arbitraging would eliminate them.

12.3.3 Small firm and neglected firm effects

The shares of small firms, the shares of firms neglected by analysts, and shares with low price–earnings ratios all seem capable of outperforming the returns on shares of larger firms with comparable risks.[8] One possible explanation of these effects is that institutions find it cost-effective to trade only in the larger issues. To save on transactions costs, institutions typically buy or sell in large amounts, as already discussed. Institutions are less willing to invest in small issues, because blocks of small companies' shares are less liquid than those of larger companies. Since institutions screen only the issues they regard as potentially suitable for investment, there is more institutional research available regarding the performance of the larger companies. Thus the prices of larger issues are more likely to reflect fundamental value as revealed by this information.

A second possible explanation of small firm effects is that investment strategies sometimes have a faddish component, and some firms may be unpopular for a time. The two explanations are not conflicting, but the first provides economic reasons for neglecting to analyse some firms, while the second does not.

12.4 BOND MARKETS

This section first discusses the conceptual differences between stocks and bonds. It then examines the nature and importance of the bond markets, and the interest rate spreads in them.

12.4.1 Differences between stocks and bonds

Bonds convey a priority claim on value, whereas stocks convey a residual claim. To see why bonds are normally regarded as less risky than stocks issued by the same firm, suppose as in Table 12.1 that one period hence a firm could have two possible amounts of funds available to pay off bondholders and stockholders (for simplicity, assume the firm is to be wound up at the end of the arrangement). The two different possible values, only one of which will actually be realised, are shown in the right-hand column of the example. The first line of numbers represents best case earnings, in which the cash available to pay all security holders is 30. The second line of numbers represents worst case earnings in which the cash available is only 10. Only one situation (one row) can actually obtain, but when agents contemplate the future they recognise that either of the two possible scenarios might be realised.

The main difference between bonds and stocks is that bonds get first claim on funds up to a certain amount (equal to 8 and representing both principal and interest in the example), while stockholders are entitled to the funds remaining after the debtholders are paid. In this sense you can think of bonds as being designed principally to avoid downside risk, stocks to take advantage of upside potential.

By changing Table 12.1 to reflect a different situation, it is also possible to show why bondholders sometimes ask for more equity (more investment by stockholders) as a condition for buying the bonds. Suppose the amount of debt previously considered was issued by a firm whose possible earnings were as shown in Table 12.2, and bear in mind that bondholders suffer if they are not paid in full. If the cash available is only 6, it will all be paid to the bondholders, but the rest of their debt will have to be written off because the firm has no other resources. Many bondholders would not find this arrangement attractive. They might, for example, find it difficult to assess the legal and other costs, including waiting to recover their funds, of not being paid in full. That is, potential bond buyers might well prefer to avoid any consequences of a possible writeoff, and place an upper limit of 6 (principal and interest) on the debt they would be willing to purchase. If the client asked for 8 as in the first case, the potential bond purchasers might respond with 'you need more equity', meaning that the proposal to invest the present value of the promised repayment of 8 was too risky for the bondholders, and that the bondholders would expect the shareholders to put up the rest of the needed funds.[9]

Table 12.1 Claims of debtholders and stockholders (first example)

Possible outcomes	Funds available for payment to security holders	To debtholders (first priority, limited claim of 8)	To stockholders (second priority, all remaining funds)
High earnings	30	8	22
Low earnings	10	8	2

Table 12.2 Claims of debtholders and stockholders (second example)

Possible outcomes	Funds available for payment to security holders	To debtholders (first priority, limited claim of 8)	To stockholders (second priority, all remaining funds)
Best case	30	8	22
Worst case	6	6	0

In practice, corporations also issue such hybrid instruments as preferred shares. These kinds of securities represent a mix of the instruments already discussed rather than a completely new type of claim. For example, a corporation may issue bonds, common shares and preferred shares. The preferred share has a claim to income that is junior to the claim of bondholders but senior to that of ordinary common shares. In the event of liquidation, the preferred share will have a claim on assets junior to that of the bondholders, but senior to that of the ordinary common shares. Hybrids are used principally when different groups of potential investors seek securities that are relatively finely tailored to the investors' individual needs, in much the same way that shareholders are usually more eager to purchase securities offering relatively large rewards, while bondholders are usually more eager to purchase securities offering relatively safe returns.

12.4.2 Importance and functions

Bond markets are composed of government and corporate sub-markets. After discussing the two markets' general features, each is examined separately. As with the money and stock markets, further information about the bond markets is developed using the United States as an example. New issues of bills and bonds are sold by the US Treasury in amounts determined by the government's financing needs. In the US, bonds are usually traded in OTC markets rather than on exchanges, but in the UK gilts are typically traded on the stock exchange. The trading is done chiefly by securities firms which act as dealers in government bonds, and as dealers or brokers in corporate bonds. The choice between acting as a dealer or a broker is made according to the ratio of inventory risk to typical trading profits, as discussed earlier. Most bonds are bought by financial institutions, although individuals can be relatively important purchasers, especially of government issues.

Corporate bonds are also traded over the counter, but the corporate markets are not usually as active as those for government securities. The difference stems mainly from the fact that corporate bonds are issued in smaller amounts and vary considerably more widely in quality. In order to enhance marketability, many companies pay to have their bond issues rated by an independent agency. Both Moody's and Standard and Poor's, the largest bond rating agencies in the United States, estimate creditworthiness in terms of how likely the firm is to default and the protection, if any, that creditors have in that event. Both agencies use letter grade systems to indicate their estimates of creditworthiness.[10]

Corporate bonds are sold both through private placements and through public offerings; the proportion of funds raised through public offerings peaks more or less with the business cycle. The ratio of private placements to public offerings has increased since 1990 as a result of regulatory changes in the US Securities and Exchange Commission's rule 144a, which permits privately placed issues to be resold to institutions without registration of the primary issue.

The markets for most bond issues are very much less active than their money market counterparts. There is less activity in bonds because the instruments offer a very much wider range of qualities than do money market instruments. The wide range of qualities, plus the fact that individual issues are frequently for relatively small amounts, tend to make information production somewhat uneconomic, and the lack of available information further inhibits trading activity.

12.4.3 Determinants of interest rate spreads

The principle of pricing by arbitrage establishes that interest rates on instruments of the same quality and terms will be equalised by profit-oriented trading. Thus any persistent differences between, say, government and corporate bonds need to be explained using differences in risk or differences in the details of an issue's terms. Insofar as risk is concerned, default risk is almost always greater for domestic corporate issues than for domestic government issues. The lower a bond's quality rating, the greater the spread between it and a government security of comparable maturity and coupon is likely to be.

Call risk refers to the possibility, reflected in a bond's terms, that it may be redeemed prior to maturity. The effective yield on a callable bond will be higher than the effective yield on a comparable non-callable bond, because the firm has an option to redeem the bond should interest rates fall relative to the rate the issue promises. A callable bond presents its purchasers with the possibility of facing a reinvestment risk as and when the issuing firm exercises the call privilege, and investors require to be compensated for the risk. Thus if two bonds are issued on the same terms, apart from one having a call feature that the other does not, the effective yield on the bond with the call feature is likely to be higher to compensate for the reinvestment risk.

Marketability risk refers to the possibility that dealers may not be willing to provide continuous quotes for an issue. This risk will be especially prominent in cases where bonds are redeemed partially prior to maturity, say through a form of **serial redemption**.

> **serial redemption bonds** bonds whose terms provide that a certain number of the issue will be redeemed at regular intervals. The bonds to be redeemed are chosen by either selecting their serial numbers in a lottery or simply buying the bonds in the market.

A corporation or junior government planning to retire a bond issue serially may set up a fund, called a **sinking fund**, to provide for repayment of the issue. The serial retirement will impair marketability, but the existence of a sinking fund may enhance the bond's quality. Quality will also be enhanced if a sinking fund is set up, not to finance serial retirement, but simply to provide funds for retiring bonds at their maturity.

---

sinking fund bonds bonds issued on terms which provide for gradually building up a repayment fund, called a sinking fund, to finance retirement of the bonds. The bonds may be retired either all at once or serially at several points in time.

Event risk refers to such possibilities as industrial accidents or takeover actions. The more likely is event risk, the greater the spread between the bond in question and comparable issues not subject to the same risks.

12.4.4 High yield bonds

The late 1980s boom in leveraged takeovers of public companies greatly increased the popularity of negotiated financings, especially those using high yield or junk bonds (bonds whose quality ratings are Standard and Poor's BB or below; Moody's Ba or below). The amount of junk bonds outstanding in the US increased from US$20 billion in 1977 to about US$240 billion in 1990 (Fabozzi *et al.* 1994: 429). This huge increase in popularity reflects the importance of junk bonds as a financial innovation. Essentially, the bonds represented a new way of channelling institutional funds to corporations which had previously relied principally on bank borrowing or privately negotiated financings. Institutions were willing to purchase junk bonds because studies suggested that the risk premium on a diversified portfolio of junk bonds more than offset the increased risk of holding them.[11] Junk bond financing is cheaper than bank debt for some corporations, and it is also advantageous because it is typically longer term than the bank borrowings.

Like many other financial innovations, the junk bond market's development led to a mix of effects. The development presented profit opportunities for innovators, increased the financial markets' allocative efficiency, and at the same time created its own set of new problems. So much junk bond financing was used during the 1980s that firms became over-levered and vulnerable to cyclical declines in their profitability. This in turn led to an increase in the rate of defaults on junk bonds, and as the defaults increased the bonds became very much less popular, and new issues declined precipitously. With the passage of time, a more balanced point of view has come to prevail – high yield bonds present higher than normal risks, but when used judiciously they do not need to create extraordinary risks – and junk bond activity is again on the increase.

12.5 MORTGAGE MARKETS

This section discusses the importance and functions of both the residential mortgage markets and the institutionally operated markets in which blocks of mortgages are traded. The former are private markets in which individual mortgage loans are arranged between an intermediary and a client. The latter encompass both public and private market securities issues, designed to appeal to institutional investors and collateralised by blocks of outstanding mortgages.

12.5.1 Importance and functions

Consumers use mortgage loans to finance construction, purchases, extensions or improvements of their primary residences. Most mortgage borrowing is to finance investment in the residence itself, although consumers also borrow against their homes to finance the purchase of summer cottages or to invest in rental housing. Even mortgage loans to finance consumption can be found. While the latter are now uncommon, they may become less so, especially in the form of the reverse discussed below, as an ageing population seeks new sources of retirement financing. An equity position in a home is the largest investment most households have, and it offers possibilities for sizeable capital gains or losses. Calculated comprehensively, the returns include shelter service, security of tenure, and capital gains or losses.

Most lenders require individual mortgages to be insured against default. This provision reduces the lender's risk and also makes it easier to securitise a portfolio of mortgage loans, as discussed below. Since the mid-1940s, the North American mortgage loan market has seen depository institutions replace insurance companies as the principal providers of mortgage funds, and the principal suppliers of mortgages are now banks and other depository institutions.

12.5.2 Innovations

During the 1980s the traditional level payment, fixed rate forms of mortgages created problems for both borrowers and lenders. During an inflationary period, interest rates rise. Insofar as borrowers were concerned, fixed rate mortgages made at relatively high interest rates accelerate the rate at which purchasers build up equity in their home during the early years of the mortgage, as shown in Table 12.3. As interest rates rise, mortgage payments rise at a much more rapid rate, and this change in the terms of mortgages can present fairly serious cash flow problems for both new borrowers and borrowers whose mortgages have to be renewed. For such borrowers, the ratio of payments to income rises much faster than interest rates themselves.

For lenders, the problem with fixed rate mortgages arises because they have traditionally funded their mortgage lending with short term deposits. When interest rates rise, deposit costs rise. However, interest earnings on fixed rate mortgages do not similarly rise, and the borrowers face profitability problems.

Table 12.3 Interest sensitivity of level payments on mortgages

Principal	Term	Interest rate	Monthly payment	Index of payments
$100,000	5 yr	5%	$1,887.12	(1.00)
$100,000	5 yr	10%	$2,124.70	(1.13)
$100,000	5 yr	15%	$2,378.99	(1.26)
$100,000	25 yr	5%	$584.59	(1.00)
$100,000	25 yr	10%	$908.70	(1.55)
$100,000	25 yr	15%	$1,280.83	(2.19)

Adjustable rate mortgages are one response to the problem with level payment mortgages instruments; adjustable payment mortgages are another. Adjustable interest rates stabilise financial institutions' net interest earnings, but pass interest rate risk on to their clients. Thus adjustable rate mortgages solve lenders' problems, but not borrowers'. Adjustable rate, level payment mortgages create the cash flow problems for borrowers illustrated in Table 12.3. Graduated payment mortgages have been designed for use with adjustable rates to resolve borrowers' problems.

Reverse mortgages are means of selling a house owned by a retired person who wishes to have the income for the remainder of his or her life. In effect, the reverse mortgage allows the owner of a house to sell off the equity piecemeal to obtain income while continuing to live in the house. Reverse mortgages may become increasingly popular because of ageing populations in many countries. However, so far the effective interest rates on these instruments seem to have been atypically high in comparison to other mortgage loans, and there has not been much demand for them. Finally, there have been innovations in a related product: mortgage insurance that pays off the outstanding principal if the borrower dies. Banks and near banks are strong proponents of such insurance, and offer it at relatively low cost.

12.5.3 Secondary markets

Growing areas usually have a demand for mortgage financing that is greater than the supply of savings to finance them. Mature areas often have a supply of savings greater than the demand for mortgage financing. Thus local mortgage lending institutions face supply–demand imbalance problems that can best be solved by improving the markets to trade portfolios of outstanding mortgages.

The institutional markets for trading blocks of residential mortgages owe their origin mainly to primary mortgage lenders' needs for funding. Liquidity needs are generally regarded as a less important contributory factor. Since some mortgage lenders can originate more mortgages than they can fund by raising deposits, it was natural for them to design instruments capable of raising additional funds from such institutions as pension or mutual funds. By encouraging trading of securities collateralised by blocks of mortgages, the mortgage lenders were thus able to increase primary market activity as well. In addition, the trading made it easier for lenders to raise liquid funds as and when needed.

Trading in mortgages was originated by mortgage brokers, but greatly enhanced by the use of securitisation, a concept introduced in Chapter 9. To create a market for securities based on portfolios of mortgages, it was necessary to design securities that would appeal to such institutions as life insurance companies and pension funds. This appeal to institutional investors was premised on minimising both their risks and their administrative costs. Risks are minimised by appropriately choosing the terms of the securities issues, while administrative costs are usually minimised by leaving the actual collection of payments with the original lender.

One form of securitisation involved instruments called mortgage **pass-through securities** devised for sale to financial institutions. In the US, many of these transactions use Government National Mortgage Association (GNMA) pass-through certificates. These certificates are issued by private lenders against pools of mortgages, both those insured by federal agencies and uninsured mortgages. The federally insured pass-through certificates are guaranteed as to payment of principal and interest by GNMA, thus reducing the default risk faced by the institutional purchaser of the certificates. Institutional investors regard the certificates as high quality instruments, and find them attractive investments. The attraction of the certificates is increased because their standardised terms and guarantee also enhance secondary market trading.

Pass-through certificates may be created without a GNMA guarantee, but in this case they are usually covered by private sector insurance to create the higher quality ratings similar to those enjoyed by the former. Pass-through certificates function as substitutes for long term bonds if the underlying mortgages are mid to long term maturities which carry both a fixed term and rate of interest. Interest rates on such certificates, as on the underlying mortgages, should thus also be close to long term bond rates. The principle of pricing by arbitrage predicts that rate differences not attributable to differences in risk will quickly be eliminated.

---

pass-through securities securities created when mortgage holders pool mortgages and sell shares or participation certificates in the pool.

Many mortgages are not fixed term, and in this case pass-through certificates function more like equity than like a bond. Both the cash flows and the earnings of the pool are passed on in proportion to the holders of the pass-through certificates. As a result, the investor in pass-through securities faces the risk that mortgages in the pool will not be paid down as scheduled. The first of these risks, similar to that risk faced by the holder of a callable bond, is called contraction risk. When interest rates fall, holders of flexible term mortgages may pay them down more quickly than forecast, creating contraction risk. On the other hand repayments on adjustable term mortgages can become slower than forecast when interest rates rise, resulting in a diminution of cash flows known as extension risk. The combination of contraction and extension risks is referred to as prepayment risk.

Collateralised mortgage obligations (CMOs) are securities of different maturities backed by pools of mortgages and designed to minimise the prepayment risk to the institutional investor by promising fixed cash flows. Essentially, CMOs function as bonds secured by a pool of mortgages. Any cash flow not needed to meet the terms of CMOs is called the CMO residual. In that it is a residual, it functions like equity. It is, however, a form of equity that increases in value as interest rates increase.

12.6 SUMMARY

This chapter examined financial market activities, focusing on US markets as an example. Domestic financial markets take specialised forms, which are determined by the economics of market operations, the economics of the firms operating in these markets, and the economics of information production. These explanations were used to organise a discussion of the main characteristics of the money markets, stock markets, bond markets and mortgage markets.

REVIEW QUESTIONS

Exercise 1 The Chicago Board of Trade set up the Chicago Board Options Exchange in 1973. What would have been the principal advantage that the founding members of the Exchange expected to gain from establishing the new market?

Exercise 2 In Canada, Gordon Capital invented the bought deal, which effectively put Gordon in the position of acting as a dealer rather than a broker for new shares. Give two reasons why this might have looked like a good idea to the executives at Gordon when they initiated the practice.

Exercise 3 Why do real estate firms normally act as brokers rather than as dealers?

Exercise 4 Suppose two securities, issued by the same government and having the same maturity, regularly traded at different yields. What might explain the difference?

Exercise 5 Are there any fundamental differences between Gordon Capital's use of the bought deal and third market dealing? Why or why not?

Exercise 6 What is the largest value of riskless bond that could be issued by the firm in Table 12.1? Explain your reasoning.

Exercise 7 First City Savings in Vancouver used to have problems raising enough money to satisfy its clients' demands for mortgages. How would the emergence of securitisation help such a firm?

Exercise 8 Why are money market transactions so closely integrated? Where would you expect to find the closest links between the money market and other financial markets?

Exercise 9 What are the main differences between the stock and the bond markets? How do these differences affect the organisation of each?

Exercise 10 There are many dealers in government bonds, but corporate bonds are usually traded by brokers. What explains this difference in practice?

Exercise 11 Why do firms issue both bonds and shares?

Exercise 12 What role is played by listing requirements? What analogue to listing requirements might increase trading in an electronic OTC market for little known shares?

Exercise 13 Many computer networks exhibit economies of scale in their operations. How might scale economies affect the future organisation of computerised share markets?

Exercise 14 Distinguish the economic functions of brokers and dealers. Why are homes almost never traded by dealers?

Exercise 15 How are the mortgage markets different from the markets for government treasury bills? In what ways do these differences matter?

13 Markets for risk trading

13.1	Introduction	214
	13.1.1 Risk trading	214
	13.1.2 Why risks are traded	215
13.2	Options markets	216
	13.2.1 Importance and functions	217
	13.2.2 Understanding options	217
	13.2.3 Transactions data	219
13.3	Futures markets	221
	13.3.1 Importance and functions	221
	13.3.2 Using financial futures	222
	13.3.3 Transactions data	223
13.4	Foreign exchange markets	224
	13.4.1 Trading	224
	13.4.2 Dealing banks	225
	13.4.3 Covered interest arbitrage	226
13.5	International risk management	228
	13.5.1 Exchange risk	229
	13.5.2 Currency and interest swaps	229
	13.5.3 Long term swaps	230
	13.5.4 Evolution of risk trading	231
	13.5.5 Managing country risk	232
13.6	Summary	232

LEARNING OBJECTIVES

After reading this chapter you will understand

- how markets for risk trading serve as a vehicle for risk management
- how and why the following market instruments are used for risk management:
    options
    forward and futures contracts
    interest and currency swaps
- how and why some risks are managed by non-market means

13.1 INTRODUCTION

This chapter focuses on the markets for trading risks, with a view to explaining how risks are actually traded in practice. It applies the portfolio governance theory of Chapter 9 to develop the explanations. The discussion examines the markets' economic similarities and differences, and explains why risk trading has grown at such phenomenal rates since the early 1970s. The chapter also introduces intermediaries' risk management activities, to explain why intermediary activity complements market trading.

13.1.1 Risk trading

Risks are traded, in one form or another, in every market-oriented economy. However, specialised markets for trading risks are found mainly in the major cities of the world's largest and most developed economies. In early 1995, the countries with the largest daily turnover in derivatives were Japan, Britain and the United States, as shown in Table 13.1. The table also shows that the next two most important countries, France and Germany, posted much smaller amounts of trading.

Although press discussions sometimes create the impression that risk trading is a casino-like activity that is of little importance to agents other than speculators, in fact the trading is of considerable economic importance. First, by performing the functions of dividing up and exchanging risks, risk trading creates economic value. Second, risk trading produces information by establishing market prices for different kinds of tradable risks. Third, the trading enhances entrepreneurs' ability to undertake new risks in the first place, just as an active secondary market for a company's shares enhances the company's ability to float a new share issue. For example, it is easier for exporters to do business when foreign exchange risk can readily be hedged through market transactions than it is when exporters must take all the risk on their own books.

The kinds of risks that can be traded profitably in the marketplace are those which have readily ascertained payoffs, conform to agreed contract standards,

Table 13.1 Approximate daily turnover, all derivatives contracts (foreign exchange and interest rate instruments), April 1995 (US$ billion)

Japan	$560
Britain	$600
United States	$370
France	$130
Germany	$100

Source: Bank for International Settlements, as reported in *The Economist*, January 13, 1996.

and do not require continuous, intensive monitoring. For example, purchasing a put option written on a well-known stock is a typical example of risk trading, at least so long as the put is traded on an options exchange. Exchange-traded options have standardised terms and contract performance is almost always guaranteed by the exchange's clearing house.

This chapter focuses mainly on risk trading in the marketplace. Intermediaries also trade risks, sometimes acting as principal and holding one side of the transaction on their own books, at other times acting only as agents. Intermediary risk trading, an important complement to market trading, will be introduced in this chapter and examined more extensively in Part IV.

13.1.2 Why risks are traded

Agents trade risks for at least three reasons: they may have different attitudes towards a given risk, they may estimate its distribution differently, or they may wish to tailor portfolio returns. Consider first how different attitudes affect risk trading.[1] **Risk averse** individuals are motivated to sell risks, either to less risk averse agents or to **risk lovers,** as the following example shows. Suppose as in Table 13.2 three individuals are interested in an investment which offers three possible outcomes, each believed to be equally probable, so that the investment's expected value is $50.00.

---

risk aversion a preference for less rather than more risk when the expected return on an arrangement is kept constant.

---

risk loving a preference for more rather than less risk when the expected return on an arrangement is kept constant.

The attitudes of different investors toward the investment can be illustrated by recalling the put-call parity condition (7.2). To employ put-call parity in the present example, suppose for ease of illustration that the options have a strike price of $50.00 and that interest rates are zero. Then the investment can be

Table 13.2 A risky investment proposition

Value of outcome	Probability	Sure payoff (S)	Call payoff (C)	Payoff to short put (–P)
25.00	1/3	50.00	0.00	–25.00
50.00	1/3	50.00	0.00	0.00
75.00	1/3	50.00	25.00	0.00

decomposed into a sure payoff of $50.00, an upside potential (represented by the call payoffs) and a downside risk (represented by the payoffs to the short put position) as shown in the last three columns of Table 13.2. The risk neutral investor will place equal personal values on both the call and the put, and value the whole investment at $50.00, its expected value. The risk averse investor, who weighs the possibility of downside risk relatively heavily, will value the same investment at something less than $50.00, thus placing a negative personal value on the put position greater than the positive value he places on the call. Finally, a risk lover will weigh the upside potential relatively heavily and value the investment at more than $50.00, thus placing a higher personal value on the call than on the put.

Agents may also trade risks because they place different estimates on the payoff distribution. In the foregoing example, one risk averse agent might be able to sell a put to another, equally risk averse agent if the first thought that the probability of a price decline in the underlying stock was lower than the second estimated it to be. Finally, agents may trade risks for portfolio reasons. For example, Chapter 9 showed how a put could be used to limit the downside risk of investing in a given stock.

13.2 OPTIONS MARKETS

Options markets have grown enormously since the early 1970s. Throughout the world, daily turnover in options is now measured in trillions of dollars, as Table 13.1, which shows the average turnover for all derivatives, suggests. (Options account for something like one-half of the trading reported in Table 13.1.) The current importance of options trading stems from several sources. First, the financial environment has exhibited more variability since the 1970s than it did in the 1950s and 1960s. As a result, since the 1970s there have been substantial increases in the demand for risk management services.

On the supply side, financiers have learned to standardise and to guarantee options, making them cheaper and more attractive instruments. Standardising terms both increases liquidity and reduces transactions costs. Exchange-sponsored guarantees of option contracts eliminate the need for traders to investigate the credit ratings of individual option writers.[2] Thus the guarantee permits anonymous individuals to trade more cheaply with each other than would be possible if it were necessary for trading parties to investigate each contract's default risk. Third, financial theorists have shown, using the concepts introduced in Chapter 7, that many different kinds of risk trading can be interpreted as involving combinations of options. Fourth, financial theorists have also shown how options can be used to tailor portfolio returns, a subject introduced in Chapter 9. The theoretical insights have increased the popularity of options trading, both because they have shown how options can be used to emulate the risks of underlying securities and because trading options can be less costly than trading in the underlying assets. Less capital is required to trade in options than in the underlying shares, and sometimes transactions charges are proportionately lower for options trading.

13.2.1 Importance and functions

Options are written on individual shares, share indices, bonds, money market securities, commodities, or on such instruments as futures contracts. Traded options are presently used in such a large variety of risk management transactions that they cannot all be detailed here. For further discussion the reader is referred to such works as Cox and Rubinstein (1985), Hull (1989) or Jarrow and Turnbull (1996). The present discussion attempts only to outline the principal ideas motivating option trading.

Options are used both for hedging and for assuming risks. For example, a call option may be purchased to ensure that, until the option's maturity, the underlying security can be bought for no more than the exercise (or strike) price specified in the option contract. The call has value to its purchaser only if the share price rises above the exercise price. In effect, the call purchaser pays an insurance premium to limit the costs the purchaser would bear if the share price were to increase. Similarly, buying a put on a share is a purchase of insurance against a share price decline. If the price of the share remains above the exercise price of the put, the put will be worthless. However, if the share price falls below the put's exercise price, the purchaser can still sell the share, at the exercise price specified, to the writer of the put contract. With regard to speculative transactions, some investors might assemble a portfolio of options rather than a portfolio of shares. Options are riskier than shares in the sense that, relative to the amounts invested, the price changes on the options are much larger than on the underlying shares.

13.2.2 Understanding options

The options pricing model of Chapter 9 valued an option extending over two periods. As shown next, the same model can be extended to more time periods. The extension permits examining how changes in the share price and in the option value are related over time. The extension also shows that the option value will usually fluctuate over a wider proportional range than the underlying price. Table 13.3 extends the example of Table 9.2 to value a European call option with an exercise price of $100.00 over four periods. Possible share prices are represented by the first number in a cell, option values by the second number.

The model assumes share prices evolve multiplicatively by a factor of 1.10 or 1.10^{-1} as in Chapter 9. For example, if the share price starts at $100.00 at time zero, it can either rise to $110.00 or fall to $90.91 at time 1. If it is $90.91 at time 1, it can either rise back to $100.00 or fall to $82.64 at time 2. For simplicity of calculation it is also assumed that the risk free interest rate is zero. Finally, some cells in Table 13.3 have no entries, indicating that only some time–price combinations are attainable. For example, when the share price is $100.00 at time zero, the only possible time 1 values are $110.00 or $90.91. In the process assumed here, the share price can return to its original value after two periods, but cannot remain the same in the intervening period.

At time 4, the option values are

$$\max\ (S_4 - 100.00,\ 0)$$

where S_4 is the time 4 share price. That is, the option value is the larger of zero or the share difference between the share price and the assumed exercise price of $100.00. At time 3, the option values are computed for each share price using time 4 option values and the risk adjusted probability

$$p^* = (1.00 - 1.10^{-1})\ /\ (1.10 - 1.10^{-1})$$

found in Chapter 9. To focus on the essential aspects of the calculations, the example continues to employ the Chapter 9 assumption that interest rates are zero. For example, if the time 3 share price is $133.10, the associated option value is

$$p^*(\$46.41) + (1 - p^*)(\$21.00) =$$

$$(0.4762)(46.41) + (0.5238)(\$21.00) = \$33.10$$

Table 13.3 Relations between share and call prices

Time 0	Time 1	Time 2	Time 3	Time 4
				146.41 / 46.41
			133.10 / 33.10	
		121.00 / 21.00		121.00 / 21.00
	110.00 / 12.49		110.00 / 10.00	
100.00 / 7.14		100.00 / 4.76		100.00 / 0.00
	90.91 / 2.27		90.91 / 0.00	
		82.64 / 0.00		82.64 / 0.00
			75.14 / 0.00	
				68.31 / 0.00

In this particular case, the option value is just $100.00 less than the current price, because the same exercise price has been deducted from both outcomes. Once all the time 3 option values have been found, the time 2 option values can be computed from them, and so on.

In exactly the same way, the calculations can be continued backward in time to find the time zero value of the European option.[3] To give another example, when at time 1 the share price is $110.00, the option value of $12.49 is found from

$$p^*(\$21.00) + (1 - p^*)(\$4.76) =$$

$$(0.4762)(21.00) + (0.5238)(\$4.76) = \$12.49$$

Table 13.3 displays two important properties of option prices. First, it shows that for a given share price, the longer the time to maturity, the more the option is worth. Second, it shows that for a fixed time to maturity, the value of a call increases as the share price increases. It can also be inferred from this second property that the value of a put increases as the share price decreases.

In theory the effect on share prices of any new information is reflected simultaneously in both the share market and the related options market. Option pricing theory assumes there is active arbitraging between options and the underlying instruments. Moreover, since arbitrageurs use all available information in carrying out their trades, whatever information affects the underlying instrument's price also affects the option price. In practice, information reaching one market is usually transmitted to the other market with a lag. However, in markets that are closely related by arbitraging the lag may be very short, say on the order of a few minutes.

13.2.3 Transactions data

While options have been traded over the counter for many years, they were first traded on an organised exchange – the Chicago Board Options Exchange – in 1973. Currently there are five major options exchanges in the US: the New York Stock Exchange, the Chicago Board Options Exchange, the American Stock Exchange, the Philadelphia and the Pacific Stock Exchanges. Options on both listed shares and OTC shares are traded on these exchanges.

Market quotations, obtainable from the press and from securities firms, are available in forms resembling Table 13.4.

The closeness with which the put-call parity relation developed in Chapter 7 holds in practice can be assessed from the data in Table 13.4. Recall that Equation 7.6 stated:

$$v(S) \equiv v(X) - v(C) + v(P) \tag{13.1}$$

where $v(\cdot)$ means 'determine value using the risk adjusted probabilities' and the capital letters S, X, C and P refer to the option exercise price, the payoffs to the underlying risky prospect, and the call and put payoffs respectively. From

Table 13.4 Trans Canada Options: quotations for June 20, 1995

Options	Maturity and strike price	Volume	Open interest	Last price	Stock close
Alcan	Jul $40.00	51	826	1.80	40.375
Alcan	Jul $30.00P	50	217	0.05	40.375
Alcan	Jul $40.00P	275	742	0.85	40.375

Source: *The Globe and Mail*, June 21, 1995.
Definition of headings:
Options: the underlying security on which the option can be bought or sold.
Maturity: the month until which the option can be exercised or expires (3rd Friday of the month at 3:00 p.m.).
Strike price: the price at which the holder of the option can buy (call) or sell (put) the security.
P: a put option. Data without this symbol refer to call options.
Volume: the daily number of contracts traded. Note that each contract applies to 100 shares.
Open interest: the number of outstanding contracts, i.e., contracts unexpired and unexercised.
Last: the last market quotation and market value of the contract in cents.
Stock close: the closing price of the underlying security for that day.

Table 13.4, the values of the different instruments to be substituted into the right-hand side of (13.1) are

$$v(X) - v(C) + v(P) = \$40.38 - \$1.80 + \$0.85 = \$39.43$$

Similarly, the value to be used on the left-hand side of (13.1) is

$$v(S) = \$40.00 / (1 + r_f)$$

For the period in question, about one month, a reasonable value for the risk free interest rate is about one-half of 1 percent, making the left-hand value equal to a little less than $40.00. The example shows the put-call parity relationship holds relatively closely, even though trading in this particular market is rather thin.

The July $40.00 call in Table 13.4 is said to be 'in the money'. That is, its exercise price is below the market value of the underlying share, and this determines the minimum value of the option as shown in Equation 13.2.

$$\text{Minimum Value} = \text{Share Price} - \text{Exercise Price} \qquad (13.2)$$

$$\$0.38 = \$40.38 - \$40.00$$

Although the minimum value is $0.38, as can be seen from Table 13.4 the market value of the contract is $1.80. The call sells for more than its theoretical minimum value because there is some probability the underlying share will appreciate between the valuation date used and the July expiry date. For example, if before the July expiry date the share price were to rise to $45.00, the call would then be valued at something more than $5.00. The value in excess of $5.00 would arise from the probability that the share price might increase still further before the option expires.

Table 13.4 also shows a July $30.00 put. This put is said to be 'out of the money' because the exercise price is below the market price. The agent who created (wrote) this put probably believed the price of Alcan shares would rise, or at worst would not be likely to fall, below the exercise price of $30.00. (Indeed, he may have believed the share price would not fall much below its current $40.375.) Therefore he was willing, in exchange for a relatively small premium, to create an obligation to buy 100 shares of Alcan at a fixed price of $30.00. The contract remains in effect from the issue date until the third Friday in July, after which it expires.[4]

Recalling the valuation relation (13.2), a similar relationship can be developed for the minimum value of the put. In this case, the equation is

$$\text{Minimum Value} = \max\,[(\text{Exercise Price} - \text{Share Price}), 0.00] \quad (13.3)$$

$$\$0.00 = \max\,[\$30.00 - \$40.375, 0.00]$$

because options do not sell at negative prices. Extending the reasoning used to develop Table 13.3, it can be shown that puts decrease in value, as share prices rise. Thus in this case the market value of the put is $0.05 because market participants believe there is still some slight chance the share price may fall from its present $40.375 to below $30.00 before the expiry date.

13.3 FUTURES MARKETS

Financial futures and forwards offer alternative risk management instruments. While options trading has grown spectacularly since the early 1970s, forward contracts have long been important in foreign exchange trading and are currently of growing importance in managing interest rate risk, as are such financial futures contracts as interest rate futures, currency futures and share index futures.

As Chapter 7 pointed out, both forward and futures contracts create obligations (not privileges as with option holders) for the holder to buy or sell a specified asset at a time and price written into the contract. The differing nature of the two types of contracts reflects the history of their development and the specialised requirements of the agents trading in them. Although futures contracts were first written against physical commodities, a large proportion of the contracts currently traded are written against financial instruments, while forward contracts continue to be written mainly against physical commodities and foreign exchange. Futures contracts are usually written by individuals and trade on futures exchanges, while forward contracts are usually written by banks and are not actively traded. This section, 13.3, examines market trading of futures contracts. The main uses of forward contracts are discussed in section 13.4 on foreign exchange, and in Part IV on financial intermediaries.

13.3.1 Importance and functions

Futures contracts are used for trading the price risks of the commodities or financial instruments against which they are written. Hedgers will sell off risks to those willing to bear them, providing the two parties can find a mutually acceptable price. For example, some portfolio investors find it cost-effective to use interest rate futures to reduce the interest rate risk of an investment position, as shown in section 13.3.2.

As Chapter 7 pointed out, futures contracts are marked to market as the value of the underlying asset changes. Futures contracts present smaller default risks than forwards, partly because marking to market means capital gains or losses are realised rather than remaining unrealised as they do in the case of a forward contract. The marking to market process creates a difference between a forward and a futures contract that is somewhat like the difference between holding a long maturity bond and rolling over a series of short maturity bonds. In comparison to forwards, the default risks of exchange traded futures contracts are also smaller because both seller and purchaser formally treat the exchange as the official counterparty to the contract, and performance under the contract is almost always guaranteed by the exchange's clearing house.[5] The demand for trading futures contracts is enhanced by the guarantee because it means that the agents entering the contracts do not have to assess counterparty risk.[6]

Financial futures are traded in many of the world's developed economies. Some of the larger futures markets include the International Monetary Market of the Chicago Mercantile Exchange, the New York Futures Exchange and the London International Financial Futures Exchange. These exchanges typically trade government bill futures contracts, bond futures contracts and Eurodollar CD Futures. Japanese government bond futures trade on the Tokyo Stock Exchange as well as on the Chicago Board of Trade Options Exchange. Futures contracts of similar sorts are traded on France's MATIF,[7] and Germany's DTB.[8]

US futures exchanges and the LIFFE in London conduct trading according to the open outcry method, where members of the exchange are physically present in an area called the trading pit and complete their orders by a combination of shouting, hand and eye signals. Some continental exchanges, like the DTB, conduct screen trading, and the LIFFE offers after-hours screen trading. Brokers both enter orders, and accept others' orders, by entering their transactions into a centralised computer. The computer displays outstanding orders and other information on members' screens.

13.3.2 Using financial futures

Interest rate futures are used frequently in the daily operations of lending intermediaries. Currency futures and share index futures are presently used by security dealers, insurance companies, trust companies, pension funds and multinational firms. Hedging against interest rate changes is often carried out using futures contracts on treasury bills or bankers' acceptances.

As the conceptual discussion of Chapter 7 indicated, a long position in a treasury bill futures contract (also called an interest rate futures contract) will increase in value as the underlying bill increases in value. However, the bill itself will decline in value if interest rates rise, so that a short position in bill futures is needed to generate a capital gain to offset any decline in the value of the bill. If there is an interest rate increase and if the short sale of bill futures is in the correct amount, the capital losses on the treasury bill will be offset by a capital gain on the short position in the futures contracts. The reverse is true if there is an interest rate decrease: the bills increase in value but there is a capital loss on the short position in the futures contract. Thus the combination of treasury bill and short position in bill futures creates a hedged investment. The cost of the hedging is not great: treasury bill futures contracts usually require posting margins amounting to 5–10 percent of the value of the underlying bills, and competitive interest rates are usually paid on margin accounts.

To illustrate the mechanics of hedging a position with a futures contract, suppose that a bank has a floating rate asset funded by a fixed rate liability such as a time deposit. The net interest revenues on this transaction will increase if interest rates increase, and decrease if interest rates fall. The risk of these changes in net interest revenue can be alleviated by hedging the difference in dollar amounts between the floating rate assets and fixed rate liability on the interest rate futures market. Table 13.5 shows the qualitative gains or losses on both the loan and the futures contract depend on the interest rate environment. If a bank buys interest rate futures and rates rise, the bank gains on the original loan-deposit deal but loses on its interest rate futures position. If interest rates decline, the bank loses on its loan portfolio but makes compensating gains on the value of its futures contracts. If the appropriate size of futures transactions is made, the sum of gain and loss in either cell can be made equal to zero, and the income risk on the transaction will be completely hedged.[9]

Table 13.5 Interest hedging with a futures contract

Transaction	Rates increase	Rates decrease
Floating rate loan, fixed rate deposit	$gain	$loss
Buy interest rate futures	$loss	$gain

13.3.3 Transactions data

Table 13.6 provides data for representative Eurodollar interest rate futures contracts. To interpret Table 13.6, consider the September 1995 Eurodollar contract which closed at 94.33. The standard Eurodollar contract is for three months (i.e., one-fourth of a year). Market quotations are given according to the formula

$$\text{Quote} = 100.00 - \text{Per Annum Forward Interest Rate}$$

In the present example the quote implies

$$94.33 = 100.00 - 5.67$$

that is the annual interest rate implied by the contract price is 5.67 percent. This system of quotations is used for convenience; traders do not need to make any computations other than those shown to establish annual interest rates on an instrument. The method is also convenient because futures markets are very

Table 13.6 Daily quotations for Chicago Mercantile Exchange Eurodollar Futures three month contract, $1 million

Season high	Season low	Expiry month	Daily open	Daily high	Daily low	Daily close	Open interest
95.43	91.59	Sep. 95	94.37	94.40	94.31	94.33	390608
95.81	91.18	Dec. 95	94.43	94.46	94.34	94.38	321642
95.10	91.20	Mar. 95	94.49	94.53	94.41	94.44	283655
94.95	91.59	Jun. 95	94.43	94.45	94.34	94.36	199729
94.83	91.61	Sep. 95	94.32	94.37	94.25	94.27	162517
94.59	91.57	Dec. 95	94.12	94.17	94.05	94.08	129882

Source: *The Globe and Mail*, June 21, 1995.

closely related by arbitrage to the money markets, and interest rates in the two markets follow very much the same pattern over time. The headings of the remaining columns in Table 13.6 are self-explanatory, except possibly for open interest. This term refers to the number of contracts outstanding on the date to which the table refers. It is not a good indicator of exposure risk because some of the contracts might be held as long positions, others as short positions by the same party. For example, if there were only two contracts outstanding, the open interest would be two, even if both parties each had a long and a short position such that neither had any net exposure.

13.4 FOREIGN EXCHANGE MARKETS

The short term foreign exchange markets are highly active marketplaces in which transactions are made to settle accounts arising from trade in goods and services or from investment or speculative transactions. Market prices are closely related to each other by arbitraging and other trading intended to profit from emerging price differences. Interest arbitraging deals are used to take advantage of perceived short term atypical interest differentials among countries. Currency arbitraging follows a similar rationale. The chief arbitrageurs are the world's dealing banks, although multinational firms and speculators also play important roles.

13.4.1 Trading

Whatever the purpose of the deal, if it provides for immediate delivery of foreign currency it is called a **spot transaction**.[10] Deals providing for delivery at some time in the future are known as **forward transactions**; settlement is made on the day the contract matures. Over the post-war years, the forward markets have taken on increasingly greater importance, and the proportion of spot to forward trading has been gradually falling. In its 1995 survey of the London foreign exchange market, the Bank of England reported that trading for spot accounted for just over 40 percent of turnover, while forward trading represented almost 60 percent (Bank of England 1995: 361).

> **spot transaction** a foreign exchange transaction in which immediate delivery is specified. The term 'immediate' means 'at once' for small amounts of currency, but with a delay of two or fewer working days in the case of larger electronic funds transfers. For example, in Canada, large amounts of US dollars purchased in the spot market are usually delivered on the following working day. In the US, large amounts of say French francs are usually delivered on the second working day after a deal is done.

> **forward foreign exchange transaction** a transaction in which parties agree to exchange currencies at some future date.

13.4.2 Dealing banks

The world's dealing banks conduct transactions in both currencies and the instruments used for managing currency risk. Very large transactions in the currencies themselves may be negotiated individually, as may more complex and less standard risk management transactions. Smaller and more common transactions are handled either by banks or by foreign exchange dealers on standardised terms.

A dealing bank's traders are responsible for managing their bank's foreign currency positions. Much of their work involves trying to offset positions the bank has assumed in its dealings with clients. Most dealers reduce these position risks through offsetting transactions. Thus spot purchases are usually offset by spot sales as quickly as possible. Forward transactions are usually first offset in the spot market and only later in the appropriate forward maturity, mainly because trading in spot markets is more active than in the forward markets. The strategy of offsetting a forward position with a spot position permits laying off some risk while waiting for the appropriate offsetting forward transaction to present itself.

For example, suppose a dealing bank buys US dollars three months forward. If it is unable immediately to sell US dollars three months forward, it will sell them spot. The sale reduces the risk of the position, since the unhedged forward position is subject to fluctuation in the value of the currency, while the forward–spot combination is only subject to fluctuation in changes in value between spot and forward contracts in the same currency. This latter, smaller risk is known as interest rate risk. When it becomes possible later to sell US dollars three months forward, they will be bought back on the spot market, thereby netting out the initial spot position. Large orders in some lesser traded currencies may take several days, or even possibly weeks, to offset completely.

Traders who speculate on their inventory positions place their employers at some risk, and as a result trading positions are usually subject to several kinds of limits. First, traders must end the day with a limited position in each foreign currency, so that the bank will not be exposed to undue foreign exchange risk overnight. Second, the amount of forward exposure in a given currency is also constrained, in this case with a view to managing the interest rate exposure associated with differences between spot and forward rates. There are customary differentials between bid and ask rates in both spot and forward markets, but these differentials can widen or narrow as time goes by and various kinds of news regarding a currency's value are announced. For example, in the event of a major expected change in a currency's value, the forward markets first show a widening bid-ask spread, and, if the uncertainty continues to mount, may cease functioning for a time. Third, the amount of transactions a trader can arrange with a given bank is constrained to manage what is known as settlement risk (i.e., the risk that the other bank will not pay for the transactions as arranged). Finally, banks themselves are limited by regulations governing their allowable exposures to foreign exchange risk.

The spot and forward transactions carried out by traders in the dealing banks are referred to using a somewhat peculiar terminology. The most common interest arbitraging transaction involves a spot–forward combination and is called a swap transaction. This terminology seems to have evolved because dealers make crude profit calculations using the difference between buying and selling rates, a difference known as the number of swap points. On the other hand, since to traders a forward transaction by itself is unusual, it is called an outright forward or just an outright, drawing attention to its uncommon nature.

13.4.3 Covered interest arbitrage

Like securities denominated in domestic currencies, securities denominated in foreign currencies, and indeed the foreign currencies themselves, can be regarded as financial instruments. The principle of pricing by arbitrage, discussed in Chapters 6 and 7, helps to relate the values of these exotic opportunities when there are no transactions costs or other impediments to trade. Further insight into how interest rates are related can be gained by considering how you might approach the question of whether to invest at home or abroad.

To begin developing your answer, suppose funds can be transferred freely between countries, at least for investments covering relatively short periods of time. Then, if any risk of change in the value of foreign currencies can be eliminated, the principle of pricing by arbitrage suggests that you invest in the country whose securities give you the higher rate of return. However, the principle of pricing by arbitrage actually goes further to argue that since all investors will make this calculation, the same interest rate should be earned in either of two countries, even though their securities appear to offer different interest rates. Once we have developed this last point, we can return to the puzzle of where you should invest.

Recall that a **forward contract** is a contract, entered today, which specifies a quantity of some asset to be delivered at some future time, and at a specified price to be paid at or near the time of delivery. An appropriately designed forward foreign exchange contract can be used to eliminate foreign exchange risk on investments in other currencies. If the investment also involves purchasing foreign government obligations with no (or little) default risk, the foreign investment would not pose risks much different from those of investing in a domestic government bond. Finally, if the two risks are regarded as identical, then in the absence of arbitrage opportunities the two different ways of investing should yield the same interest rate in domestic terms.

To illustrate the situation, suppose that today US$1.00 will buy exactly A$1.08 (i.e., exactly 1.08 Australian dollars). In foreign exchange terminology, the Australian dollar **spot rate** is assumed to be US$1.08.[11] Suppose further that US treasury bills can be purchased to yield 6 percent over one year, while similar Australian bills yield 11 percent. Since the hedged Australian investment should, by the principle of riskless arbitrage, yield the same 6 percent in US dollar terms as the US domestic investment, the Australian dollar must be expected to fall relative to the US dollar, that is one year from now the US dollar must be expected to buy more than A$1.08.

Denote the **forward exchange rate** for Australian dollars, expressed in US dollar terms, by F. Since a $1.00 investment in US treasury bills returns US$1.06 after one year, the principle of riskless arbitrage predicts that US$1.00 invested in Australian bills and hedged against changes in the value of the Australian dollar (relative to the US dollar) will also yield 6 percent to the US investor when no profitable arbitrage opportunities remain. The deal is hedged by purchasing Australian dollars in the spot market, using them to purchase the Australian dollar denominated securities, and simultaneously selling the Australian dollar proceeds forward.

> **forward exchange rate** a rate at which two parties agree to exchange currencies that will be delivered and paid for at a future time, specified in the forward contract.

In the absence of arbitrage opportunities, either deal should earn the same 6 percent for the US investor. That is, in US terms

$$\text{US\$}1.00(1.06) = \text{A\$}1.08(1.11) / F \qquad (13.4)$$

or $F = 1.11(1.08)/1.06 = 1.1309$, which means that US$1.00 will A$1.1309 forward, for delivery one year from now. In other words, the Australian dollar one year forward price, in terms of US dollars, is 1.1309 if there are no arbitrage opportunities between the two countries. This means the Australian dollar is expected to fall, since US$1.00 will buy only A$1.08 in the spot market, but A$1.1309 in the forward market.

The above example illustrates the **interest parity theory** to be developed further in Chapter 14. The theory states that the ratio of the forward to the spot price of a foreign currency (when the prices are stated in terms of the domestic currency) is equal to the return on an investment in the foreign country divided by the return on a similar investment in the home country. Symbolically

$$F/S = (1 + r_f) / (1 + r_d)$$

You should be able to work out the derivation of the formula from the interest arbitraging example just given. However, in case you want to see a more formal demonstration, it will be given in Chapter 14.

Transactions intended to take advantage of interest rate differences, and hedged against the foreign exchange risk, are called **covered interest arbitrage transactions**. When covered interest arbitrage transactions can be arranged, any difference between countries' interest rates (hedged against the foreign exchange risk) is likely to be offset by an adjustment in currency values. The country with the higher interest rate will have a currency that is declining in value relative to the country with the lower rate. Indeed, higher interest rates can be used, if other circumstances between countries are equal, as a predictor of a subsequent decline in currency values.

> **covered interest arbitrage** a transaction in which a resident in one country invests short term in another country, covering the foreign exchange risk of the transaction through a forward sale of the investment returns.

Now, returning to the question of where you should invest, we have an answer, given the circumstances assumed above, to the question of whether it should be in the US or in Australia. If you can carry out the Australian investment on terms that allow you to exchange A$ forward at a better rate 1.1309 per US dollar (for example, if you can get US dollars for a forward price of A$1.10, meaning you have to surrender fewer A$ to get the same number of US dollars), you should do so! By so doing, you would be one of the investors who were actually helping to establish the interest rate parity theorem in this particular case. (Incidentally if there are transactions costs, you need to take them into account before deciding whether the deal is still profitable.)

13.5 INTERNATIONAL RISK MANAGEMENT

Exchange risks can be managed through hedging, as in the transaction just discussed, or through currency and interest rate swaps. Some hedging transactions can be completed in markets, others can be negotiated only with counterparties. Still others, such as country risk, do not usually trade at all. Nevertheless, even risks that cannot be traded require to be recognised and managed.

13.5.1 Exchange risk

Foreign exchange risk exposure is frequently classified as translation exposure, transaction exposure and economic exposure. Translation (accounting) exposure refers to possible gains or losses when the results of foreign transactions are converted into their domestic equivalents. Translation exposure is often measured by the difference between foreign currency assets and foreign currency liabilities. Transaction exposure refers to the risk incurred when a foreign currency is to be converted into its domestic equivalent at some future date, and its value is not currently known with certainty. Economic exposure refers to the possibility of changes in the market value of the net worldwide assets of a firm, determined in its domestic currency, as a result of changes in exchange rates used to value net foreign assets.

Foreign exchange exposures are often hedged either by generating earnings in the same currency as the obligation or through arranging explicit hedging transactions. Active markets exist only for hedging short term risks, because the risk–return ratios are uneconomic for longer maturity forward and futures transactions. For example, an established market exists in US dollars, Canadian dollars and pounds sterling up to ten years, in Australian dollars up to approximately two years, and in Spanish pesetas up to twelve months. Within each of the foregoing markets, the bulk of the trading is for instruments of one year or less to maturity. Beyond the time bands for established markets, swaps can be arranged by banks and by various investment banking companies in such major financial centers as New York, London and Tokyo.

13.5.2 Currency and interest swaps

The first kinds of swaps were interest rate swaps; **currency swaps** followed not long afterward. When they were first originated in the early 1970s, swaps were usually negotiated individually. As transactions became more frequent, and as agents became more familiar with swap techniques, the cost and informational conditions under which they could be completed also changed. As a result, swaps can now be arranged and traded in a highly active marketplace.

---

currency swap an arrangement whereby one economic agent exchanges a payment in one currency for a payment in another, with the intention of subsequently reversing the transaction at a later date. Currency swaps are normally entered in order to reduce accounting measures of foreign exchange risk.

Interest rate swaps are now frequently combined with currency swaps, and are forging increasingly stronger arbitrage links between markets. For example, in 1990 it became profitable for British investors to borrow sterling at floating

rates in London (**LIBOR**) and to use the funds for purchasing Italian government fixed rate ECU bonds. An interest income swap from fixed to floating
was used to stabilise the interest earnings, and a swap of sterling for ECUs was
used to stabilise the foreign exchange risk of the British investor. The currency
swap meant the British investor arranged to exchange pounds sterling for ECUs
when making the investment, and ECUs for sterling when disinvesting. The net
result of this deal, after transactions costs, was a profit of about 0.80 percent
(eighty basis points) per annum on the sterling funds invested. As such transactions become increasingly commonplace, the effects of arbitraging, as
discussed in Chapters 6 and 7, are likely to reduce their profit potential.

LIBOR the London Interbank Offered Rate for short term Eurocurrency
loans. It is the most responsive money market price in the world, changing
quickly in response to changing supplies or demands. LIBID, the London
Interbank Bid Rate, is offered to market participants for large deposits.

There is also growing use of exchange traded currency futures and options
for risk management purposes. Many such deals are pure market transactions,
standardised according to terms set by the exchanges on which they trade. These
kinds of options and futures market trading have some characteristics of retail
trading, because the amounts involved are typically smaller, and because the
contracts are often shorter term. Both large securities firms and banks act as
agents in these markets.

13.5.3 Long term swaps

Most forward transactions involve one, three or six month maturities, although
longer maturities can be arranged in major currencies such as the US dollar.
Because the inventory risk is large in relation to customary returns, it is usually
necessary to hedge a long term transaction through a bank that will act as a
broker to find an offsetting transaction of approximately equal maturity between
the same two countries. This kind of swap arrangement involves an exchange of
funds at the outset, and one or more reversing transactions at time(s) of payment.

The mechanics of a long term swap are most easily explained with an
example. Suppose Alcan, a Canadian firm, has a need for pounds sterling while
Imperial Chemical Industries, a British firm, has a similar need for Canadian
dollars. Today the parties exchange $10 million Canadian for £4.5 million. They
agree that ten years hence they will re-exchange at the same 1986 exchange
rate. In the meantime ICI pays Alcan the difference in ten year interest rates
minus a concession fee; for example,

$$(14.25\%) \cdot (10.75\% + 0.75\%) = 2.75\%$$

the annual fee. Both firms eliminate foreign exchange risk in this transaction.

Although in the previous example the spread is fixed, arrangements with a floating spread are also possible. The cosmetic advantage of such a swap is that it is not shown on the balance sheets of the corporations. The substantive advantage is it provides protection for creditors who can sue for liquidated damages. In this transaction, different formal arrangements may be used to alter the credit risk borne by the different parties.

13.5.4 Evolution of risk trading

Like other kinds of financial deals, some forms of risk trading have evolved from intermediated to market transactions. One reason for the evolution is that some deals, originally negotiated on an individual basis by intermediaries, become so popular that their terms are standardised, making the deals suitable for market transactions. For example, options have traded on organised exchanges only since 1973, when standardisation decreased the cost of trading. A second reason for the migration of some deals from intermediaries to markets, also illustrated in the development of the options markets, is that contract guarantees make it cheaper for parties to trade without investigating each others' creditworthiness. Finally, the first theoretical model for pricing options was published in the same year (Black and Scholes 1973), helping to define relations between market and theoretical prices, and thus giving its own impetus to trading activity.

Many of the innovations in risk trading have occurred in the options and futures markets, largely because these markets were set up by securities firms familiar with performing the functions of market agents. On the other hand, foreign exchange trading was mainly originated by banks and is not always as standardised as options and futures trading. In part, the lack of standardisation is due to the larger size of individual transactions in foreign exchange. Since most large banks have at least a rough idea of other banks' credit risk, the need for contract guarantees is not as important as in the options and futures markets. Default risk is usually managed by restricting the quantity of orders placed with any single counterparty in a given day. However, as the foreign exchange markets continue to expand and the number of traders increases further, the need for guarantees may increase.

The explosive development of the swap market is due to changes in both demand and supply. On the demand side, both financial and non-financial firms have learned to manage interest rate and currency risks using swap transactions. With the increasing number of participants, search costs have been reduced by the emergence of well-known market agents, and transactions costs by standardising swap terms. On the supply side, banks originated the use of both interest and currency swaps, but are no longer the principal actors in all parts of this market. Interest and currency swaps can presently be arranged most cheaply using the standardised terms agreed by the International Swaps and Derivatives Association. The Association was organised by securities firms, which currently do more standardised swap business than the banks which originated the transactions. As yet, swaps do not bear performance guarantees like those under-lying futures contracts, but the economic value of such guarantees seems likely to become clearer as the swap markets continue their present explosive growth.

The evolution of some deals toward greater standardisation and market gover-nance provides a case study of increasingly discriminating alignment of deal attributes and governance capabilities. The changes occur gradually because agents learn incrementally, and change the ways they do deals accordingly.

13.5.5 Managing country risk

Country risk refers to the possibility that a sovereign borrower may be unable or unwilling to fulfill its borrowing obligations. Country risk has both political and financial dimensions. Foreign governments are immune from most legal processes, and hence do not face the same default obligations as private sector firms. Political risk encompasses such possibilities as forced expropriation, while financial risk involves such factors as inability to meet payments necessitating rescheduling of loans. Another dimension of country risk is that borrowers in a given country may be unable to meet external obligations because of foreign exchange controls imposed by the country's government, a risk known as transfer risk. Whatever the source of the difficulty, lenders can find some small comfort in that default can seriously affect a country's international credit standing. Perceptions of credit risk affect both the supply of new funds and its cost.

Bank and investor practices for assessing country risk vary considerably, but still have some common features. Financial factors are usually of greatest interest to lenders. The debt owed to foreigners in relation to foreign exchange earn-ings provides an indication of a country's ability to service the debt. The liquidity of a country may roughly be assessed by measuring its foreign exchange reserves in relation to its imports. The amount and diversity of exports provides a measure of the country's ability to earn foreign exchange. Measures of economic growth indicate how the country's foreign earnings are likely to grow.

Political and sociological factors may also be assessed. For example, splits between different language, ethnic and religious groups can threaten political stability. A strong degree of nationalism can lead to preferential treatment of local interests and nationalisation of foreign holdings. Extremes of wealth can lead to unfavourable social conditions. Social conflict and the presence of disaf-fected radical groups are, of course, even stronger indications of political instability. Brewer and Rivoli (1990) observe that frequency of regime change has a significant impact on country creditworthiness. Armed conflict and polit-ical legitimacy are less significant.

13.6 SUMMARY

This chapter examined the principal markets for risk trading: the options, futures and foreign exchange markets. In each case, the market's importance and func-tions was discussed and the organisation of trading activity presented. Market transactions were used to illustrate the various forms of risk management. The chapter also examined the advantages and disadvantages to using different instruments. Finally, some specialised aspects of international risk management were examined, and the reasons for using non-market instruments presented.

REVIEW QUESTIONS

Table 13.7 A risky investment proposition (Exercise 1)

Outcomes	Sure payoff (S)	Call payoff (C)	Payoff to short put (−P)
25.00	50.00	0.00	−25.00
50.00	50.00	0.00	0.00
75.00	50.00	25.00	0.00
55.00	50.00		

Exercise 1 Table 13.7 shows the values a risk lover would place on a risky outcome and a sure thing. Using put-call parity, what can you say about the value of the call in relation to the value of the put?

Exercise 2 Using the data in Table 13.3, find the value of a call option with an exercise price of $105.00. (Use the risk adjusted probabilities used in Table 13.3.)

Exercise 3 Suppose you have borrowed $1 million today. The interest rate on your loan will be set six months from now, and you will pay the loan plus interest in one year. Would it take a short or a long position in a treasury bill futures contract to offset your interest rate risk?

Exercise 4 The long term swap discussed in section 13.5.3 handles some kinds of risks, but not others. The C$/£ exchange rate in the example is $2.22. Who would be the loser, in an opportunity sense, if the C$/£ exchange rate ten years hence turns out to be $2.10?

Exercise 5 Describe one form of hedging. Be sure to indicate what instruments are involved, and explain how they are used to create the hedge.

Exercise 6 Why are options, futures and forward exchange markets so closely integrated with their underlying spot markets?

Exercise 7 Do hedgers and speculators necessarily have different attitudes toward risk?

Exercise 8 Discuss at least two uses which the manager of a mutual fund might have for options.

Exercise 9 How might a bank use the interest futures markets in risk management? How does this method compare with using the swap markets?

Exercise 10 How does the forward exchange rate compare, as a predictor of currency values, to the current spot rate? Why?

14 International financial markets

14.1	Introduction	236
14.2	International finance and the balance of payments	236
	14.2.1 International balance of payments	236
	14.2.2 Exchange rate systems	239
	14.2.3 Interpreting imbalances	242
	14.2.4 International financial flows	243
14.3	Foreign exchange markets and exchange rates	244
	14.3.1 Effective exchange rates and arbitrage	244
	14.3.2 Fisher relation	245
	14.3.3 Interest parity	245
	14.3.4 Purchasing power parity	247
	14.3.5 Forward parity	249
	14.3.6 Central bank intervention	250
14.4	International financial markets	250
	14.4.1 What are Euromarket transactions?	250
	14.4.2 Origin of Eurocurrency markets	251
	14.4.3 How are Eurocurrencies created?	251
14.5	Eurosecurity markets	252
	14.5.1 Eurobond market	252
	14.5.2 International equity markets	254
	14.5.3 Eurocommercial paper	254
	14.5.4 Eurocurrency futures markets	255
14.6	Summary	255

LEARNING OBJECTIVES

After reading this chapter you will understand

- the meaning of the balance of payments and how it is related to financial flows between countries
- how international trading establishes interest parity, purchasing power parity and forward parity
- how a central bank's ability to manage currency values is restricted by arbitrageurs
- the meaning of Eurocurrencies and how they are created
- the nature of Eurosecurity markets and their importance

14.1 INTRODUCTION

Chapter 13 described markets for trading risks, including the risks of dealing in foreign currencies. This chapter examines additional details of international transactions, both short and long term. It first defines the international balance of payments accounts, then shows how the accounts summarise international financial transactions. Next, the chapter examines exchange rate relationships. Finally, it discusses the origin and importance of the world's first truly international financial markets, the Eurocurrency and Eurosecurity markets.

14.2 INTERNATIONAL FINANCE AND THE BALANCE OF PAYMENTS

To show how exchanges of funds between countries can be traced, we first examine the balance of payments accounts. It is then possible to interpret the nature of an imbalance, and to see how international financial flows offset payments imbalances. Offsetting financial transactions can either be long term, in which case they usually represent international investment, or short term, in which case they usually reflect arbitraging and speculative activity. Short term transactions also play a residual role in settling payments imbalances.

14.2.1 International balance of payments

The balance of payments is determined using an accounting procedure which links the balance on trade in goods and services to their offsetting financial transactions. The major categories reported in the accounts are given in Figure 14.1.

The components of the **balance on current account** defined in Figure 14.1 represent sources and uses of foreign exchange. If exports exceed imports, the difference in their values represents a source of foreign exchange, while if exports are less than imports, the difference is a use of foreign exchange. Investment income and the sale of services are sources, citizens' travel abroad

minus	Exports Imports
equals	Merchandise trade balance
plus minus	Investment income and services provided to other countries Travel abroad, remittances to other countries, and government grants
equals	Balance on current account
plus	Balance on capital account (net long term investment)
equals	Balance on current and capital account (basic balance)
offset by	Short term private and official financial transactions

Figure 14.1 Balance of payments accounts

uses of foreign exchange. A country with a current account surplus is a country whose sources of foreign exchange exceed its uses. It is therefore a net generator of foreign exchange earnings.

> **balance on current account** the difference between a country's imports and exports of goods and services, adjusted to include such other items as investment income.

A country's actual needs for foreign exchange are the difference between its net earnings (balance on current account) and what it borrows or lends. This difference, called the **basic balance**, recognises that long term investment in a country can be a source of foreign exchange, just as investment abroad is a use. Thus a basic surplus reflects availability of foreign exchange, while a basic deficit reflects a need for foreign exchange. A basic surplus is offset by short term lending or the accumulation of foreign exchange reserves, a basic deficit by short term borrowing or the sale of official reserves.

> **basic balance** the difference between a country's balance on current account and its long term borrowing or lending transactions.

In most circumstances, payments imbalances are affected simultaneously by trade, domestic production capability and savings. To see this, define national income as Y, where

$$Y \equiv C + I + G + X - M \tag{14.1}$$

and

C: consumption expenditures of households and business
G: consumption expenditures of government
I: investment expenditures of households and business
X: exports of goods and services, adjusted for investment income, travel and remittances
M: imports of goods and services, similarly adjusted.

Define total expenditures, E, by

$$E \equiv C + I + G$$

Then

$$Y = E + X - M$$

$$Y - E = X - M \tag{14.2}$$

Domestic Income – Domestic Spending = Current Account Balance

= Capital Account Balance

Condition (14.2) indicates that a country's balance of payments has both financial and trade dimensions. The left-hand side of (14.2) shows the spending calculation, the right-hand side the resulting current account balance. If the whole of the current account balance is offset by a long term financial transaction, the two previous magnitudes also equal the capital account transaction. Thus, for example, (14.2) shows that a country with a deficit on current account both spends more than its income and borrows the difference.

Also,

$$Y - C - T \equiv S$$

where T represents government tax collections, S represents savings. Rewriting the above as

$$Y - C = S + T$$

and substituting into (14.1) gives

$$Y - C = I + G + X - M$$

$$S + T = G + I + X - M$$

and finally

$$S - I = G - T + X - M \tag{14.3a}$$

If the government's budget is in balance (i.e., if $G = T$), then (14.3a) simplifies to

$$S - I = X - M \qquad (14.3b)$$

Savings – Investment = Current Account Balance

Condition (14.3b) indicates that with a balanced government budget, a country that has less domestic savings than domestic investment will also have a current account deficit. Condition (14.3a) shows more explicitly how government imbalances can affect the balance on current account. For example, if the government has a budgetary deficit, then either the current account balance or the amount of savings must change from the values they would take on if the government's budget were balanced.

More generally, the combination of (14.2) and (14.3) says that the capital account balance, the current account balance, the government's budgetary balance, and the difference between domestic savings and investment are all interlinked. An imbalance on current account can thus be regarded either as an imbalance in international financing in the amount of domestic saving available for fixed investment, or in the government's budget.

14.2.2 Exchange rate systems

As a country's trade patterns and international financial transactions change, the value of its currency is likely to be affected unless exchange rates are fixed.[1] Under one arrangement, the gold standard, exchange rates are fixed by international agreement in relation to gold. To maintain its obligations under the gold standard, a country must limit its currency issue to a prespecified multiple of its gold reserves. If it tries to exceed the ratio of currency to gold reserves, it faces a credibility problem: holders of currency may not believe the country can maintain the currency's value in relation to gold, and will thus try to redeem their currency for gold before others come to the same belief.

Assuming that its currency is at or near the maximal levels permitted by its gold stock, a country with a trade deficit must surrender an amount of gold equal in value to the excess of its imports over its exports.[2] Since the amount of currency outstanding is assumed to be at or near its permissible maximum in relation to gold reserves, and since agreements with other countries prevent its letting the value of the currency fall, the amount of currency outstanding must be reduced as gold reserves are surrendered.

Adhering to a gold standard means that an automatic adjustment mechanism is called into action if a country's price levels increase faster than those of other countries. To illustrate the adjustment, suppose the country in question has a current account deficit. Then as domestic price levels increase the deficit will also increase, as buyers throughout the world substitute cheaper foreign goods or services for the more expensive domestic goods or services. To compensate for the increased trade deficit, greater gold outflows will occur, and the outstanding amount of the country's currency will have to be reduced. The effect of reducing the amount of currency outstanding is to curtail economic activity, which in turn reduces the current account deficit by limiting imports. While the chain of events is lengthy and requires macroeconomic analysis, the reduction in imports comes about because curtailing economic activity reduces national income, and imports are regarded as an increasing function of national income. Then, if imports fall faster than exports, the deficit on current account is also reduced.

The adjustments that occur in the event of a current account surplus are not dissimilar. In this case adhering to the gold standard means that the surplus will lead to an increase in the domestic money supply that will in turn ultimately increase domestic prices. The increase in domestic prices then leads to a chain of adjustments analogous to those already discussed. In particular, if exports become more expensive on world markets, the current account surplus is likely to be reduced.

The purpose of a gold standard is to stabilise currency values in relation to gold, and hence in relation to each other. This stability serves both to reduce foreign exchange risk and to encourage trading among countries. On the other hand, adhering to the gold standard limits the amount of currency outstanding, and implementing the standard therefore means that the value of transactions in a given period cannot exceed a certain maximum – the product of the currency outstanding and the rate at which it is exchanged betwen parties. Thus the gold standard can encourage trade by making countries' announced values of their currencies credible, but at the price of restraining economic growth through limiting the maximal value of transactions in any given period. The tradeoff between stable currencies and growth is known as the Triffin Dilemma, after Professor Robert Triffin, who first pointed it out in the 1960s.

Under a flexible exchange rate system, the linkages between current account imbalances and adjustments to national income are loosened. A flexible exchange rate offers a country greater freedom in choosing economic policy, because its policymakers can allow the burdens of adjustment to fall either on the exchange rate or on the growth of national income. Some observers believe that flexible exchange rates can impair trade by creating uncertainty about relative currency values. However, these risks have diminished, at least for shorter-term deals, as the growth of derivatives and currency trading has made hedging foreign exchange transactions easier and cheaper than formerly.

With flexible exchange rates, relative currency values are determined by market forces rather than by agreement: changes in currency values can occur independently of changes in the amount of currency outstanding. Thus, a current account deficit can be eliminated by currency values falling on the international markets, so long as the decline in currency value leads to exports rising relative to imports. However, if countries employ tariffs, duties, quotas and domestic price controls, adjustments can be impeded and exchange rate flexibility may be translated, at least partially, into changes in real output.

Perhaps the most severe criticism of a flexible exchange rate regime is that it does not impose sufficient discipline on a country to keep its domestic costs in line with the rest of the world. For example, a country can tolerate large wage increases and yet offset most of the effects on the international price of its exports by devaluing its currency. Even with devaluations, however, in an environment of continued wage increases a country's costs are likely to rise faster than those of its international competitors, weakening the country's ability to compete for a share of world trade.

Essentially, these concerns underlie the European countries' willingness to join the European Monetary System (EMS). While a full discussion of the advantages and disadvantages of the EMS is beyond the scope of this survey, mention of the principal issues is relevant to discussing the meaning of fixed and flexible exchange rate regimes. Each member of the EMS agrees to restrict the fluctuations in the value of its currency relative to those of other members, thus making it difficult for special interest groups in any one country to obtain increases in income over and above those obtained by counterparts in other countries. Thus the EMS promotes anti-inflationary, pro-competitive conditions that individual countries sometimes find politically difficult to create on their own. During the years 1979 to 1992 the EMS worked relatively well, largely because member countries grew at about the same rate and had roughly the same rates of inflation. The necessary adjustments following on differences in growth rates and in inflation were made using relatively frequent, but small, realignments of currency values.

Strains began to show in September 1992 when Finland, which had unilaterally pegged the Finnmark to the ECU, had to abandon its link and lower the value of its currency. The Swedish krona was next to forgo its link to the ECU, and subsequently Spain devalued the peseta. In late September 1992 both Italy and Great Britain dropped out of the EMS, and capital controls were imposed by Spain, Portugal and Ireland. Despite all these actions, France and Germany were able to maintain a fixed French franc/deutschemark exchange rate, and the EMS continued to function in relatively quiet markets until the summer of 1993.

At that time the economic pressures of German reunification tested the EMS much more severely. To aid the East during reunification, the German federal government incurred relatively large deficits, and Germany's attempts to offset the inflationary effects of such a policy caused serious policy disagreements among EMS members. In order to resist inflationary pressures in Germany, the Bundesbank wanted to restrict monetary growth, largely by keeping interest rates high. The relatively high German interest rates meant that in order to maintain the values of their currencies relative to the deutschemark, other EMS members were also under pressure to raise interest rates. However, the German policy conflicted with the preferences of other countries for promoting economic growth through lower interest rate policies. In particular, as France indicated a preference for not letting interest rates rise too sharply, the policy disagreements with Germany became serious enough that market agents began to speculate on a devaluation of the French franc. Despite official attempts to stabilise currency values, speculation continued and the EMS intervention band had to be raised from its former 2.25 percent to 15 percent, in effect suspending the workings of the EMS.

There has been no subsequent return to the former stability of currency values, but at this writing hope still remains that at least some of the EMS members will be able to effect a convergence of their economies in future years. The ultimate aim of the EMS members is to establish a single currency to be used in all member countries, thus in effect fixing the exchange rate between those countries.

14.2.3 Interpreting imbalances

Persistent payments imbalances can be interpreted in a number of ways. There are several factors which explain, solely or in combination, why some countries have chronic surpluses, and others chronic deficits, in their balance of payments accounts. There are also several reasons why some currencies appreciate in one period, and decline in another. The explanatory factors include the portfolio decisions of investors, trade elasticities and the size of a country's output relative to domestic demand for it.

The portfolio approach to payments imbalances considers the supply of currency, and bonds denominated in domestic currency, relative to investors' demands for these instruments.[3] If the quantity of currency and securities supplied at current market values is not equal to the quantity demanded, an imbalance results. Under fixed exchange rates, the disequilibrium will lead to a payments imbalance, but under flexible exchange rates it will lead to a change in the value of the currency (measured relative to the values of other currencies). For example, if the demand for a given country's currency and securities increases under fixed exchange rates, the country's balance of payments will move toward surplus. Under flexible exchange rates the country's currency will appreciate in value on the international markets.

If central banks are able to influence international financial flows by changing domestic credit conditions they may also be capable of sterilising reserve flows, that is to offset the effects entirely. A central bank must be able to sterilise reserve flows if it wishes to pursue an independent monetary policy while maintaining a fixed exchange rate. However, international capital markets are large, and a central bank's ability to sterilise reserve flows is limited by the amount of resources it can muster for that purpose. Since world-wide daily trading in foreign exchange now exceeds the total reserves of all central banks, no one central bank, even with the help of others, can withstand market pressures for very long.

The elasticities approach to payments imbalances is concerned mainly with conditions under which a devaluation will improve the trade balance. If both exports and imports are price elastic, a change in relative currency values will quickly affect a trade imbalance. However, the less elastic are demands for exports, imports, or both, the less likely it is that a change in currency values will offset the imbalance. If volumes of trade are unaffected by price level change, changes in the value of the currency will not improve an imbalance much, and may even worsen it.

Suppose, for example, that both imports and exports are price inelastic in some country with a trade deficit. If the value of the currency falls, the volumes of imports and exports will be unaffected, but imports will cost relatively more and exports will bring in about the same as before. In this case the trade deficit can actually worsen, at least in the short run. In the long run the demands for exports, imports, or both, are likely to be more elastic and volume adjustments will take place.

The absorption approach views a trade imbalance as the difference between the quantity of domestic production supplied and the quantity demanded. If domestic output is held constant, the trade balance can only improve if domestic demand for the output falls, permitting more domestic output to be exported. A devaluation can bring about this effect if it decreases the proportion of total production absorbed domestically.

The foregoing three explanations of why trade imbalances arise are not necessarily exclusive. In fact, trade imbalances are determined simultaneously by financial disequilibria, the price elasticities of trade transactions and individual economies' absorption capacities. Nevertheless, for analytical purposes it is useful to develop each of the explanations separately, showing how each works while assuming other factors are held constant.

As the world's financial system becomes increasingly integrated, a fourth factor, changing expectations, is becoming increasingly important to explaining the volatility of currency and securities values. For example, in the mid 1990s a weakening of the Mexican peso created a similar weakening in the Canadian dollar. Even though the two countries' economic fundamentals are quite different, expectations for the two countries' currencies seemed to be related in the eyes of some of the world's currency traders.

14.2.4 International financial flows

A current account deficit implies capital inflows; a surplus implies outflows. The financial offsets to a current account imbalance can be either short term or long term, depending on the country's financial picture and on investor preferences. Money market transactions occur mainly in response to changing interest rate differentials between countries, and involve such short term instruments as treasury bills, bankers' acceptances and commercial paper. International bond market transactions usually involve borrowing initiated by domestic firms and governments, while share transactions are often initiated by foreign investors seeking to acquire equity positions in either existing or new domestic firms.

Foreign investment means a country is raising long term funds from the rest of the world. It can take the form of either **direct investment** or **portfolio investment**. Direct investment, which means the purchase of equity in order to acquire control, depends on risk–return considerations as well as such other factors as country risk. Moreover, direct investment is often motivated by a perceived need for high capability financial governance. For example, technology transfer is often carried out internally to an organisation, because of the complexity of arranging contracts at arm's length in the marketplace when the actual terms of the transaction cannot readily be described.

> **foreign direct investment** the purchase of equity by non-nationals in order to acquire control of a company's operations.

Portfolio investment means investment for portfolio return only, and is mainly determined by the risk–return considerations developed in portfolio theory. Portfolio investors, whether they actually buy debt or equity, do not seek to acquire control positions in the companies whose securities they purchase. However, most investors have not diversified geographically to the extent portfolio theory would predict. In practice, they are inhibited by such factors as government capital controls, the threat of nationalisation and the absence of information regarding investment opportunities.

> **foreign portfolio investment** the purchase of shares or bonds by non-nationals for holding in an investment portfolio. Control over the firm is not sought by portfolio investors.

At some time a country might not have sufficient domestic savings to finance its total planned investment. If the investments are all to be carried out, the country must then raise funds abroad, which means it incurs the obligation of repaying the borrowings with interest. Sometimes a nationalistic press will be critical of such a policy, but if the investment projects financed yield returns higher than the cost of funds, and if they could not have been financed using domestic funds, the country can still benefit from the international borrowing.

14.3 FOREIGN EXCHANGE MARKETS AND EXCHANGE RATES

This section first explains how arbitrage-based trading influences relations between different currencies. It then examines four theoretical exchange rate relationships established primarily by arbitraging. The Fisher relation, introduced in Chapter 6, is recalled here and related to the remaining three: the interest parity, purchasing power parity and forward parity theorems. The section also examines some of the deviations from theoretical relations that are observed in practice, and discusses reasons for their occurrence. Finally, the section examines how central banks intervene in the foreign exchange markets in attempts to affect currency values.

14.3.1 Effective exchange rates and arbitrage

As Chapter 6 explained, arbitraging establishes well-known interest rate relationships between securities traded in perfectly competitive markets with no transactions costs. The same kinds of arbitraging arguments can be used to derive theoretical relations between the values of different countries' currencies, as the remainder of this section shows. In practice, the actual relations between countries' currencies are more complex than arbitraging arguments suggest: deviations from the theoretically predicted values can quite frequently be observed. These deviations are usually attributable to market imperfections or central bank intervention designed to offset the workings of market forces. They occur more often and are larger in the short run, but some of them can last for periods measured in years, as will be discussed further below.

14.3.2 Fisher relation

Chapter 6 explained that the **Fisher relation** results as lenders try to advance funds in ways intended to preserve the real rather than the nominal value of their loans or investments. To do so, lenders set interest rates according to

$$(1 + R_D) = (1 + r)(P_{D1}) / (P_{D0}) \tag{14.4}$$

where

R_D = current nominal interest rate
r = current real interest rate
P_{D1} = expected domestic price level at time 1
P_{D0} = domestic price level at time 0.

Equation 14.4 restates (6.11) in a form useful for this chapter. It says that lenders or investors attempt to strike terms that will offset possible future declines in purchasing power. When interest rates and inflation rates are both relatively low, the Fisher relation can be approximated by

$$(1 + R_D) = (1 + r + i) \tag{14.5}$$

where i represents expected inflation over the period and the other variables are defined as before.

The Fisher relation probably holds more nearly over the long run, but it is difficult to measure inflation expectations over long periods of time.[4] Expected inflation is less difficult to measure over the short run, and Fama and Gibbons (1984) show that the Fisher relation provides an adequate description of how nominal interest rates on US short term money market instruments behave up to the early 1980s.

14.3.3 Interest parity

> **interest parity theory** a theory which explains that arbitrage is likely to remove differences between real interest rates obtainable on investments of the same risk but in different currencies.

According to the **interest parity theory** the ratio of forward to spot exchange rates will equal the ratio of foreign to domestic nominal interest rates:

$$(F / S) = (1 + R_F) / (1 + R_D) \qquad (14.6)$$

where

F = forward rate (foreign currency units per domestic unit)
S = spot rate (foreign currency units per domestic unit)
R_F = current foreign interest rate
R_D = current domestic interest rate.

Since the interest parity theory is established by arbitraging arguments, it says in effect that individuals will invest in a foreign country if the net return to them is greater than could be earned on domestic investments. Interest parity theory goes further to predict that if returns differ, then the short term investment flows will continue until currency values, interest rates or both will adjust until the two investment possibilities offer equal returns:

$$(1 + R_D) = S(1 + R_F) / F \qquad (14.7)$$

To illustrate the workings of interest parity theory, consider Figure 14.2, which displays the three logical possibilities regarding two countries' interest rates.

Assumptions	Domestic = foreign interest rate $R_D = R_F = 0.10$ $S = 0.75$	Domestic > foreign interest rate $R_D = 0.10$ $R_F = 0.09$ $S = 0.75$	Domestic < foreign interest rate $R_D = 0.09$ $R_F = 0.10$ $S = 0.75$
Predictions of equilibrium forward rate from interest parity theory	1.10 = 0.75(1.10)/F F = 0.75 = S	1.10 = 0.75(1.09)/F F = 0.7432 < S	1.09 = 0.75(1.10)/F F = 0.7569 > S
Interest arbitraging activity	If F* < 0.75, Canadians should invest in US. If F* > 0.75, US citizens should invest in Canada.	If F* < 0.7432, Canadians find it profitable to invest in US on a covered basis. US investors could invest at home, borrowing in Canada.	If F* > 0.7569, US investors find it profitable to invest in Canada on a covered basis. Canadians can invest at home, borrowing in the US.

Figure 14.2 Covered interest arbitrage activities

The figure assumes a one year maturity for all instruments, and considers various kinds of profitable actions depending on the nature of interest rates and forward exchange rates. A spot rate S of 0.75 means $1.00 Canadian buys 0.75 dollars US. The three columns display three possible interest rate scenarios. In each column, the first group of figures lists assumptions, following which Equation 14.7 is used to calculate the equilibrium forward rate. Next, the equilibrium forward rate is compared to the assumed spot rate. Finally, if the actual forward rate F* differs from the equilibrium forward rate F, actions to take profit advantage of the situation are listed.

Interest parity theory applies to international trade in the most liquid financial instruments, but not to others. For example, the theory has been observed to hold relatively closely in the Eurocurrency markets (Taylor 1987). On the other hand, interest parity theory does not well describe relations between ECU bonds and their synthetic equivalents, where the latter are made up of individual countries' government bonds held in a portfolio duplicating the currency composition of the ECU. Such observed deviations from interest rate parity seem to be attributable primarily to a lack of liquid instruments to trade. Nevertheless, if arbitrage between ECU bonds and their synthetic equivalents can be made profitable, the currently observed deviations would likely be reduced or eliminated.

14.3.4 Purchasing power parity

> **purchasing power parity theory** a theory which says that agents think in terms of buying power rather than in terms of local prices.

Purchasing power parity theory is similar to interest parity theory. Suppose there are two economies in which only one consumption good is traded. The Absolute Purchasing Power Parity Theorem says that if exchange rates can adjust freely and if there is free movement of the good between countries, the good should be offered for sale in either country at the same price, after adjusting for exchange rate differences using the prevailing exchange rate. In other words, changes in the exchange rate offset differences in prices stated in local currencies. The theorem can, of course, be expressed in terms of a representative basket of consumer goods rather than just the single good used in our introductory illustration.

Temporal adjustments to exchange rates can be expressed using a related concept, relative purchasing power parity, which compares exchange rate changes to differences in price level changes, between home and abroad. Formally,

$$(S_1 / S_0) = (P_{F1} / P_{F0}) / (P_{D1} / P_{D0}) \qquad (14.8)$$

where

S_1 = spot rate at time 1
S_0 = spot rate at time 0
P_{F1} = expected foreign price level at time 1
P_{F0} = foreign price level at time 0
P_{D1} = expected domestic price level at time 1
P_{D0} = domestic price level at time 0.

For example, if Canada has zero inflation and the US experiences a 10 percent inflation over some period, the US dollar should fall 10 percent relative to the Canadian dollar over that period. To illustrate, consider Equation 14.6 and assume all values at time 0 are unity. Then the right side will equal 1.1, because of the 10 percent inflation differential. Therefore the ratio of spot rates will also equal 1.1, meaning that at time 1 a Canadian dollar will buy 10 percent more of the US dollar, or that the US dollar has declined in value against the Canadian dollar by 10 percent. More generally, a currency will appreciate or depreciate in relation to another depending on whether the first country has a lower or a higher rate of inflation than the second.

Both the absolute and the relative purchasing power theorems have been tested. It might be expected that the tests would not strongly confirm either version of the theorem, because there are many impediments to the emergence of purchasing power parity in the short run. These impediments include costly information, shipping costs, the presence of differentiated goods, and trade barriers (such as tariffs, quotas and administrative delays). As an example of a crude test, *The Economist* surveys of purchasing power parity use the Big Mac hamburger as a proxy for a basket of goods. The observed prices of Big Macs vary widely between countries after adjusting for exchange rate differences, suggesting that absolute purchasing power parity does not hold closely with respect to this standard.

If price changes caused exchange rate changes and if purchasing power parity theory were a good predictor, one would expect that exchange rates would change slowly over time, but in fact exchange rates exhibit frequent, sudden, and relatively large changes. There are several reasons for these deviations from the predictions of purchasing power parity. First, not all goods are traded among countries, so purchasing power parity might be expected to exert only one of several influences on exchange rates. Second, the goods that do trade are exchanged in relatively imperfect markets, and so can exhibit relatively large deviations among countries. Third, purchasing power parity theory ignores the effects that financial transactions can have on exchange rates. 'It is more likely that the short-term variation in exchange rates is caused by interest rate changes, or news about the relative state of the domestic and foreign economies, or even changes in the prices of other assets' (Sercu and Uppal 1995: 367) . In a survey of formal work, Rogoff concludes there are large deviations from purchasing power parity, which die out at the rate of about 15 percent per year (1996: 664). Rogoff observes that the frictions preventing faster adjustment probably include 'transportation costs, threatened or actual tariffs, nontariff barriers, information costs, (and) lack of labor mobility' (1996: 664).

14.3.5 Forward parity

---

forward parity theory a theory which concludes that when arbitrage opportunities are eliminated, countries' real interest rates are equal.

The Fisher relation, interest parity theory and purchasing power theory together imply a fourth result: **forward parity theory**. The first three effects together imply that real rates of interest between the two countries will be equal. The forward parity theory then says that the forward exchange rate must equal the future spot rate. Recall the conditions:

$$(1 + R_D) = (1 + r)(P_{D1}) / (P_{D0}) \tag{14.4}$$

$$(1 + R_F) = (1 + r)(P_{F1}) / (P_{F0}) \tag{14.4'}$$

$$(F_0 / S_0) = (1 + R_F) / (1 + R_D) \tag{14.6'}$$

$$(S_1 / S_0) = (P_{F1} / P_{F0}) / (P_{D1} / P_{D0}) \tag{14.8}$$

The first two state the Fisher relation for domestic and foreign countries respectively, using the notation defined earlier in this chapter. The third states the interest parity result, using notation which now takes timing into account. The fourth is the purchasing power parity condition. The ratio of Equation 14.6' to Equation 14.8 is

$$(F_0 / S_1) =$$

$$[(1 + R_F) / (1 + R_D)] / [(P_{F1} / P_{F0}) / (P_{D1} / P_{D0})] =$$

$$[(1 + R_F)(P_{F0} / P_{F1})] / [(1 + R_D)(P_{D0} / P_{D1})] = \tag{14.9}$$

$$(1 + r) / (1 + r) = 1$$

using (14.4) and (14.4') to eliminate $(1 + R_D)$ and $(1 + R_F)$. That is, $F_0 = S_1$ as claimed. In practice this relation may be affected by risk premia incorporated in estimates of future interest rates. As stated, (14.9) is derived under an assumption of certainty which does not recognise the importance of risk premia.

Real gains or losses can be made in foreign investments if the actual spot rate at time 1 differs from its time 0 expected value. (These two values are the same under the certainty assumptions made above.) If S_{R1} (the realised spot rate at time 1) differs from S_1 (its expected value calculated at time 0) real gains or losses would be made according to

$$(1 + g) = S_{R1} / S_1 \tag{14.10}$$

where g measures the real gain or loss from investing in foreign rather than domestic assets. By Equation 14.9 the time 1 spot rate is anticipated by the time 0 forward rate (i.e., $S_1 = F_0$). We therefore have

$$(1 + g) = S_{R1} / F_0 \tag{14.11}$$

This result assumes the two countries' real interest rates are equal and shows only the earnings resulting from unanticipated changes in the spot rate. It says that investors should take a long position in a foreign currency if they expect the realised spot rate to rise above that predicted by the current forward rate; a short position if they expect the realised spot rate to fall below the value predicted by the current forward rate.

For example, referring again to Figure 14.2, if investors believe that the US dollar will fall by more than is implied by $F = 0.75$, say $S_{R1} = 0.76$, forward speculators will take a long position. That is, they will buy Canadian dollars forward at 0.75, and on maturity sell the contract in the spot market at 0.76, making 0.01 per dollar traded if things turn out as they expect. On the other hand, if they believe the US dollar will revalue more than is implied by $F = 0.75$ (say $S_{R1} = 0.74$), forward speculators will take a short position. That is, they will sell Canadian dollar forward contracts at 0.75, with the intention of buying spot at 0.74 when the contract matures. If they turn out to be right, they will make a profit of 0.01 per dollar traded.

14.3.6 Central bank intervention

Attempts by authorities to alter exchange rates away from their market-determined levels can affect relative currency values for a time, but international financial markets are so large that eventually currency speculation can overcome any attempts by authorities to maintain an exchange rate at a non-market level. When a central bank intervenes, it does not usually intend to resist fundamental changes in the value of the currency, but rather to smooth temporary changes. The central bank monitors potential supplies and demands in the market in attempts to offset short term price changes, and also influences the currency indirectly by changing interest rate policies. For example, to offset downward pressures on its currency, a central bank will restrict monetary growth to keep interest rates somewhat higher than they would otherwise be.

As a point of interest, the monetary authorities in the United States rarely intervene in the markets for US dollars, and did not do so at all between 1973 and 1985. However, in September 1985 when a major realignment of currencies was desired, the Federal Reserve System did attempt to influence the exchange rate.

14.4 INTERNATIONAL FINANCIAL MARKETS

Some financial deals are effected in markets that can truly be called international. The most important of these markets are the Euromarkets.

14.4.1 What are Euromarket transactions?

The distinguishing feature of a Euromarket transaction is that it is denominated in a national currency, but booked in a foreign city. Sometimes the term offshore market is used as a synonym for a Euromarket. Originally most Euro-transactions were short term US dollar transactions booked in London. Now a number of major currencies can be used, there are both money and capital market transactions, and the deals can be booked in a number of the world's major cities.

14.4.2 Origin of Eurocurrency markets

The Eurodollar, the first Eurocurrency, appeared in the late 1950s. The innovation in creating Eurocurrencies was not the use of dollar deposits outside the US, since that had been done earlier, particularly in Canada where US dollar deposits first appeared in 1860. Rather, the distinguishing feature of Euromarket transactions was their profitable placement and active use outside the US domestic money markets and domestic banking system.

The regulations applying to Eurocurrency deposits are usually less stringent than those applying to domestic deposits. This difference contributed importantly to the markets' origin and continues to be important even now. Some of the first Eurodollar deals took place in the 1950s, and were arranged to circumvent UK government restrictions on using sterling to finance foreign trade. British banks substituted US dollar for sterling trade credits, increasing sharply the demand for offshore dollars in Europe. The British banks raised some of the necessary deposits from the Moscow Narodny Bank, which for political reasons did not wish to place US funds in domestic US banks. The supply of offshore deposits was further increased by US balance of payments deficits which placed more dollars in international circulation, and still further by restrictions on the interest rates payable on US dollar deposits booked in the United States. Finally, since there were no compulsory reserve requirements on offshore deposits, their effective cost to financial intermediaries was lower than it was for domestic deposits.[5]

The emergence of the Eurocurrency markets was one of the most important developments in post-war international banking. Originally serving as a source of short term funds for trade financing, the markets expanded to facilitate banks' foreign exchange transactions and to provide money market trading facilities. Not long after the first transactions occurred, the Eurocurrency market became the central mechanism for channelling international funds flows among banks, and the London Interbank Offer Rate (**LIBOR**) became one of the best known and most important international interest rates. Now most Eurocurrency transactions are priced in terms of LIBOR plus a premium reflecting the risk of the arrangement, just as domestic loans are priced in relation to prime.

14.4.3 How are Eurocurrencies created?

As one example of how Eurocurrencies are created, consider a Eurodollar deposit, that is a US dollar denominated bank deposit placed outside the United States. The deposit might be placed in a foreign branch of a US bank, or in a non-US bank. Any such deposit involves a transfer of ownership on the books of banks in the US, say from the account of a US citizen living in the US to the account of a foreign bank. On the foreign bank's books the same transaction is recorded as both an asset – the bank's deposit with the US bank – and a liability to the depositing client. If the funds on deposit are repeatedly lent out and redeposited in other foreign banks, the original amount of funds can be multiplied many times.[6]

The centre of the Eurocurrency market is a group of banks which bid for deposits and use the funds raised for relending to other banks or to non-financial businesses. Other Euromarket participants include investment banks, merchant banks, multinational corporations, government agencies, OPEC (Organisation of Petroleum-Exporting Countries) countries, governments and central banks of less developed countries, and international organisations. The 1996 annual report of the Bank for International Settlements estimated that the outstanding amount of banks' net international financing was approximately $6,440 billion in 1995. With respect to net international lending over the year 1995, about 40 per cent was in US currency. Other major Eurocurrencies in order of importance include the deutschemark, the Japanese yen, the French franc and the British pound.

14.5 EUROSECURITY MARKETS

Eurosecurity markets include the Eurobond market, international equity markets, the Eurocommercial paper and Eurocurrency futures markets.

14.5.1 Eurobond market

The Eurobond market is an international long term bond market which, like the Eurocurrency market, came into being because of regulatory restrictions. One of the first restrictions avoided by issuers of Eurobonds was the US Interest Equalization Tax (IET) which was levied against non-residents borrowing funds in the United States. Even after the removal of the IET in 1974, the Eurobond market continued to flourish because of other regulations placed on bonds issued in domestic capital markets. For example, in the United States registration of foreign bonds involves meeting stringent SEC requirements, and there are similar requirements in other countries.

Eurobonds are not floated in a domestic capital market. Rather they are issued in the international Euromarket and underwritten by an international banking syndicate not subject to any one country's laws. Because Eurobond issues need not satisfy any country's regulatory requirements, it is usually possible to market an issue more quickly and cheaply in the Eurobond market than in a domestic capital market. Eurobonds may be denominated in an individual currency, such as US dollars or deutschemarks, or in units such as **European currency units** (ECUs). The latter are popular with some European investors because their market value depends on a portfolio of currencies which is usually more stable in value than a single currency issue.

European currency unit a unit of account and a medium of exchange between participating central banks whose countries are members of the European Union (EU). The ECU is a composite currency formed by a basket of EU currencies. The currencies are held in weighted averages according to the economies' sizes and importance to trade, and the weights are adjusted periodically to reflect changes in the criteria. The value of the ECU is determined by the value of the individual currencies in the basket.

Value of one ECU = $1.12US = £0.67 (December 6, 1997. *Source: The Economist*)

Table 14.1 illustrates the size and composition of international bond issues for 1989 through 1992. International bonds consist of foreign and Eurocurrency bonds. Foreign bonds are issued by a borrower who is of a nationality different from the country in which the bonds are issued. Such issues are usually underwritten and sold by a group of banks of the market country and are denominated in that country's currency. In contrast, Eurocurrency bonds are those underwritten and sold in various national markets simultaneously, usually through international syndicates of banks.

Eurobonds are issued because their net costs are lower than those of domestic issues. Of the Eurobond issues, the most important currency used is the US dollar, which accounts for one-third to one-half of the amounts raised. The ECU, the yen, the British pound, the deutschemark and the Canadian dollar are of about equal importance, accounting for some 5 percent of amounts raised in the years covered by Table 14.1. Of the international issues, the most important country is Switzerland, which accounts for 40–50 percent of the total amounts raised. Issues in the United States and Japan each account for another 10 percent or so of the amounts raised.

From 1979 to 1988 Eurobonds grew much more rapidly, by a factor of 9.4, than foreign bonds, which grew only 2.2 times. In 1988 foreign bonds (issued in domestic capital markets) represented only about one-fifth of value of all the international bond issues; the rest were Eurobonds. International bond issues have increasingly been floated by industrial countries and international

Table 14.1 International bond issues and placements, 1989–92

	(billions of US dollars)			
	1989	*1990*	*1991*	*1992*
International issues	212.8	180.1	258.2	276.1
Foreign issues	42.9	49.8	50.6	57.6
Totals	255.7	229.9	308.8	333.7

Source: OECD (various issues) *Financial Market Trends, Financial Statistics Monthly.*

organisations. Centrally planned economies and developing countries are beginning to gain access to the markets, but in the mid-1990s accounted for only a small portion of the total.

Borrowers will usually refrain from issuing long bonds when they judge interest rates to be unusually high. Thus as in domestic bond markets, primary Eurobond issues increase (decrease) when interest rates decline (increase). The Eurobond market has another characteristic similar to that of domestic markets. It began like most fledgling markets as a primary market, but following on primary market successes, secondary market trading increased significantly. In contrast to primary transactions, secondary market trading takes place within domestic capital markets because it is not usually subject to the same regulations as primary trading.

14.5.2 International equity markets

International equity markets are not as well developed as the bond markets just described. International trading of equities is hampered by international differences in trading and price setting methods, and by difficulties in obtaining information regarding the issues. Companies interested in attracting shareholders world-wide currently have to list their shares on as many different share exchanges as the number of countries from which they wish to attract investors. Thus trading in the international equities markets essentially involves a few hundred large, well-known companies. As of the mid-1990s, the most important international stock trading takes place on the London International Stock Exchange, where it makes use of London's SEAQ (Securities Exchange Automated Quotation) system. SEAQ turnover of foreign shares is about as great as that of British shares, and SEAQ claims about half of the world's cross-border trading in equities.

Some regional cross-border trading is better developed than the Euroequities markets. As one example, it is quite common for Canadian companies to float equity issues in the United States, and this practice has increased since SEC regulations were revised to make it easier for Canadian firms to float private placements in the United States.

The International Finance Corporation, an arm of the World Bank, now provides information regarding developing countries' stock market prices. This information is intended to provide international investors with some of the data they require to purchase stocks issued in these countries, and thus to enhance the flow of funds to development. Currently most purchases of this type are initiated by investment companies.

14.5.3 Eurocommercial paper

Since the 1980s, the Euromarkets have also witnessed the emergence of trading in short term instruments, including commercial paper, promissory notes and other instruments only referred to as notes. Commercial paper and promissory notes are typical money market securities, which are issued on a discount basis and have maturities up to one year. Notes are medium term paper having maturities from one to seven years, and usually bear coupons. Banks also issue Eurocurrency certificates of deposit which, apart from being issued and traded in an international market, are just like the domestic certificates of deposit discussed in Chapter 12.

14.5.4 Eurocurrency futures markets

The first Eurocurrency futures contract was a Eurodollar contract traded on the International Money Market of the Chicago Mercantile Exchange. Eurodollar futures are currently also traded in London and in Singapore. Nearly all Eurocurrency contracts are used to manage interest rate risk, and the contracts trade according to the principles discussed in Chapters 7 and 12. Many developed countries also have contracts written in their own currencies on the local interbank interest rate. For example, a contract known as the French franc PIBOR contract is traded in Paris on the market known as MATIF (Marché à Terme Internationale de France).

14.6 SUMMARY

This chapter considered international currency and capital markets. It defined international financial transactions and showed how they affect the balance of payments. Exchange rate relations were discussed, as were the origin and importance of the Eurocurrency and Eurobond markets. These markets, which owe their origin to domestic financial regulation or taxation, now trade a range of securities quite similar to that traded in the larger domestic markets.

REVIEW QUESTIONS

Exercise 1 Which of the following transactions would increase a current account deficit? An increase in foreign travel. More long term borrowing by the US Treasury. A decrease in exports. An increase in remittances abroad?

Exercise 2 From identities (14.2) and (14.3), you can see that if savings is less than investment, the balance is likely to be made up by long term borrowing from abroad. Using an analogy with corporate finance, under what conditions might such long term borrowing be of benefit to a country?

Exercise 3 Suppose a country is borrowing from abroad to finance a new power project that will provide badly needed infrastructure. What is the difference between raising the funds in the form of foreign direct investment as shares, and in the form of portfolio investment as bonds?

Exercise 4 Calculate the returns to a C$100.00 investment in the US if domestic and foreign interest rates are the same 10 percent as in Figure 14.2 and if F*, the forward rate, is 0.73.

Exercise 5 What might be some of the costs that would be saved by borrowing in the Euromarkets as opposed to issuing foreign bonds?

Exercise 6 How does an increase in its citizens travelling abroad affect a country's balance of payments? How is the same country's balance of payments affected by a decline in its imports?

Exercise 7 Explain how the Eurocurrency markets are creations of domestic regulation.

Exercise 8 Can international banks create Euromoney?

Exercise 9 In the late 1980s the Eurobond markets seemed to present quite important arbitrage opportunities between the interest rates on domestic bonds and Eurobond issues in the same currency. Many of these arbitrage opportunities were not taken up. Why do you think that might be? Does your answer deny the workings of the principle of riskless arbitrage?

Exercise 10 Under what circumstances might a country become better off by borrowing from abroad?

Exercise 11 Covered interest arbitrage brings short term interest rates between Canada and the United States close together, but they also exhibit small random deviations from each other. Why do you think this might be? That is, why does interest parity theory not seem to hold exactly?

Exercise 12 A central bank can resist, but not withstand, the pressures of international currency speculators. How does this statement reflect the workings of the principle of riskless arbitrage?

Exercise 13 Why is there country risk in lending money to, say, a copper mining company with operations in the Andes? That is, why might the loan's risk differ from that of lending to a copper mining company with operations in North America?

Part IV

Financial intermediaries

This part examines domestic and international intermediaries. Chapter 15 discusses principles of intermediation. The principles are applied to the problems of managing domestic intermediaries in Chapter 16, and to international intermediation in Chapter 17.

15 Principles of intermediation

15.1	Introduction	260
15.2	Economics of intermediation	260
	15.2.1 Economies of scale and of scope	261
	15.2.2 Intermediary size	262
	15.2.3 Specialised activities	263
	15.2.4 Information processing and screening	263
15.3	Operating issues	264
	15.3.1 Technological change	264
	15.3.2 Gap management	265
	15.3.3 Risk management	266
	15.3.4 Liquidity management	267
	15.3.5 Managing capital positions	268
15.4	A strategic management model	269
	15.4.1 Model structure	269
	15.4.2 Model properties	272
	15.4.3 Sensitivity analyses	275
15.5	Summary	276

LEARNING OBJECTIVES

After reading this chapter you will understand

- why there are both financial supermarkets and specialised financial firms
- how the economics of information processing affects intermediaries' organisation
- why technological change is so important to intermediaries
- how intermediaries manage their portfolio risks
- how the gap serves as a rough risk management tool
- how intermediaries manage their liquidity and capital positions
- how a simple model can be used to help study tradeoffs between management goals

---

15.1 INTRODUCTION

This chapter examines strategic management in financial intermediaries. One of the most important of an intermediary's strategic decisions is choosing its organisational structure. A second, equally important challenge is preparing the firm to respond to future changes – either in its markets or in the technology it might employ. The chapter first outlines the factors affecting profitability when intermediaries consider whether their organisational structure might better be that of a multiproduct or a specialised firm. Next, the chapter examines economic issues that arise in adapting to changing markets or to technological change. Third, the chapter outlines the basic economics of intermediary operations. Finally, the chapter develops a model explaining how balancing expected profitability against risk can be studied.

15.2 ECONOMICS OF INTERMEDIATION

Like any financial firm, intermediaries structure themselves to meet and if possible outperform the competition. Management tries to lead or at least keep abreast of market developments, and at the same time tries to operate as profitably as possible. Meeting these two challenges means that intermediaries adapt their business to changing opportunities. As one example, intermediaries still perform their traditional role of raising funds through deposits and repackaging the funds as loans, but they are increasingly also acting as agents for financings they do not retain on their own books.

In performing their traditional roles, intermediaries gather savings deposited in small individual accounts and then lend out the funds in typically larger amounts – an activity sometimes called denomination intermediation. They employ maturity intermediation when they use their short term funds (i.e., funds deposited in chequing and savings accounts) to finance medium term loans.

Intermediary operations also transform risk: the depositing client of an intermediary does not face the same default risk as she would if she lent funds directly
to one of the intermediary's clients. The depositor's risk is related to the diversified risk of the intermediary's asset portfolio rather than to the credit risk of the
borrowing client. Risk is also transformed when portfolios of intermediary loans
are securitised: the original loans are repackaged into a diversified portfolio which
is then offered as collateral for securities purchased by institutional investors.

Despite the advantages of diversification, the uninsured depositor can still
face default risk: unsound lending practices can cause an intermediary to fail.
Thus when deciding where to place their short term funds, large depositors are
wise to take the intermediary default risk into account. On the other hand, small
depositors do not face default risk in jurisdictions where their funds are protected
by deposit insurance.[1]

In performing their newer roles, intermediaries usually act as agents, say to
find a group of investors willing to place funds with a business client. For
example, an intermediary might arrange a financial lease that involves a pension
fund as an investor and an airline as an equipment operator. Although it is still
commonplace for the intermediary to assume some of the default risk in these
kinds of arrangements, in some cases the whole of the default risk will be
assumed by the investing client.

15.2.1 Economies of scale and of scope

Scale economies provide intermediaries with reasons to specialise. For example,
there are usually fixed costs to setting up a screening facility for a particular
type of loan application, meaning that the unit cost of this type of screening
will decrease as the number of screenings increases. Similarly, most intermediaries enjoy scale economies in portfolio administration. Evidence shows that
small intermediaries can realise scale economies through asset growth, and there
is little or no evidence showing that large financial intermediaries encounter
scale diseconomies.[2] Recent mergers of data processing operations in banking
suggest that scale economies are realised in these operations as well as in the
administration of their asset portfolios.

Intermediaries can also sometimes enjoy scope economies by placing related
types of deals on their books. Scope economies (cost complementarities) stem
principally from sharing inputs across transactions that are not too different in
type. For example, the skills needed to lend operating funds to medium
sized business may be transferable to a consumer lending division. Similarly,
economies of scope might be realised from cross-selling agreements between
banks and securities dealers or between banks and insurance companies. If they
prove to reduce costs significantly, agreements of this type might also have significant impact on product pricing. For example, a 1992 study of the Consumers
Association of Canada suggested that combining banking and insurance activity
could save consumers up to 20 percent of the current retail price of life and
general insurance policies, largely through standardisation of contracts and their

delivery through bank branches. Similarly, securities firms might realise scope economies in offering cash management accounts or term deposits.

Scope economies do not necessarily extend to all combinations of transactions, especially those which differ considerably. There may, for instance, be scope economies in combining the sale of fire and property insurance, but these economies would probably not extend to offering both insurance products and venture investments within the same business unit. As a second example of the limits to realising scope economies, a life insurance representative may not initially be qualified to sell such financial products as registered retirement savings plans (RRSPs) and mutual fund shares or guaranteed investment certificates, and perhaps can do so only after relatively costly on the job training. Neverthless the development of expert systems which take the form of computer programs used to guide the marketing efforts of intermediary personnel could change this picture, so that cross-selling of presently dissimilar products may eventually become more cost-effective than is now the case.

15.2.2 Intermediary size

Many transactions can be performed most cheaply by large, multipurpose financial institutions. Larger institutions' abilities to reduce transactions costs stem mainly from the scale and scope economies discussed in the preceding section. New technologies can yield both scope and scale economies, through such ways as remote delivery of financial services and making it possible to develop common accounting schemes for different financial products. In recognition of these possibilities, many intermediaries are making impressively large investments aimed at keeping their computing and communications capabilities abreast of rapidly changing technology. The firms' resultant abilities to offer services at convenient locations, and for relatively low prices, mean that financial supermarkets are likely to continue capturing increasing shares of certain kinds of financial business. In particular, technology-intensive intermediaries are likely to perform the bulk of routine transactions in the future.

Size can affect portfolio risk, because large intermediaries usually have greater opportunities for geographical diversification than their smaller counterparts. Financial system observers also argue that large intermediaries are sometimes able to command government support in the event they encounter financial difficulty, an argument known as the 'too big to fail' argument. For both these reasons, larger intermediaries are perceived to be less risky than smaller ones, allowing them to benefit from lower overall costs of funding.

Even so, some small and specialised intermediaries still flourish. Niche firms can emerge and survive over the longer run so long as they retain cost advantages and are not vulnerable to takeover by larger firms. The smaller firms' cost advantages may stem from less burdensome regulation than that applying to larger firms, or from possessing the kinds of specialised skills needed to serve a small market. Small firms may also be more flexible than their larger counterparts, and thus able to adapt more rapidly and more cheaply to changing market conditions.

The size an intermediary can economically attain depends on both its operating costs and the markets it serves. Intermediaries expand until they exhaust their sources of operating economies, at least if the markets they serve are large enough to permit the expansion. As the foregoing discussion of scale and scope economies suggested, there are large potential efficiency gains associated with bank mergers. However, there is little empirical evidence that merged banks have reaped any economies of scale or scope in terms of returns on asset portfolios. Most of the gains appear to be through cost reduction rather than improved asset selection, and most of the value thus created appears to accrue to shareholders (Berger and Humphrey 1991, 1992). No intermediary can attain a large size if it serves only one or a few small markets. Even a specialised intermediary faces fixed setup costs, and if these setup costs are sufficiently large, some markets may not be served at all.

15.2.3 Specialised activities

Specialised divisions concentrate the activities of highly skilled, costly personnel. They can also provide more powerful performance incentives than larger units. Some intermediaries segregate their activities into semi-autonomous groups, and these specialised divisions may avoid the scale diseconomies that would be incurred if the activities were combined into a single large unit. For example, some life insurance companies and some trust companies have divisions operating specialised funds, such as fixed income, share or mortgage funds.

Lending and investment intermediaries specialise for other reasons as well. As shown by the example of venture capital firms, there are relatively high setup costs to screening those kinds of potential investments for which some or all of the necessary screening skills are experientially acquired. Venture investors remain specialised because their experientially acquired skills do not usually transfer readily to more traditional types of lending. Another factor contributing to specialisation is that venture capital firms usually need to show annual profits on their investments in order to satisfy the demands of the institutions funding them. A venture capital fund that needs to show short term profits cannot invest entirely in investments with very long run payoffs, even if these investments are likely to prove relatively rewarding. Yet, the typical firms in which a venture capitalist invests are likely to show profits only after several years of operation, and therefore a judicious balancing of fund raising and portfolio returns is necessitated.[3]

Regulatory restrictions also provide a stimulus for specialisation. Some kinds of institutions, such as mortgage companies, are permitted to make only certain kinds of investments. In other cases, financiers lose tax advantages unless they specialise.

15.2.4 Information processing and screening

All intermediaries screen proposed loans or investments to determine which are acceptable. Screening costs differ by type of deal, but screening operations usually exhibit both a relatively large fixed cost and a relatively small marginal cost component. As a result, unit screening costs usually decrease with the volume of deals screened. A screening cost function can shift downward as intermediary personnel learn to acquire additional skills or additional experience with a new type of deal.[4] For example, it takes about five years to train an investment officer in the venture capital industry. A reasonably experienced officer has the capacity to govern six to eight active investments, and to conduct some additional deal generation and screening activities. Intermediaries evolve different screening capabilities as a result of differing business experience. These different capabilities affect both their current screening costs and their likely future evolution – financial firms are more likely to enter lines of business related to their current expertise rather than businesses with which they have no experience. To the extent an intermediary has lower costs earned through learning by doing, it has an effective barrier to the entry of new competitors. The barriers are particularly effective if a market is small and potential entrants are therefore unsure whether they would be able to recover their fixed costs.

While intermediaries produce large amounts of information regarding their clients, they do not always make the information public. For example, lending intermediaries produce information on a deal by deal basis to be used privately in negotiations with the client.[5] Other kinds of intermediaries such as mutual funds, which spend relatively large sums on research, sometimes function as both information producers and information sellers. They may, for instance, sell or promulgate some of their research information as part of their marketing activities.

15.3 OPERATING ISSUES

The operating issues of concern to senior management include managing technological change and managing the balance sheet to achieve desired risk, liquidity and capital positions.

15.3.1 Technological change

In finance as in many other service industries, the cost of human resources relative to technology has risen steadily since about the 1960s, and is likely to continue rising. These changing costs mean that financial institutions will continue to substitute relatively cheap machines for relatively expensive labour: the trend begun by the proliferation of automatic banking machines and their electronic linkages will continue for some time. Various forms of communications media, including telephone and cable television facilities, will enhance future access to financial services, and it is likely that most routine financial transactions will eventually be effected using communications devices in the home or office. At this writing, client inquiries regarding credit card and account balances are handled automatically over the telephone or through the electronic media by many financial institutions, as are account transfers, bill payments, securities transactions, and other similar transactions. As more and more transactions are conducted using automated banking machines and communications media, the accounting for them is completed automatically after they have been entered by the client. In addition, the services provided by machines are increasing in number and type. Some automated banking machines can now dispense travellers cheques, different forms of ticketing, information on savings products and on loans, and can even serve as convenient communications points for institutions offering tax preparation services.

Technology has brought impressive productivity gains to routine operations, and there are more to be realised. It is now possible to use debit cards in retail establishments to pay for goods electronically, eliminating the necessity for paper cheques. Direct debit terminals have met with some resistance in the US because the client loses chequebook float, but eventually higher charges on cheque and credit card transactions will alter the current attitudes. In Canada, debit cards first came into use in 1990. Growth of debit card transactions has been so rapid that by 1995 they accounted for one-third of non-cash retail transactions.

As routine financial transactions are increasing automated, intermediary personnel will spend more time selling products and providing clients with advice. Management by exception will become the rule as most human activities come to focus on less readily programmed activities, such as generating some kinds of new business and supervising the non-routine collection of slow-paying loans. Industrialised forms of providing services will likely emerge as one way of realising scale economies in computing and communications technologies. Financial services franchise operations will probably use commercially available computer programs to realise economies in routine financial applications, both personal and corporate. For example, production-line income tax services operated on the same principles as fast food outlets are presently in business.The total number of offices will also decline as more and more of the financial system disappears into communications and information processing infrastructures.

As technological applications continue to spread, financial firms will likely centralise some activities, decentralise others. For example, client information is being increasingly centralised in a bank's computers. However, the information is readily available for use by different divisions, as well as by the clients themselves. Interdivisional communications using a common client base mean that combinations of different centers' services can be provided as the institutions involved attempt to serve their clients' total needs. In another technological application, some institutions are now able to determine unit profitability more precisely than has been possible heretofore, and their services are increasingly being priced to reflect their true costs.

15.3.2 Gap management

In the 1950s and 1960s the typical intermediary borrowed short and lent long (i.e., had a balance sheet consisting chiefly of floating rate liabilities and fixed rate assets). The strategy of borrowing in short term markets and lending in longer term ones is called straddling the term structure. The policy generated relatively steady profits when the yield curve remained in essentially the same position, year after year. However, interest rates have been more variable since the early 1970s, changing both more frequently and over a wider range, and in that more turbulent environment the interest rate risk inherent in a policy of straddling the term structure has become more evident.

As market conditions change, the interest patterns on long term assets do not behave in the same way as on short term liabilities. The inherent interest rate risk is said to result from a mismatch of assets against liabilities. Recognition of this risk led to the development of **gap management** as a way of stabilising earnings.

---

gap the difference between an intermediary's floating rate assets and its floating rate liabilities. An intermediary with more floating rate assets than liabilities is said to have a positive gap, and one with more floating rate liabilities than assets is said to have a negative gap.

A gap management strategy attempts to manage interest rate risk by matching floating rate liabilities against floating rate assets. In the 1970s, banks and other intermediaries implemented the new gap management strategies by changing the interest terms of intermediary assets to match those on intermediary liabilities. In particular, long term fixed rate loans were changed to floating rate loans, so that interest revenues responded to market conditions in much the same ways as the interest costs on deposits.[6]

For example, at one time mortgages were written at interest rates fixed for the life of the arrangement, but now the interest rate is usually renegotiable at regular intervals, usually between one and five years in length, and in some cases as frequently as quarterly or monthly. Mortgages whose interest rates float with market conditions transfer interest rate risk from the lender to the borrower.[7]

To the extent that intermediaries still offer fixed rate loans, they attempt to fund them by a portfolio of fixed rate deposits. Should that tactic prove unsuccessful, interest rate swaps or other means of hedging the interest rate risk are used with increasingly greater frequency. Over the shorter term, intermediaries have also implemented other strategies aimed at increasing their interest earnings, reducing the risk of those earnings, or both. For example, over an interest rate cycle the typical intermediary attempted to shorten the maturities of assets relative to liabilities when rates were rising, and reversed this pattern when interest rates were falling.

15.3.3 Risk management

In practice, risk management involves both gap management – that is matching interest earnings patterns against interest cost patterns – and using derivative products to achieve a more desirable balance of portfolio return and risk. Insofar as product terms are concerned, changing from fixed to floating loans probably represents the most important risk management decision for any institution that funds most of its loans using short term deposits.

It is not always possible to change the terms of products so they are perfectly matched, and the interest rate swaps introduced in Chapter 13 have become an increasingly important tool for intermediary risk management. To understand the rapidly growing demand for swaps, consider a mortgage lending institution which makes fixed rate loans and has only one source of funds – floating rate deposits. It is, of course, vulnerable to fluctuations in the cost of funds. But it might be able to find a bank in another country (Japan proved to be a good source in the 1970s and early 1980s) that has borrowed using long term fixed rate notes and has relent the money as variable rate commercial loans. The swap means that each takes on the other's interest obligations, and consequently each has a better matched portfolio after the swap has been arranged.

Intermediaries also use forward commitments to offer their clients a risk management service by guaranteeing the interest rate a client will pay on a loan. For example, if a forward commitment specifies a fixed interest rate, the issuing intermediary assumes the risk that rates might rise after giving the undertaking. The intermediary does not assume the interest rate risk if it only agrees to provide a line of credit at the market interest rate prevailing when the loan is actually drawn down, but competitive pressures might dictate prespecifying the rate. In this case the intermediary may wish to hedge the risk in the futures markets.

15.3.4 Liquidity management

The problem of liquidity management is to ensure that the intermediary holds enough liquid assets, usually short term government securities,[8] to meet operating cash needs. Day-to-day cash losses result mainly from cheques drawn on clients' deposit balances, and presented to the intermediary through the clearings. If the intermediary holds too little in the way of liquid assets, it must meet cash outflows by selling off less liquid assets at a possible loss. On the other hand, since government securities are both low risk and low return, the intermediary forgoes earnings if it either holds too large a proportion of liquid assets or acquires them as a result of clearing gains.

Thus the problem of liquidity management is one of balancing two kinds of costs: the cost of having to sell illiquid assets when unexpected demands for cash must be met, and the opportunity cost of holding too much in cash or short term assets bearing low rates of return. In principle, the liquidity management problem is resolved by choosing a level of cash which minimises the expected value of the two costs as shown in Figure 15.1. Liquidity management problems cannot usually be addressed effectively by attempting to forecast future interest rates, largely because such forecasts can be highly imprecise, even over relatively short time periods.

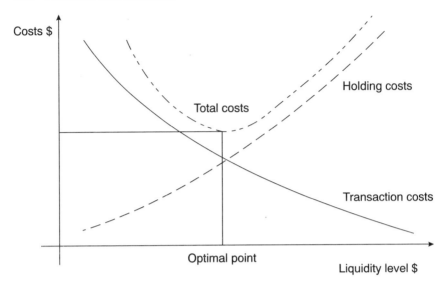

Figure 15.1 Liquidity management

15.3.5 Managing capital positions

The role of capital in a financial intermediary is to absorb earnings risks. If an intermediary's capital is insufficient to absorb earnings losses, the intermediary will become insolvent as and when any such losses are posted. Losses can result either from changes in net interest earnings or from defaulted loans. The first type of loss is primarily cyclical, whereas the second can increase gradually over several years if unsound lending policies have been followed. While capital regulations may reduce solvency risk to a degree, the capital account is actually an accounting provision to absorb losses as they occur. The surest protection against insolvency remains sound lending, adequate liquidity and the resultant capacity of the intermediary to raise additional funds when the need arises.[9]

The proportion of capital to assets is not regulated for all financial intermediaries. However, most jurisdictions regulate the capital to asset ratios of banks, and many jurisdictions apply similar requirements to near banks. Most countries have signed international agreements that their banks will adhere to capital standards developed by the Basle Committee under the sponsorship of the Bank for International Settlements. According to the Basle agreements, banks in twelve different countries are expected to achieve a minimum target ratio of total capital to risk weighted assets of 8 percent, of which at least 4 percent must be in the form of common equity. The risk weightings reflect different kinds of business; for example, commercial loans have a weighting of 100 percent, while government securities have a weighting of 0 percent. In many banks, the risk weightings mean that capital is about 5 percent of the assets held on the books.

In practice, capital ratios vary widely between intermediaries: from about 1:45 for some depository intermediaries in some countries to about 1:8 for some lending intermediaries. Obviously, if all intermediaries earned the same rate of return on total assets and if their risks were the same, the more highly levered intermediaries would earn much higher returns on their shares. But different asset portfolios generate both different average incomes and different income risks, as the model next presented shows.

15.4 A STRATEGIC MANAGEMENT MODEL

A financial intermediary can be regarded as an investment portfolio operated to generate income for the owners of its common equity. Income risk also needs to be recognised. Portfolio theory argues that a portfolio should generate as large a return as possible for a given degree of risk, because in competitive markets this strategy will maximise the value of the owners' equity in the firm. Both portfolio composition and portfolio trading strategies affect the risk–return tradeoff, as will be shown.

Portfolio theory must be modified to apply to organisations other than publicly owned firms. For example, a mutually owned intermediary might try to maximise its market value, but that value might not be clearly defined. In addition, the management of a mutually owned intermediary might not be motivated to pursue the goal of market value maximisation. In particular, since the mutually owned firm's management does not face the possibility of being ousted through a takeover bid, management can pay somewhat less heed to public acceptance of its decisions than can the management of a publicly owned, for-profit company.

Some other intermediaries may not even attempt to maximise value, focusing instead on other goals. A goal such as providing cheap loans subsidises some clients at the expense of others, but it may still be chosen by, say, some credit unions. If such firms have no publicly traded stock, resolving the conflict between different clients is not easy. Management cannot usually look to industry standards for assistance, because the same goals may be given different weights in different institutions. While the model to be developed next is most directly applicable to value maximising firms, it also has relevance to the exceptional cases just mentioned. By offering guidelines indicating what the wealth maximising firm would do, and how the wealth maximising firm would be affected by regulatory constraints, the model provides a standard of comparison for all firms, even those which choose not to maximise value.

15.4.1 Model structure

An intermediary's risk–return tradeoff is affected by the types of assets and liabilities it holds, and by its proportions of reserves and capital. The following model recognises how the relations between these variables can be examined, and in so doing explains several practical decisions taken by intermediaries.

Since the model focuses on important aspects of the management problem in a simplified way, it helps to shed light on the principal variables affecting the risk–return tradeoff.

The variables in the skeleton balance sheet of Figure 15.2 indicate that an intermediary's value maximising problem involves

1   raising funds through deposits which can then
2   be invested in earning assets, most of which are loans of one maturity or another. The process is managed with a view to
3   maximising the return to the owners' equity that can be obtained for
4   a given degree of risk.
5   Most jurisdictions require intermediaries to hold a specified proportion of their liabilities in the form of cash reserves.[10] Even banks which are not subject to reserve requirements usually hold some reserves voluntarily. When these banks address the problem of determining optimal holdings of liquid assets, they often make some allowance for offsetting uncertain cash flows. The following model implements the ideas of either a reserve requirement or a voluntary decision to hold reserves using a simple cash reserve constraint. The details of current practice will be discussed further in subsequent chapters.
6   Similarly, many intermediaries face regulations requiring them to hold certain proportions of capital, as indicated in the previous mention of the Basle agreements. Even unregulated intermediaries usually adopt a target capital ratio voluntarily. A simple version of the capital requirement is used in the model, again leaving the details of current practice to be discussed later.

The balance sheet in Figure 15.2 states schematically that

$$R + L = D + E = A \qquad (15.1)$$

cash reserves plus loans form the bank's total assets, while deposits and equity are its only two sources of funds. Accounting convention requires that total assets equal liabilities plus capital.

Assets	Liabilities and equity
R = cash reserves	D = deposits
L = loans (or investments)	E = owners' equity
A = total assets	A = total liabilities and equity

Figure 15.2 Structure of intermediary balance sheet

To recognise regulatory constraints, consider the following two balance sheet relations:

$$E \geq bA \tag{15.2}$$

$$R \geq kD \tag{15.3}$$

These fixed proportions can be interpreted as reflecting the minimum amounts of capital and cash reserves the intermediary is required to hold. We next assume that, as a policy choice, the intermediary holds only the minimum required cash reserves and maintains only the minimum required capital position. This permits treating replacing the inequalities in (15.2) and (15.3) with equalities,[11] and then the resulting equalities can be incorporated conveniently into the balance sheet shown in Figure 15.3.

To focus on the effects of the reserve and capital policies, it is useful to restate the whole balance sheet in terms of total assets, eliminating R, D, E and L. Formally,

$$D = (1 - b)A \tag{15.4}$$

Then by substituting (15.4) into (15.3), we obtain

$$R = k (1 - b)A \tag{15.5}$$

Also since $L = A - R$ from (15.1) we can write

$$L = [(1 - k)(1 - b)]A \tag{15.6}$$

The effects of the substitutions are summarised in the balance sheet of Figure 15.4.

It is now possible to relate the balance sheet items to the income statement. Assume that loans yield an effective interest rate r per period, while deposits

Assets	Liabilities and equity
R = kD	D = deposits
L = loans (or investments)	E = bA
A = total assets	A = total assets

Figure 15.3 The balance sheet restated

Assets	Liabilities and equity
R = k(1 − b)A	D = (1 − b)A
L = [1 − k(1 − b)]A	E = bA
A = total assets	A = total assets

Figure 15.4 Balance sheet showing relations to total assets

have an effective interest cost c per period. Then net interest income per period is

$$NI = rL - cD \tag{15.7}$$

and using (15.6) for L and (15.4) for D

$$NI = [r - rk(1 - b) - c(1 - b)]A \tag{15.8}$$

$$NI = [r - (rk + c)(1 - b)]A \tag{15.9}$$

Net interest income is now expressed as a function of total assets, interest rates, cash reserves and minimum equity requirements. Schematically, the income statement can be written as in Figure 15.5.

Now consider NI in relation to assets A. The proportion NI/A, usually termed the interest spread, is expressed in this case as a fraction of total assets.[12] The ratio of net interest income to equity, here referred to as ITE, can be written

$$ITE = NI / E = NI / bA$$

$$= [r - (rk + c)(1 - b)] / b \tag{15.10}$$

$$ITE = r[1 - k(1 - b)] / b - c(1 - b) / b \tag{15.11}$$

ITE is a thus a measure of relative earnings power. For a given degree of risk, maximising ITE will maximise the equity's market value if, as is quite reasonable to assume, non-interest operating costs do not change much with changes in asset size. If in these circumstances the risk of ITE can be reduced without affecting its average value, the intermediary's market value will increase.

Interest revenue			
Interest on reserves	0·R	=	0
Interest on loans	rL	=	rL
Total interest revenue		=	rL
Less: interest paid on deposits		=	−c·D
Net interest revenue		=	rL − cD

Figure 15.5 Income statement

15.4.2 Model properties

First, note from (15.9) that if net interest income is positive, it will increase as assets increase. Thus Equation 15.9 shows why, and under what conditions, an intermediary will try to expand its assets. Second, (15.11) shows that ITE decreases with k, which means the intermediary has a profit incentive to minimise its reserve holdings. The reason is clear: cash reserves earn no interest, while loans do. Moreover, ITE increases as b (required capital) decreases, at least so long as interest earnings net of reserve requirements exceed the cost of funds. Hence the intermediary faces an incentive to minimise the proportion of equity capitalisation. Again the reason is clear: the more earnings that can be supported by a given amount of equity investment, the greater the return to equity will be.[13]

While these effects can be seen by taking partial derivatives in (15.11), most readers will probably prefer a less formal exploration. Figure 15.6 numerically illustrates the workings of the two effects. Reading down the columns of the figure shows that ITE decreases as b increases and k is held constant. Reading across the rows shows that ITE decreases as k increases and b is held constant.

To assess how risk affects the return on equity, consider, as in portfolio theory, the variance of ITE as a risk measure. Begin by simplifying ITE in (15.11) as follows. Define

$$X \equiv 1 / b$$

and

$$Y \equiv X - 1 = (1 - b) / b$$

Then Equation 15.11 can be written more simply as

$$ITE = r(X - kY) - cY \tag{15.12}$$

Then treating r and c in Equation 15.12 as random variables (i.e., supposing that interest revenues and interest costs fluctuate unpredictably as a result of changes in market conditions) the variance of ITE is given by

$$\sigma^2(ITE) = \sigma^2(r)(X - kY)^2 + \sigma^2(c)Y^2 \tag{15.13}$$
$$- 2\rho(r, c)\sigma(r)\sigma(c)(X - kY)Y$$

where $\sigma^2(ITE)$ refers to the variance of ITE, $\sigma(ITE)$ to its standard deviation, and $\rho(r, c)$ to the correlation between r and c.

ITE = {r[1 − k(1 − b)] / b} − {c(1 − b) / b}		
	k = 0.04	k = 0.10
b = 0.04 b = 0.10	0.965 0.437	0.792 0.372
Assume r = 0.12, c = 0.08		

Figure 15.6 Effect of reserve and capital requirements on ITE

Treating X and Y as constants, the negative sign of the third term in (15.13) shows that σ^2(ITE) decreases as $\rho(r, c)$ increases from 0. That is, the closer a bank comes to matching its pattern of interest earnings with its pattern of interest costs, the lower its earnings risk.

Figure 15.7 shows how increasing the correlation between r and c stabilises ITE. In the figure, r and c are positively correlated for the numerals on the main diagonal (moving down and from left to right), negatively correlated on the other diagonal. The ITE hardly changes as one reads down the main diagonal, but it changes radically as one reads up the second diagonal. This shows that an intermediary with high positive correlation between loan revenues and deposit costs minimises the effects on profits of changing interest rates, and that a less well matched one faces more interest rate risk.

The entries in the body of Figure 15.8 are return and risk respectively. Reading down the columns shows that, under the assumptions of the model, increasing the proportion of equity decreases both earnings and earnings risk. Reading across the rows shows that increasing reserve requirements decreases both earnings and earnings risk, and that the effect is proportionately smaller than the effect of changing capital requirements.

ITE = {r[1 − k(1 − b)] / b} − {c(1 − b) / b}			
	c = 0.0600	c = 0.0800	c = 0.1000
r = 0.0800	0.3384	−0.0416	−0.4216
r = 0.1000	0.7080	0.3280	−0.0520
r = 0.1200	1.0776	0.6976	0.3176
Assume k = 0.08 and b = 0.05 throughout			

Figure 15.7 Effects of interest rates on ITE

ITE = {r[1 − k(1 − b)] / b} − {c(1 − b) / b}		
	k = 0.04	k = 0.10
b = 0.04	0.965, 0.115	0.792, 0.109
b = 0.10	0.437, 0.017	0.372, 0.016
Assume r = 0.12 and c = 0.08. Also, $\rho(r, c) = 0$, so that $\sigma^2(ITE) = \sigma^2(r)(X - kY)^2 + \sigma^2(c)Y^2$. Finally, let $\sigma^2(r) = \sigma^2(c) = 0.0001$		

Figure 15.8 Effects of b and k on ITE and σ^2(ITE). Entries are ITE and σ^2(ITE) respectively

15.4.3 Sensitivity analyses

The practical aspects of profit planning are most readily demonstrated with an example. The example illustrates the principles involved, although in practice planning calculations would involve more detail. The example shows how combinations of fixed and floating rate instruments are capable of affecting both the return on an intermediary portfolio and the return's sensitivity to changing market conditions (i.e., its risk).

Consider an intermediary which makes consumer loans on a fixed rate basis, funding them by issuing savings deposits bearing current market interest rates. The intermediary is assumed to remain fully loaned up at all times in that whenever existing payments on consumer loans are received the funds will be reinvested in new instalment loans, at a new but still fixed rate reflecting current market conditions. For simplicity, equity, fixed assets and cash holdings are all ignored in the example.

Assume a four-year interest rate pattern of 14, 16, 12 and 10 percent on new consumer loans, along with a pattern of 8, 10, 6 and 4 percent on savings deposits as shown in Table 15.1. The loan rates apply to all new loans, while existing loans carry their original rates. The new deposit rates apply to all deposits, regardless of their date of origin. Note the 6 percent differential between current loan rates and current deposit rates.

The example assumes that the assets are fixed rate, but liabilities are floating, so that the intermediary has a negative gap. While a negative gap means interest revenues will fall when rates rise and vice versa, the pattern is not always a simple one. As Table 15.1 suggests, in practice the timing of cost and revenue

Table 15.1 Example of an intermediary's profit planning problem

Years	1	2	3	4
Consumer loans				
14%	1,100	900	800	700
16%		200	180	160
12%			120	108
10%				132
Total loans	1,100	1,100	1,100	1,100
	1,100	1,100	1,100	1,100
Savings Deposits @	8%	10%	6%	4%
Net interest revenue	66.00	48.00	89.20	105.76
Earnings on assets	6.00%	4.36%	8.11%	9.61%
Deviations from 6%	0.00%	−1.64%	2.11%	3.61%

changes do not correspond exactly, and a finer analysis is needed to establish the intermediary's interest rate sensitivity.

The time pattern of change in the interest spread depends on the relations between average and marginal interest costs, average and marginal interest revenues, and these are dictated by the mix of assets and liabilities. The marginal return on consumer loans does not equal the average return because loans at different rates will be outstanding at the same time. On the other hand, for savings deposits average interest cost equals marginal cost, because the rates on all deposits change together. At the margin, the difference between interest revenue and interest cost is assumed to be a constant 6 percent, but this still does not mean that net interest earnings will equal 6 percent. That is, fixed markup pricing does not guarantee a fixed spread, even though many persons hastily conclude that it ought to.

The last example can be related to the portfolio model of section 15.4. First recognise that, for simplicity, the present example uses the values $k = b = 0$. Since this means the ITE ratio is undefined, we now focus on the interest rate spread rather than the interest to equity ratio. The risk of the realised spread can then be measured straightforwardly by examining the deviations from 6 percent, as shown in the last line of Table 15.1. Despite the simplifying changes used in Table 15.1, the model of section 15.4 can still be used to suggest how the intermediary could reduce its earnings risk. All future consumer loans might be converted to floating rate loans, or if the deposit markets permitted, fixed rate deposits might be offered. Either of these changes would increase the correlation between interest earnings and interest costs, reducing the amount by which the spread fluctuates as interest rates change. To assess the practical impact of such changes, the computations of Table 15.1 could be repeated. In practice, the computations would likely be repeated for different interest rate environments, providing additional information about the sensitivity of interest rate earnings to the policy changes.

15.5 SUMMARY

This chapter discussed intermediaries' strategic choices. The first topic considered was the economics of intermediation and how it affects the choices to specialise or to operate as a multiproduct firm. Next a number of operating issues were addressed. The first issue was how the intermediary can benefit from technological change; the remainder of the section examined the principal aspects of risk management, gap management, liquidity management and managing capital positions. Finally, a strategic management model was presented and its properties analysed.

REVIEW QUESTIONS

Exercise 1 List two sources of scale economies in the operations of a bank and the operations of an insurance company.

Exercise 2 Give two examples of technological change other than those related to the increasing use of ATMs.

Exercise 3 Suppose that loan writeoffs increase as interest rates rise. What kind of position in interest rate futures would show capital losses as interest rates rise? Would the correlation between these two instruments usually be important? Why or why not?

Exercise 4 Suppose a bank had a large percentage of fixed rate loans, but its deposits were all floating rate. What kind of gap would it have? Would you want to manage such a bank when interest rates were rising? If you had to manage such a bank, what kinds of changes would you seek?

Exercise 5 Canada's banks now face a zero reserve regime. Does this mean that they will never hold any cash? Why or why not?

Exercise 6 Suppose a bank faced large loan writeoffs that reduced its capital below the minimum level. Why would the bank likely be reluctant to fund the deficiency by floating a new share issue?

Exercise 7 Suppose in Equation 15.11 that $k = 0.08$, $b = 0.05$ and that deposit costs c are 0.06. What average rate of return would you have to earn on loans in order just to break even? Would this be the return you would charge the customer? Why or why not?

Exercise 8 Suppose in Figure 15.7 that $r = 0.10$ and $c = 0.08$, so that the net interest earnings per dollar of equity return are 32.8 cents. Suppose the fixed costs of running the bank are $100. Ignoring taxes, what is the minimum amount of equity the bank must have to break even? Since assets are twenty times equity, how big must the bank be in order to break even?

Exercise 9 Why does technological change pose important strategic issues for financial intermediaries? (Example: the data processing of many North American transactions takes place in Ireland or in Puerto Rico.)

Exercise 10 What economic forces contribute to the emergence of financial supermarkets? Of specialised institutions?

Exercise 11 How do lower computing and communications costs alter the economics of developing new financial products? Of marketing them?

Exercise 12 What are some ways in which intermediaries can realise scale and scope economies? What limits these possibilities?

Exercise 13 Would it be a good idea to reduce an intermediary's ratio of capital to equity? Why or why not?

Exercise 14 How would an intermediary's liquidity management problem be affected if the return on treasury bills increased relative to the average return on loans?

Exercise 15 Why does offering floating rate loans increase the correlation between interest revenues and interest costs?

Exercise 16 If you had only floating rate deposits, but the opportunity to make a fixed rate loan, what would you do?

Exercise 17 Some observers think that banking and investment banking activities can be combined in the same business units. Would you agree or disagree, and why?

16 Domestic intermediation

16.1	Introduction	280
16.2	Banks	280
16.3	Other depository intermediaries	283
16.4	Lending intermediaries	285
	16.4.1 Term lenders and venture capital companies	285
	16.4.2 Finance companies	286
	16.4.3 Financial leasing companies	286
16.5	Securities firms	287
16.6	Investment companies	288
16.7	Insurance companies	289
	16.7.1 Life insurance companies	289
	16.7.2 Property and casualty insurance companies	290
	16.7.3 Reinsurance	290
	16.7.4 Industry change	291
16.8	Pension funds	291
16.9	Financial conglomerates	293
16.10	Summary	294

LEARNING OBJECTIVES

After reading this chapter you will understand

- the principal management problems in banking
- how the management of near banks differs from that of banks
- the principal issues in managing a long term lending institution
- the several roles of securities firms
- some of the special management problems arising in investment companies, insurance companies and pension funds
- how financial conglomerates perform both an intermediation and an internal allocation role

---

16.1 INTRODUCTION

This chapter employs the principles of Chapter 15 to examine some of the management problems faced by domestic intermediaries. The intermediaries considered are: banks, near banks, lending intermediaries, securities firms, investment companies, insurance companies, pension funds and financial conglomerates.

16.2 BANKS

From their inception, banks have accepted deposits from commercial enterprises. In the 1930s and 1940s, banks gradually began to emphasise their willingness to accept individuals' deposits as well. The funds raised from both types of deposits were principally lent to businesses, usually in the form of working capital loans. In the 1950s, North American banks also began to offer consumer loans and residential mortgage loans. The banks discovered that consumer credit was a relatively low risk business which they could conduct profitably even while charging lower interest rates than their then competitors, the finance companies. Banks also discovered that mortgage lending was a profitable line of business, and once having made this discovery, pursued the business even in the face of regulatory obstacles. For example, in some jurisdictions where banks were hampered from making mortgage loans directly, they set up non-banking subsidiaries to carry out the business.

Even though banks face certain costs that other intermediaries do not, banks' costs of funds can be lower than those of such competitors as finance companies. First, banks raise a substantial proportion of their funds through deposits which bear lower interest rates than finance companies must pay on their principal source of funds – money market borrowings. To be sure, banks incur additional costs when they accept deposits. They usually hold some of the deposit balances to satisfy reserve requirements,[1] and some banks provide depositors with other banking services for which they do not charge explicitly. But even after taking these additional costs into account, the net costs of funds to banks have historically been lower than those of their retail competitors.

When banks concentrated on working capital, consumer and mortgage loans,[2] both risks and screening costs were relatively low. However, in the late 1960s and the 1970s competition for banking assets increased, and the products offered in response took such new forms as term financing, loans to the resource extractive industries, and project financing. Most of the world's largest banks developed their international lending, both to international businesses and to foreign governments, during the 1970s and 1980s. As they entered the new businesses, the banks' costs and earnings risks both increased, leading them to search for still other sources of profit.

While North American banks had originally focused management attention on their asset portfolios, in the late 1960s they began to engage in actively managing their liabilities. As traditional forms of deposit growth slowed and interest rate patterns became more variable, banks shifted their emphasis from demand to time deposits in attempts to sustain growth.[3] This change meant that banks' fund sources became both more costly and more volatile. Liability management was later carried beyond aggressively seeking term deposit funds to raising funds in both domestic and foreign money markets. The practice of writing loan commitments and then raising deposits to fund the commitments became increasingly important.

During the 1950s, 1960s and 1970s, North American banks developed extensive domestic branch networks wherever legislation permitted. (In the US, bank holding companies effectively created a kind of interstate branch banking even though legislation technically prevented it.) Branching was mainly aimed at capturing larger market shares of retail deposit and lending business. In the 1980s the profitability of branches began falling. During this period and into the 1990s many branches were reduced in size or eliminated by an increasingly extensive use of automated banking machines and by reliance on electronic communications to carry out routine banking transactions.

As Chapter 5 suggested, since the mid-1970s the banking sector has faced increased competition from other intermediaries. From the 1970s through the mid-1990s bank portfolios show a declining percentage of assets held as business loans, and an increasing percentage of assets held as mortgage loans. Business loans have declined mainly because large corporations now use the money and securities markets to satisfy some of their funding needs. At the same time banks' mortgage holdings increased, mainly because of their profitability. However, in the US the banks' larger shares were also attributable to the 1980s difficulties experienced by the traditional mortgage lenders, the thrift institutions.

The percentage increase in mortgage holdings is the more remarkable given the growth of securitisation during the same period. Much securitisation has involved selling off mortgage assets, reducing the percentage of mortgage assets held from what it would otherwise have been. While banks still earn most of their revenues from traditional forms of intermediation, fee-related business such as arranging **syndicated** international or domestic **loans** is becoming increasingly important, especially in the 1990s. In these ways, banks are emphasising their capabilities to act as financial agents to a greater degree than formerly (see Saunders 1994: 4).

Providing information to clients, and processing information on behalf of clients, are also growing areas of business. For example, in 1989 the Royal Bank of Canada announced that by the year 2000 it expected to earn about half its revenues from selling information processing and information services. In 1997, this emphasis on information processing was proceeding much as had been forecast eight years earlier.

---

syndicated loans loans to a given client provided by a number of banks. They are usually arranged by a single lead bank which, in addition to the interest it receives on its own portion of the loan, receives a commission for arranging the entire transaction.

During the 1980s, banks began acquiring other intermediaries such as trust companies, insurance companies and securities firms.[4] At the retail level, combinations such as banking and insurance offer scope economies in selling services to customers. At the corporate level, banks have entered the securities business both because they hope both to realise scope economies from the combination and because they wish to retain corporate fee business, particularly in securitisation, that might otherwise be lost to market agents.

Profit and cost analyses are as important a part of managerial activity as is supervision of daily operations. Indeed, in the more stable economic environments which prevailed up until the late 1960s, profit and cost analyses were almost the only management tasks emphasised. In the 1950s and the 1960s the financial environment exhibited little change, and such problems as managing interest rate risk did not attract the attention they have since received. In the 1980s and 1990s, cost control, management of non-interest expenses, and marketing risk management products are all important activities. Despite the enormous emphasis since the mid-1970s on risk management products, however, risk–return analyses of the banks' entire asset and liability portfolios are still in their early stages. Most of the risk management products are market traded, and banks have yet to integrate the assessment of risks in their loan portfolios with the risks in their portfolios of marketable securities and risk management instruments.

The model of Chapter 15 postulated that banks seek to maximise return relative to risk. In practice, bank management implements this goal by seeking to achieve specific financial targets. For example, as long ago as 1988 the Royal Bank of Canada stated in its annual report that in 1989 it would strive to attain an annual return on assets (ROA) of 0.85 percent and an annual return on equity (ROE) of 19 percent. The report continued by specifying ways to achieve these targets, which included finding the value of the financial products and services the bank offers. Still more specifically, products and services were defined in terms of the markets in which the bank aimed to achieve its targets. Aggressive product marketing was an important feature of this thrust. The same kinds of targeted returns have been pursued since that time.

16.3 OTHER DEPOSITORY INTERMEDIARIES

Other depository intermediaries, very often called near banks, resemble banks which specialise in retail business. In most countries near banks have operated almost exclusively in domestic markets, although in the 1980s some began to participate in syndicated lending. Near banks mainly raise funds through savings deposits and relend the monies in the form of mortgage and consumer loans. Some near banks emphasise their role as savings institutions, others their lending activities. In both cases, liabilities are mainly savings and term deposits with maturities ranging from a few months to as long as five years. On the asset side, the proportion of mortgages to consumer loans is generally large. In the past regulation restricted investments, most frequently to mortgages and government bonds. When other assets were permitted, the proportions were usually restricted. However, with financial deregulation, most jurisdictions have granted near banks greater freedoms and in many instances the firms are gradually evolving toward full service retail financial institutions.

Asset management in near banks has mainly involved increasing the flexibility of earning on what were traditionally fixed rate level payment mortgage loans. As interest rates on deposits became increasingly variable in the 1970s and 1980s, near banks began to offer adjustable rate mortgages, allowing them better to match interest revenues against interest costs over changing market conditions. They also began to use graduated rather than level payment mortgages in order to address the problem of borrowers' cash flows being adversely affected by increases in interest rates, as discussed in Chapter 13.

Liability management has mainly emphasised attempts to raise longer term deposits with the intent of providing a better match for interest revenues, since even in the later 1990s most mortgage lenders still hold some proportion of fixed rate assets on their books. But, since most consumers prefer short term deposits, the attempt to raise long term fixed rate funds has not been very successful, and most interest-bearing deposits carry floating rates. Most near banks now also offer chequable deposit accounts, some of which are interest-bearing.

In North America the near banks form one of the main links between deposit markets on the one hand, mortgage loan and consumer credit markets on the other. On the whole, the near bank industry has been at least as innovative as the banking industry, and the near banks have actively marketed new products. For example, near banks developed flexible mortgages and various forms of retirement savings plans, and were early to introduce daily interest savings accounts. Despite their innovativeness, however, few near banks have experimented with reverse mortgages, an instrument designed to provide income to retired persons by making loans against equity in the person's residence. Such loans are liquidated by the sale of assets at the time of the person's death. The lack of aggressiveness in marketing this instrument is rather curious, since the near banks are so familiar with mortgage lending and since the percentage of retired persons continues to increase in many western countries.

The model of Chapter 15 can be used to explain the principal operational problems of near banks, as exemplified most dramatically by the US thrifts. Until the early 1970s, US thrifts financed fixed rate mortgages with floating rate deposit liabilities, which meant the correlation between interest revenues and interest costs was close to zero. With a correlation close to zero, the thrifts' profit risk was relatively high, as can be verified by reading across a row or down a column of Figure 15.7 and noting that the return varies more than it does when reading down the main diagonal.

Although US thrifts had been prosperous since about 1900, they began to experience operating difficulties in the mid-1960s as short term interest rates began to rise. At that time the thrifts' principal investments were fixed rate mortgages, and rises in interest rates presented the possibility that formerly positive interest rate spreads would turn negative. During the 1970s costs continued to rise while revenues remained largely fixed, and the possibility of losses became a reality. A thrift can reduce its risk by increasing the correlation between its interest earnings and its interest costs, a change that would principally be brought about by using flexible rather than fixed rate mortgages. Indeed, attempts to stabilise accounting profits form the main reason why thrifts and other similar mortgage lenders began to offer floating rate mortgages, that is to invest in floating rate assets. However, it took the US thrifts about two decades to make the shift fully, and they experienced severe operating difficulties before completing the adjustments.

The first attempt to keep the US thrifts profitable was to stabilise their costs by imposing legislated ceilings on the rates they and banks could pay on savings accounts. However, savers then withdrew their funds from savings accounts in a process referred to as **disintermediation**, which meant taking deposits from intermediaries and investing them in more lucrative forms of assetholding, such as marketable securities. After being found unworkable, the interest rate ceilings were removed, and the thrifts' potential profitability problems became real ones. The profitability problems were then further exacerbated by increases in interest rate volatility which faced the thrifts with variable as well as rising costs of funds.

---

disintermediation the process whereby depository institutions, unable to pay market rates of interest because of restrictive regulation, lost deposit funds to alternative sources of savings, such as government securities.

Eventually, following on changes in regulation that removed constraints from the kinds of liabilities the thrifts could issue and that also permitted them to offer floating rate mortgages, the thrifts began to restructure their portfolios.

During the restructuring of the later 1970s and early 1980s, however, the thrifts' profitability problems worsened and many firms became insolvent. The insolvencies were actually encouraged by fixed rate deposit insurance, which created a moral hazard problem to which many thrifts succumbed. Deposit insurance allowed any thrift, no matter how risky, to compete equally with other, safer institutions for savers' funds. But the thrifts also faced strong incentives to improve profitability by acquiring highly risky earning assets. Since many were already near insolvency, their shareholders had little to lose if the risks did not pay off, much to gain if they did.

Thrift depositors also faced strong incentives to direct their deposits toward the riskiest thrifts, because these institutions offered the highest interest rates. Depositors did not face additional risks on high yield deposits, because the deposits were insured. Effectively, the depositors held a put option written by an agency of the US government. If the thrift failed, the deposit insurance corporation (in this case the subsequently restructured Federal Savings and Loan Insurance Corporation, FSLIC) paid off the depositor losses. Deposit insurance losses and recognition of the moral hazard problem led to further legislation, revision of deposit insurance schemes, and strengthening of thrifts' capital requirements. By the mid-1990s, the thrifts are returning to profitability, but the process of adjusting their portfolios to achieve floating rate earnings has been a long and painful one.

16.4 LENDING INTERMEDIARIES

Lending intermediaries are institutions with specialised loan portfolios. For example, they may finance vehicle and equipment purchases, act as factors, provide export trade finance, or venture capital financing. Typically, lending intermediaries raise their funds in the money markets and by borrowing from other financial institutions; relatively small proportions are raised by soliciting deposits from the public. In relative order of importance, their funds are raised from short term financial paper, long term debt, loans from affiliates, owners' equity and bank loans. Many of the financings the lending intermediaries arrange are ultimately placed with such institutions as pension funds, meaning the principal role played by the lending intermediary is that of an agent rather than of an intermediary *per se*. Some of these lending intermediaries are set up as divisions of banks or other large diversified financial firms.

16.4.1 Term lenders and venture capital companies

Term lenders' chief purpose is providing medium term loans to medium sized businesses. Term lenders are often bank affiliates, set up to perform specialised functions requiring skills not possessed by most branch personnel. Specialised institutions are needed because of the scale economies in screening applications for term credit and because much of the skill in longer term lending is acquired on an experiential (learning-by-doing) basis. The requisite skills are those of raising funds from institutional investors such as pension funds or life insurance companies, and of investing in portfolios of longer term commercial loans or ventures. In addition, some lending intermediaries are specialised because they serve relatively small markets and cannot readily extend their skills to other markets.

Venture capital companies offer an example of intermediaries serving specialised markets. Venture capital companies provide medium term loan and investment capital to selected firms with relatively high earnings growth prospects. While they usually extend higher risk forms of financing than do the capital companies, most venture investments are placed in existing businesses rather than in new ones. Typically they accept about 1 per cent of the applications they consider. Venture capital companies seek high rates of return on their investments – on the order of 50 percent per annum – but realised returns are lower, since a substantial proportion of a venture firm's investments are unsuccessful and do not yield the target returns.

Other lending intermediaries have been set up to raise funds from financial institutions with a view to investing them in portfolios of residential and commercial mortgages originated by still other institutions. These firms, known as real estate investment trusts and mortgage investment companies, channel funds raised by institutions like pension funds and life insurance companies into mortgage investments. In some jurisdictions they have had tax advantages not available to other organisational forms, but recently these advantages have been attenuated and the activity has lessened.

16.4.2 Finance companies

Finance companies mainly provide credit to consumers and to wholesale organisations engaged in selling consumer and to a lesser extent industrial durables. Usually the two activities are combined within the firm. Acceptance companies have little contact with the public, mainly financing conditional sales contracts generated by retail or wholesale sales. They can be subdivided into retailers, car and truck manufacturers, and farm equipment manufacturers, some of which also provide term loans and financial leases to their clients. General acceptance corporations also purchase instalment finance contracts, but are not tied to one organisation. Consumer loan companies form a fifth type of finance company.

Finance companies generally fund their operations through money market instruments and bank borrowing. Finance companies usually have high costs of funds because they do not have access to retail deposit markets. Their asset–equity ratios are usually lower than those of the banks, and their ability to generate a return on equity is also lower. In some cases, these features of finance company operations have led finance companies to restructure their operations as banks.

16.4.3 Financial leasing companies

Financial leasing companies mainly finance fixed capital equipment, offering advantageous terms to some companies, particularly those which cannot use depreciation allowances to reduce their taxable incomes. A leasing company can obtain depreciation tax shields not available to the lessee firm either because the prospective lessee's income is not taxable or because its income is not large enough to create a tax liability. Apart from possible tax advantages, financial lease contracts really offer an alternative to debt or term financing. For some firms, financial leasing is an important alternative to borrowing. At present, financial leasing companies in the US, such as GE Capital Services, Associates Commercial Corp., AT&T Capital Corp., IBM Credit Corp., and others, are very fast growing parts of the financial services industry. These firms provide strong competition for banks in some areas of corporate finance, especially areas where relatively complex financial structuring is required. Some banks are hampered in these areas because their traditional capabilities have been developed mainly to provide working capital loans to business and are unsuited to structuring more complex arrangements.

16.5 SECURITIES FIRMS

The securities industry is comprised chiefly of investment bankers, retail securities firms and discount brokers. All these firms engage in some combination of investment banking, trading, market making, custody and other service functions. Most retail securities firms emphasise trading, custody and other services functions, while discount brokers are principally securities traders operating at the retail end of the market. The largest and most important firms in the securities industry are investment banking firms.

One widely accepted definition of investment banking is that it covers 'all capital market activities, from underwriting and corporate finance, to mergers and acquisitions (M&A) and fairness opinions, to fund management and venture capital. Excluded . . . are the selling of securities to retail customers. . . . Included is merchant banking, when investors work and invest for their own account. Also included is the nonretail trading of blocks of securities for financial institutions' (Fabozzi and Modigliani 1992: 61). Larger investment banks conduct the following principal types of business: underwriting new securities issues, private placements, asset securitisation, mergers and acquisitions, merchant banking, creating and trading risk control instruments, securities trading and money management (Fabozzi and Modigliani 1992: 63). The extent to which a given investment banking firm engages in these different activities is largely determined by its views of whether each such function can be shown to be profitable.

Investment banking firms enjoy scale economies in performing research. Hence larger firms are more likely to conduct research than smaller ones, which may instead emphasise specialised forms of, say, trading activities. There also appear to be scale economies to the data processing and accounting activities (back office activities), and some of the 1980s mergers in the North American securities industry can be explained as attempts to realise one or both of these sources of scale economies. Investment bankers trade both on behalf of clients and take positions on their own account. Taking positions in securities, especially when arranging mergers or acquisitions, can demand large amounts of capital; another reason for the spate of mergers in the late 1980s.

In some jurisdictions commercial and investment banking activities are being combined, at least within the same financial groups if not within the same business units. Investment bankers in the US have offered deposit accounts for some time, and a few US banks acquired discount brokerage firms in the 1980s. Most of Canada's largest investment banking firms are now controlled by banks. These acquisitions by banks and financial holding companies have an economic rationale in that control of a securities firm seems important to competing effectively in both investment banking and risk management.

16.6 INVESTMENT COMPANIES

Investment companies (mutual funds in North America) are financial intermediaries that sell shares to the public and invest the proceeds in diversified securities portfolios. They fall into three types: **open-end fund**, **closed-end fund** and unit trusts. The shares of open-end funds are sold to the public on a continuing basis, while a closed-end fund has fixed capitalisation. Open-end funds operate according to two fee bases: load funds for which investors pay a commission to acquire the shares, and no-load funds for which there is no sales commission. No-load funds usually charge a higher annual administration fee than load funds to cover their operating costs.[5] Closed-end funds issue non-redeemable shares which are generally traded on the over-the-counter market, although some are listed on stock exchanges. A unit trust is set up for a fixed period of time, issues trust units to the public, and typically holds the same bond portfolio for its lifetime. It is like a form of closed-end fund whose portfolio is not actively changed and whose shares do not trade.

---

open-end fund an investment company which continuously issues shares in response to demand for them. An open-end fund will also redeem shares at the current market value of the investment.

---

closed-end fund an investment company with a fixed capitalisation. The shares of a closed-end fund may trade either on an exchange or in the over-the-counter market.

The shares of open-end funds trade at a price determined by their net asset value per share. Open-end funds usually make a market in their own shares, selling them to the public on a continuing basis and buying them back at prices determined by the net asset value per share. The shares of closed-end funds trade either on exchanges or in the over-the-counter market. Typically, the shares of closed-end funds sell at a discount from their net asset value, but as the price is determined by investor demand relative to the existing supply, the shares can and sometimes do sell at a premium over net asset value. The shares of unit trusts do not usually trade, but are retained by their original purchasers until the fund is wound up.

Mutual funds pursue a variety of goals. Some emphasise growth stocks, others mixed portfolios of bonds and stocks, still others just bonds. The principal service provided by any investment fund is to form a diversified portfolio at lower costs than can individual investors. However, many studies of investment companies show that their portfolios usually earn a return, after adjusting for administration expenses, no greater than that on a comparable market index portfolio. Nevertheless, investors are attracted to the funds whenever they offer the prospect of relatively lucrative returns. For example, in the late 1980s and early 1990s sales of mutual funds were exceptionally large. While new sales fell off and redemptions increased around 1993 or so, subsequently new sales have again strengthened and investment companies are an increasingly popular vehicle for household savings. In the US, investment companies are federally regulated under legislation similar to, but less stringent than, that governing pension funds.

16.7 INSURANCE COMPANIES

Insurance companies are financial intermediaries because they collect premiums that remain invested until paid out in claims or transferred to earnings. Life insurance companies insure against policyholder death or loss of income, while property and casualty insurance companies against such events as fire or hurricane damage to a building. Insurance companies strive to profit from the premiums they charge for underwriting (assuming) risks. In effect, an insurance company writes put options on assets possessed by the insured parties, and sells these puts, in a form called insurance policies, to policyholders. The premiums it collects from policyholders are the prices at which it sells the puts. Most insurance policies are written for one year or more, and are arranged by individual negotiation with the party purchasing the insurance. Life insurance, fire insurance and mortgage principal insurance are all well-known examples.

Some insurance companies establish regional underwriting limits in an attempt to diversify risks geographically. If the regional constraints are smaller than the demand for insurance in a particular period, the intermediaries are able to write policies only until the allocation is exhausted. Such constraints create financial market imperfections similar to legislation placing geographical lending restrictions on mortgage lenders. It is not clear why the insurance companies use underwriting limits instead of charging higher premiums in regions with particularly buoyant insurance demand, unless they perceive political or public relations difficulties to implementing rate policies of this sort.

16.7.1 Life insurance companies

Some life policies offer both insurance and a form of savings, and continuing industry growth depends partly on continuing to appeal to savers. The industry has not always been successful in this regard. From the 1960s through the 1980s life insurance captured only a declining proportion of North American savings, largely because many policies did not pay competitive interest rates on the savings element of the policies. In attempts to recover lost ground, new products such as universal life insurance have been developed to provide savers with rates of return commensurate with those on other kinds of savings vehicles. To compensate the insurance company, premiums paid for life protection are usually subject to increases when higher rates are paid on policyholders' investments, and vice versa when rates are lower.

The actuarial values of life insurance companies' liabilities are generally easier to calculate than those of property and casualty insurance companies, a fact which explains most of the differences in their investment policies. Life insurance companies face less demanding liquidity management problems than property and casualty companies, and as a result hold smaller proportions of liquid assets than property and casualty companies. On the other hand, since it is important that they have predictable rates of investment return over the longer run, life insurance companies invest mainly in long term bonds, holding them to maturity. This investment policy allows life companies to fix a minimum rate of return on their invested funds, and thus ensure that premiums plus investment income will be actuarially sufficient to cover their outpayments on claims.

Regulations applying to life insurance companies chiefly restrict the kinds of investments they can hold. In addition, investments must meet earnings and dividends tests similar to those faced by pension funds.

16.7.2 Property and casualty insurance companies

Property and casualty insurance companies write policies on which the claims are less predictable than on life insurance policies. As a result, property and casualty insurance companies' investment portfolios are more liquid. Their portfolios can also be quite specialised; for example, in the United States, property and casualty insurance companies are the most important purchasers of municipal bonds because interest on the bonds is not regarded as a part of their taxable incomes.

The property and casualty insurance businesses are cyclical; several years of profits are likely to be followed by several years of losses. This phenomenon occurs primarily because profits attract new entrants to the business and these new entrants typically acquire business at lower premiums than those currently being charged, leading to periodic industry overcapacity.

16.7.3 Reinsurance

During the 1970s and 1980s the reinsurance business, in which international companies purchase large proportions of policies originated by small companies, has grown rapidly. For example, in 1985, when issuing $900 million worth of default insurance on Citicorp's loans to less developed countries, CIGNA corporation resold most of the liabilities in the reinsurance market. The extent to which the growth of the reinsurance business allows diversification to offset cyclical profit risks (at least for the reinsurance companies if not for the smaller originating companies) does not yet seem to have been explored.

Insurance exchanges are markets offering an alternative method of redistributing risks. The most famous exchange is Lloyd's of London, but there are similar exchanges in New York, Chicago and Miami. As an alternative to reinsurance and exchange transactions, the US securities industry has also attempted to sell catastrophe futures, and more recently bonds whose payoffs depend on catastrophes. The bonds, used as a means of diversifying and trading the risks associated with large-scale storm, flood and earthquake damage, offer an increased payoff in the event of industry losses due to natural disasters.

16.7.4 Industry change

As financial services become increasingly integrated, insurance companies are experimenting with new distribution systems, and selling such new products as trust company deposits and mutual fund shares. American insurance companies are attempting to obtain regulatory permission to sell their products through banks. In Canada insurance products are now sold through credit unions, trust companies, banks and some investment dealers.[6]

Several life companies are selling each others' products and two trust companies are selling life annuities through life insurance agents. In the future, larger companies will likely dominate the industry to a greater degree than presently. Large national retailers will likely offer life insurance on credit purchases and there will also likely be sales of general insurance, financial counselling services, mutual and money market funds and securities brokerage. They may also offer deposit accounts, perhaps focusing mainly on accounts from which funds can be withdrawn electronically. Banks will probably sell insurance by making sales and distribution agreements with existing life companies. Banks have for some time utilised affiliated insurance companies to write life insurance against various kinds of personal loans they offer.

Technological change in insurance companies was rapid when computers first appeared on the scene around 1960, but since then the rate of change has slowed. The insurance companies attribute this to the cost and indivisibility of computer systems as well as to a shortage of skilled personnel, but other financial companies have not found these factors as limiting. Insurance companies will probably need to acquire state-of-the-art technology to cope successfully with increased competition in the 1990s.

16.8 PENSION FUNDS

A pension fund represents employee savings accumulated to finance payment of retirement benefits. Pension funds have gained an increasing proportion of North American savings flows since the 1950s. Society's increasing wealth, and increases in the proportions of persons attaining retirement age, are both contributory factors. Although there are thousands of pension funds in the US, the largest twenty held about 25 percent of all pension assets in 1989 (Fabozzi and Modigliani 1992). As Table 5.4 showed (see p. 62), households pension fund and insurance assets amounted to more than 30 percent of total household assets in 1993.

Pension funds are financed by contributions from both employers and employees, and cannot be used, even as collateral for a loan, until the employee retires. The success of this illiquid form of saving seems to be due to the facts that contributions are tax-exempt, and that pension fund membership is a condition of employment with many large firms. Finally, many persons find it difficult to save voluntarily, and thus actually seek out compulsory forms of saving.

A pension fund may be a **defined benefit plan**, in which case payouts are specified, or a **defined contribution plan**, in which case only the contributions into the fund are specified. Defined benefit plans whose payouts are guaranteed by insurance products are known as **insured plans**; others are called non-insured plans. Some insurance companies offer standard plans for small firms. Since most pension funds operate as non-profit organisations, they are not usually subject to income taxation.

---

defined benefit plan a pension plan with specified payouts. It is contrasted with a defined contribution plan which specifies only the contributions into the fund.

---

insured pension plan a pension plan whose payouts are guaranteed by an insurance company.

Pension funds are important buyers of corporate stocks and bonds, but the larger funds view capital market securities as only temporary outlets for their investments. They also invest directly in real estate, mortgages, oil and gas development. Some pension funds have even entered merchant banking activity, helping finance corporate mergers and acquisitions. Many funds are managed by advisory firms, the number of which has grown rapidly over the 1980s. Pension advisory firms are usually independent, although some trust and insurance companies have also set up investment counselling subsidiaries. During the 1990s, individuals are increasingly supplementing their other sources of pension income with private saving. This private saving takes the form of mutual fund purchases, bond purchases and bank deposits. In some jurisdictions at least some of the contributions to these funds can be made out of pre-tax income, with the taxes being collected at the time the funds are used to provide pension income.

Many individuals have a large proportion of their life savings invested in a pension fund, and some jurisdictions regulate pension fund operations closely.

For example, in the US they are governed by the Employee Retirement Income Security Act (1974). This Act establishes minimum funding standards, requiring that assets be held to meet the fund's actuarially calculated liabilities. Funds must be governed by trustees who are legally responsbile for the prudent investment of assets. Minimum vesting standards are established, and a guarantee corporation insures payment of vested benefits.

Although the large amounts of funds invested in pension funds are reason enough for their regulation, there are also other justifications for supervision. Pension fund managers face an incentive to strive for high rates of return on pension investments, since higher returns reduce employer contribution costs. But higher return investments carry higher risks, and risk taking is by definition not always successful. Thus the managers of weaker pension funds can be tempted to take relatively large risks with employees' savings. In addition, some private sector funds hold relatively large amounts of their firm's stock, so that the security of employees' pension assets is tied to the fortunes of the firm.

The US Pension Benefit Guaranty Corporation alleviates these risks, but not all jurisdictions treat pension assets with equal care. Canada has no federal pension plan insurance corporation, although Ontario provides pension insurance for funds established under the laws of that province. The UK is revising its pension legislation following on the misuse of pension fund assets by the Maxwell Group of companies, which resulted in the almost total loss of Maxwell employees' accumulated pension funds. So long as insurance premiums rise with risk, an insurance plan will not create perverse incentives for its managers.

16.9 FINANCIAL CONGLOMERATES

Some combinations of financial and non-financial firms, called financial conglomerates, fund investments internally rather than through market agents or intermediaries. In effect, a financial conglomerate operates an internal capital market, and a major part of the conglomerate form's effectiveness stems from its ability to use expert initial screening, and a high degree of monitoring and control capabilities to govern its internal allocations of funds. For example, some real estate developers own trust companies in order to enhance their capabilities for financing the development business.

American Express Company (Amex) was once upheld as another model of a modern financial conglomerate, pushing aside barriers between banking, insurance and stockbroking, and moving into cable television, the medium that could become the best way to deliver financial services. At one time it owned Fireman's Fund Insurance, brokerage firm Shearson/Amex, investment services Shearson Lehman/Amex and Warner Amex Cable Communications. More than half its earnings came from travel-related services, mainly travellers cheques and credit cards. (Amex gets charges on average of about 3.5 percent commission on all the retail sales charged to its cards.) The combination of businesses did not prove particularly successful and in recent years American Express has restricted

its focus, spinning off some of the businesses formerly acquired and emphasising its travel and leisure business.

In Canada, financial conglomerates have assets equal to about two-thirds of
those held by the domestic banking system. Some of the conglomerates combine
traditionally separate activities such as insurance, banking or near banking,
trustee functions and securities dealing. The firms are usually organised as
holding companies with subsidiary firms conducting various forms of financial
business.

16.10 SUMMARY

This chapter compared and contrasted different types of intermediaries typical
of domestic financial systems, focusing on the principal nature of their economic
activities and on the principal differences in the management problems they
face. The chapter began by discussing how the management of near banks differs
from that of banks, then turned to examine the principal issues in managing a
long term lending institution. The several roles of securities firms were then
examined, after which the discussion turned to some of the special management
problems arising in savings intermediaries: investment companies, insurance
companies and pension funds. Finally, the internal capital market functions
performed by financial conglomerates were discussed.

REVIEW QUESTIONS

Exercise 1 Suppose you were in charge of a region with high branch expenses.
You know that much of the time spent by branch personnel is in marketing
routine products, but you also believe that the existing branch network is an
expensive way to continue doing the marketing. How might you attempt to
retain some personal service and at the same time control costs to a greater
degree than is now possible?

Exercise 2 How does level premium deposit insurance provide the management
of a savings intermediary with perverse incentives?

Exercise 3 What kinds of governance are needed by venture capital firms that
are not needed by banks when making working capital loans?

Exercise 4 Why might a leasing company be able to make profits on equipment
leasing deals? (Remember that the firm using the equipment could do the deal
itself, and the leasing company has to make a profit if it does the deal.)

Exercise 5 Explain how scale economies in performing research might make it
profitable for a securities firm to conduct research on behalf of individuals, who
would then pay for the results of the research.

Exercise 6 What services can mutual funds perform that investors cannot
perform as economically on their own?

Exercise 7 Explain why the asset portfolio of a property insurance company is likely to be more liquid than the asset portfolio of a life insurance company.

Exercise 8 In what ways do the non-market investments of a financial conglomerate resemble the activities of a venture capital company? In what ways do they not?

Exercise 9 Try to invent a new banking transaction and argue the case for its potential profitability.

Exercise 10 Suppose deposit costs increase. How will banks attempt to adjust their portfolios to compensate?

Exercise 11 When Canadian banks were freed of some portfolio constraints that had formerly restricted their ability to make mortgage loans, very little happened to the availability of mortgage finance. Why do you think this might be so? What does the example say about the likely impact of some kinds of deregulation?

Exercise 12 If banks can offset interest rate risk, why might they still be more reluctant to make fixed rate loans following on a sudden increase in the rate of inflation?

Exercise 13 Banks sometimes spend more than the amount they originally lent to collect individual bad loans. Why might this be a rational economic decision? Why don't they just write the loans off?

Exercise 14 Some near banks have attempted to enter the commercial lending market, which is well served and highly competitive, but have avoided the market for reverse mortgages. Why do you think this might be so?

17 International intermediation

17.1 Introduction   297

    17.1.1   Rise of multinational business   297
    17.1.2   Rise of international banks   298
    17.1.3   International financial centers   299

17.2 Euromarket activity   300

    17.2.1   Eurocredits   300
    17.2.2   Investment banking   302

17.3 Contemporary issues   302

    17.3.1   International indebtedness   302
    17.3.2   Capital shortages: a possibility?   304
    17.3.3   Risk management   305

17.4 Summary   305

LEARNING OBJECTIVES

After reading this chapter you will understand

- the forces contributing to the rise of multinational corporations
- the forces contributing to the rise of international banks
- how banks developed the Eurocredit markets
- the nature of an international financial center
- the problem of international indebtedness and why it has arisen
- why a world capital shortage is unlikely
- why the explosive growth of risk management needs careful monitoring

17.1 INTRODUCTION

This chapter outlines the rise of international financial activity since World War II. It first discusses the forces contributing to the rise of multinational corporations and international banks. It then examines the forces promoting the development of Eurocredit markets, offshore financial centers and international banking facilities. Contemporary issues regarding international finance are also examined, including whether it is possible to have capital shortages in a developed economy and the importance of monitoring risk management activities.

17.1.1 Rise of multinational business

After World War II international intermediation grew rapidly, largely in response to measures that successfully promoted world reconstruction and trade. Following the creation of the European Common Market and the European Free Trade Association in the early 1950s, the next two decades witnessed a rapid growth of international trade. The establishment of the International Monetary Fund, the World Bank and the General Agreement on Tariffs and Trade further enhanced prospects for trade by promoting exchange rate stability, providing assistance to developing countries, and reducing tariffs that restricted international trade.

Trade growth provided strong incentives for the growth of multinational corporations, which offer several advantages over simply exporting goods or services. First, multinationals can compete in host countries without paying import tariffs. Second, they are likely to be more sensitive to the nuances of host markets than are foreign-based firms. Third, they may have lower production and labour costs than firms which do not consider finding the best world markets for different forms of resources. Fourth, subsidiaries can provide some defence against competitors in the host country. Finally, they may also offer means of avoiding restrictive regulation in the home country.

17.1.2 Rise of international banks

Between the 1930s and the late 1950s international banking was inactive. The reconstruction activities that began immediately after World War II were not at first financed by the private sector, but rather by the World Bank and through assistance programs like the Marshall Plan. However, during the 1960s the growth of trade stimulated a resurgence of private sector international banking. In many cases, banks followed businesses into new markets with a view to protecting existing client connections. Once established, both the banks and the multinationals contributed to still more growth in international business, both financial and non-financial. The development of international banking was further enhanced by the fact that European countries, while applying stringent controls to domestic banks, allowed substantial freedom to their foreign counterparts. As Chapter 13 showed, this lack of regulatory restriction contributed importantly to the growth of the Eurodollar, Eurocredit and Eurobond markets.

International banking activity can be divided into three principal types – offshore banking, arm's length banking and host country banking. Offshore banking is like an assembly plant in a low wage country: it represents an economically advantageous means of carrying out the banking. Offshore banks thus carry out business for their domestic customers in a low cost jurisdiction. The jurisdiction's tax laws are often the source of the cost advantages, but labour and other resource costs also play a role. For example, a substantial proportion of the world's data processing is carried out in such locations as Ireland and Puerto Rico.[1]

Arm's length banking is based on comparative advantage, and means that international banks can profitably make loans or investments which domestic banks are less qualified or too small to offer. As one example, US banks familiar with making relatively risky cash flow loans were able to do so profitably in small markets like Canada's before an indigenous capability developed. To the extent this kind of activity occurs, the average costs of the international bank are lower than the average costs of the indigenous bank, principally because the international bank has a larger volume of business over which to spread the fixed costs of originally entering the business.

Finally, host country banking is full fledged foreign direct investment whereby banks accompany their countries' investors to provide financing for the capital projects in the foreign country. At the present time, many of the world's largest banks have full fledged operations in a number of countries. These operations are largely international in character, but can also include retail operations in host countries.

Most foreign banks are wholesale firms which make loans to medium or large sized corporations, raising the funds through both money market instruments and time deposits. In addition to some forms of retail business, international banks serve the interbank deposit market, the market for syndicated loans, and agency markets where banks act on behalf of clients. The risks in these businesses include credit, interest rate and foreign exchange risks.[2]

In a number of North American instances, the retail operations were acquired by purchasing troubled domestic banks. They were usually purchased as a means of obtaining more favourable regulatory treatment than would usually be afforded a foreign entrant establishing a new business. A second way of easing entry is for two countries to negotiate reciprocal arrangements with each other.

The extent of any scope economies between domestic and international banking operations has not yet been established by empirical research. However, since operating costs in international banking appear to be lower than in domestic banking, lower spreads in the international banking business can generate as high a return to equity as can domestic business.

17.1.3 International financial centers

International financial centers (IFCs) are distinguished from domestic banking activity in that they

- deal in external currencies
- are operated primarily for non-resident clients
- are generally free of the taxes and exchange controls imposed on domestic markets.

The money markets of international financial centers both facilitate market exchanges of funds and create profit opportunities for the institutions involved.

The practices of IFC banks are not always the same as those of their domestic counterparts. The international banks borrow and lend like domestic banks, but unlike the domestic banks they raise more of their funds in the money markets and are therefore relatively vulnerable to large changes in their deposits. Hence an active secondary market for trading deposit funds has emerged. On the asset side, large loans are usually syndicated rather than being granted only by a single bank, diversifying the credit risk. In most cases loan rates are specified as floating, say with LIBOR. Floating rate loans reduce the profit risks associated with maturity mismatch, as discussed in Chapters 15 and 16.

Many major cities have international financial centers. In the mid-1990s the largest in terms of trading activity are London, New York, Tokyo, Singapore and Hong Kong. In all of these cities international financial activity is a major source of foreign exchange earnings. A cluster of international banks creates a cluster of expertise that in turn stimulates a greater degree of financial activity than would otherwise take place.

International Banking Facilities (IBFs) have been permitted in the United States since 1981. A United States IBF is a special US-owned banking facility, located in the US, and permitted to participate in the Eurocurrency markets under the same regulations as an offshore bank. That is why they are sometimes called onshore offshore banks. The major IBF cities are New York, San Francisco, Los Angeles and Miami. IBFs are allowed to service non-resident clients and other IBFs free of local reserve requirements, interest rate ceilings and of some taxation requirements. IBF deposits are not supported by deposit insurance, and the banks are not allowed to issue certificates of deposit in domestic market transactions.

Japan and Canada have both permitted IBFs to be set up since the late 1980s. While a large city like Tokyo can profit from setting up an IBF, smaller cities such as Montreal and Vancouver probably cannot profit in any substantial way. While any international financial center needs to make sure that its regulatory constraints are no more restrictive than those of competing centers, freedom from overly restrictive regulation is not sufficient to stimulate international financial activity to any appreciable degree. An international financial center can be successful only if it can attract and retain a large pool of financial skills and trading activity based on using those skills.

17.2 EUROMARKET ACTIVITY

Most international intermediation takes place in the international financial centers of major cities. As discussed in Chapter 14, Euromarket transactions in these cities can be less costly than comparable domestic transactions because they are not subject to the same kinds of regulation.

17.2.1 Eurocredits

Eurocredits are medium or long term bank loans with floating interest rates tied to short term Eurodollar rates. Since they are usually in large amounts and provided to foreign borrowers, the loans are normally provided by a syndicate or consortium of international banks. In addition to spreads over LIBOR, the syndicate's managing or lead bank usually charges a **management fee**, a **participation fee** and a **commitment fee**. In addition facility and negotiation fees may also be added. Because of the fees, a borrower can effectively pay a relatively large spread over LIBOR, but the announced interest rate on the loan may be only a few basis points in excess of LIBOR. In part, this arrangement is struck to bolster the prestige of borrowers by making it technically possible for them to announce that they have obtained international loans at relatively low rates of interest.

---

management fee fee for performing the administrative work of arranging a syndicated loan.

---

participation fee fee charged by an international bank for actually providing some of the funds to a borrower under a syndicated loan arrangement.

> **commitment fee** fee charged by an international bank for agreeing to provide funds to a borrower under a syndicated loan arrangement.

Floating rate Eurocredits emerged in the 1970s, a period when banks were reluctant to make medium or long term commitments at fixed rates. The floating rate formula at a spread over LIBOR eliminated the profit risk the banks faced due to changing interesting rates, while the syndication of larger loans permitted the banks to diversify the default risk inherent in large trnasactions.

Credit lines called euro-facilities include Eurocommercial paper, medium term notes (MTNs), revolving underwriting facilities (RUFs) and note issuance facilities (NIFs). Eurocommercial paper, which is similar to domestically issued commercial paper, represents the most important component. RUFs are medium term financial arrangements to enable borrowers to issue short term notes, typically three to six months in maturity, up to a prescribed limit over an extended period of time, commonly by means of repeated offerings to a tender panel. If, at any time, the notes are not sold by the panel at an acceptable price, an underwriting bank (or a group of them) undertakes to buy the notes at a prescribed price or guarantees the availability of standby credit. NIFs are similar to RUFs except that the bank underwrites the facility only on a 'best efforts basis' with no undertaking to buy unsold notes or to make standby funds available.

Like larger domestic loans, Euroloans are often written as a package that includes options on interest rates. The options may be caps, floors, or more exotic combinations of these instruments. In addition, there are forward contracts on interest rates, taking the form either of a forward forward (FF) contract or of a forward rate agreement (FRA).

The first, FF contract, merely fixes an interest rate today for a loan or deposit starting at some future time and, usually, extending over some fixed maturity. A forward rate agreement stipulates an interest rate to be paid or charged at the time a loan or investment is originated, and thus offers a means of either speculating on or hedging against interest rate change. For example, a borrower wishing to arrange a loan for three months hence could fix the interest rate on the loan using a FRA. Like a swap, the FRA is based on a notional amount. Its worth is determined by the difference between a contracted interest rate of, say, a deposit of fixed maturity, and the actual rate prevailing on that deposit when the contract expires. The deposit is not actually made, and settlement of the instrument is in cash at the time specified in the contract.

FRAs are used mainly to help financial institutions manage maturity mismatches. According to Sercu and Uppal (1995) they offer the following advantages over financial futures. First, they are not marked to market, and therefore do not nominally carry the interest rate risk associated with a futures contract.[3] Second, because there is no marking to market, there are no intermediate cash flow problems associated with the instrument.[4] Third, again because there is no marking to market, there is an exact arbitrage relationship between spot and forward rates that is easy to calculate. Finally FRAs are tailor made and can therefore suit two parties' interests more closely than can standard futures contracts. On the other hand, both the absence of a clearing corporation and the absence of marking to market mean the holder of the FRA is presented with a larger default risk. In sum, since FRAs have the advantages of non-standard, negotiated arrangements, they are more suitable for use in intermediated rather than in market transactions.

17.2.2 Investment banking

International investment banks carry out the same activities as the domestic investment banks discussed in Chapter 16. Based mainly in London, New York and Tokyo, they advise businesses and governments on how to raise capital, underwrite the sale of new bonds and shares, distribute new securities issues, carry out mergers and acquisitions, and effect corporate divestitures and privatisations of government owned firms. As relations between international capital markets continue to become stronger, and as domestic banking and securities activity continue to become more closely integrated, banks are becoming increasingly aggressive in pursuing the same business. At the same time, international investment banking is becoming more concentrated and investment bankers are unbundling their services as clients become increasingly sophisticated.

The successful international investment banks of the future are likely to be well capitalised, have a broadly based and efficient distribution network, and employ top quality people skilled in a particular set of activities. These firms are likely to emerge from the largest American investment banks, the Japanese securities firms, the largest global commercial banks,[5] and newly formed financial conglomerates.

17.3 CONTEMPORARY ISSUES

A number of policy and regulatory issues arise from the conduct of international banking activity. This chapter will discuss three contemporary issues, and Chapter 19 will examine regulatory responses to them. The issues involve assessing and managing international lending risks and international indebtedness, the question of whether capital shortages are a possibility, and the implications of the explosive growth of risk management activity.

17.3.1 International indebtedness

In addition to the kinds of risks in domestic lending, international lending involves the problems of assessing country risk and the risks of dealing in unfamiliar legal environments. In the 1970s these difficulties were compounded as banks, flush with liquidity, made international loans with little regard to the risks they posed. Partly as a result of the first oil crisis at the end of 1973, a number of countries ran up international debts considerably beyond their ability to service, at least in the short term. Between 1973 and 1983 non-oil developing countries' debt increased at a rate of about 19 percent.

By early 1982 the non-oil developing countries, as well as Mexico, Brazil and Argentina, not only had to reschedule existing debt repayments, but also were in need of new financing. At the time the loans were made, bankers gave little thought to the possibility that sovereign loans – that is, loans to national governments – might not be repaid. The sovereign loan fallacy held that a country could not default, because its government always had the taxing power to raise the funds to pay the debt. The argument is fallacious because it ignores the possibility that a country might not earn the necessary foreign exchange required to make the debt payments. In other words, as the discussion of sources and uses of foreign exchange in Chapter 14 suggests, a country's income might not be sufficient to meet its international obligations.

The problems of repayment were exacerbated whenever US interest rates increased, since most of the loans are floating rate obligations, with interest rates related either to LIBOR (which is affected by US rates) or to domestic US rates themselves. The inability of debtor countries to repay the loans has been dealt with by rescheduling them, that is, deferring payments on them.

While the debt problems of non-oil developing countries and other major borrowers have yet to be resolved completely, the situation had begun to improve by the end of the 1980s. The improvements followed on major adjustment efforts by both debtor countries and their creditor banks. Sharp declines in current account deficits were achieved by severely curtailing imports and increasing exports, in many cases at the cost of sharp reductions in debtor countries' living standards. These changes were supported by increased IMF assistance as well as by official and private creditors. The amortisation period for rescheduled debt was stretched and an initial grace period was granted. In some cases lenders entered into multi-year rescheduling agreements which made debt servicing requirements more predictable and hence more manageable. Lending spreads and fees were reduced. Some non-US banks even offered to switch the currencies of outstanding loans.

Default risks, the most prominent risks in international lending, have traditionally been handled through screening loan applications and writing off loans which were not repaid. The emergence of a secondary market in international debt helped individual banks to manage their loan losses in the then novel way of selling off some debts at a discount. Secondary market trading also helped banks to diversify existing risks by changing the proportions of their loans to individual countries. In a 1984 move foreshadowing the emergence of **credit derivatives**, Citibank insured $900 million in loans to less developed countries (LDCs) against default losses. For a price, the action both shifted the risk from Citibank to insurers, and improved the bank's solvency.

> **credit derivatives** instruments which pay the holder (usually a lender) in the event of a loan default. The idea of a credit derivative is similar to default insurance or to that of selling (putting) an asset to the issuer of a put for more than its current market price.

Problems still persist because some developing countries have assumed more debt, and issued less equity, than their earnings can sustain. The International Finance Corporation, the World Bank's private sector development agency, is one of many institutions to propose a solution. The IFC proposes establishing investment trusts for individual developing countries. Shares of the trust would be issued to banks in exchange for the country's foreign currency loans. The trust manager would then try to swap the loans into local currency equity positions in business. The shares of the trust would be listed on the country's stock exchange as well as on such major exchanges as London, New York and Tokyo. The main advantage of the scheme rests on the marketability of the trust shares, which would allow them to be sold to institutional investors such as pension funds.

17.3.2 Capital shortages: a possibility?

From time to time the press raises the issue of whether the world might face a capital shortage, but the reasons offered in support of this possibility are mostly spurious. As one instance of drawing mistaken conclusions, net international bank lending to developing countries declined in real terms since these countries faced payments difficulties beginning in 1982. However, this change followed on a reassessment of the credit risks involved rather than from a world-wide shortage of funds.

To take a second example, some observers argue that the heavy external financing requirements of the US in the 1980s and 1990s have both increased world interest rates and crowded out private sector domestic investment. These pressures are likely to increase in the 1990s as a result of the need to finance development in China and in Germany, along with Japan's diminishing ability to continue supplying large proportions of its savings to the rest of the world. Are any or all of these changes evidence that capital shortages can occur?

First, recall that Chapters 3 and 5 showed that not all of a country's capital formation expenditures are financed from domestic savings. The willingness of foreigners to invest in a country depends on their estimates of returns and of political stability. As these perceptions change, the terms on which a country can obtain financing from abroad are likely to change. The country then has little alternative but to try to raise more funds through domestic saving. However, this is no more evidence of a capital shortage than the fact that a corporation sometimes runs into limitations on its ability to raise funds is evidence that financial markets are somehow not working.[6]

In all these cases, potential borrowers with differing credit ratings have to compete for funds. The flow of available funds is not permanently fixed, but depends on interest rates. Thus as world demand for financing increases, interest rates may temporarily rise. But if an increase in world savings were to follow on the increase in interest rates, the longer term result could be an eventual return to something like former interest rate levels. As this process of competing for funds occurs, countries with weak credit ratings may be outcompeted by countries with stronger ratings.[7] But this is evidence, not of a world-wide shortage of funds, but rather of the kind of allocation process that normally takes place in markets.

17.3.3 Risk management

During the late 1980s and into the 1990s risk management activity has been growing explosively, both in terms of market trading and in terms of intermediated deals. In some cases, the risks of the newly invented instruments are not well understood by the firms purchasing them. Many of the participants in risk trading take particular points of view, and suffer losses when their points of view are not realised.[8] It may also be that the risks in some of the more complex positions currently being taken are not always well understood by the institutions arranging the deals.

In addition, risk control systems in some institutions are so weak that management cannot determine when institutional survival is being jeopardised. There are also aggregate problems, because the failure of one institution can bring about failure of others. Finally, there are presently few sources of aggregate statistics that would permit informed observers to assess exactly what the potential dangers in individual institutions' positions might be. On the positive side, the percentage of capital at risk in derivatives trading has been estimated at some 10 percent of the total capital of the world's banks. In addition, individual companies have sustained large losses from derivatives trading without creating serious externalities. For example, when Barings Bank failed in 1995, many of the other banks trading with Barings had become aware of the unusual risks it was taking and had reduced their positions with Barings.

17.4 SUMMARY

This chapter outlined the rise of international financial intermediaries and international finance. It discussed aspects of the Eurocredit markets, correspondent banking, offshore financial centers and international banking facilities. Managerial approaches to risk management in international financial markets were considered in the context of international indebtedness, the possibility of capital shortages, and the possible difficulties posed by rapidly growing risk management activity.

REVIEW QUESTIONS

Exercise 1 Banks sometimes enter one form of international business, then later withdraw from it. Is it possible that both these actions are rational? Why or why not?

Exercise 2 Some observers argue that Canada's banks should stick to their domestic business, because anything else is just an ego trip for senior management. Name at least one group that would be disadvantaged by following this advice.

Exercise 3 Explain why it might be rational for a country to get a loan at LIBOR and then effectively pay more for it through agreeing to pay additional fees.

Exercise 4 It has sometimes happened that large international banking transactions of essentially the same type are arranged at widely differing costs. Does this indicate to you that the markets are competitive? Does it help explain the attractions of international investment banking to ambitious senior executives? Is the situation likely to change over time? Why or why not?

Exercise 5 In addition to being subject to the sovereign loan fallacy, many bankers failed to note the possibility of moral hazard in lending to other countries' governments. Yet in some of the borrowing countries, the facilities on military establishments are unusually lavish. Why is this a clue to the presence of moral hazard?

Exercise 6 Certain African countries are so poor that it is very difficult for them to obtain agricultural development loans. Is this evidence of a capital shortage? If not, what does such a situation indicate?

Exercise 7 In recent years there have been several scandals in derivatives trading. For example, the activities of a Barings Bank trader incurred such heavy losses that the bank failed. Similarly, a copper trader at Sumitomo lost the company nearly US$2 billion over ten years. Are these incidents evidence of a need for tighter regulation of derivatives trading? Is tougher regulation likely to prove the most effective way of attempting to address such problems?

Exercise 8 Discuss the popular concern over capital shortages in light of increased integration of the international financial markets.

Exercise 9 How does increasing instability of foreign exchange rates contribute to the development of international finance?

Exercise 10 What is the function of an international lender of last resort?

Exercise 11 Suppose Frankfurt is an international financial center but Berlin is not. Are international transactions in Berlin at any serious disadvantage? Why or why not?

Exercise 12 Can a country have a credit limit like a corporation? Why cannnot the country just use its taxing powers to pay off international loans?

Exercise 13 If a country's government continues to devalue its currency at unpredictable rate, what is likely to happen to financial transactions within the country?

Part V

Assessing and improving performance

This part discusses mitigating financial system performance problems and how the financial system of the future is likely to evolve. Chapter 18 describes government financial activity, while Chapter 19 addresses principles of regulation. Both these activites are intended to affect aspects of financial system performance. Chapter 20 discusses the system's likely future evolution.

18 Government financial activity

18.1	Introduction		312
	18.1.1	Principles	312
	18.1.2	Remedial activity	313
18.2	Government programs		314
	18.2.1	Government lending intermediaries	314
	18.2.2	Loan guarantees	317
	18.2.3	Savings intermediaries	317
	18.2.4	Pension plans	317
18.3	Target sectors		318
	18.3.1	Financing small business	318
	18.3.2	Financing agriculture	319
18.4	Government financing		320
18.5	Summary		321

LEARNING OBJECTIVES

After reading this chapter you will understand

- why governments intervene in private sector financial activity
- the principal ways in which governments can intervene
- how governments select target sectors for intervention
- some of the problems arising in assisting targeted sectors
- the importance of government fiscal policy for financial activity

---

18.1 INTRODUCTION

Governments have a pervasive impact on most countries' financial systems. Their influence is registered through the conduct of monetary and fiscal policy, through programs intended to alleviate performance problems, and through legislation governing financial system operations. A full discussion of monetary and fiscal policy would distract from the principal purpose of this book, to explain the workings of the financial system itself. Moreover, there are many excellent texts that consider monetary and fiscal policy questions. Hence this book limits itself to examining the financial system impacts of government activity.

Typically, government activity is aimed at mitigating the effects of capital market gaps or at absorbing financial system externalities, a particular form of market segmentation. (The concepts of externalities and of segmentation were both introduced in Chapter 11.) Sometimes, governments address other goals such as increasing the level of national saving. Whatever the goal of intervention, and whatever benefits it is expected to bring, government activity is costly. Therefore, deciding whether a given activity would be worthwhile is an exercise in cost-benefit analysis.

The effects of government extend beyond attempts to improve the system: government's everyday operations also affect the financial environment. In particular, since the budgetary or fiscal operations of governments affect interest rates and other credit conditions, the chapter considers these effects as well.

18.1.1 Principles

Most attempts at improving financial system performance represent efforts either to mitigate the effects of capital market gaps or to capture positive externalities – social benefits that are not realised through the mix of private sector activities taking place. Government can justifiably intervene in financial system activity if

1 the social benefits from intervention are estimated to exceed intervention costs

2   the private sector cannot profitably secure the benefits through the prices it charges for financial products and services
3   the government activity can be curtailed if the original estimates on which it was based either change for the worse or prove not to have been well founded.

When it is successful, government intervention can secure social benefits deriving from such activities as employment creation, or improvements to the environment. However, the circumstances in which intervention can actually be justified occur rather infrequently. Even when justifying circumstances are present, an apparently pressing need for intervention can become less pressing over time: programs which make a positive impact at one point in time can later come to have no or even a negative impact. Finally, there is almost always more than one way for government to attempt to mitigate a given performance problem, and if society's benefit is to be maximised the form of intervention should be chosen with a view to maximising its cost-effectiveness.

18.1.2 Remedial activity

When considering whether an attempt to mitigate an alleged problem might be worthwhile, policymakers should ask the following kinds of questions. First, is there a realistic hope that the problem can be addressed cost-effectively? Second, which of the possible forms of intervention is likely to maximise the benefit–cost ratio in the particular circumstances? Finally, can the proposed remedial activity be reviewed at intervals, and terminated if its effectiveness diminishes or disappears?

Not every financial system performance problem is worth addressing. It is worth attempting to mitigate the effects of a financial market gap, or to secure social benefits by removing externalities, only if society can gain net benefits after taking the cost of the program into account. If there is a relatively strong possibility of realising net social benefits, and if these social benefits are not capable of being secured through the private sector's acting on its own, government intervention might be expected to improve matters. However, it must also be realised that the anticipated benefits might not turn out to exceed the costs of intervention, either because the benefits do not materialise or because the costs prove higher than originally expected.

If the case for realising net benefits is sufficiently persuasive, the manner of intervention also requires consideration. Since the problem being addressed is assumed to be of a type that profit-oriented private sector activity will not alleviate on its own, one obvious question is to ask whether the problem might be addressed by changing the incentives the private sector faces. Incentive schemes can quite often lead to cost-effective solutions, but the circumstances of a particular problem might render some other method of intervention more effective. Thus it is also necessary to examine various forms of direct intervention before reaching a conclusion regarding the most desirable way of addressing a particular problem.

Whatever their nature, remedial programs are based on estimated net benefits. Astute observers understand that any net benefits actually secured can differ from their original estimated values. Yet, once a remedial program is in place it can be politically difficult to terminate it, because any such program creates its own constituencies. For these reasons, any new program is probably best set up with a fixed termination date. Fixed termination means the proposed remedy is afforded a trial which, if successful, can be used to make a case for extending the program's operation. If the trial is unsuccessful, the program will terminate automatically and the initiating government is not saddled with an activity that will continue indefinitely.

18.2 GOVERNMENT PROGRAMS

The principal forms of government intervention are either setting up government lending intermediaries or providing loan guarantees and other incentive programs.

18.2.1 Government lending intermediaries

A **financial market gap** is a form of market segmentation in which potential users of funds cannot raise funds at market rate of interest appropriate for the deal's risk. The existence of a gap means that financial markets are operating in an allocatively inefficient manner, and as a result it might seem a good idea to set up a government intermediary to make loans or investments that would help fill the gap. However, a number of questions need to be answered before such a conclusion can be drawn. First, does the gap actually exist or is the situation simply one of a particular interest group seeking a governmental subsidy? Second, if there is a gap, why has private sector activity failed to remove it? That is, what is preventing arbitrage or intermediation from supplying the funds? Third, how much might it cost to set up a government intermediary, and would it be as capable of addressing the gap as private sector firms, assuming the latter could be induced to do so? Fourth, would the anticipated benefits from mitigating the gap outweigh the costs of addressing it? Fifth, is setting up an intermediary the most cost-effective remedy available? Sixth, if an intermediary is to be set up, what performance criteria should it adopt?

---

financial market gap a situation in which potential users of funds cannot raise funds at the market rate of interest for deals presenting that risk. If they can raise funds at all, their cost of doing so is higher than the market rate.

In some cases the alleged existence of a financial market gap may prove merely to be an effort by a special interest group to obtain a form of government assistance. Many groups claim they need lower interest financing for one reason or another, but if they can obtain financing at market rates, there is no gap. The claimants may have other problems, such as lack of profitability, but if there is no gap the problems they face are not financial system performance problems, and should not be addressed as such.

If a financial market gap actually exists, some kinds of financing will not be obtainable at market interest rates commensurate with the risk they present. For example, if second mortgage loans on homes in one locale have a market interest rate of 10 percent, and if in some other locale comparably risky financing cannot be obtained for less than, say, 15 percent, a capital market gap could be said to exist. Such situations may not appear to be very likely, because financial theory argues that in any such cases arbitrage opportunities present themselves. When an arbitrage opportunity is detected, lenders are likely to find a way to profit from the unusual interest rate differential, and subsequent profit-seeking activity may well cause the gap to disappear.

On the other hand, if some kind of market imperfection (such as lack of knowledge regarding a profit opportunity) does seem to inhibit arbitraging, it is at least possible that a gap exists. The proponents of intervention then need to face the question of why, if the proposed deals are so attractive, the private sector has apparently failed to detect them? Answers to this question can help determine the kind of intervention most likely to be successful.

If government is considering whether an intermediary could mitigate the effects of a gap, its first task is to assess the benefits and costs of setting up the intermediary. The social benefits will usually be the increased economic activity from providing the financing, and may be difficult to quantify. But an effort to do so should be made nevertheless, because the social benefits need somehow to be measured against the social costs of intervention. The social costs may be easier to establish. They are principally the resource costs of setting up the intermediary, including the costs of raising funds to carry out the lending or investment activity. Since it can be presumed that the private sector could not profit from the activity, the expected losses from government's doing the business need to be deducted from any expected benefits before it can be concluded that intervention is socially worthwhile.

Assuming the social benefits and costs have correctly been taken into account, the question of assessing the proposed intermediary's performance then arises. Would intermediary profitability be a useful criterion? The answer to this question is negative for several reasons. In the first place, if profitability could be used as a criterion the principles of arbitrage suggest that private sector firms would have had an incentive to enter the business. Moreover, any profits reported by government agencies may be illusory, because government accounting methods do not always recognise the full cost of the resources they employ. For example, premises are sometimes provided at low or no cost to a government intermediary. As another example, government intermediaries sometimes borrow funds from their governments, at interest rates that are lower than market in view of the risks involved. In still other instances a public sector intermediary may be able to raise funds on favourable terms in financial markets because the government appears morally responsible for its debts.

Another problem with assessing the profitability of a government intermediary involves determining an appropriate standard for loan losses. The size of loan losses will depend on the target group of clients: high risk financing cannot be provided without incurring loan losses. Yet quite often government intermediaries (for example, those financing high risk small businesses) may be unwilling or unable to make the high risk loans their mandate requires. In particular, the skills of their credit officers and the incentives these officers face may bias them against making relatively high risk investments. Such persons frequently argue that they are doing a good job when in fact they are working hard to keep loan losses unrealistically low by directing loans toward clients presenting lower risks than the intended target group.

Government lending intermediaries also suffer from other forms of goal confusion. It is usually argued that government intermediaries can assist their clients by making low interest financing available to them, but this argument conceals two quite different reasons for intervention. For example, government intermediaries should not be set up to make low interest rates to farms on the grounds that farming is otherwise uneconomic. If there is a capital market gap, the loans should be at market rates of interest so that resource allocation is distorted as little as possible. If farmers can already obtain financing at market rates of interest, but claim they need low interest rate financing to survive, then any relief they obtain should be justified in the political arena rather than being disguised as a capital market gap problem.

Even if the foregoing questions can be answered satisfactorily, government intermediation may not prove the best way of mitigating the effects of the gap. Setting up a government intermediary may be more costly than, say, providing the private sector with incentives to do the job. For example, some loan applications are so expensive to assess that the private sector will not consider them. Yet, if the financing were available the jobs created from implementing the projects would be worth more than the investigation costs. In this case it would be possible to set up a loss-making government intermediary to grant the loans, but it might also be possible to defray some of the private sector's expenses and thus induce them to make the loans. The second alternative might prove both cheaper and more effective, because it takes advantage of skills already available in the private sector.

As a second example, private sector insurance to cover risks in the export trade will not be readily available if it is uneconomic for the private sector to offer the coverage, say because there are not enough risks of the type in question for private sector companies to earn profits from setting up that line of business. However, if government judges that it is worth securing the social benefits of encouraging exports, it could prove cost-effective to offer subsidies that would encourage the private sector insurance industry to take on the risks.

Sometimes when public lending intermediaries have been operating for a period of time, it may be possible for them to sell off parts of their loan portfolios to the private sector. Such a transaction allows outside observers to evaluate the intermediary's financing activity. Just as with securitisation, both the quality of the investments and the extent to which they were being subsidised are assessed using market criteria. If the instruments sell readily, it is likely the original rationale for operating the government intermediary has changed, or perhaps never existed in the first place.

18.2.2 Loan guarantees

Loan guarantees can encourage the private sector to provide financing it would otherwise regard as excessively risky. A guarantee scheme may well prove cheaper than setting up a government intermediary, at least so long as the guarantee programs are carefully administered. For a guarantee program to be successful, interest rates must not be set below market levels, or the private sector will have no incentive to advance any funds. On the other hand, care must be taken to ensure that the private sector assumes a proportion of loan losses. Unless some loan losses are borne by the lenders, they will likely underemphasise their screening responsibilities and make loans irrespective of their risk.

18.2.3 Savings intermediaries

Government savings intermediaries date back to the late nineteenth century. Their initial purpose was to offer a safe depository for wealth in locations where private sector financial institutions did not operate. However, their principal current purpose seems to be that of gathering up savings to be used for purchasing government debt, and thus helping to meet government financial needs. There are at least two reasons to believe that these intermediaries no longer serve their original purposes. First, the private sector can efficiently gather up retail savings even in remote communities. Second, well-run governments have little difficulty in tapping financial markets for funds.

18.2.4 Pension plans

Public sector pension plans are usually set up with a view to providing retirement income to persons who have been unable to accumulate pension assets themselves. The importance of public sector pension funds is indicated by the household assets invested in them. In the United States in 1993, total household assets amounted to $17,230 billion, while total liabilities were $4,393 billion. Thus households' net assets, or accumulated savings, amounted to $12,837 billion. The amount households had invested in pension funds was $4,776 billion, of which $1,396 billion represented public sector managed funds.[1]

Public sector pension programs are humane in intent and capable of generating social benefits, providing they are appropriately administered. Sadly, however, the administration of governmental pension programs is usually flawed in several ways. First, the investment policies of government pension funds are generally not as sound as those of well-run private sector pension plans. Assets are frequently invested entirely in government securities and earn a lower rate of return (after adjusting for risk) than if the funds were permitted to follow a less restrictive investment policy. Second, government funds are not usually funded on an actuarial basis, but operate on a pay-as-you-go basis. For example, the US Social Security plan makes payments out of current premiums. Like other pay-as-you-go plans, the US plan is vulnerable to demographic change and, given its current structure, will likely be unable to cover its liabilities as the average age of the population increases through the remainder of the 1990s and into the twenty-first century.

In order to remain solvent, the program will have to be revised to include some combination of increased contributions (i.e., increased payroll taxes), reduced benefits, or both. Likely, benefits from the programs will eventually be restricted to persons of little means. Benefits may also be restricted by removing current indexing provisions that increase pension payments in line with inflation. Since some other current proposals for pension reform include extending benefits to cover homemakers and thereby vastly increasing the operating expenses of the fund, it is evident that contribution and benefit rates merit further serious consideration.

Still another means of dealing with the increasing cost of public sector pension funds is to encourage the public to provide more retirement assets of their own. Many countries, including both the US and the UK, have governmentally approved plans intended to encourage savings by providing tax deferral privileges on contributions up to some maximum.

18.3 TARGET SECTORS

Traditionally, most forms of intervention have been aimed at four sectors: small business, agriculture, exports and housing. Regardless of which sector is targeted, the arguments for intervention employ the principles already cited. For example, attempts to stimulate residential mortgage financing have usually been justified on the basis of the external benefits to the economy (construction jobs, more stable living conditions) that could be enjoyed if housing construction activity were to be increased. In North America, housing has received much attention in the past, but in the 1990s problems of improving the housing stock are less acute than formerly. Similarly, problems of financing exports are less acute than formerly. Accordingly, this section discusses only the remaining two target sectors: financing small business and financing agriculture.

18.3.1 Financing small business

The pattern of small business finance in most developed countries is quite different from that of the incorporated business sector. Small business depends heavily on loans, trade credit, conditional sales contract and debt financing. The principal problem in small business financing is raising equity funds, and the new business with no track record has real difficulty in finding startup financing. First, the fixed costs of public issues are relatively high, ruling them out as a likely source of equity finance. Second, venture capitalists who might be expected to make equity investments in new businesses, also have high fixed investigation costs which prevent their considering relatively small applications for funds. Moreover, since even venture capitalists find the governance of small business financing relatively difficult, they tend mainly to invest in businesses with strong track records.

Many countries have set up government intermediaries with the mandate of providing small business with the funding that the private sector does not find profitable. Unfortunately, such intermediaries often become competitors with the private sector for relatively low risk forms of financing, and avoid the high risk investments they are mandated to provide. Government agencies rarely provide startup equity financing, and sometimes even refer clients to venture capital firms. The principal problem is that the officers of the public sector intermediaries are not rewarded for risk taking, but are rather penalised in terms of career prospects if the risks they do assume turn out badly.

A subsidy to private sector financiers might be preferable to relying on a government intermediary, but it is also necessary to recognise the difficulties with such schemes and to address them through proper program design. Subsidies are frequently misused and can channel funds toward unintended targets. For example, if there is a subsidy for screening applications, financiers may look at a great many without even intending to invest in any of the applicant firms. One way of ensuring that screening is not done simply to earn the subsidy is to have applications audited by representatives from other firms in the same industry. As a second example, subsidies through tax legislation can be difficult to target and subject to considerable abuse. Thus it is usually more cost-effective to allow the tax authorities to exercise administrative discretion, rather than to provide the subsidy through legislation. To ensure compliance of the private sector firms without using unduly costly forms of administration, licensing arrangements are probably advisable.

18.3.2 Financing agriculture

The problems of financing agriculture are mainly those of finding long term funding for a class of business with relatively uncertain annual cash flows. Such a business would normally make use of equity financing, but the only traditional form of equity financing in farming involves sharecropping arrangements, in which the operator of the farm has equity in the crop but not in the land. Alternatively, a form of debt insurance to cover bad crop years might help farms that are profitable in the long run, but such loan insurance schemes are not currently available either.[2]

Debt does not always help even profitable farmers, since one of the main sources of their returns is capital gains on their land, and capital gains are not normally available for defraying mortgage payments. For such cases, a form of mortgage with relatively small interest and principal payments might help the farmer's cash flow problems. In return, the financier would require some compensation, such as an equity interest in the land value of the farm, that would permit profiting from an increase in the value of the land. Of course, such an instrument would only provide compensation if the capital gains could be realised, either by selling the land or by trading the equity interest in it. Such a new instrument might also have to be insured against default to overcome financiers' lack of familiarity with it.

Another assistance proposal suggests the use of tax-exempt bonds, thus reducing the cost of the funding to the borrower while at the same time offering investors an attractive after-tax yield on long term investments. A similar idea has been used in the United States to raise funds for industrial development purposes, and municipalities in the US have long enjoyed the ability to issue tax-exempt securities. The main difficulty with these proposals is that they are really disguised subsidies, and it is not clear whether maintaining marginal farms through subsidies is in society's best long run interest. At the very least that issue is a matter better resolved through open political debate rather than through providing hidden subsidies.

Confusion of loans to finance viable farm operations with soft loans essentially representing income redistribution to uneconomic farms is a major problem for public sector agricultural finance. The confusion makes it difficult to administer financing programs efficiently, because few organisations can successfully pursue the disparate goals of lending to viable enterprises and income redistribution.

18.4 GOVERNMENT FINANCING

Government financial operations are the counterpart of fiscal policy: a government operating at a surplus has funds to lend or invest, a government operating at a deficit must raise funds. The more serious problems with government finance usually arise when government operates at a deficit. In those circumstances, government competes with the private sector for capital market funds, and the increased demand for funding can cause short term increases in nominal interest rates. The interest rate increases can contribute to the phenomenon known as crowding out. Because its risk is relatively easy to evaluate, many financiers regard government debt as an attractive alternative to corporate or individual debt, thus potentially exacerbating the crowding out effect. Government deficits, and the high interest rates created by their financing, usually create capital inflows in an open economy with fixed exchange rates. These capital inflows can offset any immediate possibilities for crowding out. However, the government deficit may increase inflationary pressures, which may in turn reduce private sector investment. Moreover, if many countries' governments incur deficits at the same time, the high interest rates they jointly pay can attract funds away from corporate investment.

Government borrowing may either be for account of the government itself or for its agencies. Some government agencies relend funds to private sector borrowers, thus acting as a recycling mechanism, directing more funds to some borrowers than they could otherwise obtain.

18.5 SUMMARY

This chapter considered government programs aimed at improving system functioning, and the related matter of government financing. Most government intervention is aimed at remedying the effects of capital market gaps, absorbing externalities, or such other goals as increasing the level of national saving.

REVIEW QUESTIONS

Exercise 1 Suppose, as is usually the case, that business can get ample short term credit at market rates of interest. Should the government help small business by arranging for lower cost loans in this circumstance?

Exercise 2 Government business support agencies sometimes rent premises from governments at non-market rates, and sometime obtain their funds at below-market rates. How does this affect any profits they might report? Should a government lending agency strive for profits in any case?

Exercise 3 When governments set up guarantee schemes, they sometimes also limit the rate of interest that the banks providing the loans can earn. Why is this a self-defeating policy?

Exercise 4 The California Public Employees' Retirement Scheme has invested most of its assets in state securities. Why has this policy worked against the interests of persons drawing pensions from the fund?

Exercise 5 Under what circumstances is it clearly in the economy's best interests for a government to borrow from abroad?

Exercise 6 Outline a situation in which you either favour or do not favour government intervention. Show how the principles of this chapter can be used to defend your choice.

Exercise 7 Is it a good idea to set up a program of low interest rate loans for business? Why or why not?

Exercise 8 Try to find an example of a government program that has outlived its usefulness. Defend your choice of example.

Exercise 9 What are some of the effects of fiscal policy on interest rates?

Exercise 10 What is crowding out and to what extent can it be attributed to fiscal policy?

19 Supervision

19.1	Problems and principles	323
	19.1.1 Problems	323
	19.1.2 Principles	324
	19.1.3 Importance of competition	324
	19.1.4 Costs of supervision	325
	19.1.5 Effectiveness	326
	19.1.6 Self-regulation	326
19.2	Supervision in practice	327
	19.2.1 Securities business	327
	19.2.2 Intermediation	328
	19.2.3 Taxation and its impacts	329
19.3	International issues	330
	19.3.1 Banking supervision	330
	19.3.2 International securities supervision	331
	19.3.3 Lender of last resort	331
	19.3.4 Capital adequacy	332
	19.3.5 Supervision of derivatives	332
19.4	Summary	333

LEARNING OBJECTIVES

After reading this chapter you will understand

- the kinds of problems addressed by financial supervision
- why regulators stress the importance of competition
- why supervision is costly
- why supervision is not always effective
- some of the regulatory impacts of taxation
- how regulatory issues arise from the financial system's changing operations

---

19.1 PROBLEMS AND PRINCIPLES

This chapter discusses how supervision can mitigate financial system performance problems. The problems to be addressed must be selected carefully because regulators' ability to improve system performance is limited. First, regulators almost always have limited resources, and there is little point in giving the regulators powers they cannot use. Second, regulation imposes costs on the regulated, and such costs should not be imposed unless there is a strong case that at least commensurate social benefits are being obtained.

The chapter first considers the principal kinds of problems that supervision attempts to address. It then examines the principles according to which problems can be tackled, and discusses the kinds of regulatory actions best suited for particular kinds of problems. The chapter also discusses why some popular policy choices are not particularly suitable, and are therefore likely to be ineffective. Finally, the chapter examines how some current regulatory issues arise from financial system changes.

19.1.1 Problems

The problems regulators must address are numerous, and discussing them on an individual basis would be a very lengthy task. Therefore, we consider the usual types of problems with which regulators are likely to be concerned. Taking a long run performance perspective, supervisors usually address the following kinds of questions:

- whether the financial system provides the types of funding needed to finance economic growth
- whether public confidence in the financial system can be strengthened, and if so, how
- whether the public is reasonably well informed about the risks inherent in making different kinds of investment
- whether financiers have incentives to operate as responsible custodians of others' funds.

Insofar as funding is concerned, regulators cannot usually do much more than try to ensure the financial system operates as competitively as possible.[1] With respect to enhancing public confidence, legislation can try to establish expectations that financiers will deal with the public fairly and openly, handling the public's money with the care of a prudent trustee. A public that is reasonably well informed will make its investments in a more discriminating fashion than a public without information. For example, as and when the public appears to be misinformed about the safety of some type of investment, regulators should try to ensure that information about the risks is promulgated more widely. Finally, sound supervisory principles can be implemented more effectively if financiers face positive incentives to deal honestly with their clients, and if they face penalties should they violate principles of good conduct.

19.1.2 Principles

Since a well-operated financial system can enhance economic growth, forward looking supervisors will try to ensure that viable projects can readily obtain funding at market rates of interest (commensurate with the risks or uncertainties involved). In this way funding will enhance investment, and that in turn can both maintain competitive rates of economic growth and foster technological change. These goals are best pursued by encouraging the development of different kinds of governance capabilities. It is not easy to tell what kinds of deals the future might present, and regulators should try to foster a climate that is open to innovation rather than just encouraging one or two types of deals that seem currently to be needed.

In designing their supervisory approaches, regulators face a mix of political and economic problems. For example, political concerns regarding the foreign ownership of domestic firms arise as an almost inevitable result of importing capital over long periods of time. After a period of borrowing from abroad, observers are likely to begin asking about the extent to which it is desirable for a country to allow equity ownership of its real assets to lie in the hands of non-residents. Equally, they may become concerned about the proportions of equity ownership acquired by foreign investors. On the other hand, economics suggests asking whether it is possible for a growing country to provide realistic alternatives to foreign equity investment. Economists will question whether a policy of relying solely on domestic funds might not negatively affect the amount and type of capital formation taking place. Assessing these kinds of tradeoffs forms the essence of a pragmatic regulatory policy, as will be considered further below.

19.1.3 Importance of competition

Most policymakers stress the merits of competition. First, competition is one way of ensuring that profit opportunities provide incentives for innovation. Financiers who compete keenly for new profit opportunities will be alert to changes in demand for new or evolving financial services, and will strive to supply the new demands in innovative and cost-effective ways.

If markets are not competitive,[2] the interest rate charged on a loan product can exceed financiers' marginal cost of funds, or the interest rate paid on a savings instrument can fall short of financiers' value marginal product. Competitive financial markets help ensure that interest rates, when appropriately adjusted for the risk of the deal, reflect the marginal value of funds in both borrowing and saving. Competition further ensures that above-normal profits will not persist. Rather new entry and the consequent competition for profitable business will mean that financiers try to bid business away from each other, diminishing the above-normal profit margins.

19.1.4 Costs of supervision

While press discussions sometimes seem to suggest the opposite, nearly all supervision imposes costs on the financial system. Hence it is important for policymakers to ask whether imposing a given regulation, or a given piece of legislation, creates benefits commensurate with the costs it brings. Policymakers must also recognise that different supervisory approaches – whether through detailed rules, broad principles or self-regulation – can have different cost impacts. Supervision based on broad principles is more flexible than detailed rules, and therefore avoids costs of creating rigidities. On the other hand, not all regulatory purposes can be achieved by pronouncing broad principles, and in some cases detailed regulations must be imposed. Nevertheless, a good principle is to avoid detailed regulations whenever it is possible to achieve the same or similar results with statements of regulatory principle.

The costs of supervision imply that indiscriminate supervision should be avoided. Many regulators have a bias against self-supervision of any type, and yet self-supervision can be quite effective in markets where a small number of large firms are both competitive and gain long term benefits from policing themselves.[3] For example, Canada's foreign exchange market has been effectively self-regulated for several decades, since the major players have a large stake in maintaining confidence in the market's operations, and since the major players compete actively for domestic business. On the other hand, self-supervision will work poorly in an industry with many small firms that can easily enter the industry, especially if they are likely to be present for relatively short periods of time. For example, firms which promote the primary issues of small resource exploration companies are poor candidates for a self-regulatory organisation, because typically such firms do not have a stake in maintaining an impeccable reputation over long periods of time.

Both existing and proposed legislation need to be examined carefully to see if the advantages the legislation is intended to bring are worth the costs, both those borne by the firms involved and those incurred by society at large. In particular, legislation which restricts financial activity may enhance safety, but it may also reduce competition. In such cases supervisors need to ask whether the benefits (safer operations) are worth the costs (less competition, less innovation). For example, in the interests of safety financial firms are sometimes restricted to conducting only certain types of business. Such restrictions can come at a price: they can both reduce competitiveness, meaning consumers pay higher than competitive interest rates, or prices for financial services. In addition, the restricted firms have fewer incentives to innovate, and thus may fail to adjust sufficiently quickly to changing conditions.The US thrift organisations' operations in the 1950s and 1960s are a good case in point: during this period there was a less than desirable amount of innovation in the thrift industry, because firms thought they were protected by the interest rate ceilings on savings deposits.

19.1.5 Effectiveness

Not all regulations create the effects they were intended to bring about. If legislation attempts to prevent financiers from doing profitable business, they may find innovative ways to avoid the legislation. For example, the 1970s development of the US money market fund stemmed in part from the Federal Reserve Board's Regulation Q interest rate ceilings imposed on banks and, through similar regulation, on such other savings institutions as thrifts. Originally intended to encourage mortgage lending by keeping the mortgage lenders' costs of funds low, the Regulation Q interest rate ceilings turned out to work perversely when market interest rates rose quickly to unexpected levels. Institutions could not retain deposits when market interest rates rose above the ceilings: at those times large amounts of deposits were withdrawn from banks and near banks in a process known as **disintermediation**. These financial institutions therefore faced incentives to circumvent the interest ceilings.

The difficulties with interest rate controls such as those embodied in Regulation Q came to be better understood; in the US, interest rate ceilings were eliminated by the mid-1980s. Credit controls and foreign exchange controls are other examples of intervention that are equally unlikely to be successful. They may appear to be successful when business does not wish to carry out the transactions covered by the controls, but their lack of effectiveness quickly becomes evident when the controls attempt to limit transactions that business views as profitable. In this case the controls become ineffective largely because they are easy to frustrate or circumvent.

19.1.6 Self-regulation

Some parts of a financial system are likely to be self-regulated. The main argument in favour of self-regulation is its sensitivity to industry concerns. The sensitivity is, however, also the main disadvantage of self-regulation: industry may make the rules to its own advantage in ways that do not coincide with either the interests of industry clients or of society in the larger sense.[4] The effectiveness of self-regulation depends in considerable measure on whether the firms in the self-regulated industry are likely to have long term horizons.

If they do, they are much more likely to keep client interests prominently in mind, recognising that the industry will most likely prosper if it treats clients honestly and efficiently. However, as mentioned above, self-supervision will work poorly in an industry with many small firms that can easily enter the industry, especially if they are present for relatively short periods of time. At the present time, the rapid growth of mutual funds in North America has led to many new funds being established, and the new funds' managers have not always conducted themselves as prudent trustees. Abuses of position and apparent conflict of interest have stimulated a number of observers to argue for more formal regulation of what is currently an informally and self-regulated industry.

19.2 SUPERVISION IN PRACTICE

North American legislation still separates certain kinds of financial business, and thus works to restrict competition in some areas. This legislation, now largely vestigial, was originally established in response to pressures from industry representatives who managed to convince legislators that orderly division of functions was a desirable end. Even today, some legislators are persuaded by such arguments, particularly if the representations are couched in terms of preserving financial system safety or in terms of preserving employment in a changing industry. The legislators sometimes hear the self-interested arguments of the financiers presenting them, and overlook the costs of restricting competition.

While avoiding restrictions is a generally desirable principle, in some instances the costs of restricting competition can be justified, from a social point of view, as a means of preventing what could otherwise be serious problems. For example, the separation between commercial lending and trustee functions addresses a potential conflict of interest. Without the legislation, trustees working for a bank could recommend, with impunity, that their clients invest in companies to which the bank was a lender. In this way the trustees might serve the bank's interests by increasing the client company's capitalisation. However, in the assumed circumstances they would not serve the interests of their trust clients, who could be induced to place funds in weak investments.

19.2.1 Securities business

Securities legislation attempts primarily to achieve adequate reporting, or disclosure, and the prevention of fraud. To ensure the viability of the firms in the industry, securities regulators also supervise the capital and liquidity positions of securities companies and those firms trading in risk management products. Regulators also seek to obtain full disclosure of pertinent information, to reduce the possibilities for insider trading and self-dealing, and to promulgate additional information regarding securities markets transactions.

It is difficult to ensure that dealings are in the public interest when there is lack of adequate disclosure. One example of abuses involves securities firms using insider information to trade on the Vancouver Stock Exchange. In another instance, the US Securities and Exchange Commission (SEC) intervened in the profit reporting of America's then (1984) fastest growing mortgage banking group, Financial Corporation of America. The SEC required a change in accounting methods that turned a second quarter 1984 profit of $31.1 billion into a loss of $107.5 billion in order to reflect capital losses on acquisitions of fixed rate assets during periods of rising interest rates.

19.2.2 Intermediation

Legislation governing intermediaries is concerned mainly with enhancing competitiveness, with ensuring the safety of depositor funds, with obviating potential conflicts of interest and self-dealing, and with preventing fraud. The first of these goals is pursued mainly by encouraging freedom of entry to financial businesses. Safety is sought primarily through providing deposit insurance,[5] and through supervising intermediary solvency. Many countries now employ guidelines established under the auspices of the Bank for International Settlements, as discussed below.

Deposit insurance offers a mix of advantages and disadvantages. The provision of insurance enhances competition by making the liabilities of different financial institutions perfect substitutes from a credit risk point of view. That is, deposit insurance makes it easier for small new intermediaries to compete for savers' funds. Deposit insurers could maintain this advantage through better administration than is now commonly used, but to do so they must ensure they do not provide weaker institutions with perverse incentives. Although many countries do not now follow the practice, any insurance scheme should provide that intermediaries pay higher premiums as they take on greater risk. Without risk-based premiums, insurance effectively subsidises the risk takers at the expense of better run institutions.

Similar considerations arise with respect to solvency legislation. In the past, legislation has restricted the assets in which intermediaries can invest. For example, banks were restricted as to the percentage of conventional mortgages they could hold, a restriction partially reflecting an attempt to prevent the banks from competing for the lending business of other intermediaries. Similarly, near bank investments were largely restricted to residential mortgages and government bonds. Insurance companies and pension funds are permitted to purchase only the securities of companies which meet certain earnings and dividends standards. None of these restrictions has convincingly been shown to enhance safety, but they all reduce financial system adaptability and the profitability of the restricted firms.

During the 1980s both US and Canadian banks made incursions into the securities business by acquiring discount brokerage firms. Up to that time, North American banking regulation had prevented banks from entering the securities business directly, and the discount brokerage acquisitions were attempts to test the regulations' legality. Canada now permits banks to acquire securities firms' affiliates, but the US is not yet as accommodating. Nevertheless, in the future closer combinations will probably emerge in both countries, since it is at least arguable that there are economies of scope to combining retail securities sales with domestic banking activity.

Prudential regulation is a key element in maintaining the confidence of the public in the stability and integrity of financial institutions. Prudential regulation attempts to protect invested wealth by constraining high risk transactions or investments, by imposing obligations on directors to ensure appropriate institutional behaviour, and by providing for audits and other inspections to ensure that financial managers act as prudent trustees. In some countries prudential regulation needs urgently to be strengthened. For example, the UK employees of the Maxwell Group of corporations suffered serious losses when their pension funds' assets were misused. Many countries do not yet have the kinds of pension fund insurance schemes set up in the US. Some other countries have established pension insurance schemes, but the regulations governing them are not fully enforced. Moreover, the countries that do insure their pension schemes rarely use risk-based premiums, and therefore the same perverse incentive problems that affect level premium deposit insurance also plague pension schemes.

As earlier chapters have shown, some kinds of commercial–industrial links make possible the financing of projects that could not otherwise obtain funds. However, commercial–industrial links can create conflicts of interest, particularly if the institutions are closely held. For example, real estate developers with a controlling interest in a near bank might be tempted to use depositors' funds to finance speculative real estate projects. The developers would have even more incentive to do so if their near bank could obtain level premium deposit insurance. To balance the advantages and disadvantages of commercial–industrial links, it is probably better not to restrict them. Rather, supervision should be better aimed at intensive oversight of any closely held financial institutions that are likely to abuse the linkages.

In North America, regulation continues to be reformed, largely according to the following agenda:

- integration of financial functions through common ownership of institutions and extension of powers
- a stronger framework for prudential regulation
- a pragmatic ownership policy of checking the growth of commercial–financial links in the economy while maintaining competition within the financial services sector.

Integration of functions is being driven by a search for economies of scale and of scope, and regulation promoting integration is primarily a response to these economic realities.

19.2.3 Taxation and its impacts

Tax laws affect many financial arrangements. Since interest is usually a tax deductible expense and dividends are not, the effective cost of debt securities is often lower than that of equity. As a second example, flow-through partnership arrangements allow original investors to write off the exploration or research expenses incurred by the companies in which they invest. This scheme reduces investors' cost, meaning that the exploration or research activity can obtain its financing more cheaply than would otherwise be possible.

Some countries tax non-profit investment pools such as pension funds if their portfolios contain more than a certain maximum percentage of foreign securities. Such schemes cannot improve the lot of investors, since a constraint cannot increase the flexibility of investment policy or the rate of return the invested funds might earn.

19.3 INTERNATIONAL ISSUES

With the rapid growth of international finance, national jurisdictions do not always have the power to supervise transactions adequately. As a result, certain forms of international regulatory coordination are desirable. Some of the areas in which the need for coordination arises are discussed below.

19.3.1 Banking supervision

There is currently little international coordination of banking supervision, except for that carried out by the Basle Committee – a committee of the governors of the central banks of the G-10 countries.[6] The Basle Committee attempts to coordinate national supervision to take account of banks' international business, and to assist national authorities in monitoring the overseas operations of their own banks. The Basle Committee, in negotiations hosted by the **Bank for International Settlements (BIS)**, has worked out the so-called Basle agreements to cover the following points. All foreign banking establishments should be supervised, and supervision is a joint responsibility of host and parent authorities. Supervision of liquidity is a primary responsibility of the host country (to assure conformity with local practice), but supervision of solvency is primarily a responsibility of the home country. Every effort should be made to exchange information needed for these supervisory tasks.

Bank for International Settlements (BIS) acts as a central banker for other central banks which are its shareholders. Founded in 1930 in Basle, Switzerland, its primary purpose is to handle and coordinate foreign exchange settlements between member central banks. It also closely monitors major developments in world capital markets and extends collective but limited guarantees as a lender of last resort for the Eurocurrency banks. Recently it has taken a more active position by actively participating in some international debt rescheduling operations.

The Basle Committee has also developed guidelines for the assessment of country risk, liquidity risk, solvency risk and risk-based capital adequacy standards for the world's banks. The guidelines are intended to restrict international firms from endangering each other by engaging in a competition to carry out more and more business with increasingly smaller percentages of capital. Financial firms are motivated to do so because financial markets do not seem to adjust share valuation to increasing risk. Thus without restrictive regulation international banks have an incentive to lever highly, to the detriment of sound system operations.

International banks' Eurocurrency dealings are regulated primarily by their home countries, but their other operations are usually regulated by the host country. There are several arguments favouring international coordination of supervision affecting Eurobanks. The failure of a major Eurobank might trigger collapse of the international banking system. Domestic banks facing more stringent regulation are at a competitive disadvantage relative to more loosely regulated Eurobanks. One counterargument is that attempts at more stringent regulation will merely move Eurobanks to new jurisdictions; any country initiating offshore regulation on its own will only decrease its own market share of offshore banking. A second counter is that the Euromarkets are mainly conducted by sophisticated players, for whom additional regulation would be superfluous.

Some standard practices, such as legal contracts covering Euromarket loans, have evolved without regulatory intervention. The documentation of long term syndicated loans is the most complex type. Choices of applicable law and jurisdiction are made, and government obligants must give their consent to be subjected to legal proceedings.

19.3.2 International securities supervision

The principal international body concerned with securities supervision is the International Organisation of Securities Commissions (IOSCO). In its meetings, IOSCO has worked on such issues as establishing international capital adequacy standards for securities firms. It supervises international financial conglomerates, establishes international auditing standards, and is concerned with trading between cash and derivatives markets. Finally, it is also concerned with trying to keep a check on money laundering, and with promoting transparency in international financial transactions (OECD 1993).

19.3.3 Lender of last resort

A lender of last resort stands ready to provide credit to solvent but temporarily illiquid financial institutions. There is general agreement regarding the need for an international lender of last resort, but there is no single authority empowered to play this role. As international interdependence of financial institutions continues to increase, the need for a lender of last resort facility will become greater. In 1974 the Bank for International Settlements stated that its governors were satisfied that means to provide temporary liquidity did exist, even though no fixed arrangements had been struck. In 1995 the arrangements gained greater force as the US joined the Bank for International Settlements.

19.3.4 Capital adequacy

A bank's capital is the source from which its loan losses must be covered, at least if current earnings are insufficient to do so. The adequacy of a bank's capital is related to the degree of government support it enjoys, for if a bank is backed by the public sector, less capital is needed to protect depositors and creditors. Determination of an adequate level of capital for a private sector bank is difficult because adequacy depends on the value of its loan portfolio. Since value depends on loan quality, it can be exceptionally difficult to establish.

As mentioned above, risk-based capital adequacy regulations were implemented in 1988 under the auspices of the Bank for International Settlements. Banks in twelve different countries are expected to achieve a minimum target ratio of total capital to risk weighted assets of 8 percent, of which at least 4 percent must be in the form of common equity. The framework sets forth: a definition of capital for risk-based capital purposes; a system for assigning risk weights to balance sheet assets and off-balance sheet items; and a schedule, including transitional arrangements, for achieving a minimum supervisory target ratio of capital to risk weighted assets. The risk weights recognise that some assets are more likely to suffer losses than others. For example, government bonds have either zero or a relatively low risk weighting depending on the type of issue, while commercial loans have a relatively high risk weighting, largely because the loss experience for the latter is greater.

19.3.5 Supervision of derivatives

Risk management activity has grown at an explosive rate over the 1980s and early 1990s, as both international banks and investment banks increased their derivatives activities. As discussed earlier, the new risk management activities involve both creating and trading instruments. At least two issues arise in supervising derivatives trading. First, do the firms involved employ appropriate risk management technologies? Second, is there adequate international supervision of trading so that any externalities created by a single firm's failure would largely be confined to that firm?

Both issues have recently been addressed in the US. Six of Wall Street's largest investment banking firms, in cooperation with the Securities and Exchange Commission and the Commodities Futures Trading Corporation, have worked out standards whose implementation will create a pattern of regulatory oversight for OTC trading. The standards address four groups of issues: the nature of management controls for monitoring derivatives risks, enhanced reporting to regulators, assessment of whether a firm's capital is adequate in relation to the scope of its derivatives trading and the risks it creates, and assessment of each firm's counterparty relationships. The reports to regulators will cover the structure of each firm's derivatives portfolio, including its twenty largest exposures by trading partner, and the partner's location and credit risk. The assessment of counterparty relationships includes both assessment of the credit risk of trading partners and providing clients with written statements about the risks involved in purchasing a derivatives product.

Although the growth of derivatives trading has been so rapid that individual financial firms may have less than adequate risk management systems in place, the real difficulty from a regulatory point of view arises from the possibility that a chain of failures might follow on the default of a single institution. Any individual financial firm can learn to manage its dealings with any other firm, but to be successful some international deals require that an entire complex of other deals be completed successfully. As a result, financial firms do not always find it easy to establish key features of their possible vulnerability. At this writing the possible extent of losses from system risks seems to account for a relatively small percentage of world institutions' financial capital, but the possible effects of a chain of failures are still not well understood.

19.4 SUMMARY

This chapter described goals and principles of supervision. Taking a longer term perspective, the chapter defined classes of structural problems and discussed the potential of legislation for dealing with them. With a view to learning from historical experience, some forms of intervention that have proven unsuccessful were also discussed.

Supervision should be designed first of all to improve economic activity by ensuring that the climate favours a spectrum of financial arrangements. Supervision should balance the advantages of encouraging competitiveness against the need to protect the public from some of its costs.

Regulatory reform should try both to recognise past financial system change and to anticipate future change. Encouraging change can conflict with protection of the public, but the tradeoffs can be clarified using the economics of change and of learning. It is important for regulators to inform the public about financial system change so that whenever possible perceptions adjust gradually rather than suddenly.

REVIEW QUESTIONS

Exercise 1 If regulators possess information they do not release to the public, is their policy likely to maintain confidence in the financial system? Why or why not?

Exercise 2 Is the current debate about whether banks should be permitted to sell insurance in their branches primarily an economic or a political debate? Explain your reasoning.

Exercise 3 In a competitive financial system, is it likely that small business will be able to find financing at market rates? Why or why not? If some kinds of financing are not provided by a competitive system, what can you infer about the way financiers regard the deals?

Exercise 4 What is the principal reason that some regulations prove ineffective?

Exercise 5 Explain why Canada's banks might be effective self-regulators of foreign exchange trading, while firms trading speculative securities might not be as effective at self-regulation.

Exercise 6 Suppose you owned several non-financial firms (give examples of the firms you are supposed to own) and also held voting control of the shares of a thrift institution. What kinds of uses for the thrift institution's funds might you find? Would these uses conflict with depositor interest in any way?

Exercise 7 Draw parallels between the US Federal Reserve System and an international agency as providers of emergency liquidity and lenders of last resort. Use the parallels to develop a case for establishing an international lender of last resort. How might the international agency obtain the funds needed to conduct its activities?

Exercise 8 One of the issues arising in regulating derivatives trading is the following. A given firm's trading losses might prove large enough to lead to its failure. The failing firm would likely default on at least some of its obligations, and as a result other firms might also fail. What regulatory actions might be taken in an attempt to limit the effects of such a failure? Can regulators devise effective means of supervision that do not overly inhibit trading activity? Try to base your answer on lessons from the 1995 failure of Barings Bank, which followed on the bank's trading losses from speculating on the Nikkei Index. (Essentially Barings bet on the index not moving over a very wide range, after which the Kobe earthquake drastically affected the Japanese stock market and moved the Nikkei Index sharply downward.)

20 Toward the future

20.1	Introduction	336
20.2	Evolution	337
	20.2.1 Changing organisational forms	338
	20.2.2 Increased competition	339
	20.2.3 Technological change	339
20.3	Tomorrow's payments system	339
	20.3.1 Electronic funds transfer systems	339
	20.3.2 Intermediaries and payments	340
20.4	Evolution in intermediation	340
20.5	Evolution in financial markets	341
20.6	Increasing internationalisation	342
20.7	Importance of legislative change	342
20.8	Summary	343

LEARNING OBJECTIVES

After reading this chapter you will understand

- how the economics of financial change can be used to help forecast the future evolution of financial activity
- how the following components of the financial system seem likely to evolve:
    the payments system
    intermediaries
    financial markets
- why the world's financial systems are likely to become still further integrated

---

20.1 INTRODUCTION

This book has shown how the financial system has evolved continuously, albeit at changing rates, since the 1940s. It has examined how typical financial systems have adopted new technology, expanded their international character, and increased in competitiveness. This final chapter attempts to sketch the course of system evolution over the next few years, by recalling some of the major developmental forces and their impacts on the world's financial systems.

The financial system of the future is likely to be even more highly integrated than it now is, and to use still more electronic equipment. Both consumer and business transactions will increasingly be handled by electronic communications media: large parts of the financial system will disappear into the communications infrastructure. Consumers and corporations will have greater access to the financial system through remote terminals and other communications media such as cable television systems. The remaining, visible parts of the financial system will consist of fewer traditional offices in which more automated service equipment will be available. Most of the remaining work in these offices will involve completing specialised transactions not easily handled by machines. The personnel assisting with the transactions will spend more time marketing products and giving advice, less time handling routine transactions, than they now do.

The proportion of international deals will also probably continue to grow, mainly because the availability of electronic equipment is altering both the kinds and locations of transactions. For instance, stock markets are becoming internationally linked, and securities firms are becoming internationally integrated. As another example, electronic retail banking is starting to move abroad. For example, ING Bank of the Netherlands begain offering retail banking services electronically in Canada in 1996; in the United States the First Internet Bank opened for business in the same year. As a result of readier access, demand for financial services will probably become more price sensitive than it has previously been. Firms offering financial services will probably use common networks to sell their services, but will probably also make strong efforts to differentiate the products or services they offer through the common networks.

20.2 EVOLUTION

As it has in the past, the financial system will continue to change. The kinds of changes that occur will depend on how the economics of doing deals changes, and on how financial managers perceive the emerging profit opportunities. A brief historical review will provide a background for predicting the broader outlines of likely future change. The 1950s and 1960s were periods of relatively stable interest rates and relative currency values. In contrast the 1970s, the 1980s and the early 1990s were much more turbulent. During the later 1990s, some domestic financial environments have returned to stability as inflationary expectations adjusted downward. But even during the later 1990s, the international environment has remained relatively volatile, and large swings in the values of some currencies, notably the Mexican peso and the Thai baht, have been posted.

In the stable and relatively unchanging environment of the 1950s and 1960s, financial institutions served both as safe repositories for wealth and as steady providers of funds to good credit risks. The financial markets chiefly handled domestic transactions. The financial system was not especially innovative, and high quality deals were largely defined in terms of their familiarity. New business, and small rapidly growing business, did not always receive favourable treatment. Risk management using derivatives trading was almost unknown: exchanges for trading derivatives did not emerge until the 1970s.

The less stable environment of the later 1970s, the 1980s and early 1990s faced financiers with greater competitive pressures than they had previously experienced. Competitive pressures were increased both by slower rates of deposit growth and by changing computing and communications technologies. The changing environment meant that both interest rates and currency values began to change more frequently, and over wider ranges, than had been experienced since World War II.[1] Changing technology meant there was more information available about market conditions and financial assets' characteristics, which in turn meant that interest rates were more competitively determined.

In response to the increased competition, new types of deals proliferated as changes in technology made it possible to offer innovative products and services both more cheaply and more closely tailored to individual client needs. One of the most rapidly growing areas has been risk management. Banks built up interest rates and currency swaps from virtually nothing at the beginning of the 1980s to several trillion US dollars in the later 1990s. In retail financial services, some forms of money management accounts now make automatic transfers between high yield balances and chequing balances without human intervention. Consumers can now also withdraw funds from securities-based accounts or from investments with life insurance companies as well as from bank deposits, meaning that a variety of asset forms are now more accessible than previously.

20.2.1 Changing organisational forms

In the mid-1990s, most financial intermediaries are evolving towards a common type of full service firm. For example, banks and trust companies are increasingly offering similar financial services, and the number of separate firms offering the services is shrinking through mergers and acquisitions. These forms of financial integration are occurring mainly because of scope economies – a variety of products can be marketed at lower unit costs jointly within a single firm rather than by separate financial firms. Changing technology, increasing competition and the gradual removal of restrictive regulation are the additional factors inducing formerly specialised financial firms to enter each others' traditional businesses. The remaining specialist firms serve particular niches, but even specialised financial activities are sometimes incorporated into larger financial firms and organised as profit centers.

Industry understanding of what is currently cost-effective changes as financiers experiment with new forms of organisation. When they are perceived as cost-effective, technological innovations spread rapidly. If one firm perceives the possibilities of using a new technology, and earns profits from doing so, other firms are soon likely to follow suit. For example, once it was realised that consumer loans could be administered more cheaply by using computers, computerisation of loan management and accounting was rapidly implemented. Financial institutions are now adapting to continuous and rapid change by using an assembly form of organisation, in which new products or traditional activities are outsourced to specialised providers. For, example, a bank-dominated financial group may now acquire a specialised insurance company to create products which it then markets, and may at the same time contract out its data processing activities to another specialised firm. The same financial group may strike alliances with software providers to make it possible, say, for the group to offer its financial products over the Internet.

Economic conditions and current industry practice affect industry perceptions of new opportunities, whether they involve expanding markets, reducing costs, or both. Most of the world's larger banks expanded rapidly into international investment activities in the later 1970s and early 1980s. By the late 1980s the international banks began curtailing some of their investment activities even though their rates of entry into this arena were most rapid in the years just prior to the subsequent curtailment. The change of strategy suggests the banks may originally have overestimated the effect of scope economies on profitability, possibly because they underestimated the costs of acquiring the requisite skills for competing with international investment houses. Alternatively, they may have correctly anticipated the net benefits to expansion of their own business, but neglected to adjust their profit forecasts for similar moves by competitors. Virtually all international banks took the same actions simultaneously, and their combined moves may well have changed the economics of their individual expansion plans in ways that these firms' planners did not originally anticipate.

20.2.2 Increased competition

Increased competition means that entry into new forms of business continues to be likely. Product changes follow rapidly on emerging new profit opportunities, and the assembly type of organisation favoured by many larger financial groups facilitates developing and marketing new products. For example, at the same time as they have lost a share of the corporate lending business to the securities markets, banks have increasingly promoted their agency role in arranging market financings for their former borrowing clients.

20.2.3 Technological change

Advances in technology have led to the discovery of both new arbitrage possibilities and new ways of intermediating deals, as illustrated by the growth in interest rate and **currency swap** markets. Intermediaries first promoted many of the new risk management instruments, using computers to keep track of the payments involved. The instruments soon proved so popular that the instruments were standardised and more formal markets for their trading began to evolve. Advances in communications and computing technology then provided further opportunities for cost reduction. For instance, terminal equipment is gradually becoming more intelligent, that is acquiring more internal data processing capability and hence less need to communicate with central computers.

Banks and other financial institutions are currently exploring the use of digital networks which enable them to blend voice, video and data transmission services using a single terminal. Photocopying machines now make electronic images of records, and computers are now able to scan printed forms, both important new developments in the ability to transform and transmit information.

20.3 TOMORROW'S PAYMENTS SYSTEM

The payments system will gradually become electronically based and paper transactions will continue to reduce in volume until eventually most of them are eliminated.

20.3.1 Electronic funds transfer systems

Tomorrow's payments system will be even quicker, cheaper and more efficient than today's. While cash and cheques will not disappear altogether, **electronic funds transfer systems (EFTS)** will increasingly replace costlier and less efficient paper-based systems. Settlement risk is being reduced as EFTS moves toward netting of transactions and, in some cases, continuous settlement which ensures final payment is made immediately rather than with the delays to which agents have been accustomed.

In retail transactions, EFTS will make even greater use of automated banking machines, point-of-sale terminals and both debit and credit cards. At this writing, debit card transactions are rapidly replacing paper cheques in some jurisdictions. The growth of the smart card or 'electronic purse' will reduce the use of currency, as will the development of small cash accounts which can be used to pay for such Internet transactions as the copyright fees for reading or using portions of documents.

In wholesale transactions, electronic equipment is enhancing the use of cash management systems, pre-authorised payments and electronic payments. All these developments make both domestic and international transactions easier to initiate and to complete. International payments are being made increasingly swiftly by electronic means: it is now possible to make same-day transfers of funds between almost any two points in the world.

---

electronic funds transfer system (EFTS) a paperless funds transfer system. Examples of EFTS developments within the banking industry are automated clearing houses, point-of-sales payments systems and automatic teller systems.

20.3.2 Intermediaries and payments

Intermediaries are investing huge amounts of funds in upgrading their communication and payments systems. Such is the value of instantaneous data access and transmission that investments to facilitate electronic data interchange assume a scale never before seen: banks' outlays are expected to reach about 35 percent of non-interest expense before the end of the 1990s. The main focus of these investment programs is to provide intermediaries with on line, real time connections of their computer centers across the country, to link the banks' computer operations on a world-wide basis and to establish a round-the-clock communication network. As a part of the program, intermediaries are committed to providing their retail and corporate customers with the widest possible array of payments instruments and financial services. Clients will be offered the choice between conventional means of payments like cash and cheques and electronically based ones like credit cards, debit cards and home banking facilities.

20.4 EVOLUTION IN INTERMEDIATION

The financial system is restructuring itself in several ways. A variety of new financial service companies is entering the industry and existing intermediaries are doing new kinds of business. Insurance companies, financial co-operatives and capital corporations are entering commercial lending, and pension funds are beginning to play an important role in longer term corporate finance.

One of the major changes in financial intermediation has been a movement from consuming information to marketing it. For example, banks are now selling access to their databases. Cheaper communications and computation mean that the electronic exchange of information will become much more widely dissem-inated, and at lower costs, as the technological advance continues. At the present time it appears the most formidable competitors for financial intermediaries during the first decade of the new millennium will be the computing and commu-nications firms, for example, IBM, AT&T, Telerate and Reuters.

An important strategic question for financial intermediaries is whether they should be investing or acquiring internal expertise to take advantage of these new technological developments. For example, should banks be buying satel-lite communications systems, whose operating costs are not distance sensitive? Should intermediaries be buying cable TV companies or working out arrange-ments with telephone companies for offering such services as home banking or computer links with business clients? Are licensing arrangements with specialised providers a better way to proceed?

20.5 EVOLUTION IN FINANCIAL MARKETS

The chief developments in the financial markets are likely to be their greater integration and automation. The advent of new technology helps established markets cope with volume increases and also opens up new markets. As the spread of technology continues, financial markets will become increasingly inte-grated, increasingly international, see much greater use of automatic arbitraging and transactions routeing to take advantage of emerging price differentials.

As new markets emerge, they provide new opportunities of diverse forms, from information processing on the one hand to speculation and risk manage-ment on the other. With regard to information processing, Yu (1997) argues that stock prices in the more developed markets reflect the influence of more information processing than takes place in developing markets. Stock prices move much more independently in markets with highly developed information processing capabilities, because those markets facilitate the evaluation of indi-vidual companies rather than just the evaluation of economic trends that takes place in less developed markets.

With regard to risk management, stock index futures (which began trading in 1982) are now among the most successful instruments in the financial futures market. Broker-dealers make use of stock index futures to hedge their inven-tories of stocks; mutual funds use the instruments for hedging. Previously, risk management focused on hedging foreign exchange transactions and ways of transforming interest rate risks, but banks are now turning their attention to the management of non-financial risks through acting as agents or principals in arranging commodity swaps. Banks consider that their involvement in commodi-ties is a natural extension of their financial engineering activities. 'As engineers, bankers see their role as helping their customers to eliminate risks that could upset their business. Now they are trying to treat other risks, such as changes in commodity prices, with the same techniques. The simplest commodity swaps allow end-users to fix the price of their supply and suppliers to fix their incomes' (*The Economist*, September 2, 1989, p.76). The foregoing observation continues to be relevant in the mid-1990s. For example, during the 1990s banks began trading credit derivatives, an instrument which allows them to sell off some of their loan risks.[2]

Stock exchanges are competing more vigorously for business as securities trading increasingly becomes a global activity. Core markets for internationally traded financial assets have become increasingly integrated by the establishment of links between products and geographical markets. Electronic linkages between stock exchanges, and between securities dealers and their clients, are becoming increasingly commonplace. In the US, market makers must now route orders to the exchange offering a client the best price.

Currency futures contracts traded on either the Chicago Mercantile Exchange or the Singapore International Monetary Exchange can now be substituted for each other, in an activity representing a major step toward 24-hour trading in currency futures. Automated exchanges, such as one in Bermuda on which orders entered from terminals in such locations as London and New York are matched automatically, have been in operation since 1984.

Extrapolating from the experience of the US securities business, likely future changes in the securities industry include the following. Markets will see greater degrees of automation and interlinking. As this occurs, spreads are likely to decrease, volumes increase, and errors decrease. Liquidity of instruments will improve, as will the productivity of firms. Increasingly, these effects will be observed in developing as well as in previously developed markets as experience gained in developed economies spreads to the financial systems of those economies which are still developing.

20.6 INCREASING INTERNATIONALISATION

The financial system's environment is one of increasingly interlinked transactions between different parts of the world, as well as between different parts of domestic markets. Cheaper, more rapid communications and the recognition that many financial transactions are similar in terms of their information processing requirements are the main forces contributing to this increasing integration. In addition, technological change means that the arbitraging and intermediation transactions establishing these linkages take place much more rapidly than used to be the case. In some cases, such as dealing with rapidly fluctuating interest rates, new transaction types emerge as a result of institutional learning; in other cases they emerge because technological change in the computing and communications industries has made them possible.

20.7 IMPORTANCE OF LEGISLATIVE CHANGE

Is effective regulation possible or does it serve merely to legitimise the status quo? Probably either interpretation is possible depending on whether one wishes to discuss the forces that determine evolution, of which regulation is not a major factor, or to discuss the ways in which evolution can be shaped, an area in which regulation can sometimes prove to be a significant factor. The search for profits is the main force driving system evolution, and it is also the search for profits which leads sometimes to self-dealing and fraudulent transactions. The job of regulation is to try to assist evolution while limiting opportunities for dishonest dealing.

Few new profit opportunities arise from legislative change, although tax law constitutes an exception. The reasons that most kinds of legislative changes do not create new profit opportunities have been discussed in the previous chapter; for present purposes, it suffices to recall that legislation usually changes the appearance of an activity rather than its reality. For if profits can be earned the financial system will likely have found legal ways of making them even though the original spirit of restrictive legislation is circumvented.

Gerald E. Corrigan, President of the Federal Reserve Bank of New York, outlined key legislative priorities for the US in a 1989 speech whose contents still have considerable relevance for the financial system of the future.

> Looking around the globe, it is quite clear – especially in wholesale banking and financial markets – that the interrelated forces of technology and financial innovation are rendering segmented financial systems, such as we have in the United States, increasingly obsolete. Indeed, in virtually all other industrialized countries the clear trend is toward more integrated financial institutions, with elements of commercial and investment banking, securities activities and, to a limited but growing extent, insurance activities coming under common ownership and control. . . .
>
> The other possibility is that maybe – just maybe – we have to begin thinking in terms of something that leans in the direction of the so-called universal bank model. . . .
>
> [Another important task is to] do all we can to move more fully and more forcefully in the direction of greater coordination and harmonization of supervisory and prudential policies both domestically and internationally. . . .
>
> [I]n all of this, we are trying to hit a very rapidly moving target in a setting in which the risks of competition in laxity and regulatory arbitrage, nationally and internationally, are very real.

Finally, as the financial system becomes ever more dependent on the world's communications infrastructure, jurisdictional issues are likely to take on increasingly greater importance. For example, how can prudential regulation best be structured in a world where a consumer has access to several countries' financial systems from a home computer, especially when it may not be easy for one consumer to ascertain the legal system under which she is making her transactions, or for another consumer to assess the credit rating of the foreign bank in which he is placing his deposits?

20.8 SUMMARY

This chapter provided an evolutionary view of the financial system of the future. It first considered the economic forces driving system evolution, and drew inferences regarding the possible impacts of these forces. The chapter then discussed the possible evolution of the payments system, again drawing inferences using the economics of financial transactions. Evolution of financial intermediation and of financial markets was also discussed. The increasing internationalisation and integration of the system was predicted to continue, and the ability of legislation to guide the changes was discussed.

REVIEW QUESTIONS

Exercise 1 Currently three of Canada's banks are outsourcing their document processing to a common facility. What is the principal reason for this change?

Exercise 2 Would competition likely increase or decrease with each of the following changes: if banks sold insurance products in their branches? If Sears (a large retail firm) is allowed to own and operate ATMs? Give your reasons in each case.

Exercise 3 Suppose it is cheaper for both banks and merchants to encourage the use of debit cards rather than credit cards. Suppose also that there is customer resistance to using debit rather than credit cards. (Consumers seem to be quite willing to use debit cards instead of cheques; this business is growing very rapidly.) What actions could you take to encourage a change?

Exercise 4 Some companies, like GE Credit, are making inroads into certain kinds of bank lending. What cost advantages might companies like GE Credit have?

Exercise 5 Name three media on which you can currently trade stocks, and suggest a fourth future possibility.

Exercise 6 During the 1980s Sweden imposed a transfer tax on stock exchange trading. Why would you think the Swedish government removed the tax after a short trial period?

Exercise 7 Is it possible that home communications facilities (television, telephone, fax and modem) will become important media in the financial system of the future?

Exercise 8 In 1996, stocks began to be traded on the Internet for the first time. If this method of trading becomes popular, so that many stocks are traded by geographically dispersed users, how might they attempt to assess the quality of the offerings? Would quality ratings provided by a respected, well-known agency help the market to flourish? If so, why, and in what ways?

Exercise 9 Do you think securitisation will become so widespread that banks will be obsolete?

Exercise 10 Can risk management services be marketed to consumers as well as to corporations?

Exercise 11 How can an international company sell financial products that appeal to specific national markets?

Appendix
Solutions to exercises

1 INTRODUCTION

Exercise 1 It would be more than 7 percent, because the risk is higher.

Exercise 2 Banks are eager to sell insurance in their branches nowadays because they see the ability to do so as a new profit opportunity. With regard to customer demand, banks view the ability to sell insurance as an integral part of their ability to provide wealth management and financial planning services for their customers. With regard to supply conditions, at this time most bank branches have excess capacity and adding on new businesses should help contribute to their overhead costs. As a result, they regard the sale of insurance as complementary to their other activities.

Exercise 3 The main factors explaining the increased demand for risk management are that interest rates and foreign exchange rates have fluctuated more quickly and over wider ranges since the early 1970s. Increases in foreign trade have also meant that many companies have been taking on more foreign exchange risk than they formerly did. This means that foreign exchange and interest rate exposures are now viewed as more risky than they formerly were, and there is thus a greater demand to manage or lay off the risks.

Exercise 4 Fund raising: selling bonds to fund the purchase of a new computer system; borrowing to finance a new venture. Risk management: buying insurance; buying an option; arranging an interest rate swap.

Exercise 5 Yes, the second deal requires more continuing attention than the first, because if the bank fails to monitor the evolution of the business the firm might get into difficulty and default on its loan. Default on the treasury bill investment is, of course, highly improbable.

Exercise 6 If these are the only investment alternatives you have identified, and if you expect the historical returns on the equity fund to remain at 8 percent, you should probably invest in the Savings Bond, because it offers the same anticipated return for lower risk. However, if the equity fund looked like it might yield a return of, say, 10 or 12 percent, the higher return might compensate for the greater risk.

Exercise 7 A bank would typically pay little continuing attention to something like funds invested in treasury bills. It might pay some attention to whether switching into an alternative short term investment could improve returns, but such an investment doesn't usually need intensive, continuing attention. On the other hand, putting funds to work in a new company usually means making a high risk or uncertain investment, because the venture is unproven. This is even more the case if the new venture's principal asset is the talent and enthusiasm of its owners, who have little or no liquid assets to secure the investment. In this case the profitable recovery of the venture capitalist's funds depends critically on the success of the project. Therefore the venture capitalist is likely to give it continuing, detailed attention, including business advice if it looks like the untried operators might be heading for financial trouble.

Exercise 8 The major forces contributing to financial system change are changing computing and communications technology on the supply side. On the demand side, the types of investment products are changing, as are the types of risk management clients desire. Retail clients are currently looking for high return, higher risk investment vehicles such as mutual funds. Corporate clients are looking for faster, cheaper ways of hedging foreign exchange and interest rate risks. Both the supply and the demand changes present new profit opportunities of which financiers want to take advantage.

Exercise 9 These forces are having similar impacts on most market economies' financial systems because they represent the fundamental kinds of change that affect financial systems everywhere. They present the same kinds of new profit opportunities that financiers in different parts of the world all seek. Moreover, the increasing internationalisation of finance means that if local financiers don't try to take advantage of the changes, financiers from other countries will. (Sometimes foreign financiers are hampered by legislative restriction, but if profits are there to be earned, they'll try hard to find ways of end-running the legislation.)

Exercise 10 The pace of change has increased within the world's financial systems because different markets are now more closely integrated than before, and because international institutions are seeking to do business in domestic markets they formerly ignored. This means that if a development occurs anywhere in the world, it is not long before it has an impact on similar deals done in other parts of the world.

Exercise 11 Most of the current articles on changing financial regulation have to do either with an industry seeking new powers, or with an industry attempting to prevent a competitor from acquiring new powers. Banks want to sell insurance in the branches, and to enter auto leasing. Insurance companies want to make greater use of electronic funds transfer. All these new powers are sought in attempts to find and exploit new sources of profits. When the insurance companies or auto dealers oppose the banks, or when the banks oppose the insurance companies' use of electronic funds transfer, they are mainly trying to limit new competitive threats.

2 ROLES AND CLIENTS

Exercise 1 If you are resident in the US and go abroad, your vacation will cost you less when the US dollar strengthens. If you have foreign investments, the capital gains on them will be less in US dollar terms as the US dollar strengthens. If you buy imported goods, their prices will fall, or at least rise less quickly, as the US dollar strengthens.

Exercise 2 Since $2.00 is 10 percent of $20.00, if you are exchanging more than $20.00 it will pay for you to find the sort of ATM described in the question. If the ATM routes your transaction through your credit card, you have to estimate when you will repay the advance. For example, 2 months at 18 percent simple interest is about 3 percent, which is less than the 10 percent most currency dealers charge. CAUTION: do the calculations for yourself! The numbers may change depending on your particular circumstances. Don't just go around the world using ATMs without checking out the details!

Exercise 3 The return is excessively high for what is, to a financial institution, a low risk source of funds. This should make you suspicious. In fact, Caritas could pay off original depositors only by attracting new deposits – it could not earn anything like 400 percent per annum on its investments. It therefore went bankrupt after about nine months. Depositors who took the deal the first time, or even the first and second time, profited at the expense of others. The owners of Caritas made off with most of the money, after the first three months' operations had convinced the public to forget about the usual risk–reward ratios. (This kind of operation, that can survive only on continuing inflows of funds, is called a Ponzi scheme.)

Exercise 4 You'd have to find a lender on your own. Small businesses looking for startup money face this problem; their sources are sometimes called 'love money', sometimes 'country club financing'. As a result of the difficulties of finding funds, an economy with no financial system would likely have a much lower level of capital formation than a similar economy with a financial system.

Exercise 5 You would be taking the greater risk, and should therefore get a higher return than the debtholders. (If the business doesn't generate this higher return for you, maybe you shouldn't be running it.) Banks typically charge relatively low rates for loans (venture capital firms effectively charge up to 50 percent per year) and therefore they can take on only relatively low risks. If they see themselves putting up what is effectively equity capital, banks realise they are not getting a return commensurate with the risk, and will probably ask the owners to put in more of their own money.

Exercise 6 When a company issues publicly traded stocks, financial information about it is publicly available to investors. (Annual reports, including balance sheets and income statements.) Market trading then values the earnings flowing to the company's shares, using the publicly available financial information to arrive at the valuations. As the company's fortunes improve, share prices usually rise, and fall as the company's fortunes decline. (There may also be other effects on share prices that will be discussed later in the book.) If the same company borrowed all its money privately, the same financial information would usually be available only to potential investors who privately arranged to get it. In this event there would be no public valuation of the company's securities. Moreover, each investor would have to pay the costs of getting the information.

Exercise 7 The simple interest for borrowing long term at 11 percent is $5 \times \$110,000 = \$550,000$. In the case of the second alternative, the first year interest cost is $120,000, and the expected interest cost for the remaining four years is (10 percent + 6 percent)/2 = 8 percent. Thus the expected value of the remaining four years' simple interest is $4 \times \$80,000 = \$320,000$, and the total interest cost of the second alternative is $440,000.

Exercise 8 Since the effect is to expand the money supply, it is inflationary. While short term interest rates might fall, long term interest rates would be high because they include an inflation premium. (This idea is discussed further under the heading of the Fisher relation in section 6.4.1.)

Exercise 9 By making it easier for borrowers to find lenders, and vice versa, a financial system will typically increase an economy's amount of capital formation over what it would otherwise be.

Exercise 10 Each of the three transactions uses payments system information, provided by one or more communications systems. All three represent the convenient use of different kinds of financial information. The examples suggest how important communications and payments systems have become in everday life.

- Fuelling your car at a pump operated by a credit card means a payments system is used to inquire about the existence of and then to charge your credit card account.
- In this case the phone is used as a part of the information system supporting the payments system.
- In this case the phone is used as a part of the information system supporting the activities of the tax authorities.

Exercise 11 Roughly, North American prices in the late 1990s are about four times what they were in the late 1970s. Thus if someone had bought you a $1,000 bond then, its buying power would now be somewhere around $250.00. The actual worth of the investment in today's terms would be somewhat more than $250.00, because the calculation does not include interest. To put this another way, $1.00 compounded at 7 percent for 20 years becomes $3.87, while $1.00 compounded at 8 percent for 20 years is $4.66. Thus you would need something more than a 7 percent return, compounded annually, just to keep up with inflation. Most bonds issued in the late 1970s paid less than 7 percent as an annual return, meaning that even when interest is taken into account, the buying power of the investment has declined.

Exercise 12 Suppose prices and wages have both increased by a factor of about 4. Say wages were $2.50 per hour in the late 1970s, and $10.00 per hour in the late 1990s. (The precise factors depend on the basket of goods you are considering, and the kind of work you are assuming.) Then, in the late 1970s, you had to work 40 hours to buy the bond. The same is true in the late 1990s, because to get the same buying power you now have to buy $4,000 worth of bonds.

Exercise 13 In the 1990s communications and computing services are several hundred times cheaper than they were in the 1970s. These changes have made it possible for ATMs throughout the world to be networked, allowing them to communicate virtually instantaneously and allowing you to draw money from your account or credit card in many countries of the world. These changes mean the international payments system is much more extensive, much cheaper to operate and therefore much more productive than it was in the 1970s.

Exercise 14 Risk management tools are used extensively to reduce the risk of price fluctuations in many kinds of financial instruments, including stocks, stock indexes and foreign exchange. They are also used to reduce interest rate risk. Companies and other economic agents can thus stabilise their earnings from risky activities, paying a price much like an insurance premium to do so. The ability to trade risks means economic agents get more satisfaction out of undertaking risky ventures in the first place, because they can split up the risks and sell pieces of them to the agents most willing to bear them.

Exercise 15 If you were trying to start a small business and didn't have much initial capital, a financier who could make a clearheaded assessment of your firm's earnings potential would likely be very valuable. Such a person could advise you on the kinds of returns you would get from investing your energy and talent, would be able to advise you regarding the kinds of financing you could obtain from various sources, and its costs.

3 FINANCIAL SYSTEM ORGANISATION

Exercise 1 You will likely learn more about the uncertain deal than you will about the risky deal. This is why uncertain deals are usually governed in a way that allows the financier greater opportunities to monitor and to take corrective action.

Exercise 2 The financier faces only risk, because if the new route does not turn out to be as profitable as hoped, the airplane can readily be sold to another airline, assuming the client can't put it to work somewhere else. In other words, there are marketable assets with a readily ascertained market value behind this investment. The new business in Exercise 1 might not have anything but unsaleable assets if the venture doesn't succeed.

Exercise 3 The difference is in the size, the credit rating and the standardisation of the issue. Government issues are large, treasury bills are standard instruments, governments have good, widely known credit ratings. Small businesses don't borrow much, their credit ratings aren't widely known, and the particular bank loan may have features that make it non-standard.

Exercise 4 The securities sold by the bank are much like the government treasury bills of Exercise 3, except that they are probably longer term. Moreover, the bank will typically pledge the small business loan portfolio as security for the marketable instruments it sells. The bank is not selling the small business loans *per se*, but is borrowing against them. The economic functions the bank has performed are the following. It has screened these loans, and will collect the payments on them. It has diversified the borrowing risks: the portfolio of small business loans is diversified and therefore has a lower risk than does any single small loan in the portfolio.

Exercise 5 It would be greater. You could ask for any internal reports you liked, you could order changes in operations, and you could replace management if they didn't perform. The venture capitalist might have a seat on the company's board, but would serve mainly as an adviser rather than as a manager.

Exercise 6 It would be too costly to have the financial division of a conglomerate headquarters supervise a short term investment in treasury bills because the people in this division are likely to be experts in administering more complicated investments, and would therefore have higher salaries than would the typical manager of a portfolio of marketable securities.

Exercise 7 The holding company investment would be subject to more monitoring and to greater control over operations. You could ask for any internal reports you liked, you could order changes in operations, and you could replace management if they didn't perform. About all you could do with the other, liquid investment is to sell it if the interest earnings on it are turning out to be lower than expected.

Exercise 8 This is one of the most difficult kinds of financing to obtain. Since it's a new company, it represents financing under uncertainty except in the unlikely event that marketable assets are going to be purchased with the funds raised. If it's a small company, you'd think a venture capitalist might be able to help. But it often turns out that venture capitalists want to put money only into companies with track records. You would probably have to seek funds from relatives and from wealthy local business people who knew something about what you were trying to do. If it were a large new company, you might be able to find an institutional investor to buy your shares, or you might be able to find a supplier (or potential user of your product) to help with the initial financing.

Exercise 9 A risky deal is one whose payoffs can be described quantitatively, an uncertain deal is one whose payoffs can be described only qualitatively. You can write complete contracts to formalise risky deals, but not to formalise uncertain deals, because uncertainty means you don't know precisely what to put into the contract. If you were thinking about investing funds in an uncertain project, you'd want to know first of all that the client was motivated to perform. Second, you'd want the incentives to be right – if you are to profit, the client must also profit, or else the client may not be willing to put in the effort needed for the project to succeed. You'd want to know where the profits are likely to be most sensitive. In other words, if something goes wrong, is it likely to have a big effect on the project profitability and hence on your returns? If so, in what ways would the client plan to bail the project out? You'd also try to counter the client's natural optimism in forecasting the way things would likely work out.

Exercise 10 If financiers won't fund certain projects, capital formation of that type can be reduced below what would otherwise take place. Either the amount of capital formation, the type, or both can be affected by difficulties in finding finance. Since economic growth depends on the rate of capital formation, it too can be affected by financiers' unwillingness to consider funding certain types of projects.

Exercise 11 In restructuring the former planned economies, it seems likely that deals with different attributes will require financing. This means that both stock market financing and bank lending would be likely to play important roles in helping to finance the economy's restructuring.

4 CHANGE

Exercise 1 Since the mid-1980s, banks have increasingly used ATMs, and they have also increasingly used securitisation. Securitisation represents learning how to use existing governance methods in a new way. Just because you make the loans doesn't mean you have to fund them over their entire lifetime. In fact, a Vancouver mortgage company, First City Savings, was selling mortgages to other institutions long before securitisation became popular.

Exercise 2 You might want to keep writing the insurance policies, maybe for increased premiums, and sell off some of the risks to others. There are two ways for an insurance company to sell off risks – through the reinsurance market (wholesale offloading of liability) and in the (new) catastrophe futures market, where risks of things like hurricane damage are sold to any investors who want to buy the instruments. The catastrophe futures market was actually invented to spread the risks of losses from hurricane damage policies. Of course, when you sell off risks, you have to pay others to buy them. But that may be better than losing fifty years' profits in one storm.

Exercise 3 Computer processing of a credit card account and computer processing of a business loan account involve pretty much the same operations, as do maintaining computer records for a mutual fund investment and for an insurance policy with a savings element. The fixed costs of big computer installations mean that combining the transactions they handle should yield economies of scope (reduction in unit processing costs). This is one reason why forming financial supermarkets has become so popular since the mid-1980s.

Exercise 4 Maybe you could run a small test market campaign in a representative city or area. If it went well, you could then introduce the product in other markets, but if it went badly, you could cut your losses, likely to be a lot less than $50 million.

Exercise 5 The US banks transferred the deposits to London and paid the higher rates. (Observing this, the regulators realised the interest rate ceilings were unenforceable and subsequently removed them.)

Exercise 6 You'd expect to see banks emphasising mortgage lending, and possibly selling off some bonds. Securities firms might actually increase their inventories of the bonds, for two reasons. First, if the rates on the bonds fall, the cost of financing them would probably fall also, and it would be a little cheaper to carry them in inventory. Second, the bonds would be showing capital gains, which might attract new buyers, forming a second reason to increase the inventory.

Exercise 7 In the 1990s the forces causing most financial system change are lowered costs of computing and communications, greater volatility of interest rates (at least in the 1980s and early 1990s) and of foreign exchange rates. These forces have led to financial system restructuring and to an explosive growth of risk management instruments.

Exercise 8 The financial system will not attempt to promote financial products that consumers or businesses do not want, because such products would be unprofitable. If financiers can't see a way to profit from doing something they won't do it.

Exercise 9 The difficulty in raising funds for small businesses is chiefly a problem of raising long term loans or equity for highly uncertain projects with few liquid assets. Such projects are as difficult to fund today as they were thirty years ago. This should not, however, be taken as evidence that the financial system lacks adaptability. What it means is that the deals are not often seen as profitable. Adaptability occurs only if financiers can see a chance to profit from doing something new.

Exercise 10 Asset securitisation does not mean that the banks' screening, monitoring and adjustment functions do not have to be performed. It only means that other investors put up the money for the banks to continue performing this part of their work. As long as there are deals under uncertainty around, deals that require continued monitoring and adjustment, banks should have a role to play, because they have greater capabilities to perform these functions than do market agents. At a later point in this book you will be shown how securities firms that take on credit risk rather than market risk (i.e., try to perform banking rather than trading functions) often get themselves into difficulty, because they don't always have the capability to do what they are trying to do.

5 FINANCIAL SYSTEMS: AN EMPIRICAL OVERVIEW

Exercise 1 If all other features are equal, a country that is borrowing from abroad would probably have higher interest rates, because there is a shortage of domestic savings available to finance domestic investment.

Exercise 2 If the country did not borrow from abroad, you'd expect interest rates to rise. If the country had a good credit rating and borrowers could raise funds abroad as easily as at home, there might be little or no effect on domestic interest rates.

Exercise 3 International financial transactions probably involve costlier investigation of the deals than do domestic financial transactions. Alternatively, appropriate information might not be available at all in an underdeveloped capital market. For both these informational reasons, much investment might have to be financed by domestic savings.

Exercise 4 Since companies in Germany and Japan seem to be able to lever themselves more highly than companies in the US or the UK, and since greater leverage usually means greater financial risk for the company in question, one could speculate that the difference in financing comes about because financiers with greater monitoring and control capabilities can take risks (i.e., tolerate higher leverage) than the market-oriented financiers of the US or the UK.

Exercise 5 A financial system's flows can be traced from original suppliers to final users through the sector data of the financial flow accounts. These data are developed from changes in balance sheet data, aggregated for each of the sectors in the accounts.

Exercise 6 About the only realistic way of attempting to affect flows is to affect trans-action profitability, through positive or negative incentives (subsidies, taxes). Attempts to control them directly are too easily avoided.

Exercise 7 Table 5.3 shows that in 1994 the United Kingdom was a lender to other coun-tries, in the sense that domestic savings was greater than domestic investment. Therefore, there were net flows of funds out of the UK.

Exercise 8 Table 5.6 shows that relative to the US and the UK, Japan and Germany have both historically had much smaller shares of consumer credit in relation to GNP. The picture changed for Japan in 1990, where consumer credit now is roughly the same percentage of GNP as in the US or the UK.

6 PRINCIPLES OF ASSET PRICING

Exercise 1 If the lender let your interest bill go unpaid until the end of the arrangement, the lender would lose an earnings opportunity on those funds.

Exercise 2 The risk free payment of $150.00 is worth $150.00/1.08^3 = $119.07 today.

Exercise 3 If risky prospect (6.1) is worth $87.00 today, the risk adjusted rate of interest is found from $87.00 = $100.00/(1 + r). That is, $(1 + r) = $100.00/87.00 = 1.14925$. That is, the risk adjusted rate of interest is 14.925 percent. These investors are less willing to assume risk than are those who would pay $89.00.

Exercise 4 The principle of pricing by arbitrage says you won't get something for nothing. In all likelihood, the sales person is trying to sell you something that is worth quite a bit less than the price you are being asked to pay. Have you ever heard, for example, that someone bought a piece of land dirt cheap, only to find out the whole thing is nearly always under water?

Exercise 5 $87.00 = [p*(105.00) + (1–p*)$95.00]/1.10.

Therefore

$$\$87.00(1.10) = p*(105.00–95.00) + \$95.00$$

That is

$$\$95.70 – 95.00 = 10.00p*, \text{ or } p* = 0.07$$

Exercise 6 The net present value of the project is

$$\$150.00/[1 + 0.08 + 2.5(0.04)] - 100.00 = \$150.00/1.18 - 100.00 =$$

$$\$127.12 - 100.00 = \$27.12$$

Exercise 7 According to the market consensus, the expected long term rate of inflation is approximately 7 percent. By the Fisher equation, the nominal rate of 12 percent equals the real rate of 5 percent plus the inflation premium of 7 percent.

Exercise 8 We know that $\beta(12.00 - 10.00) = 12.36 - 10.00$. Hence $\beta = 2.36/2.00 = 1.18$. An instrument with a β of 0.75 will have a market required rate of return equal to 11.50 percent. To see this, use $E(r_X) = 10.00 + 0.75(12.00 - 10.00) = 11.50$ percent.

Exercise 9 The principle of pricing by arbitrage says that if it is only total buying power that matters, there are no practical differences between the two: the five coins should exchange freely for the bill, and vice versa. On the other hand, any impediments to free exchange between coins and note can frustrate the workings of the principle. If you need a one-dollar coin to put in a vending machine at mid-night, and there is no one around to change the only five-dollar bill you have, the bill is clearly worth less to you at that particular moment in time than five one-dollar coins would be.

Exercise 10 The value today of the lump sum payment of $1,000.00 is $\$1,000.00/(1.05)^{20} = \$1,000.00/2.653298 = \$376.89$.

Exercise 11 The new value today of the lump sum payment of $1,000.00 is $\$1,000.00/(1.08)^{20} = \$1,000.00/4.660957 = \$214.55$.

Exercise 12 Present value of cash flows using market financing $X/[1 + 0.06 + 1.3(0.04)] = X/1.112$. Present value of cash flows using conglomerate financing is $X/[1 + 0.06 + 1.1(0.04)] - \$300.00 = X/1.04 - \$300.00$. If the second way of doing the deal is to have a greater present value than the first,

$$X/1.112 \leq X/1.104 - \$300.00$$

or

$$\$300.00 \leq X[1/1.104 - 1/1.112] = X(0.006517)$$

Therefore the condition becomes

$$\$300.00/0.00617 \leq X$$

or

$$X \geq \$46,036.80$$

If X is large enough, the conglomerate method of financing will be better. However, it is still necessary to determine whether the project would have a positive net present value, and that cannot be determined until any costs to setting up the project are also recognised.

Exercise 13 Complete the boxes in a clockwise direction, starting at the upper left and ending at the lower left.

Today	One year from now, 1,000 percent inflation
$100.00 (borrowed)	$1,000.00 (needed to keep purchasing power constant) $80.00 interest at real rate of 8%
$100.00 = $1,080.00/10.80 (net present value of payments, using adjusted interest rate) Interest rate = 100.00[10.80 – 1.00] = 9.80 = 980 percent.	$1,080.00 (total payment)

If you can be wrong by 12 percent in either direction, the possible range of nominal interest rates is from a low of 864.29 percent to a high of 1,109.60 percent, as shown by the following calculations. Obviously, there is a good deal of risk to making a guess here. Indeed the risk is so high that many lenders would avoid the deal altogether. That's one reason why it's so hard to borrow in a highly inflationary environment.

Today	One year from now, 1,120 percent inflation
$100.00 (borrowed)	$1,120.00 (needed to keep purchasing power constant) $89.60 interest at 8%
$100.00 = $1,209.60/12.096 (net present value of payments, using adjusted interest rate) Interest rate = 100.00 [12.096 – 1.00] = 1,109.60%	$1,209.60 (total payment)

Today	One year from now, 892.86 percent inflation (1,000%/1.12)
$100.00 (borrowed)	$892.86 (needed to keep purchasing power constant) $71.43 interest at 8%
$100.00 = $964.29/9.6429 (net present value of payments, using adjusted interest rate) Interest rate = 100.00 [9.6429 – 1] = 864.29%	$964.29 (total payment)

Exercise 14 If a one year zero coupon bond bears an interest rate of 6 percent, and a three year bond bears a rate of 8 percent, what is the return to maturity on a comparable two year bond? A two year bond is a bond issued today, maturing two years later. Call today time zero, one year hence time 1, and so on. Then the return of 8 percent on the three year bond means that

$$1.08^3 = 1.06(1 + r_{12})(1 + r_{23}) \tag{1}$$

The return on the two year bond satisfies

$$(1 + R)^2 = 1.06(1 + r_{12}) \tag{2}$$

If you assume $r_{12} = r_{23} = r$, then (1) becomes

$$1.08^3 = 1.06(1 + r)^2$$

or

$$(1 + r) = (1.08^3/1.06)^{\frac{1}{2}} = 1.090141$$

You can then plug this value into (2), amended to read

$$(1 + R)^2 = 1.06(1 + r)$$

That is,

$$(1 + R)^2 = 1.06(1.090141) = 1.155550$$

Finally,

$$(1 + R) = (1.155550)^{\frac{1}{2}} = 1.074965$$

Thus, the average return to maturity on the two year bond is 7.4965 percent.

Exercise 15 The probability of winning (or losing) is in either case 1/2, and in either case your companion is assumed to be sure to pay, as are you. Thus each bet offers exactly the same payoffs with the same probability distribution, and there are no impediments to substituting one bet for the other. Under these circumstances the principle of pricing by arbitrage says that the two bets have the same value.

Exercise 16 The value of the payment today is $100.00/1.10 = $90.91.

Exercise 17 If interest rates are 10 percent, an instrument promising to pay $110.00 one year from now can be exchanged today for another instrument promising to pay $100.00 immediately, whenever there are no transactions costs to making the exchange. Arbitrage will ensure these prices prevail.

Exercise 18 People will buy the cheaper instrument and sell the dearer. This will tend to bring the two prices closer together. If there are no impediments to trading, such arbitraging will continue until the price difference is eliminated.

Exercise 19 The bond would sell now for $1,000.00/1.04^3 = $889.00. An investor purchasing the bond for $889.00 would earn a real interest rate of 4 percent, compounded annually, if the bond is held to maturity.

Exercise 20 In terms of purchasing power the investor will be repaid only $1,000.00/1.01^3. Given that the unanticipated inflation was not taken into account, the real interest rate realised on the investment is given by

$$\$889.00(1 + r)^3 = \$1,000.00/(1.01)^3$$

or

$$[\$1,000.00/1.04^3](1 + r)^3 = \$1,000.00/(1.01)^3$$

That is,

$$(1 + r) = (1.04)/(1.01)$$

which gives a value of $r = 2.9703$ percent.

7 DIVIDING AND PRICING RISKS

Exercise 1 The payments the firm could make on an instrument that promised to pay its holder $105.00 in principal and interest at time 1 would be $105.00 if earnings were high, and $95.00 if earnings were low. These payments are exactly the cash flows of the firm, and they should therefore have the same value as the cash flows of the firm. The instrument does not conform to investors' usual idea of debt because it is not risk free. Indeed, it has exactly the same risk as the payoffs to the whole firm.

Exercise 2 A sure payment of $100.00 is worth more to a risk averter than is a risky payment with an expected value of $100.00. So, when you go from holding the firm to holding the $100.00 certainty payment, value increases. To arrange put-call parity you buy a put, sell a call. Since value is increased, this means that the call you sell will not be worth as much as the put you buy: on a net basis you would have to pay out something to acquire the options needed to give you the certainty outcomes.

Exercise 3 The equation is $(0.29 \times 10.00)/1.10 + (0.71 \times 0.00)/1.10 = \$2.90/1.10$.

Exercise 4 The equation is $(0.29 \times 5.00)/1.10 + (0.71 \times 0.00)/1.10 = \$1.45/1.10$.

Exercise 5

$$v(S) = [(0.29 \times 97.90) + (0.71 \times 97.90)]/1.10 = 97.90/1.10 = 89.00$$

$$v(X) = [(0.29 \times 105.00) + (0.71 \times 95.00)]/1.10 = 97.90/1.10 = 89.00$$

$$- v(C) = -(0.29 \times 7.10)/1.10 = -2.06/1.10 = -1.87$$

$$v(P) = (0.71 \times 2.90)/1.10 = 2.06/1.10 = 1.87$$

Exercise 6 See answer to Exercise 5.

Exercise 7 If the forward contract has a forward price of $100.00, at time zero you would have to pay someone −$2.10/1.10 before they would sign a contract to buy the firm from you at time 1 for $100.00, regardless of what it was then worth. If the forward price were set lower, you'd have to pay them less. There is a still lower forward price ($97.90) at which the forward contract has a zero value. Finally, at forward prices below $97.90 people would pay you to enter the contract.

Exercise 8 Since the forward contract is in effect a combination of a call and a short put, and since an exercise price of $97.90 gives the call and the put equal values, a forward price of $97.90 also gives the forward contract a value of zero.

Exercise 9 $[(0.29 \times 7.10) - (0.71 \times 2.90)]/1.10 = [2.06 - 2.06]/1.10 = 0.00$.

Exercise 10 The value of p* is found from

$$p^*(\$110.00) + (1 - p^*)(\$99.00) = \$93.00(1.10) = 102.30$$

Hence

$$p^*(\$110.00 - \$99.00) + \$99.00 = \$102.30$$

This means $11p^* = 3.30$, or $p^* = 0.30$.

Exercise 11 The numerical answers are shown below the table. Use the risk adjusted probability from Exercise 10, the value of the instrument whose payoffs are listed in column X/2 can be determined. Then, you can value the riskless payoff in column X/2 – C using the risk free rate. Finally, subtract the value in column X/2–C from the value for X/2 to get the value of –C.

	X/2	– C	X/2 – C
Good scenario	$55.00	–$ 5.50	49.50
Bad scenario	$49.50	$ 0.00	49.50
Today's value	$46.50		

The value in the X/2 column is $[0.3 \times 55.00 + 0.7 \times 49.50]/1.10 = 51.15/1.10 = 46.50$.
The value of X/2 – C is $49.50/1.10 = 45.00$.
Therefore the value of the call option must be $46.50 - 45.00 = 1.50$.
The exercise price of the call must be $104.50.

Exercise 12 The values needed to complete the table are calculated here.

	S	X	–C	P
Good scenario	$103.00	$110.00	-$7.00	$0.00
Bad scenario	$103.00	$99.00	$0.00	$4.00
Today's value		$93.00		

$S = 103.00/1.10 = \$93.64$
$-C = -0.30(7.00)/1.10 = -1.91$
$P = 0.70(4.00)/1.10 = 2.55$
$\$93.00 - 1.91 + 2.55 = 93.64$

Exercise 13 The numerical answers are given below the table.

	X	S	F
Time 1 high payoffs	$210.00	$206.80	$3.20
Time 1 low payoffs	$180.00	$206.80	($26.80)
Time 0 values	$188.00	$188.00	$0.00

The new risk adjusted probability is found from

$$p^*(210.00) + (1-p^*)180.00 = 188.00(1.10) = 206.80$$

That is,

$$30p* = 26.80, \text{ or } p* = 0.8933.$$

Next, set the time 0 value for S equal to 188.00. Then the certainty payoffs to S must be $188.00(1.10) = 206.80$. Enter these into column S. Then subtract S from X to get the amounts in column F. Then the values of the amounts in column F, multiplied by the risk adjusted probabilities, must come to zero.

Check: $0.8933(3.20) - 0.1067(26.80) = 2.86 - 2.86 = 0$

8 FINANCIAL GOVERNANCE

Exercise 1 The benefits to offering a new product in an uncompetitive market are that, assuming the product is well received by clients, profit margins are not severely limited by competitors. The principal problem is that developing an unknown product poses severe problems of estimating likely market size and profitability. It also poses severe problems of working out the best methods to develop and market the product. There is very little that is tried and tested in a genuinely new product. On the other hand, the rewards to success, albeit realised only infrequently, may prove relatively great. When you depart from tried and true products (which usually sell in competitive markets) both the uncertainties and the rewards become potentially greater.

Exercise 2 (i) Banks offer their clients deposits whose risk is different from the individual loans constituting bank assets. (ii) Banks can make small loans to clients who could not sell their notes in the public marketplace. (iii) Banks can keep a fairly close watch on the course of small clients' loan accounts. Individuals could perform each of these services themselves, at the same cost as they are done by banks, in a perfectly competitive market. In such a market there are no transactions cost savings, no savings from realising economies of scale to operations, no savings in information processing costs. In practice, banks perform the diversification services in (i) more cheaply than can markets, because they realise unit cost savings to operations. Banks can perform the screening tasks of (ii) more cheaply than can markets, because they are volume operations which use specialised screening methods with low unit costs. Market agents are set up mainly to do larger individual deals. Banks can perform (iii) more cheaply than markets because they are in closer contact with individual clients.

Exercise 3 The statements help keep the bank up-to-date on the operations and financial position of the client. A seat on the board would give more, and possibly more timely information than can be gleaned from financial statements. The first method of monitoring is likely the cheaper. But if it's critical to getting a reasonable return on your funds, you might find the more expensive method to be the more cost-effective, and therefore the more desirable.

Exercise 4 Trading any marketable security (bonds, shares, options) is an example of a type S deal. A venture investment in a new company is a good example of a type N deal.

Exercise 5 Securities traders have mainly type M capabilities.

Bank lenders – type Y.
Venture capital firms – type Y, but getting closer to type H than bank lenders.
Life insurance companies in their function of writing policies – type Y.
Real estate agents – type M.
Real estate developers – type H.

Exercise 6 They get different information in the performance of their jobs, and they need different information to do their jobs. A foreign exchange trader mainly needs to know about the kinds of news that influence foreign exchange rates on an hour-to-hour, or even minute-to-minute basis, if he is to earn a reasonable return on the funds his employer has invested in the trading activity. A venture capitalist mainly needs to know about what can go right, and what can go wrong, in the life cycle of a new or growing company if she is to earn a reasonable return on the funds she has invested in her client's business.

Exercise 7 A complete contract is one that specifies all the relevant features of a financial deal. A perfectly competitive world is one in which risks can be described quantitatively, and in which all parties have the same information about risks. In these circumstances it is possible to specify all the relevant features of a financial deal.

Exercise 8 If a financier and a client do not have the same information about a deal, the way the financier governs it will be designed to manage the information difference. For example, if the deal involves long term financing of a new business, a seat on the board may be a way of monitoring closely the business's growth and profitability.

Exercise 9 Since transactions costs impede arbitrage transactions, there is no guarantee that an equilibrium will establish the same pricing relationships we found when there are no costs. Even so, however, if the transactions costs are not too large, the price relationships found by assuming them to be zero may give us useful bounds on what equilibrium prices will continue to be.

Exercise 10 Standardising the terms of trade and guaranteeing the creditworthiness of instruments traded greatly increased trading in the options market. Standardisation reduced transactions costs, making it cheaper to trade. Guaranteeing the creditworthiness of instruments traded also reduced trading costs because it means that individuals could buy options without having to investigate the creditworthiness of the counterparty.

Exercise 11 Exercise 10 gave you an example. Trading any marketable security (bonds, shares, options) is an example of a type S deal that uses type M governance. A venture investment in a new company is a good example of a type N deal that uses type H governance.

Marketable security ─────────────⟶ Venture investment
─────⟶   Increasing information differences ─────⟶
            Perceived greater risk
            Uncertainty rather than risk
            Decreasing liquidity of assets financed
            Greater need for continued monitoring
            Greater need for subsequent adjustment
            Increasing cost of default

Exercise 12 Informational asymmetries do not matter if there are enough government securities available for use as collateral, because the loan or investment can then be made against the value of the collateral. Since this value is easy to estimate, there is no need, if the value is sufficiently high, to investigate the client's proposal further.

Exercise 13 You might use a loan covenant prohibiting the substitution. Alternatively, you might agree to pay out the proceeds of the loan to the suppliers of materials and equipment that would be needed to implement the less risky project. As a third possibility, you might sit on the board of the company and supervise large expenditures to ensure they were made on the originally agreed project.

Exercise 14 Financial holding companies can offer the advantages of being able to use hierarchical governance of high risk projects. They can monitor projects more closely, and effect changes in operations, thus reducing the risks below those faced by lenders or investors more remote from the actual implementation of the project. It is true that these advantages bring, as the other side of the coin, the possibility of conflict of interest. For example, if you own a trust company and direct it to lend money to your own projects, you could be using depositors' money to further your own ends rather than investing those funds in the best possible uses.

9 PORTFOLIO GOVERNANCE

Exercise 1 The covariance is:

$$(0.03)(0.09)(1/3) + (0.06)(0.06)(1/3) + (0.09)(0.03)(1/3) - (0.06)(0.06) =$$

$$0.0030 - 0.0036 = -0.0006$$

The variances are $\sigma^2(r_X) = \sigma^2(r_Y) = 0.0006$.
The correlation is

$$-(0.0006) \, / \, (0.0006)^{1/2} \, (0.0006)^{1/2} = -1.0000$$

Exercise 2 The variance of a portfolio made up of equal proportions of securities X and Y is

$$(0.0006)/4 - 2(0.0006)/4 + (0.0006)/4 = 0.0000$$

This portfolio has a variance equal to zero because high returns on one security are always associated with low returns on the other, so that the highs cancel out the lows, on average leaving an unchanging return.

Exercise 3 The calculation is $(0.4762^2)(21.00) = \$4.76$.

Exercise 4 Using the form of Table 7.8, $p^* = 0.4762$, and an interest rate of zero.

	X	S*	C	−P
Time 1 high payoffs	110.00	100.00	10.00	0.00
Time 1 low payoffs	90.91	100.00	0.00	−9.09
Time 0 values	100.00	100.00	4.76	−4.76

Exercise 5 Managing a portfolio of government bonds chiefly involves managing market risk. Managing the venture investment portfolio is principally a matter of managing default risk through continuing supervision of company operations.

Exercise 6 Securitisation means that banks sell securities against portfolios of loans like mortgage loans, credit card obligations, car loans and the like. The banking function of screening and administering the original loans still has to be performed: the securities sold in the securitisation operation are new instruments. The buyers of these new instruments don't screen the original loans, and they don't monitor them.

Exercise 7 Funding a floating rate loan by using floating rate deposits is a way of getting high interest rate earnings to occur when interest costs are high, and of letting those earnings reduce when interest costs are low (i.e., of matching the earnings of the assets against the costs of the liabilities). Asset-liability matching helps to reduce interest rate risks.

Exercise 8 The swap involves trading interest patterns between institutions so that the resulting interest earnings have a pattern similar to interest costs. If you merged two banks that had been parties to a swap, the offsets on the bank's own books would be like asset-liability matching. The effect would be the same as that created by the exchange of rate patterns using the swap.

Exercise 9 Usually, interest rate futures permit hedging the interest patterns of smaller deals, for shorter periods of time, than can be done by asset-liability matching. This means that interest rate futures would probably be used to hedge or to manage the earnings risk of a deal with an individual client. Asset-liability matching would normally be done with much larger proportions of a bank's assets and liabilities.

Exercise 10 Interest rate swaps offer an alternative to floating rate lending to the extent it is possible to arrange them at reasonable cost. With floating rate lending, the client bears the interest rate risk, while with swaps the bank first takes on the risk and then tries to offset it through arranging a swap. The swap might cost the bank something to arrange, but the ability to offer clients fixed rate loans might prove to be a compensating competitive advantage.

Exercise 11 One way of diversifying the assets of a property development company is to buy properties in different locations, say in different countries. Another is to buy a mix of commercial and residential properties. A third might be to enter the construction and the property management business.

Exercise 12 The main problem is that of remaining solvent when property prices are depressed and most lenders are unwilling to advance you funds. One possibility is to arrange for support from other developers who understand the business.

Exercise 13 The difficulty with the arrangement in Exercise 12 is that competitors may extract a high price for providing what is in effect emergency financing. Some developers might prefer to run the risks of bankruptcy rather than pay what they regard as too high a price for funds.

Exercise 14 The kinds of information you need to process are quite different, and most people are limited in their abilities to perform several tasks equally well.

Exercise 15 A conglomerate can audit books, replace management, order changes in operations if it has a subsidiary whose performance is faltering. Because it can monitor and control so closely, loose statements of what will be done in an emergency (i.e., the use of incomplete contracts) can usually be made to work quite well.

Exercise 16 Each offers advantages in certain circumstances. Interest rate futures contracts work well with individual deals, and asset-liability matching works well for most of an intermediary's asset-liability portfolio. Swaps are an intermediate arrangement offering some of the advantages of each. The three are thus complementary, each proving cost-effective in particular circumstances.

10 DEALS' TERMS

Exercise 1 The bank would likely require current lists of accounts receivable, say on a monthly or quarterly basis. Likely the receivables would have to be classified as current or in arrears, and would typically have to exceed the size of the loan by a specified margin. For example, a bank might be willing to advance 75–85 percent of accounts receivable to a borrower in relatively good standing.

Exercise 2 Suppose the accounts receivable do not fully secure the loan, and that repayment of the whole loan depends on, say, the business's developing a market for a new product. (Of course, not all bankers would permit themselves to make such a loan, but they sometimes find themselves in this kind of situation as a result of past decisions not working out.) Now the contract could be incomplete because it is difficult to specify what the lender and the client would do if the new product development scheme didn't work out as projected.

Exercise 3 Financiers will buy information rather than work it up themselves when it is more cost-effective to do so. For example, buying information from a credit rating agency is cheaper than investigating the client anew, because there are scale economies to working up such kinds of information. A second reason is the third party might be better at developing specific information. For example, a real estate appraiser may be technically more qualified to value property than would a long term lender.

Exercise 4 If the company president is a technical person, the venture capital investor might recommend the company consider getting either professional sales assistance or professional administration. A professional sales person would focus on sales development, an adminstrator on monitoring company operations. In either case a judgment would have to be made about the cost-effectiveness of adding to the company payroll. Moreover, assuming that the company president will continue in office, any persons chosen would have to be able to work with the president.

Exercise 5 Taking the proceeds of a business loan and using the funds to go on vacation is an example of moral hazard. Clients approaching a financier with stories of how they have been badly treated by other financiers suggest the financier currently being approached might be facing adverse selection. Using a capital expenditure loan to pay off trade suppliers is an example of moral hazard. (In particular, the financier might have contemplated using the fixed assets as some form of security for the loan.) When people in ill health fail to declare medical problems on their insurance applications, the insurance company faces adverse selection.

Exercise 6 The original calculation is

$$(0.99)(1.10) - 1.00 = 0.089 \text{ or } 8.9\%$$

With a default probability equal to 0.02, it becomes

$$(0.98)(1.10) - 1.00 = 0.078 \text{ or } 7.8\%$$

With a default probability equal to 0.05, it becomes

$$(0.95)(1.10) - 1.00 = 0.045 \text{ or } 4.5\%$$

Since banking can be a relatively thin-margin business, it takes only a moderate risk of default to make a project unattractive. If the interest rate on the deal cannot be increased, the deal with a default probability of 5 percent is likely unattractive if the bank needs interest margins of 4–5 percent in order to break even.

Exercise 7 A banker who likes to lend at floating rates could offer a client a fixed rate loan if interest futures contracts were used to hedge the bank's profit risk. The arrangement would likely cost the client more than the standard floating rate loan, because arranging what is effectively insurance against interest rate risk is costly. The bank would like to pass this cost on to the client, although in highly competitive circumstances it might not always be possible to pass on the full cost. If it were still to make the loan, the bank would then have to be content with a lower rate of profit on the deal.

Exercise 8 The first thing to do is determine what the nominal rate needs to be. Say you want a real rate of 5 percent, but that this rate does not take the risk of misjudging inflation into account. If you advance $100 today, you want to recover $200 principal one year from now to keep the same purchasing power, and with interest of 5 percent the amount you want back is $210. The nominal rate of interest on this arrangement is $100 \times [(210 - 100)/100] = 110$ percent. However, as already mentioned this doesn't take into account the risk of estimating inflation correctly. Some kind of risk premium would have to be added to the 110 percent to compensate for the risk. A second way of bypassing the risk is to express the loan in terms of some commodity. For example, if $100 represented the cost of two barrels of oil today, you might write a contract that specified paying back an amount, one year from now, that would buy $2(1.05) = 2.10$ barrels of oil.

Exercise 9 The loans would probably end up being cheaper to farmers (i) if there was competition between lenders and (ii) the effective after-tax interest rate provided, in the financier's judgment, a reasonable return in relation to the risk of the loan. If (ii) were not satisfied, the financiers might not extend any loans at all.

11 MARKET TRADING AND INTERMEDIATION

Exercise 1 Making a venture investment and conglomerate financing of a subsidiary are closer to each other than either is to trading treasury bills.

Exercise 2 Informational differences can inhibit arbitraging because in the presence of information differences it can be difficult to know for certain whether a riskless profit opportunity actually exists. Arbitrage depends on identifying such opportunities.

Exercise 3 Yes. Switching between investments in government bonds and in loans or mortgages tends to keep the interest rates in the different markets closer together than they would otherwise be.

Exercise 4 Yes, neglected stocks are an example of market segmentation. The neglected stocks tend to have higher interest rates, in relation to their risk, than do stocks that are not neglected.

Exercise 5 Yes. It can be argued that there are net social benefits to creating employment, and these benefits are not reflected in the profits earned by those private sector financiers who specialise in small business equity financing.

Exercise 6 Shares trade in a different market from treasury bills because specialised traders can operate more profitably than less specialised ones.

Exercise 7 If rates in the treasury bill market increase, one can suppose the risk free rate is increasing. The risk adjusted probability approach of Chapters 6 and 7 values stocks using the probabilities and a risk free rate. If the risk free rate increased, the values of stocks calculated using the risk adjusted probability approach would decrease.

Exercise 8 Yes, you would expect share prices to fall if the riskless rates rose and other things remained equal. The reason you don't always see this effect in practice is that other things almost never do remain equal.

Exercise 9 This does not deny the linkage you established in Exercises 7 and 8 because an increase in share prices can also be due to effects that were assumed to be held constant in Exercises 7 and 8.

Exercise 10 They might be able to sell securities against a portfolio of longer term instruments. This would free up additional funds.

Exercise 11 Markets where there is lending on an individual basis rather than active trading in securities such as bills or bonds. Intermediaries link the government bond market and the business loan market; they link deposit markets in different countries.

Exercise 12 The neglected shares market is an example of market segmentation. In order to profit from removing the segmentation, you'd have to be able to buy up the shares at low prices (likely possible) but then resell them at higher prices. The difficulty would lie in convincing investors to buy them. Maybe well-publicised research would help.

Exercise 13 Usually, market segmentation persists only until someone in the financial system finds a way to profit from the situation. The difficulty is finding a way to generate those profits.

Exercise 14 Possibly by providing more equity finance to small business, or by providing export insurance where it is now difficult to obtain.

12 DOMESTIC FINANCIAL MARKETS

Exercise 1 The Chicago Board of Trade members setting up the Exchange expected to profit from the trading activity they created. While the Exchange itself would not make profits, its member firms would charge commissions for trading, pay for the operations of the Exchange out of their trading revenues, and keep the difference as profit.

Exercise 2 Gordon had a distribution network that made the inventory risk seem lower to them, in relation to trading profits, than it apparently did to other underwriters. A second apparent advantage might have been that Gordon expected to gain profitable market share by being the first securities firm in Canada to offer the new method of raising corporate funds.

Exercise 3 Real estate firms normally act as brokers rather than as dealers because the inventory risk in holding real property is large in relation to typical real estate commissions.

Exercise 4 The difference might be explained by something like a difference in taxes on the incomes from the two bills. For example, at one time in Canada capital gains on treasury bills were taxed differently from interest income on bonds.

Exercise 5 Apart from the difference between a primary and a secondary issue, there are no fundamental differences between Gordon Capital's use of the bought deal and third market dealing. It's true that in Gordon Capital's case the securities represent new issues, while in the case of third market deals the securities almost always represent secondary market trades. However, in both cases the institutions holding the securities are acting as dealers.

Exercise 6 The largest value of riskless bond that could be issued by the firm in Table 12.1 is a promised payment of principal and interest equal to 10. Any larger promise could not always be met from the firm's cash flows.

Exercise 7 First City Savings would have been helped by securitisation because they would have found readier markets to sell off blocks of mortgages they had already placed.

Exercise 8 Money market transactions are so closely integrated because it is relatively cheap and easy to take advantage of any emerging arbitrage opportunities in these markets. The closest arbitraging links between the money market and other financial markets would probably be with the short term government bond market.

Exercise 9 Stocks represent risk capital, while bonds really represent borrowing against assets or cash flows. The former tend to attract investors seeking capital gains, the latter to attract investors seeking income. There is much more information-based trading in the stock markets as compared to the bond markets, mainly because more kinds of information are relevant to the price of a stock.

Exercise 10 The main reason for there being dealers in government bonds, and only brokers in corporate bonds, is that the inventory risk–return ratios are higher for corporates than for governments.

Exercise 11 Firms issue both bonds and shares to appeal to different investors. Then, the sorts of information these investors typically use also differ, leading to a difference in trading conditions between stock and bond markets.

Exercise 12 Listing requirements convey information about the minimum quality of securities being traded on a given exchange? A credible rating system (A, B, C, . . .) could play a similar role in an electronic OTC market for little known shares.

Exercise 13 The existence of scale economies in computer networks is one force leading to the merging of trading activities on different networks. Eventually, a single computer network market might emerge for each of several classes of security.

Exercise 14 Dealers assume inventory risk, brokers do not.

Exercise 15 Mortgages are much more heterogeneous in quality than are government treasury bills, and the individual mortgage usually represents a much smaller transaction. These differences affect the economics of trading to such an extent that primary bill markets are active auctions in which the suppliers of funds are money market dealers bidding for inventories, while primary mortgage markets are negotiated markets in which the suppliers are intermediaries.

13 MARKETS FOR RISK TRADING

Exercise 1 Refer to Table 13.7 in the question. By put-call parity, the values at the bottoms of colums 2 through 4 must add to the value at the bottom of column 1. In order for this to be true, the call option must have a value $5.00 greater than the put. The risk lover places a higher value on upside potential than on downside risk.

Exercise 2 The value of the call option is as shown below.

Relations between share and call prices

Time 0	Time 1	Time 2	Time 3	Time 4
				146.41
				41.41
			133.10	
			28.10	
		121.00		121.00
		17.37		16.00
	110.00		110.00	
	10.17		7.62	
100.00		100.00		100.00
5.75		3.63		0.00
	90.91		90.91	
	1.73		0.00	
		82.65		82.65
		0.00		0.00
			75.14	
			0.00	
				68.31
				0.00

Exercise 3 To offset your risk, you want an instrument that will gain in value if rates rise (because then your costs will rise) and lose in value if rates fall. Such an instrument would be a short position in an interest rate future. You would have to arrange the amount of the transaction so that the gains on the futures contract would offset the extra interest you would pay, say measured against today's interest rate.

Exercise 4 The two parties have agreed to exchange Canadian dollars for pounds at the rate of $2.22 per pound. The Canadian firm has to come up with pounds to pay its loan. It gets these pounds, under the agreement, at C$2.22. But it could have bought the same pounds in the market for only C$2.10. Thus the Canadian firm is the loser, since the Canadian dollar in effect rose after the agreement was signed. The loss is an opportunity loss.

Exercise 5 One form of hedging is using a put option to minimise the downside risk of a long position in a stock. The hedge is created by buying the put.

Exercise 6 The options, futures and forward exchange markets are closely integrated with their underlying spot markets by transactions aimed at exploiting arbitrage opportunities.

Exercise 7 Hedgers and speculators do not necessarily have different attitudes toward risk; they could each be trying to offset the risk in different portfolios. For example, someone who buys a put is trying to offset the effect of a price decline on a long position. The seller of the put might have a short position and would therefore profit from a price decline. The seller can capitalise this potential gain by selling the put for a premium.

Exercise 8 A mutual fund manager could sell calls against a portfolio to earn the call premiums, especially if the manager didn't think price increases were very likely. Another manager could buy calls as a means of ensuring that a given stock could be acquired for no more than the strike price. This transaction would be useful if the fund were waiting for cash inflows before making the purchase.

Exercise 9 A bank might use the interest futures markets to offer a client a fixed rate loan, even though the bank funded it with floating rate liabilities. Usually such transactions are smaller, and for shorter terms, than are the interest rate hedges that banks arrange in the swap markets.

Exercise 10 The two should effectively give the same predictions, because they incorporate the same information in their prices. Another way of saying this is that if one country's currency is selling for less in the forward than in the spot market, its interest rate should be higher than that of another country's. But the same information about the future decline of the currency is still taken into account in both the spot and the forward market prices.

14 INTERNATIONAL FINANCIAL MARKETS

Exercise 1 The following transactions would increase a current account deficit: an increase in foreign travel; a decrease in exports; an increase in remittances abroad.

Exercise 2 It could pay to borrow from abroad if the rate of return to the investment project financed by the borrowing is greater than the cost of obtaining the funds, that is if the net present value of the project is positive. Even if domestic savings is inadequate to fund the project, the economy will still be better off in a net present value sense.

Exercise 3 If the funds are raised as shares, investors from other countries benefit if the project earns more than expected. If the funds are raised as bonds, the total payment to foreign investors is specified in advance, at least if the borrowing is not an unhedged borrowing in a foreign currency.

Exercise 4 The returns to a C$100.00 investment in the US if US and Canadian interest rates are 10 percent and if F*, the forward rate, is 0.73, are as follows:

$100 Canadian purchases US$75.00
US$ value at 10 percent, one year from now US$82.50.
Canadian value at forward rate of 0.73 = $82.50/0.73 = $113.00
Return on investment in Canadian terms 13 percent.

Exercise 5 The principal costs that would be saved by borrowing in the Euromarkets are the costs of complying with securities commission requirements in a given country. These include legal fees, filing fees and the like. A firm borrowing in the Euromarkets would not have to pay these kinds of fees if it were well enough known to attract funds from Euromarket investors.

Exercise 6 When more people travel abroad, a country's balance on current account is decreased, other things being equal. The country's balance on current account increases if imports decline.

Exercise 7 The costs of complying with domestic regulation, and the costs of domestic taxation, have sometimes been great enough to make it profitable to carry out transactions offshore, creating the Eurocurrency markets. For example, the US Interest Equalisation Tax made it profitable to hold US dollar deposits in London banks that were not subject to the tax.

Exercise 8 International banks can create Euromoney in just the same way that domestic banks can create money by lending. In order for them to effect a multiple expansion of the funds, some of the moneys lent must be redeposited in the banking system doing the creation – either the domestic banking system if we are discussing domestic money creation, or the Eurobanking system if we are discussing Euromoney.

Exercise 9 The main reason some of the arbitrage opportunities were not taken up seems to have been a lack of liquidity in some of the instruments. For example, it was difficult to trade domestic bonds in packages that would mimic the behaviour of Eurobonds. The absence of instruments to permit riskless arbitrage does not deny the validity of the principle, but does say that in some markets there can be impediments to arbitrage-based trading.

Exercise 10 A country can become better off by borrowing from abroad if the net present value (NPV) of the project is positive, that is if its rate of return exceeds the cost of raising the funds. Presumably there is not sufficient domestic savings to permit the country to carry out all positive NPV projects.

Exercise 11 Transactions costs mean that not every covered interest arbitrage transactions is worthwhile. It is only when the deviations become large enough to more than compensate for the transactions costs that the deal will be done.

Exercise 12 If a central bank can only resist, but not withstand, the pressures of international currency speculators, the potential volume of arbitrage-based transactions must be very large. This statement says that the search for arbitrage opportunities is continuous, vigorous, and can muster a good deal of funds as and when the opportunities are judged to be present.

Exercise 13 The loan's risk might differ because the stability of the governments is different and because recovering any profits from a foreign country might be affected by changes in taxation, in regulations governing the purchase of foreign currency, and the like.

15 PRINCIPLES OF INTERMEDIATION

Exercise 1 Two sources of scale economies in the operations of a bank could be spreading the fixed costs of setting up a loan screening department, spreading the fixed costs of setting up a data processing center. In the operations of an insurance company, similar sources would be found in setting up a department for screening insurance applications, and again in setting up a department for data processing. Note that a bank screens potential assets, an insurance company screens potential liabilities.

Exercise 2 Some examples of technological change are the bar coding of cheques, so they can be processed automatically, setting up telephone banking, and the use of computer assisted queries (expert systems) for use either by personnel or clients inquiring about new products.

Exercise 3 A long position in interest rate futures will show capital losses as interest rates rise. The positive correlation between a long position in futures and loan writeoffs might be important for some banks, if the futures position were large in relation to the loan position. Even then, however, the capital losses on the futures position would likely occur quickly and over the near term, while the loan writeoffs might occur more slowly and over the longer term. The positive correlation at any point in time might therefore not be very great, even if the bank does have a long futures position. On the other hand, if analysis showed the correlation to be important, the position represents a source of risk that some risk managers have to date overlooked.

Exercise 4 The bank would have a negative gap, and it would show falling profits (mounting losses) as interest rates rose. The problem faced by a risk manager in such a bank would be to find ways of getting more floating rate loans, to swap fixed for floating interest earnings, and the like: in other words, to reduce the negative gap.

Exercise 5 Even banks facing zero required reserves might have a positive desired reserve position if they typically experienced clearing losses that were costly to cover. Similarly, banks that typically faced clearing gains might find it cost-effective to adopt a negative desired reserve position, so they didn't end up many days' business with lots of uninvested cash.

Exercise 6 When a bank announces large loan writeoffs, market confidence in management ability is usually impaired, often more greatly than is warranted. As and when a bank loses the confidence of its investors, its shares will sell at a depressed price. That is clearly a bad time to try to float a new share issue, because (if the fundamental value is actually higher than the market value – a management call) too great a percentage of the bank's future earnings is being surrendered for the price the new shares bring.

Exercise 7 In the equation

$$ITE = \{r[1 - 0.08(0.95)]/0.05\} - \{0.06(0.95)/0.05\}$$

$ITE = 0$ if $r = 0.061685$. This means that net interest earnings are zero if you charge an effective rate on the loans of 0.061685. This rate should be net of loan losses, so for that reason alone you'd have to charge the client more. In addition, ITE doesn't take operating expenses into account, so to have zero profits you'd have to increase the loan rate still further to cover operating expenses. The rate increase needed to cover operating expenses would depend on the size of the bank, as shown in the next exercise.

Exercise 8 The equation is now

$$ITE = \{0.10[1 - 0.08(0.95)]/0.05\} - \{0.08(0.95)/0.05\} = 0.328$$

Suppose in Figure 15.7 that $r = 0.10$ and $c = 0.08$, so that the net interest earnings per dollar of equity return are 32.8 cents. The amount of equity needed to cover the $100.00 in fixed expenses is therefore $100.00/0.328 = 304.88$. This means the bank must have assets of $20(304.88) = \$6,097.60$ to break even.

Exercise 9 Technological change poses important strategic issues for financial intermediaries because taking advantage of it can affect profits so profoundly. For example, automating cheque processing saves only pennies per cheque, but billions in total operating costs. As a second example, the use of ATMs has greatly reduced clearings growth over what it was expected to be in the 1990s.

Exercise 10 The emergence of financial supermarkets is mainly explained by their being able to realise scale and scope economies. Specialised institutions are able to survive by serving niche markets, using specialised skills not normally possessed by the larger multipurpose institutions. For example, a specialised investment dealer might have a client list that is not easily obtained by larger competitors.

Exercise 11 Lower computing and communications costs alter the economics of developing new financial products mainly by making it less expensive to process data for products closely related to those already offered. Long distance marketing is made easier by lower communications costs, because the products can be made available wherever terminals like ATMs are to be found. (Of course, the institutions operating the ATMs would have to be paid to provide the links.)

Exercise 12 The main limits to scale economies stem from difficulties in administering large, far-flung organisations. The main limits to scope economies stem from inability to link unrelated products to the same accounting and data processing facilities.

Exercise 13 An intermediary which reduced its ratio of capital to equity could be presenting its shareholders with greater risk of loss. This would not normally be a good idea, since existing shareholders might then well suffer declines in the price of their shares. On the other hand, if an intermediary were seriously overcapitalised and could not earn the market required return on the additional investment, a case could be made for reducing either its shareholdings or its long term debt financing, if any.

Exercise 14 If the return on liquid assets increases relative to other investment opportunities, the opportunity cost of holding too much cash would be lower. This might in turn lead the intermediary to hold more of these kinds of liquid assets than previously.

Exercise 15 Interest costs typically float in a manner closely related to market interest rates. Offering more floating rate loans makes interest earnings adhere more closely to the pattern of market interest rates (i.e., increases the correlation between interest revenues and interest costs).

Exercise 16 If you wanted to make a fixed rate loan financed by floating rate deposits, and didn't want to bear the interest rate risk, you could offset the risk by taking a short futures position. Naturally, obtaining this form of insurance would cost something, and you'd have to decide whether the client ought to pay for it. That would probably depend on how competitively other institutions were seeking the particular client's business.

Exercise 17 The principal difficulty with combining banking and investment banking activities is that bankers tend to try to minimise credit risk, while investment banking personnel are more used to assessing and to bearing market risk. These differences seem to create important cultural differences between the two types of persons, differences which are difficult to overcome. The fact that bankers are usually paid on a salary basis while many investment bankers are paid on at least a partial commission basis also leads to cultural conflict.

16 DOMESTIC INTERMEDIATION

Exercise 1 The idea would be to use as much computer support as possible, to down-size the branch installations, and to refer infrequently encountered kinds of business to a central agency where experts could deal with it. The computer support might well include using expert systems, either client or personnel operated.

Exercise 2 Level premium deposit insurance does not give management any incentive to manage risks – the intermediary pays the same premium whether it takes big risks or small ones. If the institution is in trouble, this gives the holders of its shares a no-lose proposition – they win if the risks pay off, the insurance agency loses if they don't. Risk adjusted premiums would give more balanced incentives.

Exercise 3 Venture investments need a greater degree of continued monitoring, and a greater degree of adjustment to operations, than do bank working capital loans.

Exercise 4 The leasing company could probably use capital cost allowances as a tax shelter even when the firm itself could not. (Firms that are not making any taxable profits cannot use the deductions to save on taxes.)

Exercise 5 The research yields scale economies because it involve incurring a fixed cost. The results of the research can usually be sold a number of times to different clients. Thus a securities firm can spread the fixed cost of the research over many clients, no one of whom would find it economic to pay the whole cost individually.

Exercise 6 Both investors and mutual funds can achieve diversification, but mutual funds can probably do it at lower unit costs than most investors. Like securities firms, mutual funds can gain economies of scale from research, and pass on the savings to their clients. On the other hand, investors pay mutual funds a management fee that may absorb most of the foregoing advantages.

Exercise 7 The asset portfolio of a property insurance company is likely to be more liquid than the asset portfolio of a life insurance company because the claims against the former are shorter term and more variable than the claims against the latter.

Exercise 8 The financial conglomerate exercises continued monitoring and adjustment of operations, as does the venture investor. The differences between the two are mainly differences of degree – the monitoring and adjustment capabilities are greater for the conglomerate than for the venture investor.

Exercise 9 Currently providing services to wealthy investors is being investigated by a number of banks. If banks can help these persons to find suitable investments, suitable insurance and pension schemes, and suitable banking arrangements, they should be able to charge a management fee that would compensate them for the value they add. This is especially true for clients who prefer to carry out different kinds of transactions with the same intermediary.

Exercise 10 If deposit costs increase, banks will both seek to find lower cost sources of funds (assuming they are available) and to increase their net interest revenues to compensate for the increase. They will also try to cut other costs to compensate for the lower margins. If margins get thin enough despite all these efforts, some banks would consider withdrawing from the intermediation business.

Exercise 11 The availability of mortgage finance was not greatly increased because the banks had already set up affiliates to make the mortgage loans they could not technically advance on their own books. The example suggests that some kinds of deregulation don't have much impact, because the financial system has already found ways to circumvent the regulation that is currently being removed.

Exercise 12 There is the difficulty of guessing the rate of inflation when you make a fixed rate loan. If the possible future rate is highly uncertain, the chances of guessing wrong are quite great, and in these circumstances the real return on fixed rate loans becomes difficult to assess in advance.

Exercise 13 Bankers sometimes argue that, unless they are seen to be vigilant in pursuing bad loans, the numbers of defaults will increase. It might cost a lot to collect an individual loan, but that might save losses on other loans that, because of the example, are repaid promptly.

Exercise 14 Banks have so far avoided the market for reverse mortgages because the instruments are not very popular with either their retired clienteles, or the heirs presumptive of these clients.

17 INTERNATIONAL INTERMEDIATION

Exercise 1 When banks enter a business, they do so on the basis of anticipated profits, which may be known only with a considerable degree of uncertainty. With subsequent learning and better information, the anticipated profits may disappear, and the bank will withdraw from the business. One of the most important factors affecting such changes is the degree of competition that evolves, a factor whose importance can be exceptionally difficult to judge.

Exercise 2 If Canada's banks earn profits through their international business, bank shareholders will benefit. Moreover, the profits represent a source of foreign exchange earnings that is just as important as the earnings from the export of goods. Canada, like any other exporting nation, believes that increasing its export business also benefits the country as a whole through employment benefits, spinoff activities, and the like. Britain pays very close attention to the magnitude of foreign exchange earnings from financial services, as do such cities as Singapore and Hong Kong.

Exercise 3 The rate the country pays might serve as a signal of its international credit rating. In these circumstances it could be advantageous to get the loan at LIBOR and also agree to pay additional fees.

Exercise 4 When complicated international transactions are arranged at widely differing costs, it probably indicates that the markets have not yet become highly competitive. (Terms tend to get standardised in highly competitive markets.) If markets are uncompetitive, ambitious senior executives find them attractive because they offer the possibilities of greater than competitive profits. Such situations tend to diminish over time as competition increases, being attracted by the favourable profit situation.

Exercise 5 Presumably most international loans are not made to enhance the military capabilities of the borrowing country. The moral hazard is that the loan proceeds are being misspent. If the country is spending unusual amounts on the military, it is at least a possibility that its government is attempting to bolster its position.

Exercise 6 If countries have no earning power, they may not be able to borrow from profit-seeking lenders. This is not evidence of a capital shortage. Rather, it shows that lenders are no longer as captivated by the sovereign loan fallacy. International agencies such as the World Bank and the International Finance Corporation are set up to make loans to poor countries with little or no ability to repay.

Exercise 7 The scandals in derivatives trading have primarily indicated lax internal supervision. Often, the traders' reported profits have been a basis for their supervisors to earn large bonuses. Regulation can help a little, by trying to ensure that bank management behaves responsibly and that the banks have good risk assessment systems in place. The most important thing is to ensure that bank managements have the incentive to supervise responsibly.

Exercise 8 As the international financial markets become increasingly integrated, there are diminished possibilities that countries with good international credit ratings will face capital shortages.

Exercise 9 Increasing instability of foreign exchange rates leads to greater demands for hedging foreign exchange risk, and thus contributes to the development of international finance.

Exercise 10 The function of an international lender of last resort is to provide emergency liquidity support to solvent institutions that are facing temporary problems, say because another institution has failed to meet its short term obligations to the institution with the liquidity problem.

Exercise 11 If Frankfurt is an international financial center, it should not be difficult for agents in Berlin to arrange international transactions in Frankfurt.

Exercise 12 A country can have a credit limit, just like a corporation. If a country has no foreign exchange earnings, its taxing powers are of little avail for paying off international loans. Moreover, to the extent that taxes can be used, they diminish the incomes of the country's citizens, and there are limits to the extent that such measures can be pushed.

Exercise 13 If a country's government continues to devalue its currency at unpredictable rates, there is likely to be capital flight, domestic inflation, and use of a more stable foreign currency for domestic transactions.

18 GOVERNMENT FINANCIAL ACTIVITY

Exercise 1 If government helps small business by arranging for lower-cost loans when they can readily be obtained at market rates, government is subsidising small business. In the circumstances there is no financial system reason to do so. If small business suffers from a lack of long term capital, subsidising short term sources is not a good way to solve the problem.

Exercise 2 When government agencies obtain resources at below-market rates, they are not fully carrying their costs, and any accounting reports are therefore flawed. If the agency is trying to achieve something that the private sector cannot profitably achieve, the standard of profitability is inappropriate anyhow. (Although, properly measured losses would indicate the cost of doing whatever it is the government is trying to do.)

Exercise 3 Guarantee schemes are normally used to reduce the risk of some deal to make it attractive to the private sector. Reducing both risk and return can be self-defeating, because it may still leave the deal unattractive. A better plan would be to offer a partial guarantee and allow financiers to charge market interest rates. This system will give the private sector the incentives to screen the risks carefully, overcoming the writeoff problem that can otherwise accompany a guaranteed loan scheme.

Exercise 4 By investing most of its assets in provincial securities, the California Public Employees' Retirement Scheme has earned a below-market rate of return in relation to investment risk. This means there are less funds available for payouts than would have been the case if market rates of return had been sought through a more diversified investment policy.

Exercise 5 If the present value of the project is positive and if the domestic economy does not generate sufficient funds to finance all positive net present value projects.

Exercise 6 Export credit insurance has served to increase exports, and thereby create social benefits. It has been justified in the past when the private sector was unwilling to sell the insurance because of their attitudes toward the risks involved. The judgment made by government was that the risk was more than offset by the social benefits created through increasing exports. Of course, the social benefits, such as employment creation, could not be captured by private sector financiers writing the insurance.

Exercise 7 See the answer to Exercise 6.

Exercise 8 This writer believes that Canada's Business Development Bank has outlived its usefulness. It has tried unsuccessfully for many years to provide long term, high risk capital to small business. The principal problem is that the Bank is staffed by persons who have no career incentives to take risks, yet assuming risk is the essence of providing small business long term finance.

Exercise 9 A deficit fiscal policy will lead either to borrowing from abroad or to an increase in domestic interest rates. Under flexible exchange rates the borrowing abroad may also reduce the value of the currency. The spending financed by the borrowing may contribute either to employment creation, if the economy has unused capacity, or to inflation if the economy is already working to near capacity.

Exercise 10 Crowding out means that domestic private investment is reduced because of a governmental deficit. The circumstances under which this might occur are given in the answer to Exercise 9.

19 SUPERVISION

Exercise 1 If regulators do not release relevant information to the public, the public may be harmed as a result of having false confidence in some institution. Over the long run, such a policy seems more likely to damage than to maintain confidence in the financial system. It is sometimes argued that a hint of trouble should not be given, because that might create enough difficulties to cause an institution to fail. On the other hand, regular releases of all pertinent information should give early warning of any trouble developing in an institution.

Exercise 2 Banks want to sell the insurance primarily to realise scope economies from their branch operations. The insurance industry acknowledges that its present distribution methods are high cost ones. Other countries, and the province of Quebec, permit banks to sell insurance on their premises. Most of the resistance comes from independent insurance brokers and is politically motivated in the sense that if they were strong competitors, they would have nothing to fear from bank sales of the same products.

Exercise 3 In a competitive financial system, small business will usually be able to find financing at market rates, because lenders are anxious to find profitable outlets for their funds. If some kinds of financing are not provided by competitive financiers, it is probably because they cannot see how to profit from the deals. But if they cannot profit from the deals, then why should those deals be made? Business people arguing for help in these circumstances may actually be looking for disguised subsidies.

Exercise 4 When regulations prove ineffective, it is usually because business profits are restricted by the regulations, giving business incentives to circumvent the regulations.

Exercise 5 Canada's banks are mainly in business for the long term, and are effective self-regulators because they realise that if confidence in foreign exchange trading is damaged, their long term profits will suffer. Firms trading speculative securities might not be as effective at self-regulation because they do not expect to remain in business for long. Thus if they damage confidence in their industry, they won't be around to face the consequences.

Exercise 6 Suppose the firms are real estate developers. With voting control of the thrift institution's shares, you might be able to persuade the boards to fund your real estate development activities more generously than an independent lender would do. This could put uninsured depositors and, if there were deposit insurance, the insuring agency, at greater risk than if the loans were assessed by independent outsiders.

Exercise 7 The US Federal Reserve System provides emergency liquidity to solvent banks that have temporary cash flow problems. To do so, the Fed acts as a lender of last resort. By so doing, the liquidity problems of a bank do not affect other banks in the system. Thus if the liquidity problems were initially caused by some other bank going bankrupt, the effect of the bankruptcy would not spread throughout the domestic banking system. An international agency acting as a provider of liquidity and lender of last resort would perform exactly the same function with international banks facing difficulty. The agency could obtain the funds needed to conduct its activities either by subscription from member countries or by issuing its own securities. It would, of course, have to generate an income on the funds it raised.

Exercise 8 The regulatory actions could be similar to setting up the international lender of last resort discussed in the answer to Exercise 7. Emergency liquidity would help to prevent the defaults of the failing firm from spreading to other firms. In order to avoid inhibiting trading activity, regulators might require trading firms to provide the funds to operate the emergency facility, but leave most of the risk control measures to internal supervision. Regulators might also supervise the amount of capital maintained by trading firms.

20 TOWARD THE FUTURE

Exercise 1 The principal reason for outsourcing document processing is to realise scale economies in performing the activity.

Exercise 2 Competition would likely increase if banks sold insurance products in their branches. Competition might also increase if Sears is allowed to own and operate ATMs, but as people are quite sensitive to location there isn't much movement from one ATM to another if one has a higher service fee.

Exercise 3 To encourage customers to use debit rather than credit cards, merchants could give cash discounts for the former. Banks could increase their transactions charges for using the latter.

Exercise 4 GE Credit does not have a branch network, and does not pay deposit insurance premiums. This gives it cost advantages for those kinds of loans which it can make as a natural adjunct to its existing businesses.

Exercise 5 You can now trade stocks by phone, on dedicated computer terminals in brokerage offices, and on the Internet. Trading over Cable TV is a future possibility.

Exercise 6 Brokers started trading Stockholm-listed shares in London to escape the tax. As a result, the Swedish government concluded it was uncollectable.

Exercise 7 Home communications facilities such as the telephone and the fax machine have already become popular media for some kinds of financial transactions. It seems quite likely that Cable TV links will also emerge.

Exercise 8 The problem with Internet trading is knowing something about the quality of the stock (investment grade, speculative, and so on). Quality ratings provided by a respected, well-known agency should help the market to flourish, because they would reduce the costs of individual investors doing their own research. As a result of quality ratings, some stocks would become known to more potential investors and thus their liquidity would also increase as a result of more trading activity.

Exercise 9 Before a portfolio of financial assets can be securitised, the items in it have to be screened. This is a banking function that will likely continue to be performed in the future.

Exercise 10 Risk management services in the form of life, property and casualty insurance are already marketed to consumers. If new products with an appeal to consumers are developed, they could be marketed through traditional channels. Moreover, the financial system is currently experimenting with using new channels to market traditional products and this might increase the sales of risk management products, traditional or new.

Exercise 11 Usually an international company attempting to reach a specific national market will use a business that is already established in the country. For example, Royal Bank of Scotland sells insurance in Spain, using Spanish distributors. Canadians can buy property insurance, through their own agents, from a number of international companies.

Glossary

adverse selection the possibility that a risk pool will change because of the terms offered to clients whose differing risks cannot readily be distinguished by screening.

allocative efficiency a property of a financial market in which equally risky propositions have equal access to funding at the same market rate of interest.

arbitrage trading undertaken to profit from atypical market relationships, such as buying a low priced security and later selling it at a higher price, or buying a low priced security in one market and simultaneously selling it in another at a higher price. An arbitrage opportunity is an opportunity to trade for some gain, at no risk of loss.

arbitrage opportunity (riskless arbitrage opportunity) the profit opportunity presented by a situation in which the same asset sells for one price in one market but a different price in another, and in which it is possible to trade freely between the two markets to take advantage of the opportunity.

asset-liability matching borrowing and lending on the same interest rate terms (assessed with respect to the points in time at which rates can be adjusted). For example, a bank may finance floating rate loans using floating rate deposits. Asset-liability matching is internal to the intermediary in the sense that it is arranged on its own books and does not involve any trading of assets or liabilities or of interest rate patterns.

asset securitisation the practice of issuing new securities, designed to appeal to investors, against an asset portfolio of illiquid securities.

balance on current account the difference between a country's imports and exports of goods and services, adjusted to include such other items as investment income.

bankers' acceptance money market instrument similar to **commercial paper** except that its redemption is guaranteed by a bank.

Bank for International Settlements (BIS) acts as a central banker for other central banks which are its shareholders. Founded in 1930 in Basle, Switzerland, its primary purpose is to handle and coordinate foreign exchange settlements between member central banks. It also closely monitors major developments in world capital markets and extends collective but limited guarantees as a lender of last resort for the Eurocurrency banks. Recently it has taken a more active position by actively participating in some international debt rescheduling operations.

basic balance the difference between a country's balance on current account and its long term borrowing or lending transactions.

bid-ask spread the difference between the price a dealer will pay to buy a security (the bid) and the price the dealer charges (the ask) when selling it. The difference covers the dealer's operating expenses and any profits to the transaction.

block positioner see **position house**.

block trades trades in large numbers of shares, usually defined as single trades of 10,000 or more shares. See also **third market**, **fourth market** and **position house**.

bought deal an outright purchase of a new issue of securities, which are then distributed from inventory by the securities firm arranging the deal.

bridging finance the temporary financing provided to fund the purchase of the target company's shares until more permanent debt or equity financing can be arranged.

brokers securities firms that act as agents of others in buying and selling such items as financial instruments. Brokers, unlike **dealers**, do not trade on their own account. Rather, they act only to arrange transactions between parties.

certainty equivalent value the smallest value, to be paid for certain, that the holder of a risky prospect will accept in exchange for the prospect. The certainty equivalent value will be smaller than the expected value of the risky prospect whenever the investor is risk averse.

closed-end fund an investment company with a fixed capitalisation. The shares of a closed-end fund may trade either on an exchange or in the over-the-counter market. See also **open-end fund**.

commercial banks banks which emphasise deposit gathering, retail and commercial lending, but do not generally participate actively in the securities business. See also **universal banks**.

commercial paper money market instrument issued by a corporation and sold in the market for the purpose of raising short term funds. See also **bankers' acceptance**.

commitment fee fee charged by an international bank for agreeing to provide funds to a borrower under a syndicated loan arrangement. See also **management fee** and **participation fee**.

complete contracting a situation under risk in which all important outcomes can be described completely, and in which terms governing the actions to be taken in the event of such outcomes can also be described completely.

covered interest arbitrage a transaction in which a resident in one country invests short term in another country, covering the foreign exchange risk of the transaction through a forward sale of the investment returns.

credit derivatives instruments which pay the holder (usually a lender) in the event of a loan default. The idea of a credit derivative is similar to default insurance or to that of selling (putting) an asset to the issuer of a put for more than its current market price.

credit rationing equilibrium an equilibrium situation in which not all clients of a given class can obtain financing, even though all present the same risks. See also **financial market gap**.

currency swap an arrangement whereby one economic agent exchanges a payment in one currency for a payment in another, with the intention of subsequently reversing the transaction at a later date. Currency swaps are normally entered in order to reduce accounting measures of foreign exchange risk.

dealers securities firms that trade on their own account, taking securities purchases into inventory, selling securities out of inventory. See also **brokers**.

default risk the risk that a loan or investment will not be repaid, usually because the client has no funds with which to repay it. See also **market risk** and **profitability risk**.

deficit sector see **sector**

defined benefit plan a pension plan with specified payouts. It is contrasted with a defined contribution plan which specifies only the contributions into the fund.

delivery date the date the commitments under a forward contract must be carried out.

derivative securities (derivatives) securities whose returns depend on the value of some underlying asset against which they are written. For example, a call option on a stock is a derivative security whose value depends on the value of the underlying stock.

direct exchange rate (direct quote) the number of units of home currency purchased per unit of foreign currency. For example, in the United States a direct quote for deutschemarks would be expressed as US$/DEM. In November 1996 the number of US$ that could be purchased with one deutschemark was approximately 0.67. Thus to a resident of the US, a direct quote for deutschemarks would say 'the price is $0.67 US per deutschemark', just as one would say 'the price is $0.67 per tomato'. An indirect quote is the reciprocal of a direct quote: see **indirect exchange rate**.

direct investment see **foreign direct investment**

disintermediation the process whereby depository institutions, unable to pay market rates of interest because of restrictive regulation, lost deposit funds to alternative sources of savings, such as government securities.

effective exchange rates indices which measure the relative appreciation or depreciation of a country's currency against its major economic partners. Effective exchange rates are computed using weights taking account of the relative importance of a country's trading partners in its direct bilateral relations with them, of competitive relations with other countries in particular markets, of differences in the sensitivity of wages and prices to changes in import costs, of the commodity composition of trade, and of estimated elasticities affecting trade flows.

efficient markets hypothesis a theory that, in a competitive market equilibrium, all securities prices fully reflect all publicly available information relevant to determining their value. See also **law of one price**.

electronic funds transfer system (EFTS) a paperless funds transfer system. Examples of EFTS developments within the banking industry are automated clearing houses, point-of-sales payments systems and automatic teller systems.

European currency unit (ECU) a unit of account and a medium of exchange between participating central banks whose countries are members of the European Economic Community. The ECU is a composite currency formed by a basket of European Economic Community currencies. The currencies are held in weighted averages according to the economies' sizes and importance to trade, and the weights are adjusted periodically to reflect changes in the criteria. The value of the ECU is determined by the value of the individual currencies in the basket.

externality third party effect not reflected in the market price charged on a transaction. In the case of a financial system externality, the term refers to a third party effect not reflected in the interest rate charged on a financial arrangement.

finance company paper a short term promissory note, issued in a large amount and sold in the money market on a discount basis by a highly creditworthy financial corporation, such as an automobile finance company.

financial flow accounts see **funds flow accounts**

financial market gap a situation in which potential users of funds cannot raise funds at the market rate of interest for deals presenting that risk. If they can raise funds at all, their cost of doing so is higher than the market rate. See also **credit rationing equilibrium**.

Fisher relation a relation stating that the nominal interest rate on a transaction equals the real interest rate plus a premium intended to account for expected future inflation. Named after the economist Irving Fisher (1867–1947), who first pointed out the effect in the 1930s.

foreign direct investment the purchase of equity by non-nationals in order to acquire control of a company's operations.

foreign portfolio investment the purchase of shares or bonds by non-nationals for holding in an investment portfolio. Control over the firm is not sought by portfolio investors.

forward contract a financial instrument with a fixed term which provides for the purchase or sale of some asset at a fixed price. A forward contract is usually structured to have a value of zero at the time it is originated (see Chapter 7). See also **futures contract**.

forward exchange rate a rate at which two parties agree to exchange currencies that will be delivered and paid for at a future time, specified in the forward contract.

forward foreign exchange transaction a transaction in which parties agree to exchange currencies at some future date. See also **forward exchange rate** and **spot transaction**.

forward parity theory a theory which concludes that when arbitrage opportunities are eliminated, countries' real interest rates are equal.

fourth market a broker facility used for inter-institutional trading of large blocks of stock. See also **block trades** and **third market**.

funds flow accounts trace net borrowing or lending transactions between major sectors in the economy. The sectors defined in the accounts are households and unincorporated business, private non-financial business, government, private financial business and the rest of the world.

futures contract a contract like a **forward contract** except that it provides for interim settlement of any realised capital gains or losses. Like forward contracts, futures contracts can be written against many different kinds of assets. Like forward contracts, there can be capital gains or losses on a futures contract. Unlike forward contracts, the capital gains or losses on a futures contract are realised period by period in a process depending on the price of the underlying asset. When a futures contract is first issued, the usual practice is to issue it at a futures price that makes its initial value equal to zero.

gap the difference between an intermediary's floating rate assets and its floating rate liabilities. An intermediary with more floating rate assets than liabilities is said to have a positive gap, and one with more floating rate liabilities than assets is said to have a negative gap.

index linked bond a bond whose principal and interest payments are increased according to some index measuring the rate of domestic inflation.

indirect exchange rate (indirect quote) the number of units of foreign currency that can be purchased with a unit of domestic currency. For example, in the United States an indirect quote for deutschemarks would be expressed as DEM/US\$. In November 1996 the number of deutschemarks that could be purchased with one US dollar was approximately 1.50. Thus to a resident of the US, an indirect quote for deutschemarks would say 'the deutschemark price of one US dollar is DEM 1.50'. See also **direct exchange rate**.

inflation premium the percentage by which a **nominal rate of interest** exceeds a **real rate of interest**.

informational asymmetry a situation in which two parties do not share the same view of an arrangement's risk, either because they do not have access to the same data or because they interpret them differently.

insured pension plan a pension plan whose payouts are guaranteed by an insurance company.

interest elasticity a measure of the proportional change in the quantity of a transaction type that is attributable to a proportional change in the transaction's interest rate.

interest parity theory a theory which explains that arbitrage is likely to remove differences between real interest rates obtainable on investments of the same risk but in different currencies.

interest rate swap an arrangement whereby one economic agent, usually a financial institution, exchanges a pattern of interest rates with a counterparty, usually another financial institution. For example, a United States bank might exchange a pattern of floating interest rate costs with a Japanese bank in exchange for receiving the Japanese bank's fixed rate costs. Both parties enter swap transactions with a view to reducing their earnings risks, usually as measured in an accounting sense.

law of one price the result that in perfectly competitive markets two instruments offering exactly the same payments will trade at the same price. Similarly, in a perfectly competitive financial market any two riskless instruments of the same maturity will bear exactly the same riskless rate of return. See also **efficient markets hypothesis**.

leveraged buyout a takeover bid based on using substantial amounts of debt to finance the purchase of the target company's shares.

LIBOR the London Interbank Offered Rate for short term Eurocurrency loans. It is the most responsive money market price in the world, changing quickly in response to changing supplies or demands. LIBID, the London Interbank Bid Rate, is offered to market participants for large deposits.

long position an investor who owns an asset is said to have a long position in the asset. An investor who has entered a forward contract requiring him to purchase the asset is said to have a long position in the forward contract. See also **short position**.

management fee fee for performing the administrative work of arranging a syndicated loan. See also **commitment fee** and **participation fee**.

market failure a situation in which economically viable deals cannot be agreed, usually because of informational differences between financier and client which mean that the quality of the deal cannot accurately be assessed by the financier.

market risk the risk of fluctuations in market price due to changes in demand–supply conditions. See also **default risk**.

money market market for trading highly liquid, short term securities of high quality.

moral hazard the possibility that client behaviour will change as a result of the deal being arranged.

neglected shares a term used to refer to shares whose **price–earnings ratios** are judged to be atypically low, given the degree of risk the share represents. Most neglected shares are issued by relatively small companies, and their low price–earnings ratios reflect a kind of market segmentation.

nominal rate of interest the rate of interest on a transaction collected in contemporary currency units without any adjustment for changes in price levels, that is the purchasing power of the currency units. See also **real rate of interest**.

off-balance sheet financing a process of raising funds in such a manner that the client does not incur a direct financial obligation. As an example of incurring a direct financial obligation, a client may purchase an asset and borrow the funds to pay for it. The same transaction could be financed off-balance sheet if the client arranged to lease the asset from a financial leasing firm. In this case both the ownership of the asset and the direct liability for the asset are found on the balance sheet of the leasing company and not on that of the client actually using the asset.

open-end fund an investment company which continuously issues shares in response to demand for them. An open-end fund will also redeem shares at the current market value of the investment. See also **closed-end fund**.

open outcry a method of trading assets in which interested parties gather around a trading post to signal the terms on which they are willing to buy or sell. Much of the trading activity is carried out using hand and eye signals, often accompanied by a good deal of shouted communication.

operational efficiency a property of a financial market in which agents carrying out transactions do so at the lowest possible cost.

option a contract that permits its holder to trade in a security at a fixed price, either on a given date or over a given time interval, should the holder elect to do so. A contract that permits a purchase is known as a call option; one that permits a sale is known as a put option. Options can be written to permit exercise either on a given date or over a given time interval. Instruments which can be exercised only on a given date are called European options, while those which can be exercised at any time within a given interval are called American options.

over-the-counter (OTC) markets markets for trading securities other than those listed on stock exchanges. In the OTC markets most transactions are carried out between clients and brokers over the telephone as opposed to a physical location like a stock exchange. Some OTC markets, such as NASDAQ (National Association of Securities Dealers Automated Quotation Service) in the US, have trades, especially in the larger issues, conducted by dealers as well as brokers.

participation fee fee charged by an international bank for actually providing some of the funds to a borrower under a syndicated loan arrangement. See also **commitment fee** and **management fee**.

pass-through securities securities created when mortgage holders pool mortgages and sell shares or participation certificates in the pool.

portfolio investment see **foreign portfolio investment**

position house (block positioner) wholesale dealer in securities, specialising in institutional trading of large amounts. See also **block trades**.

price–earnings ratio a share will trade in the market at a price which is some multiple of its current earnings per share. For example, if a bank has current earnings per share of $5.00, its stock might trade at $30.00, in which case the price–earnings ratio would be 6. The share would also be said to trade at a multiple of six time earnings. A low price–earnings ratio may be taken by the market as an indication that a share's price is less than its expected earnings would warrant. Clearly, there is room for difference of interpretation since the price–earnings ratio is determined by current earnings, and since different analysts might well differ in their forecasts of the relation between current and future earnings.

primary transaction one involving the raising of new funds by the creation of new financial instruments. See also **secondary transaction**.

private markets markets in which securities are traded between a small number of parties on the basis of information developed in their negotiations with each other. Thus information about private market transactions is usually less widely distributed than it is for **public market** transactions. A negotiated sale of company debt to a pension fund which buys the whole issue is an example of a private market transaction.

profitability risk the risk that a loan or investment will not yield its rate of return with certainty. See also **default risk**.

program trading using computers for automated portfolio trading. Usually large numbers of stocks are traded both simultaneously and frequently.

public markets securities markets in which large well-known issues are both floated for the first time and traded after their original flotation. Information about the nature of public market securities is usually widely and relatively evenly distributed. The New York Stock Exchange and the London Stock Exchange are examples of public markets. See also **private markets**.

purchasing power parity theory a theory which says that agents think in terms of buying power rather than in terms of local prices.

put-call parity a relationship in options pricing theory which says that the value of a sure thing can be arranged using a portfolio consisting of a long position in an asset, accompanied by an (appropriately adjusted) short position in a call and a long position in a put. Both options are written against the asset; both have the same exercise price and maturity.

real rate of interest the rate of interest on a transaction after it is adjusted for any changes in the purchasing power of the currency, that is the interest rate in constant purchasing power terms. See also **nominal rate of interest**.

risk a risky financial deal is one whose earnings cannot be determined exactly in advance.

risk adjusted interest rate an interest rate, higher than the risk free rate when investors are risk averse, that is used to discount expected values of future risky payments.

risk adjusted probability a measure, defined in the absence of arbitrage opportunities, used to value instruments in relation to each other. The measure is used exactly like a probability is used to calculate an expected value. Risk adjusted probabilities are often called an equivalent martingale measure. Valuation using risk adjusted probabilities is sometimes referred to as using a risk-neutral valuation method.

risk aversion a preference for less rather than more risk when the expected return on an arrangement is kept constant.

risk loving a preference for more rather than less risk when the expected return on an arrangement is kept constant.

risk premium the difference between the expected interest rate on a transaction and the risk free rate.

scale economies the ability to produce additional units of output at a decreasing average cost per unit. Scale economies frequently arise from spreading fixed production costs over a larger number of units of output. See also **scope economies**.

scope economies the ability to obtain combinations of goods or services at a lower average cost per unit than can be achieved if the goods or services are produced individually. Scope economies, sometimes called cost complementarities, usually result from the ability to share common inputs. See also **scale economies**.

secondary transaction one involving trades in existing securities. It represents a reallocation of existing financing rather than the creation of a new arrangement. See also **primary transaction**.

sector a group of like units for purpose of economic analysis. The financial flow accounts use households and unincorporated businesses, non-financial business, financial business, government and the rest of the world as their principal sectors. A surplus sector's savings exceeds its investment expenditure; a deficit sector's savings falls short of its investment.

segmentation the partial separation of financial markets resulting in the same arrangements being available on different terms, especially different interest rates, in different markets.

serial redemption bonds bonds whose terms provide that a certain number of the issue will be redeemed at regular intervals. The bonds to be redeemed are chosen by either selecting their serial numbers in a lottery or simply buying the bonds in the market.

short position a short position is the opposite of a long position. An investor who has sold an asset before acquiring it is said to have a short position in the asset. An investor who has entered a forward contract requiring her to sell the asset is said to have a short position in the forward contract.

sinking fund bonds bonds issued on terms which provide for gradually building up a repayment fund, called a sinking fund, to finance retirement of the bonds. The bonds may be retired either all at once or serially at several points in time.

spot exchange rate the market exchange rate at which one currency can immediately be exchanged for another. The term 'immediate' means 'at once' for small amounts of currency, but with a delay of two or fewer working days in the case of larger electronic funds transfers. For example, in Canada, large amounts of US dollars purchased in the spot market are usually delivered on the following working day. In the US, large amounts of say French francs are usually delivered on the second working day after a deal is done.

spot transaction a foreign exchange transaction in which immediate delivery is specified. See **spot exchange rate** and **forward foreign exchange transaction**.

surplus sector see **sector**.

swap contract a financial instrument providing for an exchange of currencies or of interest rate payments, valid over some fixed period of time (see Chapter 7).

syndicated loans loans to a given client provided by a number of banks. They are usually arranged by a single lead bank which, in addition to the interest it receives on its own portion of the loan, receives a commission for arranging the entire transaction.

synthetic insured portfolio a portfolio composed of proxies for riskless securities, such as treasury bills, and derivatives such as stock index futures, intended to emulate the risk–return performance of a diversified stock portfolio.

third market a specialised facility in which institutions trade large blocks of stock between themselves through dealers known as **position houses**. See also **block trades** and **fourth market**.

universal banks banks which make loans to client companies, own shares in client companies, arrange securities underwritings for their clients, engage in secondary market trading, and provide brokerage and trust services for their clients. Some, especially German, universal banks have also long been active in selling insurance. See also **commercial banks**.

upstairs market a network of trading arrangements between major securities firms and institutional investors, communicating with each other by telephone and electronic display systems, designed to facilitate trading in large amounts of individual shares or simultaneous trading in large numbers of different shares.

Notes

1 INTRODUCTION

1 Even though every effort will be made to give full explanations of technical terms, it will not always be possible to do so when a term is first mentioned. In these cases the term is shown in bold type, indicating both that it is defined in the glossary at the end of the book and that it will be more fully explained at a later point in the text.

2 ROLES AND CLIENTS

1 A risky financial deal is one whose earnings cannot be determined exactly in advance. Rather, the earnings can be described only in terms of a probability distribution.

2 Of course, not every financial system performs every one of its functions with equal smoothness and equal efficiency. The issues of how well a system serves an economy are examined in Part V.

3 Spending is defined as spending on consumption goods and on the value of services provided by durable goods. If you buy a car, for example, the amount you are deemed to spend in, say, the first year you own it is equal to the services provided by the car, and not the whole of its purchase price.

4 The terminology in the UK and the US is 'Flow of Funds' or 'Funds Flow' accounting. Some other countries, such as Canada, use the terminology 'Financial Flow' accounts.

5 Technical terms are also listed in a glossary at the end of the book.

6 Usually, the clearing houses of the exchange on which the instruments trade.

7 Over-the-counter markets are discussed in Chapter 12.

8 The statement should not be taken to mean that the financial system either does, or ought to, arrange financings at non-market rates of interest. Rather, it means that the availability of funds at market rates may be increased, that the non-interest transactions costs of arranging financings are lowered, or both.

9 Chapters 15 and 16 will show how specialised financial intermediaries can play important roles in assessing particular kinds of deals.

10 The main definition of a technical term is given in the chapter of the book which discusses the related concepts in detail. The book's glossary also provides all the definitions, intended to be useful when a technical term is raised only in passing.

11 These effects might not occur if the country can borrow abroad readily. However, if a country's credit rating is not first rate, possibly as a result of previous borrowing, it might not be possible to raise funds abroad, or at least not to raise them without increasing interest rates.

12   The analysis presumes the economy is at or near full employment. Macroeconomic theory explains that under conditions of less than full employment, government spending can result in employment creation rather than inflation.

3 FINANCIAL SYSTEM ORGANISATION

1   As Chapters 15 through 17 discuss in greater detail, even large multipurpose financial firms specialise their operations to some degree. In addition, they tend to organise particular, related functions in separate business units. For example, a bank may have a lending unit and a securities trading unit.

2   Financial engineers like to emphasise the differences between instruments used for risk management. However, for explanatory purposes it is more important to recognise the instruments' similarities.

3   As will be shown later in the book, it can be helpful in specific discussions to recognise further variations in three principal attributes.

4   In some cases, one party may see uncertainty where another sees risk.

5   Portfolios of such deals are somewhat easier to value, as will be discussed later.

6   Williamson (1988) stresses the importance of asset specificity as a deal attribute. This book uses the similar (but not identical) concepts of asset liquidity, mainly because financiers are principally concerned with the likelihood that an asset can quickly be sold in a secondary market for a price at or near its market value.

7   Without taking any marketable security as collateral.

8   Institutional investors with large shareholdings in a given company sometimes influence its board. In this case they are employing a higher capability governance structure than is usually employed by market agents.

9   Information about the quality of securitised mortgages may be public, but that is information about portfolio quality. This form of public information may well reflect the kinds of processes the intermediary uses in its screening, but will typically not reflect information about individual loans in the portfolio.

10   Keiretsu are groups of firms with interrelated shareholdings. The firms within the keiretsu typically give business preference to other keiretsu members, and the keiretsu's main bank often takes a seat on the board of client companies experiencing financial difficulties.

11   A universal bank is a bank that also performs such other functions as underwriting or selling securities. In Germany universal banks own share positions in some of their larger client companies.

12   The problem of determining asset values is particularly apparent in deals involving the privatisation of former public sector firms.

13   Technically, diversification is effective only if the different deals are not perfectly positively correlated. This topic is examined in Chapter 6.

4 CHANGE

1   'The whole forced necessity of doing things frightens me. You cannot afford to do nothing. But when things go wrong they have a habit of going wrong everywhere' (Leon Levi: quoted in *The Economist*, Survey 34, July 11, 1987).

2   'We are concerned only to emphasize the fact that knowledge is in a sense variable in degree and that the practical problem may relate to the degree of knowledge rather than to its presence or absence' (Knight 1921: 199).

3   The Big Bang was an important deregulatory move in which (i) computerised trading was established, (ii) securities firms that traded in the United States and Japan were permitted for the first time to trade on the London Stock Exchange, and (iii) fixed minimum commissions on stock trades were eliminated. One of the

most significant features of the Big Bang was that it allowed investment firms which had previously traded only in New York and Tokyo to create a nearly 24-hour operation by trading in London as well.

4   Porter (1992) argues that stock markets use myopic valuation, but the issue is controversial. Yu (1997) finds no evidence of short-termism in a body of US data for publicly traded firms.

5   These remarks describe the advantages of closely monitored individual transactions, and do not apply directly to the management of an entire financial system. Japanese and German banks, especially the former, have experienced large loan losses during the early and mid-1990s. These loan losses are attributable to a complex of factors, many of them not directly connected to their use of closely monitored transactions. In other words, the difficulties of a financial system do not imply that particular practices in that financial system are without advantage.

5 FINANCIAL SYSTEMS: AN EMPIRICAL OVERVIEW

1   The sizes of the errors also change over time, as the accounts are first presented in preliminary form, then revised in subsequent publications.

2   Direct comparisons of these ratios may be misleading. The extent to which the differences are attributable to differences in tax treatment, legislative environments, and customary practice has yet to be established.

3   For detailed analytical purposes, the sectors are sometimes divided into subsectors.

4   Changes in sector balance sheets are usually expressed in nominal currency units, and are thus affected by price level change.

5   While the discussion focuses on the main changes, the actual estimation of the accounts uses greater detail than is indicated here.

6   The financial sector does spend some funds on capital formation. To the extent these investment expenditures exceed the financial sector's savings (profits), the financial sector is a deficit sector. However, these effects are small in relation to the sector's total borrowing or total lending.

7   Including the rest of the world sector if the economy is not a closed economy.

8   Investment companies are known as mutual funds in the US.

9   While it is common to refer to shares in the UK, in the US the preferred terminology is stocks. This book uses equities to refer to shares, and bonds to refer to debt instruments.

6 PRINCIPLES OF ASSET PRICING

1   In practice, the financial markets witness both the (riskless) arbitrage opportunities discussed in this chapter and the trading of instruments in what is sometimes called risk arbitrage. The latter term, used only in practice, describes such transactions as purchasing shares of a potential takeover target in the hope of making a profit.

2   There are exceptions to this statement, regarding both convergence to an equilibrium and the credit rationing equilibrium of Stiglitz and Weiss (1981). However, the conditions under which the exceptions occur are not important for the central purposes of this book.

3   It would be more nearly accurate to say that such an opportunity is one that presents no risk of loss, since there is some chance of making zero, and some chance of making a positive profit.

4   Note, however, that financial markets must be such that you can borrow the money, and in this case at the risk free rate. In practice, an idea's value cannot always be

realised, mainly because lenders or investors may not discern the value of the project and thus may not be willing to put up the money to finance it.

5   If the prospect has only two possible outcomes, its value is sufficient for determining the risk adjusted probability distribution. If prospects have three outcomes, the values of two instruments will be needed to find the risk adjusted probability distribution, and so on.

6   The procedure is sometimes, misleadingly, called risk neutral valuation. The method uses expected value calculations that would be valid if investors required no premium to take on risks, but it uses pseudo probabilities that adjust for the risk. Under risk neutrality the lottery in the example would be worth $100.00/1.10 rather than $97.90/1.10.

7   As will be seen, there is a sense in which the first theory is a specialised version of the second.

8   The arbitraging transactions envisioned in the CAPM can be either riskless or risky. If they are riskless, they involve trading instruments with the same value of β. If they are risky, they involve trading instruments with different values of β. If they accept the underlying assumptions of the CAPM, arbitrageurs know how to value instruments with different βs relative to each other.

9   There is also a multi-factor CAPM due to Merton.

10   Some relatively close equivalents, such as inflation adjusted bonds, can be found. But even these are not entirely riskless since the inflation adjustment may be imperfect.

11   In many calculations the Fisher relation is reported as the real rate plus the inflation rate, that is as 10 percent + 5 percent in the present example. When this is done, the product $(1 + r)(1 + i)$ is approximated by $1 + r + i$, ignoring the term ri. The term ri is small if both the nominal rate and the inflation rate are small, but this is not always the case. For example, during one year in Bolivia, the rate of inflation was 30,000 percent (see p. 84).

12   Estimates of liquidity premiums appear to increase quite rapidly for a year or two, then relatively slowly in successive years.

13   But do not let this observation deceive you into believing that even the two year investment is completely riskless. It is subject to an opportunity risk, because if you decide to hold the bond for two years come what may, you cannot then take advantage of any unanticipated changes in interest rates.

7 DIVIDING AND PRICING RISKS

1   The firm may wish to tailor the securities it issues as a possible means of obtaining funding either more easily, or at lower cost. In the perfectly competitive markets of this chapter, tailoring securities will not affect their prices, and consequently the firm's cost of funds will also remain unchanged. However, when a firm has to negotiate its financings in imperfectly competitive markets tailoring may have an influence on the cost of funds. These matters are discussed further in Chapters 8 through 11 of Part II, as well as in subsequent parts of the book.

2   There are, however, exceptions. Some debt issues are accompanied by option-like instruments called warrants designed to improve the marketability of the debt. Other debt issues are convertible, meaning they have a built-in option to exchange the debt for equity.

3   The price S is referred to in an options context as an exercise price. It is called a forward price in the present context.

4   The price of $1.91 is determined under the assumption the individual promising to buy the firm will not default; if there were some possibility the contracting individual might default on her obligation, the purchaser would pay less to enter the contract.

5   There are other types of options, called exotics, not referred to in this introduction. For example, Asian options have payoffs determined relative to the underlying asset's average, rather than its current price. For further discussion, the interested reader should consult such standard references as Jarrow and Turnbull (1996) or Hull (1991).

6   If there were never any disequilibrium prices, there would never be any opportunity for arbitrageurs to make profits, and hence the function would not be performed. The practical difficulty for most prospective traders is finding disequilibrium prices before the arbitrageurs locate and eliminate them.

7   The most popular options pricing model, developed using riskless hedge arguments, is the continuous time model originally developed by Black and Scholes (1973). Detailed discussions of the Black–Scholes model can be found in, for example, Cox and Rubinstein (1985) and Hull (1989).

8   They are both performing the same function in this chapter. But in later chapters we show that bank loans differ from bond investments because typically the bank has greater governance capability than the bond investor.

9   Known, famously in this context, as the Modigliani–Miller Theorem.

10 This section is based on Jarrow and Turnbull (1996: 55–62).

8 FINANCIAL GOVERNANCE

1   While no transactions charges are paid, all deals have to pay, or earn, the ruling market interest rate appropriate for the deal's risk.

2   Practical knowledge – 'know how' – is frequently harder to transmit than theoretical knowledge – 'knowing why'.

3   Williamson (1988) demonstrates the importance of asset specificity as a deal attribute; in the present context it is useful to refer to asset specificity as asset liquidity.

4   While it may formally be possible to write down a probability distribution, if it is highly diffuse it will not be of much practical assistance in deciding on a deal's profitability.

5   The above normal profits can persist until the deal becomes standard and the markets for it competitive.

9 PORTFOLIO GOVERNANCE

1   While most bank deposits are not market traded instruments, the interest rates on them do change regularly with market conditions.

2   If the holding represents a control block or a large proportion of an issue, selling it off may not be straightforward.

3   Orthodox portfolio selection theory does not distinguish between income and default risks, since for the theory's purposes both concepts can be incorporated satisfactorily in return distributions. As a practical matter, default risk becomes more important in the case of asset specific investments, as discussed below.

4   Portfolio theory recognises that not all asset combinations reduce risk. Indeed, it is possible to construct portfolios whose risk exceeds that of its individual components. For example, a security purchased on margin forms a portfolio with greater risk than the underlying security, even if the margin loan carries a riskless rate of interest.

5   As an example of using options to increase risk, buying and holding stock options rather than the stocks themselves can be used to create a portfolio with both higher expected returns and a higher risk of achieving that return.

6   When it is contrasted with market risk, default risk is often referred to as credit risk. We use the term default risk to relate the concepts now being examined to discussions of the same concept in other parts of the book.

7   The issue is more than one of just failing to update the books to reflect changes in value. In some cases the intermediary can be unaware of any changes in potential value until default is imminent.

8   As section 9.2.4 discusses, it seems at first glance that asset illiquidity has changed with the advent of securitisation. However, the change results, not from the fact that the individual loans are more liquid than previously, but from the fact that banks and other lenders have discovered how to issue relatively liquid securities secured by portfolios of illiquid instruments.

9   Even if the default risk is insured, the insurance company will set premiums on the default risk insurance according to its estimates of how screening and monitoring are being performed.

10   While some instruments used in securitising are guaranteed as to principal, that does not obviate performing the screening and monitoring functions either. The cost of the insurance depends on confidence in the intermediary's capabilities to perform its role.

11   In the case of venture investments taking the form of public equity issues, the public does not exercise high capability governance. However, the venture capitalist doing the financing prior to the firm's going public probably did resort to higher capability governance. At the time the firm goes public, there might also be some overestimation of its worth on the part of the new purchasers of the equity. The firm would, of course, want to take advantage of any overpricing of its equity, because that lowers its cost of funds.

12   A perfect positive correlation between interest revenues and interest costs has the same effect as a perfect negative correlation between earnings on two different securities.

13   From an economist's point of view, the swap should be entered only if it increases the firm's net present value, and in perfectly competitive markets the kind of swap now being discussed could not increase net present value. In imperfectly competitive markets with transactions costs, an increase in value is a possibility, but not one that is assessed here. Rather, the approach taken here is to argue that decreasing the risk of reported accounting earnings is likely to have a positive impact on the firm's net present value. The approach is crude in the sense that decreasing the risk of accounting earnings may not maximise the increase in the firm's net present value. Even so, the approach illustrates at least some of the considerations underlying the use of swaps.

14   Whether such transactions are privately negotiated or arranged in markets depends on transaction features discussed in Chapter 3.

10 DEALS' TERMS

1   Assuming the financiers are competing for business and do not see much room to increase effective interest rates to compensate for taking on the additional risk.

11 MARKET TRADING AND INTERMEDIATION

1   Arbitraging in its technical sense means profiting from trades without taking any risk. In a broader sense, arbitraging is also used to mean trading that involves attempts to buy low and sell high, even if some risk is involved. We use the term 'trading' to refer to this second form of usage.

2   The practice is so well known that traders have a name for the reversion to normal conditions. The time when uncertainty is resolved to the traders' satisfaction is referred to as the time 'when the dust settles'.

3   For example, Domowitz, Glen and Madhavan find that 'ownership restrictions effectively segment the equity market in Mexico' (1997: 1083).

4   The statement assumes that any local optimum is also a global optimum (i.e., that only a single optimum obtains).

5   The theoretical model of a competitive equilibrium has the desirable property that prices exactly cover both the social and the private costs of production.

6   The point is not that the interest rate is somehow incorrect, but that it does not reflect the net social gain or cost to the transaction. The example of the export industry in the next paragraph argues that a bank's (private sector) interest earnings on a loan to finance exports will not typically reflect such social benefits as the employment creation following on the growth of export business made possible by the bank lending.

7   The phenomenon seemed to remain even after attempts were made to allow for inter-country differences in valuation methods.

12 DOMESTIC FINANCIAL MARKETS

1   Stock exchanges in the US have specialists who are the only traders entitled to make a market in a given stock. In return for this privilege, specialists are required to purchase or sell stocks for which they receive orders at market prices.

2   Sometimes, government bonds up to three years to maturity are regarded as money market instruments because of their high degree of liquidity.

3   Although equities are called stocks in the US and shares in the UK, the exchanges on which they trade are usually called stock exchanges in both countries.

4   The first through fourth markets are respectively the exchange markets for listed stocks, the OTC markets for unlisted stocks, the dealer markets created for block trades by independent position houses, and the market for direct trading between institutions.

5   'Only a few markets of the world use the specialist system. Most markets employ some form of the competitive dealer system. . . . Computerization has been quite consistent with the competitive dealer system' (Fabozzi, Modigliani and Ferri 1994).

6   In the UK, bonds are usually traded on the stock exchanges.

7   It is not impossible to find undervalued stocks and to earn above normal returns on them, but most portfolio managers seem unable to obtain returns in excess of the cost of finding them. On the other hand 'evidence based on the activities of insiders has generally revealed that insiders consistently outperform the stock market' (Fabozzi and Modigliani 1992: 254).

8   For a review of these effects, see Fabozzi and Modigliani (1992).

9   In the absence of arbitrage opportunities, if the value of the firm was known it would be possible to estimate the value of both riskless and risky debt. The point being made here is that the principle of riskless arbitrage does not take into account all the features of financial distress that are relevant to potential bond purchasers.

10 Standard and Poor's letter grades range from AAA (highest) to D (lowest), while Moody's range from Aaa (highest) to C (lowest).

11 Existing studies do not suggest that investing in portfolios of high yield bonds offers exceptional value, but rather an increase in return commensurate with an increase in risk (Fabozzi and Modigliani 1992: 497). However, the innovators in the market may well have received, or at least may well have believed they would receive, excess returns for establishing the new form of financing.

13 MARKETS FOR RISK TRADING

1   Other reasons for trading risks include different portfolio positions and different estimates of probabilities. These motives are discussed in later chapters.
2   Technically, the guarantee is usually provided by an instrumentality of the exchange. For example, options traded on the Chicago Board Options Exchange are guaranteed by the Chicago Board's Options Clearing Corporation.
3   With the framework just illustrated, it is easy to value American options as well. To recognise the early exercise feature, the expected values at times 1 through 3 are replaced with the maximum of the expected value or the payoff to intermediate exercise. Then the calculations are carried backward as in the illustration.
4   If there are several issuers of puts, the actual seller required to honour a given obligation is usually selected at random by an agency of the exchange.
5   Performance guarantees are not universally available. Following the stock market crash of October 19, 1987, performance under option contracts traded on the Hong Kong Options Exchange was suspended. Defaults were eventually avoided as market participants assembled an emergency fund to meet the obligations of failed or failing firms. Defaults also occurred on the London Metals Exchange about two years earlier, where contracts were not guaranteed by the Exchange.
6   The counterparties in trading forward contracts are usually well known to each other. For this reason the question of assessing counterparty risk, although important, is less urgent than in the case of trading futures contracts, where the parties are not likely to be well known to each other. Thus in the absence of a clearing house guarantee the parties trading futures contracts would usually have to investigate each others' credit ratings before they could deal.
7   Marché à Terme Internationale de France.
8   Deutsche Termin Börse.
9   That is, the accounting risk has been removed. In practice, it is not uncommon to use an accounting criterion rather than the economist's criterion of maximising the net present value of the cash flows.
10   Technically, a spot transaction in US dollars provides for delivery in one day. In most other currencies delivery is in two days.
11   This form of spot rate quotation, number of foreign currency units per unit of domestic currency, is used in the UK and is sometimes called the indirect or left quote. In Europe a spot rate is usually quoted as number of domestic currency units per unit of foreign currency. The second is, of course, the reciprocal of the first. See also the entries for **direct exchange rate** and **indirect exchange rate** in the Glossary.

14 INTERNATIONAL FINANCIAL MARKETS

1   Even under a fixed exchange rate system, currency values cannot be kept fixed for very long if the financial markets reach a consensus that the values do not reflect underlying economic reality.
2   Assuming that no long term borrowing has been arranged.
3   Investors' demands are also affected by the supplies of instruments issued by other nations.
4   If it is assessed using index linked bonds, then the Fisher relation holds by definition. For the index linked bond rate is taken to be the real rate, and the difference between this and nominal rates is attributed to inflation.
5   Lower but not zero. Even in the absence of regulatory requirements, banks hold some reserves for their own business reasons.
6   The limit on the amount of funds created depends on the amount customarily retained for reserves, just as in the domestic economy the customary reserve ratio implies a theoretical limit to the money multiplier.

15 PRINCIPLES OF INTERMEDIATION

1　According to the jurisdiction and the type of intermediary business (bank, savings intermediary, securities firm, insurance company) client insurance against losses may be provided either by public or private sector agencies.

2　The lack of evidence for scale diseconomies may simply mean that management is aware of when scale diseconomies start to manifest themselves and prevent the intermediary from reaching such a size.

3　Venture firms operating as agents or divisions of banks may not need to demonstrate annual profits on their investments, but can rather invest their funds with a view to generating longer term earnings.

4　Skills that can be taught in the classroom become an employment requirement in a competitive industry. For example, the skills needed to make working capital loans against the security of accounts receivable security are easily taught, and new personnel might be expected at least to absorb them quickly. On the other hand, at least some of the skills needed to identify good prospects for mergers or promising venture capital opportunities are difficult to teach in a classroom setting and are usually gained from experience.

5　Recently, some financial institutions have begun attempting to sell the information they have produced.

6　Gap management is a practical technique using accounting concepts to stabilise earnings. Gap management does not necessarily ensure that the present value of the intermediary's cash flows are being maximised, as economic theory would advocate. At this juncture banks have not fully worked out practical ways of reconciling the two approaches, although such models are quite likely to appear in the future.

7　To some extent the borrower's risk may be offset by capital gains on real assets purchased with the mortgage financing. But interest rate risk is experienced in the short run, and capital gains are usually realised only in the long run. Thus even when one offsets the other the borrower can still face cash flow problems attributable to interest rate risk.

8　Usually some cash will also be held, but since cash yields no return while short term government securities yield at least a low interest rate, the proportion of cash to government securities will be kept as low as possible.

9　The capacity to raise additional funds is also related to the intermediary's ability to make profitable loans.

10　International banks are not required to hold reserves against Eurodollar deposits. Since 1995, Canada has adopted a zero required reserves policy: its banks no longer face formal cash reserve requirements. The Bank of England also has a zero reserve policy, although the Bank also requires the maintenance of a cash ratio levy – currently 0.35 percent of an institution's specified liabilities – to finance the Bank's operations that are not associated with the issuance of banknotes.

11　For profitability reasons to be discussed below the intermediary will never hold more cash reserves or capital than the required minimum. Therefore, even though regulations actually take the form of inequality constraints, in the present model it is reasonable to regard them as equalities.

12　Some analysts prefer to express the spread in relation to earning assets.

13　This will increase market value, at least as long as the risk is not viewed by the market as increasing too much. In normal circumstances the market does not change its estimate of intermediary earnings risk very often or very much.

16 DOMESTIC INTERMEDIATION

1　The reserve requirements discussed in Chapter 15 add to the costs of a bank's deposits. In some jurisdictions, such as Canada, banks no longer face regulatory requirements to hold reserves. Even so, as the analysis of Chapter 15 indicated, banks will still hold funds if they anticipate cash outflows; zero required reserves does not necessarily mean the banks also have zero desired reserves.

2 Consumer loans were often secured by chattel mortgages against such assets as automobiles. Mortgage loans were secured by a mortgage against the borrower's residence.

3 Even so, traditional forms of deposits continue to remain an important source of funds, particularly for retail banks. For example, as at December 1993, UK retail banks attracted 64 percent of their funds in the form of sterling deposits, about half of which – known as sight deposits in the UK – are payable on demand.

4 The practices vary according to jurisdiction. For example, banks and trust companies have conducted combined operations in the US for a long time, while countries like Canada have just begun to permit this combination. Despite variations between countries, the trend toward combining several financial businesses is world-wide.

5 Saunders (1994: 47) implies that US load funds charge no annual administration fee, while no-load funds charge fees as high as 1.25 percent.

6 Canadian banks are not currently permitted to sell insurance products in their branches, but they offer the products over the telephone and through direct mail campaigns.

17 INTERNATIONAL INTERMEDIATION

1 Similarly, computerised textile design was largely focused in Hong Kong during the early 1990s.

2 The management of both interest rate risk and foreign exchange risks has already been discussed in earlier chapters.

3 There is still an opportunity risk, as discussed in Chapter 6.

4 When the counterparties are well known to each other, the advantage of a futures contract, that marking to market reduces default risk, has less importance.

5 Both Japanese securities firms and Japanese banks are large, but currently unprofitable. Their ability to continue dominating the international scene depends importantly on their ability to resolve their current profitability problems.

6 Feldstein (*The Economist*, June 1995) stresses the difficulties individual countries have in borrowing substantial amounts over a sustained period. The Feldstein–Horioka Paradox reflects findings that despite the growth of international capital markets, a country's long term investment is usually quite closely related to its long term savings. That is, most financing of longer term projects, for most countries, still seems to come from domestic sources.

7 There may well be political or humanitarian arguments for providing some countries with funds despite their weak credit ratings. Recall, for example, the Chapter 3 discussion of agricultural finance. However, these arguments really have nothing to do with the question of a capital shortage, but are rather arguments about whether the outcomes of market allocation processes might be altered, again for political or humanitarian reasons. Finally, if capital markets suffer from a lack of appropriate information and ability to take an appropriate form of security, both of which factors informed the case of agricultural finance in underdeveloped countries, the humanitarian arguments might also have a sound economic backing.

8 For example, the traders at Barings Bank in essence bet large sums of money on the premise that the Nikkei Index would not move outside a certain range. When it did, because of the 1995 Kobe earthquake, the bank became insolvent. Most observers would regard this as an argument for better risk control within institutions, but not as a problem with the risk management activity itself.

18 GOVERNMENT FINANCIAL ACTIVITY

1   Source: *Statistical Abstract of the United States*, 1994.
2   While not currently available, such schemes have a long established precedent: the code of Hammurabi provides that the lender to a farmer can extract no payment in a bad crop year.

19 SUPERVISION

1   Chapter 18 considered the exceptional circumstances of addressing capital market gaps and of intervention aimed at securing social benefits.
2   In practice markets exhibit widely differing degrees of competitiveness. Most would agree that markets like the New York Stock Exchange are highly competitive, while the market for exchanges of shares in a transition economy, if it exists at all, does not exhibit enough trading at or near market prices to be called competitive. In banking markets there is much controversy about whether, say, markets for deposits or loans in different locales are equally competitive.
3   This is not to claim that small numbers of firms can never earn any oligopoly profits! It is only to observe that there have been no reported problems of fraud within the foreign exchange market, largely because it has been in the long run interests of a few large incumbents to maintain the market's impeccable reputation. The question of whether profits are above competitive levels does not seem to have been studied empirically.
4   The principle is sometimes referred to as one of assigning the rabbits to guard the lettuce patch.
5   Countries that provide deposit insurance usually do so up to some limit, which may apply to more than a single account, and in addition sometimes require depositor co-insurance. For example, in the US deposit insurance limits are $100,000 and there is no co-insurance. The limit is administered per account and a depositor may be able to insure a sum of more than $100,000 by appropriate structuring of accounts. The maximum value insured in the UK is £20,000 and the percentage repaid is 75 percent.
6   The G-10 group actually consists of eleven countries: Belgium, Canada, France, Germany, Italy, Japan, the Netherlands, Sweden, Switzerland, the United Kingdom and the United States.

20 TOWARD THE FUTURE

1   Japan and Germany, as well as other Asian and European economies, had experienced unprecedented financial turbulence. However, North America and the United Kingdom (despite the ravages of war damage) had continued to maintain relatively stable financial systems, even during the height of the conflict.
2   There are obvious moral hazard problems with the sale of credit derivatives, but so far these difficulties do not seem to have been given much attention, either by the banks purchasing the risk coverage or by the institutions selling it. Yet, if a bank can sell off much of its loan risk, what happens to its incentive to pursue bad loans? If the bank does not do so, will the writer of the credit derivative? Does the latter have the same skills as the former for collecting slow-pay loans?

References

Abuaf, Niso and Philippe Jorion (1990), 'Purchasing Power Parity in the Long Run,' *Journal of Finance* 45, 157–174.

Albert, Michel (1993), *Capitalism vs. Capitalism*, New York: Four Walls Eight Windows.

Allen, Franklin (1993), 'Stock Markets and Resource Allocation,' in Colin Mayer and Xavier Vives (eds) *Capital Markets and Financial Intermediation*, Cambridge: Cambridge University Press.

Arbel, Avner and Paul Strebel (1983), 'Pay Attention to Neglected Firms,' *Journal of Portfolio Management* 11, 37–42.

Bank of England (1995), *Quarterly Bulletin* 35, 4.

Baum, Theodor (1994), 'The German Banking System and its Impact on Corporate Finance and Governance,' in M. Aoki and H. Patrick (eds) *The Japanese Main Bank System*, Oxford: Oxford University Press.

Benson, E. D. (1979), 'The Search for Information by Underwriters and its Impact on Municipal Interest Cost,' *Journal of Finance* 34, 871–885.

Berger, A. and D. B. Humphrey (1991), 'The Dominance of Inefficiencies over Scale and Product Mix in Banking,' *Journal of Monetary Economics* 28, 117–148.

Berger, A. and D. B. Humphrey (1992), 'Megamergers in Banking and the Use of Cost Efficiency as an AntiTrust Defense,' *The AntiTrust Bulletin* 37, 541–600.

Black, Fischer and Myron Scholes (1973), 'The Pricing of Options and Corporate Liabilities,' *Journal of Political Economy* 81, 637–654.

Breedon, Francis (1995), 'Bond Prices and Market Expectations of Inflation,' *Bank of England Quarterly Bulletin* 35 (May), 160–165.

Brewer, Thomas L. and Pietra Rivoli (1990), 'Politics and Perceived Country Creditworthiness in International Banking,' *Journal of Money, Credit and Banking* 22, 357–369.

Brinson, Gary P. and Richard C. Carr (1989), 'International Equities and Bonds,' in Frank J. Fabozzi (ed.) *Portfolio and Investment Analysis: State-of-the-Art Research, Analysis and Strategies*, Chicago: Probus Publishing.

Cable, J. R. (1985), 'Capital Market Information and Industrial Performance: the Role of West German Banks,' *Economic Journal* 95, 118–132.

Canals, Jordi (1993), *Competitive Strategies in European Banking*, Oxford: Clarendon Press.

Carlton, Colin (1989), 'Risk and Return in Canada's Capital Markets: A Historical Perspective,' *Canadian Investment Review*, 2, 9–15.

Catte, Pietro and Cristina Mastropasqua (1993), 'Financial Structure and Reforms in Central and Eastern Europe in the 1980s,' *Journal of Banking and Finance* 17, 785–817.

Chan, Y.-S. and G. Kanatas (1985), 'Asymmetric Valuations and the Role of Collateral in Loan Agreements,' *Journal of Money, Credit and Banking* 17, 84–95.

Chen, Nai-fu, Richard Roll and Stephen A. Ross (1980), 'Economic Forces and the Stock Market: Testing the APT and Alternative Asset Pricing Theories,' *Journal of Business* 53, 383–403.

Cheng, Pao L. and Robert Grauer (1980), 'An Alternative Test of the Capital Asset Pricing Model,' *American Economic Review* 70, 660–671.

Coleman, William D. (1996), *Financial Services, Globalization and Domestic Policy Change*, London: Macmillan.

Copeland, Thomas E. and J. Fred Weston (1988), *Financial Theory and Corporate Policy*, 3rd edn, Reading, Mass.: Addison-Wesley.

Corrigan, Gerald E. (1989), 'Legislative Priorities,' *Federal Reserve Bank of New York Quarterly Review* 13, 1–6.

Courchene, Thomas J. and Edwin H. Neave (eds) (1995), *Financial Derivatives: Managing and Regulating Off-Balance Sheet Risks*, Kingston, Ont.: Queen's University, John Deutsch Institute for the Study of Economic Policy.

Cox, John C. and Mark Rubinstein (1985), *Options Markets*, Englewood Cliffs, NJ: Prentice-Hall.

Crane, Dwight B. *et al.* (1995), *The Global Financial System: A Functional Perspective*, Boston, Mass.: Harvard Business School Press.

Domowitz, Ian, Jack Glen and Ananth Madhavan (1997), 'Market Segmentation and Stock Prices: Evidence from an Emerging Market,' *Journal of Finance* 52, 1059–1085.

Donaldson, Gordon F. (1980), Harvard University, personal conversation.

Donaldson, T. H. (1989), *Credit Risk and Exposure in Securitization*, London: Macmillan.

Edwards, Jeremy and Klaus Fischer (1994), *Banks, Finance and Investment in Germany*, Cambridge: Cambridge University Press.

Elton, Edwin J. and Martin Gruber (eds) (1990), *Japanese Capital Markets*, New York: Harper and Row.

Fabozzi, Frank J. and Franco Modigliani (1992), *Capital Markets: Institutions and Instruments*, Englewood Cliffs, NJ: Prentice-Hall.

Fabozzi, Frank J., Franco Modigliani and Michael G. Ferri (1994), *Foundations of Financial Markets and Institutions*, Englewood Cliffs, NJ: Prentice-Hall.

Fackler, J. S. (1985), 'An Empirical Analysis of the Markets for Goods, Money, and Credit,' *Journal of Money, Credit and Banking* 17, 28–42.

Fama, Eugene F. (1985), 'What's Different about Banks?' *Journal of Monetary Economics* 15, 29–39.

Fama, Eugene F. (1991), 'Efficient Capital Markets: II,' *Journal of Finance* 46, 1575–1617.

Fama, E. F. and M. R. Gibbons (1984), 'A Comparison of Inflation Forecasts,' *Journal of Monetary Economics* 13, 327–348.

Ferson, Wayne E. and Rudi W. Schadt (1996), 'Measuring Fund Strategy and Performance in Changing Economic Conditions,' *Journal of Finance* 50, 425–460.

Flannery, Mark J. (1986), 'Asymmetric Information and Risky Debt Maturity Choice,' *Journal of Finance* 41, 19–36.

Garvey, Gerald (1993), 'Does Hierarchical Governance Facilitate Adaptation to Changed Circumstances?' *Journal of Economic Behavior and Organization* 20, 187–211.

Gemmill, Gordon (1996), 'Transparency and Liquidity: A Study of Block Trades on the London Stock Exchange under Different Publication Rules,' *Journal of Finance* 51, 1765–1790.

Glosten, Lawrence R. (1989), 'Insider Trading, Liquidity, and the Role of the Monopoly Specialist,' *Journal of Business* 62, 211–235.

Grossman, Sanford A. (1988a), 'An Analysis of the Implications for Stock and Futures Price Volatility of Program Trading and Dynamic Hedging Strategies,' *Journal of Business* 61, 275–296.

Grossman, Sanford A. (1988b), 'Program Trading and Stock and Futures Price Volatility,' *Journal of Futures Markets* 8, 413–419.

Grossman, Sanford A. (1995), 'Dynamic Asset Allocation and the Informational Efficiency of Markets,' *Journal of Finance* 50, 773–785.

Hatch, James E. and Michael J. Robinson (1989), *Investment Management in Canada*, 2nd edn, Scarborough, Ont.: Prentice-Hall.

Heffernan, Shelagh and Peter Sinclair (1990), *Modern International Economics*, Oxford: Basil Blackwell.

Houston, Joel and Christopher James (1996), 'Bank Information Monopolies and the Mix of Private and Public Debt Claims,' *Journal of Finance* 51, 1863–1889.

Huang, Chi-Fu and Robert H. Litzenberger (1988), *Foundations for Financial Economics*, New York: North–Holland.

Hull, E. D. (1989), 'The Complete Story on Securitization of Bank Assets,' *Journal of Commercial Bank Lending* November (Part I) and December (Part II).

Hull, John C. (1991), *Introduction to Futures and Options Markets*, Englewood Cliffs, NJ: Prentice–Hall.

Isard, P. (1977), 'How Far Can We Push the Law of One Price?' *American Economic Review* 67, 942–948.

James, Christopher and Joel Houston (1996), 'Evolution or Extinction: Where are Banks Headed?' *Journal of Applied Corporate Finance* 9, 8–23.

Jarrow, Robert A. and Stuart M. Turnbull (1996), *Derivative Securities*, Cincinnati, Ohio: South-Western College Publishing.

Jog, Vijay (1988), 'Stock Pricing Anomalies: Canadian Experience,' *Canadian Investment Review* 1, 55–62.

John, Kose and David C. Nachman (1985), 'Risky Debt, Investment Incentives, and Reputation in a Sequential Equilibrium,' *Journal of Finance* 40, 863–876.

Johnson, Lewis D. and Edwin H. Neave (1992), 'Strategic Real Estate Management: The Case of Olympia & York,' *Canadian Investment Review* 5, 51–62.

Johnson, Lewis D. and Edwin H. Neave (1994), 'Governance and Comparative Advantage,' *Managerial Finance* 20, 54–68.

Johnson, Lewis D. and Edwin H. Neave (1995), *Governance and Financial Regulation*, Working Paper, Toronto: C. D. Howe Research Institute.

Jones, Randall S. (1989), 'Japan's Expanding Role in World Financial Markets,' *Columbia Journal of World Business* 24, 3–9.

King, Robert G. and Ross Levine (1993), 'Financial Intermediation and Economic Development,' in Colin Mayer and Xavier Vives (eds) *Capital Markets and Financial Intermediation*, Cambridge: Cambridge University Press.

Knight, Frank H. (1971), *Risk, Uncertainty, and Profit*, Chicago: University of Chicago Press. (Original publication Boston: Houghton Mifflin, 1921.)

Levine, Ross (1997), 'Financial Development and Economic Growth,' *Journal of Economic Literature* 35, 688–726.

Malkiel, Burton G. (1995), 'Returns from Investing in Equity Mutual Funds 1971 to 1991,' *Journal of Finance* 49, 549–572.

Manover, Michael (1989), 'The Harm from Insider Trading and Informed Speculation,' *Quarterly Journal of Economics* 104, 823–845.

Mayer, Colin (1997), 'Financial Systems and Corporate Governance: A Review of the International Evidence,' *Conference on Financial Institutions in Transition: Banks and Financial Markets*, Wallerfangen/Saar, Germany.

Mayer, Colin and Xavier Vives (eds) (1993), *Capital Markets and Financial Intermediation*, Cambridge: Cambridge University Press.

McCauley, Robert and Steven Zimmer (1989), 'Explaining International Differences in the Cost of Capital,' *Federal Reserve Bank of New York Quarterly Review* 13, 7–28.

McKinnon, Ronald I. (1973), *Money and Capital in Economic Development*, Washington, DC: Brookings Institution.

Merton, Robert C. (1987), 'A Simple Model of Capital Market Equilibrium with Incomplete Information,' *Journal of Finance* 42, 483–510.

Merton, Robert C. (1992), *Operation and Regulation in Financial Intermediation: A Functional Perspective*, Cambridge, Mass.: Harvard University Graduate School of Business Administration Working Paper.

Miller, Merton H. (1986), 'Financial Innovation: the Last Twenty Years and the Next,' *Journal of Financial and Quantitative Analysis* 21, 459–471.

Morgan, Iuean G. and Edwin H. Neave (1993), 'Valuing Forward and Futures Contracts,' *ASTIN Bulletin* 23, 3–22.

Nathan, Alli and Edwin H. Neave (1989), 'Competitiveness and Contestability in Canada's Financial System: Empirical Results,' *Canadian Journal of Economics* 23, 574–591.

Nathan, Alli and Edwin H. Neave (1992), 'Cost Functions of Canadian Chartered Banks,' *Journal of Financial Services Research* 6, 265–277.

Nathan, Alli and Edwin H. Neave (1994), *Profit Functions of Canadian Financial Intermediaries*, La Boule: French Finance Association.

Neave, Edwin H. (1989a), 'Canada's Approach to Financial Regulation,' *Canadian Public Policy* 15, 1–11.

Neave, Edwin H. (1989b), 'Regulation in a Global Financial System: Truths and Consequences for Canada,' *Canadian Investment Review* 2, 51–60.

Neave, Edwin H. (1990), 'How Financial Systems Evolve,' *Canadian Investment Review* 3, 11–18.

Neave, Edwin H. (1991), *The Economic Organisation of a Financial System*, London and New York: Routledge.

Neave, Edwin H. (1995), 'Governance and Directors' Control,' *Canadian Business Law Journal* 26, 106–120.

Neave, Edwin H. (1996), *Canadian Financial Regulation: A System in Transition*, Toronto: C. D. Howe Research Institute.

North, Douglass C. (1994), 'The Evolution of Efficient Markets in History,' in J. A. James and M. Thomas (eds) *Capitalism in Context*, Chicago: University of Chicago Press.

Organisation for Economic Cooperation and Development (1986), *Venture Capital – Context, Development, and Policies*, Paris: OECD.

Organisation for Economic Cooperation and Development (1989), *Competition in Banking*, Paris: OECD.

Organisation for Economic Cooperation and Development (1992), *Financial Market Trends 53*, Paris: OECD.

Organisation for Economic Cooperation and Development (1993), 'Organisation and Regulation of Securities Markets,' *Financial Market Trends 54*, 14–86, Paris: OECD.

Organisation for Economic Cooperation and Development (1995), 'Financial Market Trends and Corporate Governance,' *Financial Market Trends 62*, 13–32, Paris: OECD.

Oxelheim, Lars (1995), *Financial Markets in Transition: Globalization, Investment, and Economic Growth*, London: Routledge.

Porter, Michael E. (1992), 'Capital Disadvantage: America's Failing Capital Investment System,' *Harvard Business Review* September–October, 65–82.

Rhee, S. G. and R. P. Chang (eds) (1990), *Pacific Basin Capital Markets Research*, vol. I, Amsterdam: North-Holland.

Riordan, Michael H. and Oliver E. Williamson (1985), 'Asset Specificity,' *Journal of Economic Behavior and Organization* 3, 365–378.

Rogoff, Kenneth (1996), 'The Purchasing Power Parity Puzzle,' *Journal of Economic Literature* 34, 647–668.

Roll, Richard (1977), 'A Critique of the Asset Pricing Theory: Part I. On the Past and Potential Testability of the Theory,' *Journal of Financial Economics* 25, 129–176.

Ross, Stephen A. (1976), 'The Arbitrage Theory of Capital Asset Pricing,' *Journal of Economic Theory* 8, 343–362.

Ross, Stephen A. (1977), 'The Determination of Financial Structure: The Incentive Signalling Approach,' *Bell Journal* 8, 371–387.

Ross, Stephen A. (1989), 'Institutional Markets, Financial Marketing, and Financial Innovation,' *Journal of Finance* 44, 541–556.

Rybczynski, Tad M. (1984), 'Industrial Finance System in Europe, US and Japan,' *Journal of Economic Behavior and Organization* 5, 275–286.

Sakakibara, Eisuke and Robert Alan Feldman (1990), 'The Japanese Financial System in Comparative Perspective,' in Edwin J. Elton and Martin Gruber (eds) *Japanese Capital Markets*, New York: Harper'and Row.

Santoni, G. J. (1987), 'Has Programmed Trading Made Stock Prices More Volatile?' *Federal Reserve Bank of St. Louis Review* 67, 18–29.

Saunders, Anthony M. (1994), *Financial Institutions Management*, Homewood, Ill.: Irwin.

Sercu, Piet and Raman Uppal (1995), *International Financial Markets and the Firm*, Cincinnati, Ohio: South-Western College Publishing.

Sheard, Paul (1992), *The Role of the Japanese Main Bank when Borrowing Firms are in Financial Distress*, Stanford, Calif.: Center for Economic Policy Research.

Singh, Ajit (1995), *Corporate Financing Patterns in Industrializing Economies*, International Finance Corporation Technical Paper 2, Washington, DC: World Bank.

Smith, Roy C. and Ingo Walter (1990), *Global Financial Services: Strategies for Building Competitive Strengths in International Commercial and Investment Banking*, New York: Harper.

Stambaugh, Robert F. (1992), 'On the Exclusion of Assets from Tests of the Two-Parameter Model,' *Journal of Financial Economics* 30, 237–268.

Stiglitz, Joseph and Andrew Weiss (1981), 'Credit Rationing in Markets with Imperfect Information,' *American Economic Review* 71, 393–410.

Taylor, M. P. (1987) 'Covered Interest Parity: A High Frequency, High Quality Data Study,' *Economica* 54, 429–438.

Tinic, Seha M. and Richard R. West (1974), 'Marketability of Common Stocks in Canada and the USA: A Comparison of Agent versus Dealer Dominated Markets,' *Journal of Finance* 29, 729–749.

Tufano, Peter (1989), 'Financial Innovation and First-Mover Advantages,' *Journal of Financial Economics* 25, 213–240.

Williamson, Oliver E. (1975), *Markets and Hierarchies: Economics and Anti-Trust Implications*, New York: Free Press.

Williamson, Oliver E. (1985), *The Economic Institutions of Capitalism*, New York: Free Press.

Williamson, Oliver E. (1986), *The Economic Organization of Capitalist Institutions*, London: Wheatsheaf.

Williamson, Oliver E. (1987), 'Transaction Cost Economics: The Comparative Contracting Perspective,' *Journal of Economic Behavior and Organization* 8, 617–625.

Williamson, Oliver E. (1988), 'Corporate Finance and Corporate Governance,' *Journal of Finance* 43, 567–591.

Williamson, Oliver E. (1993), 'Contested Exchange versus the Governance of Contractual Relations,' *Journal of Economic Perspectives* 7, 103–108.

Yu, Wayne W. (1997), 'Essays on Capital Markets,' PhD dissertation, University of Alberta, Edmonton.

Index

acceptance companies 286
adaptation 44, 54, 165, 184–5
adjustment 32–4, 45–6, 55–6, 126–8, 132, 137, 144, 146, 148–9, 158–62, 239–41, 247–8
administration costs 33, 35, 129, 133, 210
adverse selection 163–4
advice 56, 60, 265, 292, 336
agent: bank as 282; intermediary as 260–1, 285; market 31–5, 55, 121–3, 129, 133, 190–1
Albert, Michel 47
alignment 33–5, 37, 130–3, 232
allocative efficiency 121–3, 149, 179–80, 193, 195, 202, 207, 314
arbitrage: change 45; efficiency 121, 144; foreign exchange 224, 244–7, 249; forward rate agreements 302; futures 224; futures-forwards 114–15; market gap 314–15; markets 176–7, 195–6, 202–3; options and shares 219; pricing by 71–3, 75–9, 81–2, 88, 95, 206, 210, 226; securities trading 171; segmentation 178, 180, 182; swaps 229–30; technological change 339, 342
Arbitrage Pricing Theory 81–2
asset 11, 14, 18, 20, 28, 30–2, 35, 53, 61–4, 147–8; pricing 70–90
asset–liability 58–60, 136, 150, 270–2, 281–3
attributes, deal 28, 33–7, 43, 121, 126–8, 130, 132, 157, 232
automation 264–5, 281, 336–7, 339, 341–2

balance of payments and international finance 236–44
balance sheet 53, 58–9, 270–1
Bank for International Settlements (BIS) 252, 328, 332
bankers' acceptances 166–7, 196–7, 222, 243
banks: capital standards 268, 270, 332; change 41; consumers 19; domestic 302; electronic retail 336; Euro- 331; federal funds 198; finance companies 286; future role 46–8, 338; governance 136; growth 56–7, 64; insurance 261–2, 291; intermediation 280–3; international 6, 297–8, 304, 330–1; loans 14, 32, 45, 148, 183, 280–2, 303; mortgages 208, 328; project financing 167; risk 146, 230–1, 341–2; securities 328–9; signalling 160; technology 340; see also by type
basic balance 237
Basle Agreements 268, 270, 330–1
Benson, E.D. 160
Berger, A. 263
bias 131, 163, 165
bid–ask spread 175, 226
Black, Fischer 231
blocks, trading 137, 201–2, 208–10
bonds: balance of payments 242; call 210; ECU 247; high yield 207; insurance companies 290; interest rate 88, 167–8; international 243; markets 14, 190, 203–7; mortgages loans 210–11; options 217; pension funds 292; risk 11; tax-exempt 320; see also by type

borrowing 12, 18–21, 26–7, 52–3, 57–8, 60–1, 265–6
bought deal 192
Breedon, Francis 87
Brewer, Thomas L. 232
bridging finance 43, 145, 184–5, 196
Brinson, Gary P. 193
brokers 172, 174–5, 193–4, 201, 210, 222, 341
business: as client 17–20, 27–8; in financial system 10–12, 14, 52, 57–8, 63; money markets 195; small 20, 203, 318–19

Canada: banking 261, 288, 298, 300, 336; certificates of deposits 179; cross-border trading 254; currency value 243; debit cards 265; discount brokerage 328–9; financial conglomerates 294; insurance companies 291; pension funds 293; regulation 325; stock market 163; US dollar deposits 251
capabilities: adjustment 55–6, 161; banks 282, 287; closely held investment 148–9; communication 262; financial conglomerates 293; financier 16–17, 27, 29; foreign direct investment 243; governance 33–5, 37, 43, 127–33, 145, 195, 232, 324; information 125; intermediaries 32; management 47; screening 27, 32–3, 35, 37, 264
capital: adequacy standards 331–2; corporations 340; formation 4, 13–14, 16, 54, 57, 61, 324; management 268–71, 273–4; market line 140; markets 242, 251, 302; possible shortage of 304–5; supervision 327
Capital Asset Pricing Model (CAPM) 79–82, 123
Capital Asset Pricing Theory 123
caps 153
Carr, Richard C. 193
casualty insurance 290
catastrophe futures 291
central banks 13, 21, 242, 250
certainty equivalent value 74–5
change, economic 5–6, 41–8
Chen, Nai-Fu 82

Cheng, Pao L. 81
Chicago Mercantile Exchange 222, 224, 255, 342
clients in deal 18–21, 26–7, 30, 33
closed–open ended funds 288
Coleman, William D. 54
collars 153
collateral 36, 56, 126, 162, 198, 210, 261, 291
collateralised mortgage obligations 211
commercial banks 35, 54–6, 145, 192, 197
commercial paper 166–7, 175–6, 196–7, 243, 301
commission, trading 173–4, 193–4, 199, 201–2
commodities 14–15, 217, 221, 341
communications media 42, 193–4, 200, 262, 264–5, 281, 336–7, 339–43
compensation 36, 72–3, 80, 153, 206, 320
competition: advantage 174; banks 56, 281, 287; change and 5, 43–4; economic 17; future evolution 336–9, 343; intermediaries 260; market 76, 176–7, 191, 269; multinational 297; perfect 120–3, 131–2, 244; position house 202; securities 184; segmentation 181; stock exchange 193; supervision and 324–8, 331; technology and 194
complementarity, dynamic 132–3
complete contracts 31, 158–60, 176–7
compound interest 72–3
computerisation 42, 194–5, 200, 222, 262, 265, 291, 337–42
conditional sales contracts 20, 286, 318
confidence 323–4, 329
conglomerates, financial 293–4
consumers 16, 18–19, 280–1, 283, 286
contingency planning 149, 160, 162
contraction risk 210–11
control 32–5, 127–8, 132, 137, 293
convergence of financial systems 4
corporate bonds 89–90, 178, 205–6
corporate finance 19–20, 27, 46, 48, 62–3, 177, 205, 207, 281–2
Corrigan, Gerald E. 343
cost–benefit 31, 140, 181, 312–15, 325

cost-effectiveness: banks 46; cross-selling 262; deals 123, 130–2, 157, 167, 171; externalities 182; financial services 325; future evolution 338; governance 33–6, 56; government 313–14; markets 195–6, 203; portfolio 140–1, 149
costs: default 127; financing 160, 167; governance 34–5; information 183; international banking 298–9; lending intermediation 286; liquidity management 267; multinational 297; *see also by type*
country: costs 240–1; risk 228, 232, 243, 302, 331
covered interest arbitrage 226–8
Cox, John C. 105, 217
credit 13, 19, 42, 54, 148, 164, 196–7, 216, 280, 298, 300–2, 305, 312, 326, 339; risk 42, 46, 166, 195, 198, 232, 299, 304
credit derivatives 342
creditworthiness 15, 196–7, 205, 231–2
cross-border trading 254
cross-selling 261–2
crowding out 320
currency: futures 221–2, 230, 342; swaps 228, 229–30, 231; value 224–6, 228, 239–42, 245–6, 250–1, 337
current account balance 236–40, 243

data processing 191, 287
dealers 172, 174–5, 193–4, 196, 199, 201, 341
dealing banks 224–6
debit cards 265, 339–40
debt 317–20; -equity 55–6, 63, 96, 108–12, 147, 161, 330
default 82–3, 85, 161, 207–8, 232; risk 29–31, 35–6, 42, 90, 112, 145–7, 152, 166–7, 184, 206, 210, 216, 222, 227, 231, 261, 301–3
delivery date 96–7, 112
demand, change and 41–2
deposit finance 11, 19, 21, 52, 63–4, 208, 283–5
derivatives 5–6, 15, 46, 95–6, 137, 141, 144, 146, 150, 177, 214–16, 240, 266, 303–5, 332–3, 337, 342

devaluation 241–3
developing countries 17–18, 48, 161, 179, 254, 297, 303–4
development of financial systems 10, 16, 17, 183, 342
direct debit 265
discount brokerage 287–8, 328–9
disintermediation 284, 326
distribution risk 215–16
diversification 79–80, 131, 137–41, 146–7, 149, 191–2, 207, 214, 261–2, 288–9
domestic intermediation 280–94
domestic markets 190–211, 254, 283, 342
Donaldson, T.H. 162

earnings risk 146–7
economics: of financial markets 190–4; of intermediation 260–4
Edwards, Jeremy 56, 63
efficiency 120–3, 144, 149, 176, 179–80, 193, 195, 202, 207, 314
efficient markets hypothesis 120
elasticity 182–3, 242–3
electronic funds transfer system (EFTS) 339–40
equilibrium 71, 75, 77, 79–81, 120–3, 176–7
equity 208, 243–4, 269–74, 319–20, 324; debt- 55–6, 96, 108–12, 161, 330; markets 47–8, 63, 190, 198–203, 254
Euro-CDs 197
euro-facilities 301
Eurobonds 252–4, 298
Eurocurrency 230, 247, 251–2, 253, 255, 299, 331
Eurodollar 223–4, 251, 255, 298, 300
Euroloans 300–1
Euromarkets 250–2, 300, 331
European currency units (ECU) 241, 247, 252–3
European Monetary System (EMS) 241–2
evolution of financial system 336–44
exchange 216, 219, 239–42, 297
expectations 86–7, 171, 243
experimentation 17, 43, 149, 165, 184
expert systems 130, 262

export credit insurance 162, 182
exports 214, 318; imports- 232, 236–7, 239–43, 303
exposure 224, 229
extension risk 211
externalities 181–2, 312–13, 332

Fabozzi, Frank J. 144, 148, 153, 160, 177, 202, 207, 287, 292
failure 164, 191, 305, 333
Fama, Eugene F. 160, 245
federal funds 196, 198
Federal Reserve Board Regulation Q 45, 326
Federal Reserve System 45, 195–6, 250
fees 124, 300
Feldman, Robert Alan 54, 60
Ferri, Michael G. 160, 207
finance companies 175–6, 280, 286
financial market gap *see* gap, financial market
financial markets 13, 314, 325, 331, 337, 341–2; international 236–55; risk trading 214–32
financial system: empirical overview 52–64; role 10–18
financier: capabilities 16–17; change 41–5; in deal 26–7, 29–31, 33, 35, 37; deal attributes 157–66; in financial system 16; governance 124–31; incentives and regulation 323–5; innovation 19; portfolio governance 141, 145, 148; profit 171; skill 5
firms, financial 6, 27, 36–7
Fischer, Klaus 56, 63
Fisher relation 82–6, 245, 249
fixed–floating rates 146, 167, 197, 208, 240–2, 267, 275–6, 283–4, 299–301
flexibility 131, 149, 158, 161–2, 262, 283, 325, 328
floors 153
flow-through partnership 330
flows, international financial 242–4
foreign exchange 45, 175, 221, 236–7, 242, 326, 341; markets 224–8, 231, 244–51; risk 214, 226–9, 240
foreign investment 21, 47, 132, 243–4, 298, 304, 324
forward contract 96–100

forward forward contracts 301
forward parity theory 249–50
forward rate agreements 301–2
forwards 28, 95–102, 108–9, 112–15, 152, 175, 221, 224–7, 267
fourth market (US) 199, 201
France 214–15, 222, 241
fraud 11–12, 327–8, 343
fund raising: business 17, 19–20; debt-equity 96; financial system 10, 12, 14–15, 52–3; financier 27; foreign direct investment 243; intermediation 32, 177–8, 260, 268, 270, 285–6; international financial centres 299; market gap 314–15; markets 172–3, 195–8, 251–2; mortgages 209–10; near banks 283
funds flow data 12–13, 27, 48, 52–3, 57–61, 182
future evolution 260, 264, 336–44
futures 14–15, 95–6, 112–15, 141, 144, 146, 152–3, 199, 217, 221–4, 230–2, 255, 301–2, 341–2

gap, financial market 265–6, 312–14
Garvey, Gerald 131
Gemmill, Gordon 193, 202
general acceptance corporations 286
Germany 47–8, 53–8, 60–4, 195, 214–15, 222, 241
Gibbons, M.R. 245
gilts 205
gold standard 239–40
goods–service trade balance 236–7
governance: change and 42–4; complementary 183–4; financial 120–33; in financial system 52, 55–7, 63; intermediaries 55; market 31–2, 48, 232; portfolio 136–54; uncertainty 160–1
government: bonds 21, 82, 146, 174, 198, 328; capital adequacy 332; as client 18, 21, 27; financial activity 16, 312–21; in financial system 10, 12–13, 52, 57–8, 60; money markets 195–6; transition economies 47
Grauer, Robert 81
gross national product (GNP) 54, 60–3
Grossman, Sanford A. 203

growth, economic 10, 13–14, 16–18, 48,
53–4, 56–7, 60, 64, 241, 323–4
guarantees 15, 82, 152, 162, 166–7,
176–7, 196–7, 210, 216, 222, 231–2,
314, 317

hedging 86, 103–5, 141–3, 146, 150,
152–3, 214, 217, 221–3, 228–30, 240,
266–7, 341
hierarchical governance (H capabilities)
33–5, 128–32, 149, 157
holding companies 148, 281, 288
households: assets 61–2, 317; in financial
system 12–13, 18–19, 27, 57–8;
savings 52–3, 288, 292
Houston, Joel 56–7, 64
Huang, Chi-Fu 79, 105, 143
Hull, E.D. 217
Humphrey, D.B. 263
hybrid governance (Y capabilities) 34–5,
128–30, 149

illiquidity 28, 30–2, 123, 136–7, 145–8,
176, 178, 291
incentives 263, 313–14, 316–17, 323–4,
326, 329
incomplete contracts 33, 131, 148–9,
158–62
indebtedness 232, 302–4
index: bonds 86–7; futures 144,
221–2
individual in financial system 10–11,
14
inflation 21, 54, 63, 83–9, 84, 208–9,
241, 245, 318, 337
information: asymmetry 30–1, 34–5,
125–6, 129, 178–81; bond markets
206; change 47–8; costs 173; as
deal attribute 157–66; disclosure
327; equity markets 199, 203, 254;
financial system 18; governance
120–1, 123–4, 126–7, 130–2;
marketing 340–1; markets 176–7;
options market 219; processing 32–3,
36, 42, 123–4, 126, 128–9, 177,
263–4, 282, 341–2; production 16,
192–3; public and financial systems
323–4; risk trading 214; trading 14,
56–7, 172–3

innovation 17, 30, 43–4, 55, 125, 180,
184–5, 207–9, 231, 283, 324–6,
337–9, 343
insiders 159, 163, 327
institutions, financial: change 42; deal
attributes 29; efficiency 193; forward
rate agreements 301; future evolution
337–9; interdependence 331, 333, 343;
as intermediaries 262; junk bonds 207;
markets 194–5, 198; mortgage 209–10;
portfolio 32; risk management 153–4;
securities 147–8; supervision 328–9;
survival 305; technological change
264–5; trading 200–3; US regulation Q
326
insurance 19, 61–2, 64, 143–4, 208–9,
261, 291–2, 328–9; companies 14–15,
136, 147, 282, 289–92, 328, 340
integration: financial systems 42, 243,
291, 329, 336, 338; markets 5, 194,
341–3
interest earnings–equity ratio 272–4,
276
interest parity theory 227–8, 245–7, 249
interest rate: balance of payments 243;
bank loans 280–1; bonds 254; capital
shortage 304–5; change and 44; credit
rationing 164; crowding out 320; deal
terms 158; differential 266; effective
36, 149, 166–7; Eurocredit 300, 301;
Euromarkets 251; foreign exchange
224–5, 228, 244–6, 248–50; future
evolution 341; futures 221–3; Germany
and exchange rates 241; governance
and 120–2, 125; government activity
312; indebtedness 303; market gap
314–17; market segmentation 178–9;
money market 195–7; mortgages
208–11; pricing 72–3, 75, 79, 82–90;
pricing by arbitrage 226–7; relations
182–3; risk 103, 113–15, 221–4, 255,
266, 282; risk management 149–54;
spreads and bonds 206; stability 337;
supervision 324–6; swaps 28, 146,
150–2, 228–31, 266, 267, 339; thrifts
284–5; trading 19–21, 171, 176–7
intermediaries: capabilities 129–31; in
deal 27–8; financial 260–76; fund
raising 10, 12–13

intermediation: change 41–2, 45, 47–8; domestic 280–94; financial system 52, 60–4; future evolution 340–1; governance 55, 183; government lending 314–17, 319; international 297–305; market gap 314; market segmentation 178–80, 182; market trading and 171–85; mortgages 208; organisation 27–8, 32–5, 338; over-the-counter 15; payments and 340; perfect market 123; portfolio governance 145–8, 150; risk trading 215, 231; supervision and 328–9; technological change 339, 342
internal governance 33–5, 129
international banks 44, 251–3, 281, 297–300, 304, 332
International Financial Corporation (World Bank) 42, 254, 304
International Monetary Fund 297, 303
internationalism 5, 15, 21, 42, 251, 299–300, 336, 338, 340, 342; financial markets 236–55; mediation 297–305; risk management 228–32
intervention, government 181–2, 312–13, 315–16, 318, 326
inventory 174–5, 193, 198, 205, 225, 230
investment: banks 44, 145, 197, 287–8, 302, 332, 338; closely held 148–9; companies 254, 288–9; dealers 195; as financial activity 16; financial system 10–12, 61–2; foreign exchange rates 246, 249; household 27, 52–3, 208; institutional 147–8, 203; intermediation 32, 263, 269; markets 194, 236–7; pension plans 318; portfolio 140–1; pricing by arbitrage 226–8; program trading 202; risk 173; supervision 324, 330; venture capital 286

James, Christopher 56–7, 64
Japan 6, 15, 47–8, 53–7, 60–4, 162, 195, 214–15, 222, 300
Jarrow, Robert A. 114, 217
John, Kose 160
junk bonds 171, 207

King, Robert G. 14

law of one price *see* allocative efficiency
learning-by-doing 132, 165, 264, 285
leasing companies 286–7
legislation 5, 29, 32, 45, 285, 312, 324–8, 342–3
lender of last resort 331–2
lending 12, 18–19, 21, 26–7, 52–4, 57–8, 60–1, 265–6; intermediaries 222, 263, 285–7, 314–17, 319
leveraged buyouts 43, 184–5
Levine, Ross 14, 57
LIBOR *see* London Interbank Offer Rate
life insurance 32, 210, 263, 289–91, 337
linkages 60–1, 171, 175–8, 182–3, 264, 329, 342
liquidity: asset 11, 14, 18, 20, 28, 30–2, 35; Bank of International Settlement 332; country 232; deals 126–8, 133; management 267–8, 290; markets 173, 195–7, 199; mortgage 209–10; options 216; premium 88; risk 331; securities 136–7, 145–9; shares 203; supervision and 327, 330
listings 194, 199–200, 219, 254, 288
Litzenberger, Robert H. 79, 105, 143
loans 32, 260–1, 266, 270–4, 286, 316–18, 320, 332, 338; *see also by type*
London Interbank Offer Rate (LIBOR) 230, 251, 299–301, 303
London International Stock Exchange 172, 194, 202, 254
long position 96–8, 102–3, 105, 222–4

McKinnon, Ronald I. 179
Malkiel, Burton G. 203
management 47, 161, 260, 264–5, 300; strategic model 269–76
market: failure 164; funding 10, 12–13, 46–8; governance (M capabilities) 128–32, 149, 157; makers 199, 202; marking to 112–15, 222, 301–2; portfolio 79–81; risk 145–7; trading and intermediation 171–85; trading risk 15; type of 171–5; value maximisation 269–72; *see also* domestic; financial; money; over-the-counter; primary; private–public; secondary; stock; upstairs

marketability risk 206–7
marketing 262, 283, 336
Maxwell Group 293, 329
Mayer, Colin 57
mergers 5, 47, 145, 191–2, 263, 287–8
Merton, Robert C. 132
Modigliani, Franco 144, 148, 153, 160, 177, 207, 287, 292
money markets 14, 175, 190, 192, 195–8, 206, 224, 243, 251, 255, 285, 286, 299
monitoring 31–5, 46, 48, 55, 57, 121, 126–30, 132, 136–7, 140, 144, 146, 148–9, 157–9, 165, 167, 215, 293
monopoly 43–4
moral hazard 163, 165, 285
mortgages: adjustable rate 209, 211, 283–4; interest rate 266; investment companies 286; loans 19, 146, 174, 280–1, 283–4, 315, 318, 320, 328; markets 190, 192, 208–11; US regulation Q 45, 326
multinational business 297–8
municipal bonds 29, 160, 178, 290
mutual funds 11, 19, 64, 140, 177, 264, 288–9, 327, 341

Nachman, David C. 160
National Association of Securities Dealers Automated Quotation service (NASDAQ) 194, 200
near banks 268, 284, 328
neglected firms effect 203
negotiable certificate of deposit 196–8
negotiation 28, 41, 129, 146, 160–1, 173–4, 176, 202, 207, 225, 229, 289
net present value 71–3
networks 193, 337, 339
niche firms 262
nominal rate of interest 21, 54, 84–90
notes 175, 197, 254–5, 301

off-balance sheet 20
off-exchange transactions 199
offshore finance 16, 18, 251, 298–300, 331
open interest 224
open outcry 199–200, 222
open-end fund 288

operating costs 27, 36–7, 130–1, 193, 199, 263, 320
operating intermediation 264–9
operational efficiency 121–3, 149, 193, 195
options 95, 100–9, 111–12, 141, 144, 153, 199, 215, 216–21, 230–1, 301
organisation 5, 260, 338–9; financial system 26–37
output and demand 242–3
outrights 226
over-the-counter markets 15, 153, 193–4, 198, 200, 205, 219, 288, 332

parties to a deal 26–8
pass-through securities 210
pay-as-you-go plans 318
payments: streams 70–7; systems 10–11, 339–40
pension funds 11, 19, 61–3, 210, 285, 291–3, 317–18, 328, 340
performance 4, 15, 36, 44, 136–7, 181, 312–13, 315, 323
policy, monetary 21, 312–13, 320
political risk 232
portfolio: balance of payments 242; credit card 42; diversification 79–80, 131, 207, 288–9; governance 136–54; investment 243–4; loan 175, 261; market 79–81, 123; mortgage 209–10; options 217; performance 202–3; put–call parity 105–6; return and risk 215; risk 36–7, 262; riskless 103; specialisation 32, 290; theory 269, 273, 276
position house 201–2
preferred shares 205
prepayment risk 211
price–earnings ratio 180, 183
pricing: by arbitrage 71–3, 75–9, 81–2, 95, 206, 210, 226; asset 70–90; relative 70–1, 82–90; risk division and 95–115
primary markets 12–14, 16, 18, 47, 172–3, 190, 209–10, 254
private sector 298, 304, 313–21
private–public: bonds 206; borrowing 21; deal 163; markets 32, 34–5, 172–4; mortgages 208

probability 29, 71, 73, 83, 127–8, 136, 138, 184
profit: adjustment 161; banks 280–2; change 41–4, 48; derivatives 97–8, 101; financier 27, 33, 35; fund flows 182; future evolution 338, 343; governance 120, 124–5, 127–8, 131–2; intermediation 260, 264, 265–6; junk bonds 207; market gap 315–16; mortgage loans 208; opportunity 6; planning 275–6; pricing by arbitrage 76–7; risk 28–9, 29–30, 31, 192, 299, 301; segmentation 178–81; supervision 324–6, 328; thrift 284–5; trading 36, 171, 174, 177, 190
program trading 202–3
programs, government fincance 312, 314–18
project finance 20, 167
property insurance 290
prudential regulation 329, 343
purchasing power 18, 83–4, 86, 167, 247–9
put–call parity 105–7, 143, 215–16, 219–20
puts 100–8, 215, 217, 219–21, 289

quotations 219–20, 223–4

rating agencies 159–61, 205
real estate investment trusts 286
real rate of interest 54, 84–8
regulation: banks 226, 280, 283–4; bond market 206; costs 323, 325–6; disclosure 172–3; Eurobonds 252; Eurocurrency 251; financial system 5, 13, 32, 44–5; future evolution 338, 342; intermediation 262–3, 268, 270, 297–300; life insurance 290; market segmentation 179; pension funds 292–3; supervision 323–33; trading 194
remedial policy intervention 313–14
repurchase agreements 196, 198
research 177, 180, 191–2, 203, 287
reserves, cash 270–4, 280
residents of other countries as clients 18, 21
resolving underwriting facilites 301

retail trading 198, 287, 337, 339
retirement finance 19, 208, 283–4, 291, 317–18
return–risk: banks 282; change 42; deal attributes 127, 132; default 83, 85; efficiency 176–7; foreign direct investment 243–4; futures 229; intermediation 123, 267, 269–70, 273–4; securities 79–82, 136–41, 149, 165, 179–81; securities firms 191; size of 11
reverse mortgages 209, 283
Riordan, Michael H. 131
risk: adjustment 73–4, 77–9, 104–7, 111; attributes and 28–31, 35–6, 126–7, 131–3; aversion 11, 215–16; -based capital adequacy standards 332; deal terms 158–9, 162–4, 166–7; diversification 14, 36, 214, 289, 303; division and pricing 95–115; experiment 149; financial governance 123; hedging 86, 266–7; innovation 43; loans 136–7, 280–1, 303; management 6, 10, 14–16, 28, 41, 137, 141, 144, 146, 149–54, 266–8, 282, 288, 305, 327, 332, 337, 339, 341; market gap 314–17; money market 196; mortgage 210; pension funds 293; portfolio 138, 140–1, 144; premium 74–5, 88, 166, 207, 249, 328–9; pricing and 70; small business 319; stocks–bonds 204; trading 178; transformation 261; venture capital 286; *see also* return–risk
Rivoli, Pietra 232
Rogoff, Kenneth 248
roles and clients 10–22
Roll, Richard 81, 82
Ross, Stephen A. 81, 82, 159
Rubinstein, Mark 105, 217

safety 131, 325–8
Sakakibara, Eisuke 54, 60
Santoni, G.J. 203
Saunders, Anthony M. 61, 282
savings 11, 19, 27, 52–4, 57, 59–62, 238, 244, 260, 283–4, 290–2, 312, 317

scale economies: banks 46, 287; capabilities 129–30; costs and 171; financial firms 27, 36–7; information 177; innovation 44; intermediaries 261–3, 265, 285; markets 191–3; regulation 329; screening 124–5, 179

Scholes, Myron 231

scope economies: banks 282, 299, 329; costs 171; deals 129, 131; financial firms 27, 36–7; innovation 44; integration 338; intermediaries 261–3; markets 191–2; security firms 172, 174

screen trading 200, 222

screening: capabilities 27, 32–3, 35, 37, 264; change 46; conglomerates 293; costs 124–6, 179, 199, 261, 263–4, 281; default 167; financier 27; governance 121, 126, 128–30, 132–3; institutions and 203; lending intermediaries 285; loans 183–4, 303; portfolio 137, 146, 148; public–private markets 173–4

search costs 124, 131, 140–1, 172, 191, 231

secondary markets: deal attributes 127, 130; domestic 190, 193–4, 196–7; equity 199; Eurobonds 254; financial system 12–16, 18, 31, 47; international debt 303; international financial centres 299; mortgages 209–10; shares 214; trading 172–3, 175

sector, economic 57–8

securities: agents 176; balance of payments 242; banks 328–9; Euro-252–5; firms 5, 15, 41, 44, 172–4, 191–2, 205, 230–1, 262, 282, 287–8, 336; foreign exchange rates 244; global trading 342; governance 120, 122–3, 130, 133; government 177; household 27–8; integration 302; management 267; markets 48; mortgages 210; options 217; portfolio governance 136–50; preferred shares 205; price relations 75–6, 82–90; return–risk 79–82; segmentation 179–80, 182–3; supervision 327–8, 331; trading 11–14, 18, 21, 52, 55–6, 61–3, 171–3, 176–7, 200; trading and

change 45–6; value 159, 165, 192–3; withdrawals 337

Securities and Exchange Commission (SEC) (US) 196, 206, 252, 328, 332

securitisation 46, 147–8, 162, 183–4, 192, 208, 210, 261, 281–2, 317

security market line 80–1, 123, 179

segmentation, market 171, 174–5, 178–83, 312, 314, 343

self-dealing 327–8, 343

self-regulation 325–7

sensitivity 275–6, 297, 326

Sercu, Piet 248, 301

serial redemption bonds 206

services, financial 37, 46–7, 60, 121, 125, 264–5, 287, 291, 326, 336–40

settlement risk 226, 339

shares 180, 203, 217–21, 243, 254, 288–9, 331

Sheard, Paul 55

short position 96–8, 102–3, 105

short–long term 165–6, 195–7, 237, 283

signalling 160

Singh, Ajit 48

sinking fund bonds 207

size: of financial firm 36–7; of intermediaries 262–3; of market 191, 263–4; of portfolio 140–1; of public trades 173

skills 5, 31–2, 44, 125–6, 261–4, 285–6, 300, 338, 341

'smart card' 340

social benefits 181–2, 312–13, 315–17, 323, 327

solvency 147, 268, 328, 330–1

sovereign loans 303

specialisation 32, 42, 129–31, 147–8, 171, 173, 191, 214, 261–3, 285–6, 336, 338

spot transactions 224–6, 227

Stambaugh, Robert F. 81

standardisation 15, 28, 35, 41, 129, 132, 175–7, 191, 195, 210, 214–16, 225, 230–2, 261–2, 339

startup finance 17, 28, 30, 263, 319

Stiglitz, Joseph 164

stock exchange 193, 193–4, 198–202, 205, 254, 288, 342

stock market 14, 48, 57, 63, 130, 163, 183, 336
stocks 11, 20, 204–5, 292, 341
straddling 266
strategic management model 269–76
stripped bonds 168
subsidies 314–16, 319–20
supervision 12, 42, 55, 127, 293, 323–33
swaps 28, 41, 146, 150–2, 226, 229–32, 301, 337, 339
syndicated loans 147, 183, 282–3, 299–301, 331
synthetic portfolio 143–4

tax 36, 63, 167–8, 178, 196, 292, 298, 329–30, 343
Taylor, M.P. 247
technological change 5, 15, 41–4, 55, 180–1, 193–4, 243, 262, 264–5, 291, 324, 336–9, 341–3
term lenders 285–6
terms, deal's 36, 157–68
third market (US) 199, 201
third party information 159–60
thrift organisations 281, 284–5, 326
Tinic, Seha M. 193
'too big to fail' argument 262
trade 238–43, 247–8, 297–8, 318
transaction costs 20, 56, 71–2, 80, 120–4, 129, 140–1, 171, 176–7, 179, 193, 203, 216–17, 226, 228, 244, 262
transfer 10, 12, 232
transition economies 12, 46–8
treasury bills 28, 153, 158, 195–7, 205, 222–3, 243
Triffin Dilemma 240
trusts 32, 263, 282, 338
Tufano, Peter 44
Turnbull, Stuart M. 114, 217
24-hour trading 194, 342
type N deal (non-standard) 126–7, 130, 132–3, 157
type S deal (standard) 126–7, 130, 132–3

UK 15, 27, 47–8, 53–8, 60–4, 148, 195, 214–15, 222, 241, 251, 293, 318, 329

uncertainty 28–31, 35–6, 123, 126–8, 131–3, 148, 158, 160–2, 166, 176, 184
underdevelopment 16, 46–8
underwriting 160, 172–3, 191–2, 199, 289
unit trusts 288–9
universal banks 35, 54–6, 63, 343
Uppal, Raman 248, 301
upstairs market 200–2
US: banks 280–1, 283–4, 298, 299, 332, 336; bonds 29, 168, 178, 205, 320; change 47–8; cross-border trading 254; direct debit terminals 265; discount brokerage 328–9; Eurodollar 251; financial system 53–8, 60–4; funds flow data 12–13; housing 318; insurance companies 290–1; interest rates 303–4; intervention 250, 328; investment 287–9; markets 27–8, 190, 195–6, 199, 200, 201, 202; mutual funds 327; options 219; pension funds 291, 293, 317–18; Regulation Q 45, 326; risk management 15; savings 178; securities 148, 210, 342; stocks 163, 222; supervision 332; third party information 159–60; thrift organisation 326; trust companies 32

valuation 96–105, 109–12
venture capital 32, 35, 125–6, 158, 263–4, 285–6, 319
volume of trade 15–16, 32, 45, 125, 176, 191, 193, 201

wealth 11–12
Weiss, Andrew 164
West, Richard R. 193
wholesale trading 198, 340
Williamson, Oliver E. 56, 131
World Bank 254, 298, 304
world, rest of, in financial system 12–13, 57–8, 60–1
Wriston, Walter 42

yield 11, 87–90, 266
Yu, Wayne W. 341